D0881285

WAR AND PEACE NEWS

Glasgow University Media Group

Lucinda Broadbent
John Eldridge
Gordon Kimmett
Greg Philo
Malcolm Spaven
Kevin Williams

Open University Press

Milton Keynes · Philadelphia

Open University Press
Open University Educational Enterprises Limited
12 Cofferidge Close
Stony Stratford
Milton Keynes MK11 1BY, England

and

242 Cherry Street
Philadelphia, PA 19106, USA

First Published 1985

Copyright © Glasgow University
Media Group 1985.

British Library Cataloguing in Publication Data

Glasgow University Media Group
  War and peace news.
  1. War in mass media—Great Britain
  I. Title
  070.4′4935501   p96.W3
  ISBN 0-335-10598-X
       0-335-15071-3 hb

Library of Congress Cataloging in Publication Data
Main entry under title:

War and peace news.

  1. Television broadcasting of news—Great Britain.
2. Falkland Islands War, 1982—Journalists. 3. Disarmament.
4. United Nations. I. Broadbent, Lucinda.
II. Glasgow University Media Group.
PN5124.T4W37 1985   070.1′9′0941   85-11594
ISBN 0-335-15071-3
ISBN 0-335-10598-X (pbk.)

Text Design by Clarke Williams
Typeset by Gilbert Composing Services
Printed in Great Britain by J. W. Arrowsmith Ltd., Bristol

ERRATUM

On page 15, lines 19–20, the quotation should read:

'There had been a firm Board ruling that there should be no such interviews under any circumstances.'

And all politicians are at it today [the General Election], but of course us, as we are the BBC, we have to play it absolutely down the middle. One day I am going to wear a red tie and one day a blue one and . . . what's that one for the Alliance thing – oh, a green one . . . And it's today that the armed forces pay rise is announced, they will all be off at 5.00 p.m. to listen to Radio One, and if they do get one my goodness they deserve it.

Radio One disc jockey,
9.45 a.m., 12.5.83

Contents

Acknowledgements

We would like to thank first of all the Joseph Rowntree Charitable Trust and **UNESCO** for providing the funds that made this research possible. Thanks also to all original group members for their advice and help through the years: Pete Beharrell, John Hewitt, Jean Hart, Paul Walton, Brian Winston. Thanks to Howard Davis, Paul Rogers and Marjorie Thompson for reading the manuscript and giving their comments.

In the production of this volume we thank especially Brian McNair of the University of Glasgow for his help in video-recording and in the preparation of research data, and thanks to Mark Fletcher for being both helpful and cheerful. Thanks also to Dan Plesch and Pat Wilson for providing original research on press coverage of the Easter demonstrations. For advice, help and information we thank Graham Murdock, Geoffrey Robertson, Duncan Campbell, Candy Atherton, Rachel Blow, Shauna Chalmers, Hilary Embling, Gaye Tuchman, Cathy Granger, Judith Hart, Rhona Watson, Gillian Parsons, Bangor Peace Information Centre, Bradford Textual Analysis Group and London Weekend Television. Thanks also to Trevor Graham and Parlane McFarlane for photographs. For preparing and typing the manuscript a great thanks is due to Kathleen Davidson and thanks also to Winnie Russell for some very sparkling contributions. Thanks also to our friends and colleagues in the University of Glasgow Sociology Department. A special thank-you to Colonel Jason Ditton, the Equipment Officer, and to all those who have helped us at Diverse Productions. Thanks especially to David Graham, Steve Hewlett, Barry Flynn, Anna Coote and Alex Graham. There are also many people who have helped by listening, contributing ideas and putting up with us. Special thanks here to Rhona Kimmett, May Philo, Rosemary Eldridge, Paul Briers and Greg Lanning.

Finally, we have many friends, associates and advisers who work inside television and have helped enormously. Thanks very much to them.

Introduction

In the 1980s issues of defence and disarmament surfaced as matters of public concern. Relations between the USA and the USSR were characterised by cold war rhetoric. In Britain, while there were widely stated criticisms of the Soviet Union concerning its role in Poland and Afghanistan, there were also considerable reservations expressed about the competence of the Reagan administration and the direction it was taking in its approach to East–West relations. Remarks by President Reagan on the possibility of fighting a limited nuclear war in Europe as part of NATO's military strategy worried many people. Much attention was focussed on the pending deployment of Cruise and Pershing II missiles in Western Europe and the European peace movement grew in size. In Britain the Campaign for Nuclear Disarmament experienced a dramatic revival in its fortunes, so much so that the Conservative government felt obliged to develop a campaign against it. At Greenham Common, the intended site for Cruise missiles in Britian, women camped in protest. Many were arrested and some were imprisoned for 'breach of the peace'. In 1981, the General Section of the British Association for the Advancement of Science debated the nuclear arms race[1]. In 1983, the General Synod of the Church of England highlighted the report produced under the chairmanship of the Bishop of Salisbury, *The Church and the Bomb*.[2] E. P. Thompson and Dan Smith edited a Penguin Special, *Protest and Survive*, which urged immediate and determined opposition to the government's policies.[3]

The role of the mass media in the coverage of defence and disarmament issues became a major dispute. Iain Elliot, for example, contributing to a critique of unilaterialism, has written:

Whatever emotions are aroused by some debate there is a tendency for those involved to complain that their views are being ignored by the media, and that is the case today. But I see no reason to believe that these complaints are valid. If the *Daily Telegraph* gives little space to the arguments of the unilateralists, the letter columns of the *Guardian* are gorged with their attacks on Western defence policy. If *The Times* gives space to those who support the government's policy, it also gives space to Judith Hart and E. P. Thompson. If television gives more space to NATO than to its critics (and this is by no means certain) the shelves of the bookshops are as full today of unilateralist tracts as they were full of Mr Gollancz's products in the 1930s.[4]

Appraisals of the role of the media from within the peace movement have appeared, of which the most accessible is *Nukespeak. The Media and the Bomb*, edited by Crispin Aubrey.[5] These include essays by working journalists, such as Andrew Wilson, a former defence correspondent for the *Observer* and accounts of particular episodes, such as the BBC's refusal to screen *The War Game* and their withdrawal of the invitation to E. P. Thompson to give the Dimbleby Lecture—subsequently published under the title *Beyond the Cold War*.[6] Elsewhere, the journalist Jonathan Dimbleby wrote on 'The media and defence: past and future problems'. The essence of his argument was this:

> if the principles which sustain democracy are to be nutured rather than violated, the media—television, radio and newspapers—must no longer be content to echo the response of the defence establishment to the anxieties — and arguments — of what is now known as the Peace Movement. Of course, the media should report the speeches and decisions of those who have their fingers on or near the nuclear button. However, it is an elementary but fundamental proposition that the role of the media in a free society is to question and analyse prevailing assumptions and attitudes and not merely to regurgitate the conclusions that flow from them for the edification of an uninformed populace. Journalists, that is, should not be town criers or toast masters.[6]

We decided to begin our research by looking at the period June to July 1982 when the United Nations Second Special Session on Disarmament took place in New York. The First Special Session had taken place four years earlier. In the Final Report of that Special Session, reference was made to the meeting taking place in the closing years of what the General Assembly of the United Nations had declared to be the Disarmament Decade. It was recognised that the effort had been a failure in that the arms race was increasing, not diminishing, and clearly outstripping efforts to curb it. The Report reaffirmed that the ending of the arms race and the achievement of real disarmament were tasks of primary importance and urgency, and described this goal as an historic challenge which was necessary to ensure genuine security and a peaceful future:

> Unless its avenues are closed, the continued arms race means a growing threat to international peace and security and even to the very survival of mankind. The nuclear and conventional arms build-up threatens to stall the efforts aimed at reaching the goals of development, to become an obstacle on the road to achieving a new economic order and to hinder the solution of other problems facing mankind.[8]

The General Assembly expressed the hope that the discussion at the First Session and the Final Document would attract attention, further mobilise world opinion and provide a powerful impetus for the cause of disarmament. However, such evidence as we have suggests that media coverage of the First Session was patchy and inadequate.[9] How would it be four years on for the 1982 Second Special Session? On the one hand the arms race had continued unabated and East–West relations had deteriorated into new cold war postures. On the other hand there was a renewed peace movement in the West which would seek to draw attention to the event.

Since the speeches given at the UN Special Session were available in text form to the world's press this did provide a basis for examining patterns of selection. Accordingly, we mobilised our own research resources to focus on this period of time. How would British television treat the event and what might this teach us about news values? However, in the course of our preparations for this study we were caught up in another issue: the Falklands conflict. We began the video-recording of all BBC and ITN news bulletins on 1 May 1982, a month ahead of the UN Special Session. Originally this was done in order to familiarise ourselves with logging requirements for the bulletins and to devise a suitable secondary log for all defence and disarmament items. What we encountered of course were bulletins that were saturated with Falklands news. Whereas our intention had been to monitor a set event–the UN Special Session—for a predefined period of time, we now found ourselves monitoring what, without exaggeration, could be called crisis news. The periods overlapped, so that Falklands news and UN news coloured each other.

Other news items, such as the Pope's visits to Britain and to Argentina, meetings of the EEC and NATO, President Reagan's visit to Europe and the World Cup football tournament in Spain, were all strongly marked by a Falklands/Argentine aspect. In addition, current affairs and topical programmes devoted a good deal of time to the dispute. Consequently, we decided to make coverage of the Falklands War a central object of our study and have analysed major samples from key areas of reporting, including coverage of the fighting, diplomatic initiatives and issues at 'home'.

Since the war a number of works on aspects of the conflict have been written, including what came to be known as the 'media war', notably Robert Harris's book *Gotcha! The Media, the Government and the Falklands Crisis*. Harris, a journalist then working with BBC's *Newsnight*, concluded:

> The episodes which caused the most disquiet, and which have been described in this book, were not necessarily unique to the Falklands crisis. The instinctive secrecy of the military and the Civil Service; the prostitution and hysteria of sections of the press; the lies, the misinformation, the manipulation of public opinion by the authorities; the political intimidation of broadcasters; the ready connivance of the media at their own distortion . . . all these occur as much in peace time Britain as in war.[10]

The Falklands experience revealed conflicts of principle and interest. The right to the free flow of information in a democratic society was set against the need for censorship in the interests of the war effort. The right to present different points of view about the issue was set against a call to speak for the 'national interest'. In the next chapter, 'Making Good News', we look at the restrictions placed upon journalists and difficulties they encountered as well as the exchanges that took place between the various groups who had an interest in what the news looked like. In our previous work we have mainly been concerned with content analysis. In this volume we also examine some of the discussions on editorial policy which informed the production process. We analyse the decisions made by broadcasters on general policy and look at some routine journalistic practices such as the workings of the lobby system. In addition we re-examine the question of what was public opinion at the time and suggest some possible links between public attitudes and the information on which they are formed. The remainder of this volume engages in a detailed content analysis. The method we use for this is essentially the same as that employed in case studies in our previous volumes. There are three dimensions to this. Firstly, the identification of explanatory themes: these are the range of explanations which exist on a specific issues; for example, why the *Belgrano* was sunk. In this instance we list the information and viewpoints available at the time. The second dimension is a quantitative assessment of the appearance of each explanation. Finally we look at how each theme is developed in specific contexts such as in headlines or in news interviews.

In later chapters we examine the 'balance' between military and diplomatic coverage of the conflict on television news. In a situation where the British government had declared that military pressure was being used to 'back up' diplomacy, and where moves for a peaceful settlement of the conflict between Britain and Argentina went on almost throughout the period, television editors and journalists were faced with a number of choices about how to deal with news from the battlefield and news from the diplomatic front.

The public, to whom all this news was conveyed, was in a sense both spectator and participant in the event. What role did the media have in sustaining public morale and how did this condition what was said and not said? We suggest that the use of opinion polls was of strategic importance here. Opinion polls tend to ask questions based on what people are already assumed to know—for example, they may assume that, unlike the British, the Argentines refused to negotiate. But such knowledge is informed by the news and probably affects people's attitudes to the war. In the portrayal of the 'home front' in Chapter 3, we show how certain connotations of family and nation are also deployed to create a sense of unity and patriotism in time of crisis.

The Falklands conflict led to an unexpected shift of emphasis as far as our original research plan was concerned. Consequently the second part of the book is more programmatic than it otherwise would have been. We give some attention to the dimensions of the debate over defence and disarmament. This is, in effect, a map with illustrations. We want to show the ways in which definitions, concepts, issues and agendas are presented. The UN Special Session on Disarmament and the coverage of the anti- and pro-nuclear movements serve as good examples of the way news-values shape coverage.

We have also taken the opportunity to comment on current affairs programmes in the area of defence and disarmament. We have given an account of a number of current affairs programmes which were shown in the second half of 1983. This is not heavily analytical but tries to convey something of the scope of the programmes, what they were about, who was involved and what kinds of format were on offer. We recognise that there is often a wide range of views within current affairs programmes. Some, for example, have treated the growth of the peace movement in Europe with sympathy. Even so, programmes which come down on the side of the peace movement may be labelled in advance as controversial or one-sided. On such grounds John Pilger's documentary *The Truth Game* was kept off the screen by the IBA until agreement was reached for another programme to be made that would 'balance' it. In such a situation the concept of balance is deployed as part of a cultural struggle. This struggle in current affairs, important though it is, takes place in something of an enclave, since the audiences for such programmes are far smaller than those who view television news. For this reason, our main focus hitherto has been on news programmes and it continues to be in this volume.

Section One
The Falklands Conflict

ONE

Making Good News

Ordinary journalism

'Corrupting', 'pernicious', 'a cosy conspiracy', 'appalling': these are all words used recently to described the 'lobby system' in British journalism. They were spoken both by people who have used the system to help their political employers, such as Joe Haines (press secretary to Harold Wilson), and by journalists who were subject to it.* It is a system in which favoured correspondents are given private and confidential briefings, mainly by the Prime Minister's press secretary and by other ministers. The journalists do not reveal where the information has come from.

The largest group of 'lobby correspondents' are the 140 political journalists based at Westminster, who have their own rules and 'officers' to supervise the system. There are also smaller groups covering areas such as education, industry and defence. Lobby correspondents have other privileges such as access to white papers and government documents before they are released to the general public. Any who break the rules may have their lobby privileges withdrawn. The system has been attacked by some journalists, especially American, since instead of encouraging investigation it produces a reliance on the government to provide pre-packaged information. This theme was taken up by a government policy advisor in a recent television programme:

> It's very tempting on the government side to use it to hand out little goodies of information like sweets to children on the assumption that the recipients will be good boys and handle the information in a nice way.[1]

*On BBC *Panorama*, 8.3.82.

1

Another advantage for the government is that they can make statements without anyone being held responsible–even if they are wrong. This is the origin of phrases in journalism such as 'Whitehall sources have revealed tonight'. On this aspect of it, Joe Haines commented:

> What we get is a cosy conspiracy which is convenient for the government–they can make statements without attribution—it's [also] too cosy for journalists; they can just go up and be spoon fed.[2]

The lobby system is not the only or even the central problem in British journalism.* But it is symptomatic of the key relationships within which the media are organised. Political authorities can assume a consensus amongst most journalists on the range of views which are to be featured in any 'serious' fashion.[3] Perhaps more crucially, they can assume that a limited number of people have the right to speak in an 'authoritative' way. Journalists tend to take such hierarchies for granted–this part of practical journalism has become 'normal' and routine through arrangements such as the lobby briefings. Such 'normal journalism' carries with it the assumption of a class society that some people are more important than others. We made this point in our earlier work, pointing out that it seemed 'natural' to journalists to take information largely from senior civil servants and ministers. We were criticised for saying this by Richard Francis, the Director of News and Current Affairs at the BBC. He simply reaffirmed the truth of what we were saying when he wrote:

The BBC's journalists do indeed find it natural to ask 'an important

---

*Two other key factors in routine journalistic practice are the general reliance on the press to define the parameters of an 'acceptable' story plus the reliance on news services such as the Press Association to supply a large amount of basic news material. Journalists in television news to whom we spoke complained of the difficulties of initiating news stories unless something like them had already appeared in the press. Attempts by journalists to initiate new themes were met by the question, 'where are the press cuttings on this?' The use of 'standard' news material as provided on the wire services of the Press Association acts as a substitute for investigative or innovative reporting. It also favours those institutions with extensive publicity and public relations departments, who routinely provide the news rooms with 'their side' of a story. One such organisation which has recently used this system effectively is the National Coal Board. It is no accident that, during the 1984–5 coal dispute, television news programmes were so frequently introduced by statements on the number of miners returning to work. Such practices in normal news productions are important in understanding news content. We focussed attention here on the additional effects of the lobby system since it highlighted the importance of the special relationship between broadcasters and official sources which was used to such effect during the Falklands crisis.

person'–a senior civil servant or government minister, for instance—for they are the people whose decisions largely determine how things will be run in our democracy.[4]

If such exhaustive consultation limits other opinion, then the media are also helping to determine how things will be run in our democracy.

Not all journalism is so respectful. A degree of criticism is acceptable and is good copy for newspapers, just as the critical interview makes 'good' television. Journalists may for example question the activities or competence of particular ministers, but do no usually question the nature of the political and social system.*

Where journalists do touch areas which are deemed too 'sensitive', the authorities have an array of controls which they can add to their informal briefing of journalists. David Leigh in *The Frontiers of Secrecy* lists the Official Secrets Act, contempt of court, libel laws and 'D notices'. The 'D' in these stands for Defence and they are basically a set of rules held by news editors, agreed between them and the Ministry of Defence. They involve voluntary censorship in a range of areas from 'defence plans' through to 'anti-interrogation techniques' and the whereabouts of Soviet defectors. The basic 'notices' can be supplemented by 'private and confidential' letters on particular issues, sent to editors from the 'D notice' committee. This is composed of government officials from the MoD, the Home and Foreign Offices, together with eleven 'responsible' journalists, and its secretary is at present a Rear-Admiral.

Of all these formal constraints, the Official Secrets Act† is potentially the most wide-ranging, since it means in effect that all government information is secret unless an 'official' statement is made about it. Although prosecutions are rare, in practice no journalist or citizen has free access to government information (even about

---

*For example, the popular newspapers and television news had a hard time explaining the 1981 riots. The popular press focussed mainly on violence and destruction, and some on the 'racial' angle. The *Daily Mail* had a headline on 'Don't Their Parents Care?' The *Daily Mirror* stood out in that it sent a journalist who was from Toxteth to report on what people there were saying about the causes of the trouble. But much explanatory journalism was on the level of the search for 'agitators', and one television programme featured an 'expert' talking about the effects of lead fumes in the air on people's behaviour. There were few headlines suggesting simpler explanations such as that people were helping themselves to what they couldn't normally afford.

† As David Leigh notes, Section 2 of the Act carries the notorious anti-press clause asserting that: 'the uttering or receipt of any information learned by a civil servant in the course of his job is a crime' (D. Leigh *The Frontiers of Secrecy*, Junction Books, 1980, p. 50 . . .).

themselves), and civil servants may not release it unless express permission is given to do so.*

There are, then, two ways of looking at the constraints on information in the media. One is from the point of view of 'official' sources and attempts at control. The second is from the point of view of the journalists and the extent to which they will accept these pressures. The two groups meet most often in the middle ground of private briefings and the lobby system. The heavy hand of control is rare but journalists are none the less integrated into the club-like atmosphere of the privileged. The book of rules which governs lobby briefings was drawn up by the journalists themselves. The rules are private and confidential and state that the workings of the lobby system should be kept completely secret. Journalists are not to talk about lobby meetings before or after they are held, especially in the presence of those not entitled to attend them (rule 3). The rulebook includes 'general lists' on behaviour, and correspondents are told that they must never run after a minister, never crowd together, never use a notebook in the members' lobby and never in any circumstances make use of anything 'overheard' at Westminster. Finally they are instructed that they must not 'see' anything in the members' lobby.[5] If one MP should punch another (as has happened) they would not report it. The most extraorindary feature of the lobby system is the manner in which journalists 'police' each other to secure confidentiality for the government. The system is so confidential that information gained from one lobby shouldn't be used to ask direct questions in a different one. A journalist is not supposed to go to a defence lobby meeting and say to a minister, 'I heard this morning from Downing Street information that directly contradicts what you are saying.' An ITN correspondent gave us this story of his own experiences at the time of the Falklands conflict:

> Information had come from a lobby briefing at Downing Street. It came to me from the ITN newsdesk. I decided to check it out and asked a question on it at the defence correspondents' lobby. Three journalists who were 'officers' of the parliamentary lobby jumped on me and said they would make a formal complaint to the political editor of ITN.

Lobby journalists now provide a great part of what becomes news, but the price of joining such clubs is dependence on 'official' sources. As David Leigh writes:

---

*A recent case of its use was in January 1984, with the prosecution of Sarah Tisdall for releasing a Ministry of Defence memo to the *Guardian*.

Deprived, in theory at least, of independent right of access to information about public affairs, the journalist depends on what he is told as a favour. The frequent reason for claiming secrecy on power-holders' operations is to allow them to present their own unchallenged version of reality: the obverse of the secrecy coin is always propaganda. From the point of view of a politician, the ideal journalist is one who will accept misleading statements and disguise their source.[6]

Many journalists contest this view – as professionals they tend to see themselves as independent and critical. But our earlier research on television news[7] did show that it tended largely to follow 'official' explanations and to justify these in its reporting. There are, of course, exceptions, where journalists in areas such as foreign reporting have departed radically from official policy. For example, some news reports on El Salvador and Nicaragua have been extremely critical of United States policy there. The conditions which make this possible are probably that Britain's immediate interests are not seen as threatened; and the sheer distance from which reports are being sent gives the journalist some latitude. This contrasts sharply with the strictures placed on journalists over the reporting of Northern Ireland. There is now a large number of documented cases of programmes being censored, delayed or banned.* For these to emerge at all into public debate meant often that journalists jeopardised their careers. Many have spoken of the process of 'self-censorship' which more often characterises reporting in this controversial area.

Defence news is highly sensitive and tends to be conservative, especially at times of crisis. Where defence is an issue in a news story it may override normal journalistic values. For example, television, operating as it does from within generally liberal and social-democratic principles, has a positive commitment to 'democracy'. Yet as we showed in earlier work[8] some television reports of a military coup in Turkey overrode this in favour of the 'defence' angle. The BBC reported:

Turkey has a long border with the Soviet Union on the southern flank of NATO, and the West have been watching with gloom the troubles building up there. So *putting aside a few crocodile tears about democracy,* most Western observers are quietly pleased that the region looks that much more stable tonight that it did last night. Particularly since it may improve the prospects of Greece returning fully to the NATO fold. The Russians, inevitably perhaps, suspect the Americans of a hand in this

---

*Liz Curtis lists more than forty such incidents between 1963 and 1983 in *Ireland the Propaganda War* (Pluto, 1984).

coup. Apart from the former Turkish government, Moscow is probably the most aggrieved by it all.*

BBC1, 21.00, 19.9.80

After the military take-over, there were a stream of reports of torture and the violation of human rights,[9] yet the struggles of people in Turkey have received scant attention, especially when compared with those of a country such as Poland. Attitudes to the Soviet Union are crucial here:[10] the fall of democracy in Turkey is related to how 'aggrieved' Moscow will be. The rise of free trade unions in Poland is again often linked to the aggravation it is causing behind the iron curtain – and this is one of the reasons for the saturation coverage it has received.

We should not be too cynical, since television does have a record of featuring 'human rights' stories, especially in countries such as South Africa. Yet even here defence interests are sometimes a priority. On the same night as the report on Turkey, the BBC featured a story on a military base in Simonstown. The reporter stresses only the advantages of the British using it:

> *Journalist*: Until five years ago, the South African naval base of Simonstown *played a vital part* in Britain's defence thinking. The Labour government ended that link . . .Simonstown has been in the past, and traditionally, *a marvellous base*, for other navies as well, but has it still got that potential . . .?
>
> *S. African naval officer:* Well, I think, at the moment it's a fantastic base for our navy. . . .
>
> *Journalist:* It's these resources, plus the recreational opportunities for sailors after periods at sea, that South Africa appears to be offering.
>
> BBC, 21.00, 12.9.80

The conservatism of defence reporting is intensified by the extreme sensitivity of the government, and by the intense lobbying that accompanies each issue. Recently, Duncan Campbell described the 'selling' of Trident missiles:

> The Ministry of Defence is making a mighty effort to massage public opinion into accepting the Trident submarine missile system – at a cost which even its enthusiasts reckon to be not less than £8 billion.
>
> Defence Secretary John Nott is now lavishing secret briefings on the national press. Two weeks ago, he leaked details of 'offset' arrangements for British firms to work on Trident, and got a front-page lead in the *Sunday Times*. On Wednesday last week he invited a group of Fleet

---

*All italics in quotes from television news throughout this volume are our own.

Street editors to a private dinner at his London home, on 'lobby terms'. They were Harold Evans of *The Times,* and editors of the *Guardian, Financial Times, Daily Express,* and *Sunday Telegraph.* The government team consisted of Nott, Sir Frank Cooper (Permanent Secretary, Defence) and Admiral Sir Terence Lewin (Chief of the Defence Staff). Ian MacDonald, acting head of MoD Public Relations, was in attendance.[11]

Some writers have pointed to the close affinity between some news staff and the military. James Bellini had this to say about the BBC's Assistant Director General:

> 'Colonel' Alan Protheroe, as he is known to his colleagues, recieved the MBE in 1980 – for his services to the territorial army. He was one of a number of senior BBC TV news staff who had connections with the military. Defence Correspondent Christopher Wain is a former major; Managing Editor Tony Crabb was an officer in Military Intelligence.[12]

Critical TV journalism does exist, but those who tread in the most sensitive areas risk much. For example, *The Friday Alternative* was a weekly programme on Channel 4, set up to give the 'other side' of the news. On 7 January 1983 a programme examined television coverage of the Falklands. It was based on research on this book and was the first time there had been any sustained account of work by the Glasgow Group shown on television. According to a later *Sunday Times* report, this was a major factor in the series being terminated. The report describes a meeting between Jeremy Isaacs, the Chief executive of Channel 4, and David Graham, the programme's editor:

> But without doubt, the programme which got *The Friday Alternative* into deepest water was one, broadcast on January 7 this year, about the media coverage of the Falklands War. This claimed that, during the war, journalists had allowed themselves to be manipulated by the government . . . Overall Isaacs had been pleased with *The Friday Alternative,* praising it with faint damns: 'Sloppy, vulgar, inaccurate — marvellous,' he called it. But after the Falklands programme he summoned Graham to say he was under pressure to take it out of the schedules. 'It annoys some very important people,' he said.
> *Sunday Times,* 28.8.83

The Falklands conflict raised special problems for 'ordinary journalism', and we turn to these now.

Television and the Falklands: making good news

The Falklands conflict will not be remembered as a highpoint of 'open news' and free information. The restrictions on what could be reported fell into three broad areas: (1) the limits imposed directly by the Ministry of Defence in the form of censorship and controls on journalists; (2) the restraints of the 'normal' system of lobby briefings; and (3) controls which the broadcasters imposed upon themselves in the name of 'taste' or in deference to what they saw as public opinion.*

The most obvious limit from the MoD was that only British journalists were allowed to go with the Task Force. Even these had no facilities for sending satellite pictures and experienced extreme difficulties in sending back copy. After the conflict, broadcasters continued to believe that it had been deliberate policy to stop the transmission of television pictures, while the MoD maintained that the failure was merely technical — that it had not been possible to arrange it. Both ITN and BBC believed that there had been an 'absence of will' on the part of the military authorities to make television pictures possible.[13]

There was a climate of opinion in military circles which regarded television as a potentially dangerous weapon in lowering morale. Rightly or wrongly, it had been blamed for the United States public's increasing disillusionment with Vietnam. As early as 1970, an MoD Director of Defence Operations had gone on record as saying: 'We would have to start saying to ourselves, Are we going to let television cameras loose on the battlefield?'[14] At the same time, Air Vice Marshall Stewart Menaul[15] had commented: 'Television had a lot to answer for in the collapse of American morale.'

When it came to the Falklands battlefields, the public had to make do with film which was weeks old. There were no pictures of casualties from the land fighting until after the final ceasefire. It is difficult to know whether more immediate visual coverage would have had much effect on public opinion. The crucial issue is not whether there were pictures, but what kind of pictures were shown and how they were used to comment on the war. This is seen in the case of still photographs from the Falklands, which were in fact transmitted. They were not allowed out by the MoD with equal speed. After the conflict there was an enquiry by a Parliamentary Defence Committee on the handling of the press and public information. On this issue it commented:

---

*The research in this volume features mainly the second and third 'limits'—since the first has been extensively commented on elsewhere.

Was it just by chance that the celebrated picture of San Carlos villager offering a Marine a cup of tea achieved such instant currency, whilst others such as the one of HMS *Antelope* exploding suffered considerable delays?[16]

The Ministry of Defence was anxious to control reporting about the Falklands, for what it called 'operational' reasons and the safeguarding of life. But it was argued at the time that its censorship extended beyond this to the 'management' of news to secure a favourable impression of the war. Copy from journalists with the Task Force was censored at two levels: by MoD officials on the Falklands and then again by public relations staff at the Ministry in London.[17] There were many examples recorded at the time of this process going beyond the needs of 'security'. The BBC complained of being told not to use a picture of a body bag and to remove the phrase 'horribly burned'. Brian Hanrahan of the BBC sent back a report of the Argentine bombing at Bluff Cove, but it was delayed until this sentence was removed: 'Other survivors came off unhurt but badly shaken after hearing the cries of men trapped below.'[18] On HMS *Hermes*, Michael Nicholson of ITN and other journalists were so annoyed by the conduct of the military authorities that they sought to prefix their reports as 'censored'; but the word was itself censored. After the ceasefire, Robert Fox of the BBC made a remarkable statement about a conversation with an MoD official. It is recorded in the BBC's confidential News and Current Affairs minutes: 'Robert Fox recalled that one press officer, following the attack on the *Sir Galahad*, had said, "We only want you to print the good news."'[19]

So many complaints were made that the BBC's Assistant Director General referred to the period as 'open season on the Ministry of Defence'.[20] For their part, there were many in the Services and Ministry itself who were intensely suspicious of journalists even with the strict controls which applied. One senior BBC producer told us that in his view there were some good reasons for this. He argued that experienced journalists could deduce new information from even the barest of Ministry statements. For example, in the early stages of the Falklands conflict on 25 May a British helicopter had ditched into the sea with serious loss of life. He commented that reporters had immediately realised that an SAS group was involved by looking at the spread of military units from which the casualties came.

The apprehension with which some in the Ministry of Defence regarded the media led to strange conflicts.[21] At the onset of the Falklands crisis, the acting head of the Ministry's public relations department was Ian McDonald. He was a civil servant in the traditional mould of the well-rounded non-specialist. By many accounts, there were major strains between his approach and that of the public relations specialists employed within the Ministry and within each group of the Services. McDonald's initial response to dealing with the media was to hold them at arm's length. Defence correspondents had been accustomed to 'unattributable' briefings from Sir Frank Cooper who was the top civil servant at the MoD. At the beginning of the crisis these were stopped, and British and foreign journalists now had to make do with short, formal statements from McDonald. He would not speak privately with the media and instructed all his staff to do the same. His intention was to develop the 'D notice' system of voluntary restraint by editors. McDonald was worried that 'off the record' briefings were difficult to control and might violate security needs. There was also in his attitude perhaps a basic lack of sympathy with the thrusting demands of the media, especially television. He explained to us a decision to announce the final sinking of HMS *Sheffield after* the television cameras had been switched off. It would not have been right, he thought, to do it in front of all the lights and cameras – 'it was like announcng the death of a child'. This was a different world from that of professional PR.

McDonald's general approach to the media was strongly challenged by the man who had been designated to take over his job later that year.* This was Neville Taylor, a PR specialist and one of a new generation of 'professionals' in the Ministry. The new attitude was that the MoD should meet the demands of the media by giving them 'hot' news, pictures, etc., but should organise and limit what was given in order to meet its own needs.† By the middle of May 1982, Taylor's ideas had begun to dominate the MoD's approch, and 'off the record' briefings were re-established.

Here we find the second major limit on information—one which was acceded to by the British media. Robert Harris, a BBC journalist

---

*This was a formal change in appointment which had been agreed before the conflict began. Although his replacement arrived in April 1982, McDonald initially retained responsibility for public relations concerning the Falklands.

†This approach to public relations has been most fully developed by the Army, following their experience in Northern Ireland and the Falklands. In October 1983 a full-scale operation was organised to give a fifty-strong group of journalists accreditation as war correspondents and take them on a military exercise. In the words of the Army's director of public relations. 'Self-censorship is what we are trying to preach' (reported in *Soldier*, 14.11.83).

himself, argues that the period in which unattributable briefings were stopped left some journalists 'gasping for information, like patients whose life-support systems had been switched off'.[22] When the briefings were re-started, the effect was to make journalists more reliant upon them and less likely to criticise. The government, for example, had no difficulty in planting the story on 20 May that there would be no 'D-Day style' landing on the Falklands and instead giving the false impression that the Task Force would engage only in small 'hit and run' raids.*

After the war foreign journalists, particularly those from the US, were very critical of the lobby system. Leonard Downie, the national editor of the *Washington Post*, wrote:

> This was the system used by the British Defence Ministry to control through the lobby of defence correspondents most information about the Falklands war. Only these correspondents were allowed into secret briefings held throughout the war, while the rest of the large body of newsmen covering the conflict from London were told little in public statements and Press conferences.
>   Few British newsmen sought to find out more from officials or senior politicians outside these government-controlled forums [lobby briefings]. The leading political correspondent for a respected British Sunday newspaper said he would not even try to contact members of Thatcher's inner 'war cabinet' because he doubted they would talk to him and he wanted to avoid 'doing anything that might endanger our boys'. As a result of such self-censorship, it was left to an American newsman to report from sources in the war cabinet that it had unanimously made the decision to sink the Argentine cruiser *General Belgrano*, one of the most important military and political events of the war.[23]

What dismayed the Americans was that the media's reliance on 'official' sources had become so routine. It was the 'normal' way in which things are done. This quality of British journalism might explain in part why television was so reluctant to criticise the authorities during the war, and to indicate to viewers at home that material was in fact being censored.[24]

Where information is given as a privilege and controls normally operate, censorship might be seen simply as an extension of what already exists. This change could perhaps occur without there being a special point where anyone notices the difference. Could this be why

---

*Complaints were made afterwards about this to the Parliamentary Defence Committee, and many regarded incidents such as this as having done lasting damage abroad to the image of statements from the British government.

broadcasters did not put the label 'censored' across news bulletins? David Nicholas, ITN's editor, was asked about this on *The Friday Alternative*:

> Looking back on it I wish we had; because we certainly put 'censored material' — a 'censored' superimposed caption [on material] from Poland and in the later stages of Zimbabwe. In a sense the censorship aspect of the Falklands sort of crept steadily on. . . . I think it would have been better had we as a practice regularly put up, 'This report was censored.'[25]

There is a final postscript to the 'briefings' system, revealed by Robert Harris. When the Pariliamentary Defence Committee was conducting its enquiry, it discovered that the 'non-attributable' briefings had all been recorded by the MoD. This would have enabled a direct comparison to be made between what was said by the Ministry and what appeared in the news. But, according to Harris, by this time Neville Taylor was

> 'mending fences' and 'trying to establish better relations and a better understanding' with the media, [he] consulted the defence correspondents concerned, and *they* voted by nine to seven not to give the committee access to the tapes.[26]

The third limit on information was imposed by broadcasters within their own organisations. The broadcasters were not against censorship as such, but they did not wish the control to lie with outside agencies. They were afraid that their own credibility would be undermined if they were not 'seen' to be independent. Consequently, they were prepared to cut material themselves on grounds of 'taste' or what they saw as the 'public mood'. For example, we were given an account of an NUJ meeting in the BBC which had discussed the editing of a script by Brian Barron. He had used the words 'tragic incident' in relation to the sinking of the *Belgrano*, and these were cut before transmission. Similarly, when film of British casualties began to arrive, both BBC and ITN engaged in their own selection and editing. Some very harrowing shots of the wounded at Bluff Cove were shown on the BBC1 nine o'clock news on 24 June, but these were edited or cut completely from all the other news programmes on both channels that day. The reasons for such internal decisions lie in part in the complex relations between the broadcasters and the government. The BBC, in particular, was under attack at this time.

What the BBC really thought

The following account is based largely on the BBC's New and Current Affairs (NCA) minutes for the period of the Falklands crisis. Each week, the top thirty producers joined the Director General and/or his aides at confidential meetings. The minutes of these were circulated at senior levels within the BBC. Where possible, we have confirmed or added to information within them by interviewing participants. The minutes are an important source of what was being thought and said at the time, but they are not the whole story. There is always a potential gap between what senior staff desire and what occurs at the level of programme makers. Also, the minutes tend to act retrospectively — as a series of comments on past programmes. One very senior member of the NCA meeting gave us his view of how the system worked: 'There are rarely hard rules laid down at the meeting. An atmosphere is generated and people act within the prevailing climate.

At times the minutes contain suggestions and warnings about future actions; sometimes on how language is to be used. For example, on one occasion we hear from Alan Protheroe, the Assistant Director General:

> To describe a successful British assault on the Falklands, [he] favoured 'repossession', and objected to the use of invasion' . . . [but] discretion of editors was required to determine the most apposite word or phrase.

> NCA, 18.5.82

The crucial issue which these minutes help resolve is how the BBC saw its own relations with the government. The BBC approached the crisis with its normal view of 'balance'. That is, it saw itself as giving access to the views of 'authoritative' and 'legitimate' sources from each side.[27] On 6 April, the Director General spelled out the issues:

> he anticipated that the BBC would come under pressure, as it had during the Suez crisis, to 'conform to the national interest'. There was a legitimate point in this: the difficulty was to define precisely the 'national interest'. Clearly the BBC should be careful not to do anything to imperil military operations or diplomatic negotiations, but it should report accurately and faithfully the arguments arising within British society at all levels. For example, Mr Benn might be advancing views which were unpopular even with most of his Tribune group colleagues, but he was entitled to be heard.

The speaker's view of arguments 'at all levels' came down to a division of opinion between MPs. As the conflict developed, even this definition of balance was to come under attack. A section of the Conservative Party sought to outlaw any criticism of sending the Task Force as being 'subversive'. Some prominent Tories such as Cecil Parkinson distanced themselves from this, seeing that attacks on the BBC might imply that the party was against free speech. But for a time the Corporation was under ferocious attack from the Tory back benches leading what turned out to be a minority of public opinion.

The biggest row was over a *Panorama* programme broadcast on 10 May, which featured Conservative and Labour opposition to the war. It was branded an 'odious and subversive travesty' by Sally Oppenheim MP. It brought to a head a number of other complaints such as the BBC's refusal to use the words 'we' and 'us' when talking about the British. In the words of John Cole, the political editor, 'the knives had been out in the House' (NCA, 11.5.82). A few days later, the Chairman of the BBC and the present Director General were verbally savaged at a packed meeting of the Conservative Party Media Group in the House of Commons. This meeting was described by David Holmes (Chief Assistant to the Director General) as 'an exercise in intimidation' (NCA, 18.5.82).

The BBC refused to apologise for *Panorama* but the Corporation was deeply shocked by the attacks. Voices were raised in the NCA meetings on the need to meet the 'emotional sensibilities of the public', rather than simply the journalists criteria of 'impartiality' and 'balance':

> It was vital that BBC reporting was sensitive to the emotional sensibilities of the public. The truth had been well told so far, especially by those on the ground, but there had been some mistakes — the BBC was not infallible. The Director General advised that, with the public's nerve endings raw, the best yardstick to use would be *the likely general susceptibility*.
>
> NCA, 18.5.82

One week earlier, another senior broadcaster had

> reminded the meeting that the BBC was the *British* broadcasting Corporation. [italics in original] It was now clear that a large section of the public shared this view and he believed it was an unnecessary irritation to stick to the detached style.
>
> NCA, 11.5.82

On the following day, the BBC nine o'clock news ended with shot of a group of people singing 'There'll always be an England'. The subsequent *Panorama* programme featured extensive support for the government position.[28] It is not clear whether such items can be attributed simply to the political attacks. It is probable that, in any event, the weight of coverage would have featured government policy. But it appears from the NCA minutes that the effect of the new climate in the BBC was to make it more difficult than usual for those who wished to pursue alternative views.

A series of directives came down via the meetings on key issues such as interviews with relatives of thos who had died in the conflict. A senior broadcaster told us that there was considerable disquiet in government circles about the effects of such interviews on morale, and he believed that this had been conveyed to the BBC. This issue first emerges in the minutes, the day after the *Panorama* storm. The present Director General encouraged editors 'to be extremely self-critical with regard to items such as interviews with the bereaved, and invitations to Argentine diplomats to contribute to programmes in one-to-one interviews (NCA, 11.5.82). Over the next three weeks, the pressures against interviewing the bereaved hardened into an absolute ruling. On 1 June, Alan Protheroe, the Assistant Director General, announced: 'there had been a firm Board of Governors ruling that there should be no such interviews under any circumstances' (NCA, 1.6.82).

Under pressure from the editor of *Nationwide* and others, a few exceptions to this rule were made. But the records of the meetings show that, to gain even these, an extraordinary number of hoops had to be gone through. One interview from *Nationwide* had been shown first to Chris Capron, the head of television current affairs. He stated:

> it had given him no concern on any score. He had referred to the Assistant Director General, and had then discussed it with the Director General, and had been given the go-ahead. He had not been unhappy with this procedure, though he conceded that a more emotional interview might have provoked greater problems.
>
> NCA, 8.6.82

What was the source of these 'problems'? Andrew Taussig took up the point and said that 'there was a danger that, by broadcasting an emotional interview, the BBC would be charged with undermining national will' (NCA, 8.6.82). Alan Protheroe stated that he did not see it in these terms and that 'the issue was intrusion into private grief, compounded by mindless questions' (NCA, 8.6.82). However, this argument begins to look a little thin when it is apparent from the minutes that the relatives themselves were striving to get on. Earlier in this meeting we hear of an interview with the mother of someone

missing from the *Sheffield*. It had been recorded and then stopped
from going out and one producer complained that 'it had been a
marvellous interview largely because she had been keen to give it'. A
week later we hear that 'The only difficulties that local radio had
experienced had been caused by the ruling against bereaved relatives:
many had wanted to participate in phone-in programmes (NCA,
18.6.82).[29]

The general ban was sustained, but on 29 June we hear that some
relatives have been approved for interviews. Alan Protheroe
'confirmed to Robin Walsh that there would be no restrictions on
interviews with the relatives of those granted posthumous awards . . .
providing those interviews were done with taste, discretion and
elegance' (NCA, 29.6.82).

The departure from journalists criteria on who should be
interviewed was justified by an appeal to the public interest and public
sensibilities – even though a section of the public was actively striving
to depart from this definition of what it wanted. The words of Lord
Reith at the time of the 1926 General Strike rise up irrepressibly:
'Assuming the BBC is for the people and that the government is for the
people, it follows that the BBC must be for the government in this
crisis.' In the name of such 'public' opinion, journalists were advised
to avoid the sensitive areas and the 'difficult' questions. On 15 June at
the NCA meeting the BBC's Director of Public Affairs gave his views.
He sensed that 'public opinion remained volatile, and he suggested
special caution, in the weeks ahead, over the question "has it all been
worth it?"'

With such a vision of the public, it is difficult to see how the BBC fell
out with the government at all. Some programme makers, mainly in
BBC current affairs, had taken the 'balance and impartiality' argument
seriously and had dipped the Corporation's toe in the waters of dissent.
When these waters proved too hot, the BBC withdrew, while
attempting to preserve its apparent independence from the
government. This was vital since the broadcasters believed that their
own credibility was at stake and that they could not be seen to bow to
outside pressure. Many regarded the rows as having a beneficial effect.
The Director General is reported as agreeing that 'one benefit to come
out of the savaging of the BBC had been the clear proof it provided to
outside countries of the BBC's independence from government'
(NCA, 18.5.82).

Yet these broadcasters were in no doubt where the weight of their
coverage had been directed. This is seen most clearly in the manner in

which they defend themselves. They believed that they were wrongly accused. In the meeting on the day after the controversial *Panorama*, a clear statement was made:

> the weight of BBC coverage had been concerned with government statements and policy. In their vilification of the BBC, the government seemed to have entirely overlooked this. The meeting endorsed this point.

> NCA, 11.5.82

The defence against all the individual charges is the same. The Producer of *Panorama*, George Carey, protested to the meeting that 'the introduction to the programme had emphasised that the British cause was utterly right' (NCA, 11.5.82).

In a *Newsnight* programme on 3.5.82, Peter Snow had used the phrase 'if the British are to be believed' and had been criticised for doing so. But Chris Capron, the head of TV current affairs, reassured the meeting that 'the comment had been quoted out of context; the script as a whole had made it absolutely clear the British claims were far more reliable' (NCA, 11.5.82). Had there been too much from Argentina? Not according to Larry Hodgson:

> There had been the accusation that the BBC had been pumping out Argentine claims: this was manifestly untrue – the vast majority of Argentine claims had *not* been reported: others had been nailed as propagandist lies.

> NCA, 11.5.82

This is hardly the language of the liberal dissident; those at the meeting seemed quite clear where the BBC stood.

What did the media want?

After the conflict the BBC joined the rest of the media in attacking the information policies of the government and MoD. There were four main areas of criticism. The most common complaint was that the inefficiency of the MoD in providing information and clearing material meant that journalists simply could not do their job. At the NCA meeting on 8 June the Assistant Director General asked what difficulties were being experienced in general coverage. He was told: 'clearances by MoD were still taking a long time . . . the previous day had seen some particularly bad delays . . . these were more the result of inefficiency than the desire to censor' (NCA, 8.6.82). At an earlier meeting, we hear that there were perhaps other purposes behind the delays. The editor of radio news commented:

> the MoD seemed, on occasions, to be indulging in brinkmanship by delaying clearances until just before air-time, even though the BBC had made it clear it was prepared to use reports if clearances were not given in time.
>
> NCA, 1.6.82

The professional needs of journalists raise here the prospect of defying the MoD. In their evidence to the Defence Committee the BBC commented that the delays were effectively increasing the credibility of Argentine information, at the expense of the MD's.[30] The delays and paucity of visual material also enraged the press. One newspaper editor summed up the limits of the briefings given by Sir Frank Cooper:

> Whenever it got a bit hot, he'd drag up 'the national interest'. Here are you screaming, 'Where's my bloody pictures?' and he says, 'It's my job to safeguard lives.' There's not much of an answer to that.[31]

A second area of criticism was that the services and the war effort could have been portrayed better if the MoD's media operation had been organised by PR professionals. This belief was particularly strong in the Army following their years in Northern Ireland. It found supporting echoes in the BBC where it was thought by some that the dominance of the administrative civil servants was doing less than justice to the Forces. The Army, Navy and Air Force all have directors of public relations. Their work was effectively suspended – in the opinion of Alan Protheroe, the BBC's Assistant Director General, the 'practised machine was shunted into a siding by the mandarins'.[32] His views were drawn to the attention of the NCA meeting on 8 June:

> The Assistant Director General said members of the meeting would be aware of the piece he had written for the *Listener* which called for an enquiry into the MoD's handling of information dissemination. He had received a great deal of support for this call from within the government information service, but the reaction from administrative civil servants had been 'sniffy' . . . there should be adequate provision of information throughout a crisis. ADG knew that the Army supported this view strongly and that the Air Force also subscribed to it, though the Navy had yet to make up its mind where it stood.
>
> NCA, 3.6.82

ITN was also clear about the direction that its news coverage should take. In its evidence to the Defence Committee[33] it said the inadequacies of the MoD had meant that 'great opportunities were missed for the positive projection of single-minded energy and determination by the British people in their support of the Task Force. For example: 'ITN sought permission to report how dockyard workers were completing tasks in record time.' The BBC *had* managed to give such an impression of a dockyard in Glasgow – although in fact 40% of this workforce had voted against lifting an overtime ban to speed up work on the Task Force ships.[34] This raised the crucial question of to what extent the British people were of a 'single mind' about sending the Task Force. ITN believed that the Falklands issue was not socially divisive and contrasted it with Vietnam: 'Vietnam divided American home opinion: the polls in Britain showed a consistent majority support for the Task Force action.'[35]

The best that can be said of such a view is that it represents the 'tyranny of the majority' and says nothing of ITN's duty to represent the approximate one quarter/one third of the population whom it believed to be against the action. The worst is that ITN had a completely inaccurate analysis of what the British people thought of the conflict. The polls showed that attitudes were very complex.[36] Until well into the crisis a majority thought that the issues did not merit losing British life. Crucial escalations of the conflict such as the British landings on the Falklands received majority support only on condition that diplomatic negotiations and other non-violent actions were impossible. A poll on this, just before the landings, also showed that 76% of the population wished the United Nations to administer the islands pending a diplomatic solution. Little of this appeared on ITN. The 'nightly offering' the ITN desired was quite different: 'Flair in high places could have led to a nightly offering of interesting, positive and heart-warming stories of achievement and collaboration born out of a sense of national purpose.'[37]

In an interview with us, two senior ITN journalists summarised what they saw as the prevailing attitude at this time:

> We're a national news service. We reflect the nation and the mood of the nation. The nation trusts us. We reciprocate that trust by giving people the truth including the bad things, unless that would undermine morale; then we wouldn't put them on.

In both ITN and BBC there were many who apparently believed that the 'British people' and the 'public' as a whole were unreservedly behind the war. None the less the broadcasters would not accept the outright fabrication of stories to secure or increase this support. They were afraid that, if they carried false information, their credibility would be undermined. The editor of BBC radio news put this clearly:

> the BBC had made it clear there were some things it could not reveal. If at the end of the conflict it had to confess to the public that it had deliberately misled it, rather than withheld certain information in the interests of safeguarding life, the BBC's credibility would be gone.

The defence of the Corporation was a paramount concern of the NCA meetings and was a further source of the criticism directed at the authorities. Many bitter words were spoken on the duplicity of politicians:

> The Assistant Director General said he was most disappointed by the calculated misrepresentation of the BBC by some MPs. The prime example was Lord—'s accusation against [a journalist]. The ADG noted the special position of politicians, but felt a good many of them had exceeded the latitude even Parliamentarians could expect and had made fools of themselves: he recognised there was no requirement on politicians to be either accurate or truthful.
>
> NCA, 18.5.82

Later we hear that 'he had copied the BBC's response to the Prime Minister's office as a precaution against more MP chicanery' (NCA, 8.6.82).

These attitudes left the BBC caught in a contradiction. In practice they were helping the government and MoD construct a particular image of the war. But as professionals they could not be seen to take part in manipulation or no one would believe them in the future. Even those in the BBC with the greatest affinity with the Forces still felt this problem. There was an extraordinary exchange at the House of Commons Defence Committee where Alan Protheroe, the BBC's Assistant Director General, was giving evidence. He was challenged by one of the MPs[38] to give an example of 'manipulation' by the MD which was different from what the BBC normally did when it 'co-operated' in 'suppressing news'. Protheroe gave the example of an MoD statement that there would only be 'raids' on the Falklands rather than the full-scale landing which actually took place. This was referred to by the *Daily Express* as 'the most blatant piece of misinformation' of the war.[39] Yet Protheroe was ambivalent:

> I would find it, frankly and honestly, very difficult to condemn the Ministry of Defence for putting out that statement in the way that they did because clearly you can interpret that as being operationally required, that the publication of that intention is to confuse the

enemy . . . I am still very troubled by a feeling that there is something wrong when a government department is seeking to manipulate and manage the news. That I find a matter of immense professional personal concern.

The MP deftly pulled the rug from under him:

Mr Protheroe, I am not seeking to embarrass you, but after several minutes of questions you have failed to give me a single example of where you think the Ministry of Defence did wrong in this area, in contradistinction from the way you performed precisely the same way in principle.

There was a further source of criticism from journalists and others who sought outrightly to condemn the government's information policy as well as the conduct of much of the media. With the exception of the *Daily Mirror*, the popular papers had largely supported the war, and even relished it. Kim Sabido, the Independent Radio News reporter with the Task Force, was sharply critical: 'We have all been acting to a smaller or larger degree like overblown egos auditioning for parts in some awful B war movie.'[41]

In the NCA meeting there were serious criticisms made of the BBC's own coverage. Some voices were raised against the too ready acceptance of MoD claims and against decisions such as the banning of bereaved relatives. On 25 May, there was a surge of dissent:

Rick Thompson said the Television News foreign desk had been in a dilemma over the *Antelope*. The MoD had been very strongly against disclosure and had confined their own reference to 'one of our frigates has sustained some damage' at the tail-end of a statement. But since the ship was on fire and the Argentines were unlikely to be in any doubt that she had been seriously damaged, it was hard to think of an operational reasons for delaying disclosures. It was difficult to eliminate the suspicion that news was being delayed because naval losses were politically sensitive. Endorsing this point, Roger Bolton [editor of Nationwide] asked if the BBC had too readily accepted the MoD claim that 5,000 troops had been landed.

NCA, 25.5.82

But the dominant trend in television news and the popular press was to support government policy and many journalists embraced the heady mix of patriotism and fascination with war.

This appetite for conflict on the part of those who were in no danger was commented on by David Tinker, a naval officer who eventually died on HMS *Glamorgan*, three days before the end of the war. He wrote:

The newspapers just see it as a real-life 'War Mag' and even have drawings of battles, and made-up descriptions entirely from their own imagination! If some of the horrible ways that people died occurred in their offices, maybe they would change their tone.[42]

This was not true of all reports and some from television journalists with the Task Force made no effort to disguise the horror and carnage of battles such as Goose Green. Against this must be set the comic-book version of the war and those fighting it which was more typical of the media as a whole. These cardboard images disguised the real thoughts, fears and beliefs of a huge number of different people. For example, the war-comic view does not permit the admission that any of the Task Force were less than perfect. After the war, Robert Fox, the BBC radio reporter in the Falklands, did make such a brief acknowledgement, while writing in the *Listener*:

> I cannot pretend these men are angels. In Port Stanley when the tension of battle was over the amount of 'proffing' by British troops was considerable – some understandable, some not, such as the thieving of a collection of gold coins from a young vet who had just lost his wife in the final bombardment.[43]

But the mass audiences received largely the overblown images of war – a tendency which extended into television, with headlines such as 'How the SAS dared to win' (ITN, 4.6.82); and 'grandiose' descriptions from the BBC, as David Tinker recorded:

> The BBC were on board and grandiosed everything out of all proportion (Antarctic wind, Force 9 gales, terrific disruption done, disrupted entire Argentinian war effort, etc.). Mostly, they sat drinking the wardroom beer and were sick in the heads: the weather was in fact quite good.[44]

This was not how the BBC saw its coverage. On 15 June, the Assistant Director General

> asked for his thanks and congratulations to be extended to everyone involved with the BBC's Falklands coverage. He had never been prouder of BBC journalism. . . . When others tried to claim (as they frequently did) that fine war reporting had died at the end of World War Two, ADG hoped his colleagues would shout aloud, in their rebuttal, the names of such as Hanrahan and Fox of the BBC and Nicholson of ITN. They had behaved in exemplary fashion, with courage and professionalism. ADG said the BBC's coverage of the Falklands crisis was a shining chapter in the history of the BBC's journalism.
>
> NCA, 15.6.82

In the period after the conflict the glow faded and many in the BBC and ITN expressed unease about the quality of the coverage. A strong impression from our interviews was that journalists believed they had been 'had' by the MoD and, worse, had fallen too readily for the atmosphere generated by Fleet Street. One very senior member of the NCA meetings revealed his opinion to us: 'The whole atmosphere in Fleet Street did somehow affect broadcasting. I accept privately that the news responded too enthusiastically . . . in its writing and presentation, it was a bit over the top.'

What sort of broadcasting do we have?

Broadcasting is not a simple tool of the government. It is incorrect to see the state itself as a single unified apparatus able to transmit its views at will, via subservient broadcasters. To begin with, there are divisions within the state – between, for example, the 'administrative' civil servants and the new PR professionals. While one sought to close down on contacts with the media, the other sought to provide certain types of information and meet the 'needs' of journalism. More crucially, there were major divisions between sections of the state – as between the government and the military and between different parts of the armed forces. There was intense jealously and rivalry between these, particularly since they saw their 'profile' in the Falklands War as affecting their own future. Max Hastings, in an article published after the conflict, commented on the divisions between the Army and Navy:

> The land forces staff were infuriated by newspaper reports – presumably inspired by the Ministry of Defence in London — commending [Admiral Woodward's] judgement for choosing San Carlos Bay as the landing zone. In reality the Navy had favoured a landing on the featureless Plain of Lafonia to the south, and it was Thompson's staff [Army Command] who insisted otherwise.[45]

Decisions on who should be featured affected the MoD's thinking on censorship; ITN were asked to remove a passage about the Second Parachute Regiment: 'The ITN representative could see no security objections. When challenged, the MoD man in London said that 2 Para had received too much publicity already.'[46] One effect of this tension between the Services was to make the policy of limiting contacts with the media difficult to enforce. As one senior BBC editor told us: 'If the Navy thought the Army was getting too much coverage, then they would leak stories about what they were doing.'

There was also tension between the government and military, since one of the government's priorities was to announce 'victories'. There are many hints in the NCA minutes that this sometimes clashed with military priorities such as the need to keep troop positions secret.

One BBC journalist who was with the Task Force revealed his suspicion that 'political pressures in London had led to premature release of information' (NCA, 29.6.82). There were other divisions between 'political' and the 'military' which had direct effect on broadcasting. Decisions over cuts in defence budgets and over the allocation of resources were extremely sensitive. The broadcasters were effectively caught in the middle of these arguments. Alan Protheroe commented in one NCA meeting on the loss of the *Sheffield*. He believed that 'accountants in the MoD had effectively sunk the *Sheffield* by denying the ship anti-missile capability: the story of delays over Sea Wolf would develop and it was bound to anger the government' (NCA, 11.5.82).

There is no absolute unity of interest between the media, the government and the military. As we have seen, conflicts arose from the professional and commercial needs of journalism for pictures and 'news'. None the less, there were some general values which linked most of the media and the various sections of the state – specifically a desire to win the war and to be seen as supporting 'our' patriotic effort to the maximum. It is not hard to see why a right-wing press should so readily embrace these values and lend support to the government during the conflict. But why should this be so for broadcasting?* There were three reasons important at this time. Firstly, many journalists relished the experience of war reporting. A senior ITN correspondent told us that as the conflict was essentially a local affair it carried none of the overriding fears of a major conflagration. Reporting from London, if not from the Falklands, was perfectly safe. In his words: 'There was never any danger that this good wonderful war could escalate into anything like *The Day After* [the nuclear war film]. It was a good gutsy war but it was a safe gutsy war.'

Secondly, the broadcasters had a professional interest in speaking on behalf of what they hoped was 'the people'. Both BBC and ITN seek the authority and prestige of being a 'national' news service. ITN especially began to deviate from the normal format of news. It

---

*Broader issues are involved, including the relationship of broadcasting to the state, and broadcasting neutrality in the face of class and cultural interests. We give a fuller account of these in *Really Bad News* (Writers and Readers Co-operative, 1982).

included, after its main bulletin, small homilies intended to catch the 'national' mood. On 25th May, Alastair Burnett gives his views on 'willpower': 'It is usually willpower, plain people's willpower, that wins wars' (ITN, 22.00, 26.5.82).

Finally, the 'normal' manner in which broadcasters represent opinion and the sources which they use meant that they would tend to support and mainly feature 'official' views. In a sense, it was dangerous for them to do anything else given the pressures they were under, but it is probable that their normal procedures would have led them in this direction irrespective of the rows with the government. Public broadcasting does not see its main function as being to feature the views of 'the people'. Rather it shows those of the people's 'representatives', reflecting the authoritative points of view which emerge via the official channels. As we have seen, government sources tend to dominate such channels, but there was a further problem which affected the coverage of the Falklands conflict: the official opposition was divided on its approach to the war, even though a substantial section of the population was against it. In the absence of a clear lead from the political apparatus, television was unable to feature anything like the public debate which existed. In the early stages of the conflict some broadcasters were clearly aware of this absence. John Cole, the BBC's political editor, commented:

> [The BBC] was most vulnerable to criticism over its limited coverage of the internal debate in the country, though many Tories would regard any coverage of this as pure speculation because the dissenting views were being kept so private.
>
> NCA, 11.5.82

Although there was apparently dissent from the government's policy on both sides of the House of Commons, much of this remained muted. Politicians were using the system of 'unattributable' quotes to avoid the dangers of making a firm stand against the war. This is the sense of John Cole's reference to 'dissenting views being kept private'. It does not mean they were private in the country as a whole. In practice, however, *because* the BBC could get its 'normal' and 'official' channels to work, the debate in the country went largely unreported. It is clear from the NCA discussions that those present knew much more than they would allow to be said on the air. We hear in the same meeting that the 'Government machine' is stressing one line while 'ambassadors and, in private, members of the war cabinet were saying different things' (on the need for negotiation). Consequently, 'the basis for reporting anything in addition to the official line was insubstantial' (NCA, 11.5.82). Again, in the case of the row over *Panorama*, the editor, George Carey, stated that its 'misinterpretation' owed much to the fact that the extensive support for the Crouch-Meyer view [the dissent] among Conservative MPs was only expressed in private' (NCA, 11.5.82).

On another occasion the BBC was attacked for allegedly revealing information on troop positions to the detriment of the British Forces. According to the BBC the information had actually been released by the MoD or by senior politicians. The argument surfaced over reports on the Goose Green attack:

> The countryside in the area was completely open and 2 Para had been desperately vulnerable to air attack. The Argentines had brought up reinforcements during the night and Brigadier Thompson had considered calling off the attack. Col Jones had discussed steps he might take on his return to the UK to protest against this: he had threatened to sue a senior MoD person, and had decided on an open letter to *The Times*. David Holmes said it appeared it had taken the ground forces some time to accept that the information about the Goose Green attack had been released by the MoD.
>
> NCA, 29.6.82

It was widely believed in the BBC that the information was being released for 'political' reasons – from the desire to announce early victories. If British troops were being endangered because of such political priorities then this was surely a very hot news story, but one not destined to see the light of day. A journalist with the Task Force gave the details:

> Brian Hanrahan suspected that political pressures in London had led to the premature release of information. He knew the surrender of the Argentine garrison at Goose Green had been announced semi-officially in London on the night of Friday 28 May; the surrender had not in fact taken place until the Saturday morning. A more glaring example was the report of the recapture of Darwin: the Task Force commanders believed this had been accomplished without the Argentinians being aware that it had happened, but any advantage that could have derived from this had been lost by the statement in London from MoD.
>
> NCA, 29.6.82

The most significant feature of these arguments is that they all take place behind closed doors. The BBC would rather suffer the attacks on itself in silence than betray its self-imposed 'confidences'. In part the silence from the broadcasters on the issue of Goose Green may be explained if they wished to defend their own information sources. It is less understandable when the issue is the premature release of military information for political reasons. The result of this style of journalism is that information which is familiar to politicians, civil servants and broadcasters is kept from the public. It is only for the ears of the 'privileged'.

Does broadcasting matter?

As the war progressed the broadcasters became less concerned with the problems of featuring dissent and used a crude notion of 'public opinion' to limit their coverage. But even if the public had all supported the war, the broadcasters must still face the problem that such support is in part conditional upon what people hear both about the war, and chances for peace. As we show in Chapter 4, the information given about UN peace attempts varies between news services and to some extent between different countries. For example, in the United States there were reports early in June that the Argentines were contemplating a ceasefire and unilateral withdrawal. But the television news in Britain gave mainly the 'official' view that the peace plans 'would have left the Argentines on the Falklands'.

Some broadcasters believe that their coverage did have an effect in shaping public opinion. Barry Cox, the Head of Documentaries at London Weekend Television, criticised the role of the Ministry of Defence in this:

> They [the MoD] were making optimistic assertions – for example of the success of the blockade and the bombing of the runway and the poor quality of the Argentine soldiers' equipment and morale. Had we as journalists not all reported in quite the way we did at the time the Peace Party would have had a better chance of turning the Task Force round and the war in the Falklands of not taking place.[47]

When the journalists use 'public opinion' as a justification for limiting coverage they create a closed circle in which information that makes dissent credible is excluded in the name of such dissent not existing. Stuart Hood was editor of BBC television news between 1958–61 and was a senior broadcaster at the time of the Suez crisis. He compared for us his own experiences then, with the BBC's performance over the Falklands:

> At Suez where the country was split down the middle, and this split was reflected in management, a decision had to be taken on editorial

policy – on whether to broadcast those [views] which reflected that split. There is evidence from highly placed officials that Eden was prepared to commandeer the BBC overseas services. The immediate question was, should the overseas services continue to broadcast these programmes (which could be heard by troops going into Suez) – or should they censor the views?

Hugh Greene decided that as journalists we had a duty to continue the services. He decided to continue and relied on a public outcry if they were stopped. In the case of the Falklands, there was certainly a split of opinion in the BBC, but they decided eventually that they had to keep in step with 'public opinion' as they perceived it – a public opinion that they had very largely created.

There is an argument which suggests that distortion in the media does not really matter – that people do not care about being misled if the 'war effort' is enhanced. This is one of the conclusions of the Parliamentary Defence Committee:

> Many principles, supposedly regarded as sacred and absolute within the media, are applied in a less rigid and categorical way by the public as a whole when it is judging its government's conduct of a war. In our judgement the public is, in general, quite ready to tolerate being misled to some extent if the enemy is also misled, thereby contributing to the success of the campaign.[49]

It is not clear how the exaggerated accounts of British successes, as in the bombing of Port Stanley airfield, could have been expected to deceive the Argentines. Such stories were presumably meant for home consumption. The Committee may, however, be correct in its conclusion if the intention of the deceit or censorship is to preserve life. Very few would argue that 'freedom of information' should extend to revealing troop positions. But there are other conditions under which deceit might not be so acceptable: if the intention was to 'manage' public opinion into accepting the high casualties of war, or to prolong a conflict by avoiding chances for peace. The public might not be so ready to accept these, and perhaps even less the possibility that politicians might reveal what the military regard as 'secret' in the cause of winning swift political victories at home. All these raise quite different questions about what the public 'thinks' and what it has the right to know.

TWO

Fighting the War

Here we look at two key areas of coverage. The sinking of the Argentine Cruiser *Belgrano* on May 2nd 1982 and the British attacks on Port Stanley airfield on the previous day. The destruction of the Argentine ship was perhaps the most controversial act in the Falklands fighting. As such it created problems for broadcasters since they were faced with a variety of different views. Many of these related to the justification or condemnation of the act—others focussed on the human consequences such as the conditions of the survivors. In choosing between these accounts broadcasters effectively illustrate their own interpretation of what is balance and impartiality within the news. For purposes of comparison we also looked at the language used about the later sinking of H.M.S. *Sheffield*. In the first two sections of this chapter we compare the coverage of the *Belgrano* and *Sheffield* looking specifically at the treatment of 'survivors' and 'casualties' as themes in the news. In the following two sections we compare the coverage of the ships again looking at the reasons which were given to explain their destruction and the arguments which surrounded these military actions.

The bombing of the Port Stanley airfield is also a crucial example since the event was used in Britain to illustrate the technical excellence of the British forces. The television coverage of the action and the extent to which official claims were questioned shows clearly the relationship that existed in practice between 'government sources' and broadcasting.

The *Belgrano*

The airport bombing and the sinking of the Argentine cruiser

produced the first major casualties of the war, yet paradoxically a
consistent theme adopted by journalists was the 'survivability' of the
crew of the *Belgrano*. This stress was apparent from the first bulletins
of 3 May in the language of the newscript, the questions posed by
newscasters to fellow journalists, to invited 'experts' and finally in the
use of visual material. Though journalists initially admitted that
knowledge was lacking about the fate of the crew they tended to
underplay the effects of the torpedo attack. The numbers killed were
peripheral to the question of how many potentially could be 'saved'
and later the numbers who had survived. For example:

> *Journalist:* The *Belgrano* was *safe from immediate destruction by her thick
> armour plating* below the waterline; *but for that there might have been
> heavy loss of life* amongst her crew of 1,000 men. As yet we don't know
> exactly when she went down, presumably her *two escorting destroyers
> were able to go alongside to take off the survivors* . . . . So victory once
> again for the Task Force.
>
> > BBC1, 21.35, 3.5.82

> *Journalist:* The sinking of the cruiser, if that indeed is what happened, is
> a major naval disaster for Argentina, only three days into this open
> conflict with Britain, and with no news yet of the 1,000 crewmen
> aboard her there must be fears of *a grave human disaster as well. But
> there is a good chance that a lot of them will have been saved.* After all the
> torpedo struck a hole in her 24 hours ago and the announcement of
> her probable loss has only now come from Argentina. *She had two
> escorts with her who may have picked up most of the men* on board *who
> could have survived* the attack *and were able to make their escape,* but
> we just don't know yet.
>
> *Presenter:* With the latest news on this, John Stapleton, I hope, has now
> come on the line to us from Buenos Aires. *Are there any details or
> indications once again about the possibility of survivors,* John?
>
> *Reporter in Argentina:* No, there's considerable confusion about that,
> Donald. Officially the government here are saying absolutely nothing
> about survivors. What we do know is, as you probably indicated
> earlier in the programme, the ship normally has a crew of about 1,000,
> maybe 1,200 men. Local radio is saying the boat is missing with only
> 500 men on board. *Now it could be that the other five or six hundred
> were rescued in time,* but officially we really don't know.
>
> > *Newsnight Special,* BBC2, 3.5.82

Reporters with the Task Force whose accounts were censored also
stressed their lack of information, but through the studio linkman the
'survivor' theme was maintained. The following account shows the
Task Force reporter to be unaware that the *Belgrano* had been

destroyed at least thirty miles outside the exclusion zone and had sunk forty minutes after being hit at 8.00 p.m. on 2 May:

> *Task Force reporter:* We don't know if she still has her own power. What we are trying to find out from Admirality staff aboard *Hermes* is whether she has power to *take herself back outside the exclusion zone,* whether there are other ships in the Argentine battle group who are at this moment patrolling outside the exclusion zone but who are nearby and would *be allowed to come in and tow her away or take survivors aboard.* We are still waiting for information.
>
> *Newscaster:* Are any of the ships of the Task Force standing by to take on any *possible survivors,* for example?
>
> *Task Force reporter:* Yes, *Hermes* broadcast an emergency message over the emergency frequency to ships in the area, and that is all ships in the area to *look for survivors.* That must include British ships too of course.
>
> *Newscaster:* And what about *life-saving equipment?* Anything like that dropped in the sea by the *Hermes?*
>
> *Task Force reporter:* No. There will be normal helicopter surveillance *and sweep for survivors.* All that can be done is being done to *pick up survivors* in the sea. We do not know whether any casualties have gone overboard or whether there are any casualties at all. We must assume that there are. Our information is that the ship is still afloat and that emergency measures have been put into operation.
>
> ITN, 17.00. 3.5.82

After the bombing of Port Stanley and the sinking of the *Belgrano,* ITN is still asking a military expert if Britain can oust the Argentines from the Falklands without killing people:

> *Newscaster:* But after three days of hostilities, where do we go from here? One view from retired Admiral Wemyss.
>
> *Admiral Wemyss:* I think we are moving in very well-constituted steps, with meticulous planning before each, remembering all the time that we are not there to kill people. We are there to get the Argentinians out of the Falklands.
>
> *Newscaster:* But will it be possible to get the Argentinians out of the Falklands without killing people?
>
> *Admiral Wemyss:* I believe – I believe so personally, and I also believe we are moving in a step-by-step manner with that aim.
>
> ITN, 22.20, 3.5.82

The emphasis is put upon survivors through the reporting of rescue attempts and the failure to describe the effects of torpedo action.

As this theme was developed, a 'survival expert' appeared on three BBC bulletins on 4 May. On the 12.30 bulletin he was interviewed in the studio:

Newscaster: Captain Greenland, first of all, *what is the chance of survival* in those seas down in the South Atlantic in craft like these?

Interviewee: Well, it depends to a great extent on the training the seamen have had. Properly trained, I feel reasonably confident myself that they could exist . . . quite easily.

Newscaster: It appears from reports we have had over the past few days that the ship was first damaged and didn't sink immediately, so *presumably there's a good chance they could have got off.*

Interviewee: Well, in my opinion they could have spent the time very wisely in preparing themselves to evacuate the ship and consequently they probably, dependent on weather conditions, have got away.

Newscaster: How would they get into them?

Interviewee: Well, the liferaft would have been thrown over the side, and they would probably have climbed in either down ropes or jumped into the water to be pulled in. But the jumping into the water idea I doubt because of the intense cold. They would probably survive between two and four minutes.

Newscaster: Well, assuming they have got into these inflatable lifecraft, how would they survive once in them?

Interviewee: Again it comes down to training. Properly trained, they would make sure they were dry inside, completely battened down, and to all extent and purposes they would probably be in a survival bag.

Newscaster: You have one here I believe. What exactly does it involve?

Interviewee: It's basically a sleeping bag that retains the body heat of the person who is wearing it, which enables them to keep hypothermia at bay.

Newscaster: And providing they are dry when they get into it, they can keep *warm and comfy* in it for a long time?

BBC1, 12.30, 4.5.82

The assumptions made by the newscaster that the crew might be 'comfy' contrast sharply with a report much later in the *Sunday Times:*

> *One severely burned man in that raft could only avoid aggravating his agonising injuries by crouching on his knees. For 30 hours* which is how long it took before help arrived he did not utter a word. He was the first man taken on board an Argentine rescue ship; half an hour later he died. In all 368 of the crew of the *Belgrano* perished.
>
> Sunday Times, 17.10.82

This description of conditions after the sinking was not available to television news on 4 May. However, the lack of information cannot explain the extraordinary minimising of the consequences of the attack. Some media abroad, from the outset, stressed the possibility that hundreds had died. On the same day as the above BBC1 bulletin, BBC's *Nationwide* interviewed Lars Neilson, a United States

journalist, via satellite in New York. He held up the front-page headlines of three US newspapers:

New York Daily News: 'Fear 500 Died on Cruiser'
New York Post: 'Fear Hundreds Dead in Sea Battle'
Washington Post: 'Argentine War Ship Sinks, 900 Missing'

As the rescue attempts following the British attack began to make progress the 'survivor' count was displayed prominently in news headings and summaries, without reference to the likelihood that hundreds may have been killed:

Newscaster: The Argentinians say that some 400 survivors have been picked up so far . . . but one agency report from Buenos Aires quotes naval sources as saying that the *majority of the 1,000 crew are safe.*
Newscaster: Well, it's certain that many governments in Europe will backtrack a little now that the *casualties don't seem to be as high as feared.*

ITN, 17.45, 4.5.82

Newscaster: Argentina says *680 rescued* from the *General Belgrano.*
Newscaster: And in another development, an Argentine tug is reported to have *picked up 400 survivors from the Argentine cruiser General Belgrano* which sank after being torpedoed by a British Navy

submarine and the report also says that fifteen more liferafts have been spotted. The ship, a survivor of the Japanese attack on Pearl Harbor in 1941, was sold by America to Argentina thirty years ago. It was torpedoed by a British submarine on Sunday, and following that, it sank. *It was feared there wouldn't be many survivors because of the extremely cold seas but now it seems many of the sailors managed to get into liferafts* that were aboard the ship.

BBC1, Newsround, 4.5.82

Newscaster: The Argentines say there were *around 700 survivors* from the 1,082 men on board the *General Belgrano* which was torpedoed on Sunday.

ITN, 17.45, 5.5.82

Newscaster: The first group of survivors from the Argentine cruiser *General Belgrano* have been brought ashore. The *General Belgrano* was torpedoed by a British submarine on Sunday; *800 men have been rescued* and the searches still continue for others.

BBC1, 9.15, 6.5.82

From 6 May film of the return of some of the crew of the *General Belgrano* was available to develop the survivor theme, already well established in the news of both channels:

Reporter in Argentina: Meanwhile the planes bringing the first of the *survivors* from the *General Belgrano* touched down . . . Each *survivor* was personally greeted by a top naval officer . . .
Considering they had spent 48 hours in fragile rafts, in the freezing sea, they all looked surprisingly well. During the day the reunions continued *as over 300 men of an estimated 800 came home,* including the captain of the sunken cruiser. *The survivors* have already asked if they can be sent back to sea, as soon as possible. The *General Belgrano* had a complement of 1,242. So far there is *no news of the estimated 200 sailors* who are still *missing presumed dead.*

ITN, 13.00, 6.5.82

This is one of the comparatively rare references using the term 'dead'. The following reports show the more usual use of terms such as 'lost' or 'missing':

Newscaster: The Argentinians say that 27 of their men have so far died in the fighting and 44 have been wounded, but that doesn't take into account about *370 men missing from the cruiser General Belgrano* which was torpedoed last Sunday.

ITN, 22.00, 7.5.82

Newscaster: The Argentine chiefs of staff have issued the first casualty figures among their forces since the beginning of hostilities. They say 19 men have died and 37 have been wounded. This doesn't take account of those *lost* in the sinking of the cruiser *General Belgrano*. Now the *Argentinians say that 800 of the 1,000-strong crew have been rescued.* One of them said the ship went down in 40 minutes after being hit by two torpedoes.

BBC1, 21.00, 7.5.82

An interesting follow-up to BBC1's 7 May report came from Brian Barron in Chile. He said that transmissions from the Argentine commander on the Falklands had been intercepted and decoded.

Subtitles of what was said were put up on the screen in both the 12.30 and 9.00 bulletins. On the 12.30 news his words were translated on the screen as: 'The sinking of the *General Belgrano* has opened the door for *maximum use of force by our side*' (BBC1, 12.30, 7.5.82). But in the 9.00 bulletin this was changed to: 'The sinking of the *General Belgrano* has opened the way for us *to kill*' (BBC1, 21.00, 7.5.82). The translations apparently refer to the same statement. It is extraordinary that a statement should be re-translated to emphasise the willingness of the Argentines to 'kill', and contrasts with the words used for British actions. The literal translation is: 'The sinking of the *Belgrano* has opened the door for us to pass through'.

BBC1 17.40 6.5.82

Argentine Army Commander
on the Falklands

"...the sinking of the General Belgrano
has opened the way for us to kill."

BBC1 21.00 6.5.82

On 9 May both channels gave prominence to the first photo taken of the *Belgrano* as she began to sink into the sea. The photo itself was news, shown on screen with the barest of narrative:

> *Newscaster:* The first picture of the sinking of the Argentine cruiser the *General Belgrano* appears on the front page of tomorrows *Daily Mail*. The ship was torpedoed a week ago *on the edge* of the 200 mile exclusion zone then in force around the Falklands.
> ITN, 18.30, 9.5.82

> *Newscaster:* Photos have just reached London of the sinking of the Argentine cruiser last Monday, the *General Belgrano*. The *Daily Mail* photographs shows the 13,000 ton cruiser going down shortly after it was torpedoed by the British submarine. The photo was taken by a member of the *Belgrano's* crew after he was taken to a lifeboat.
> BBC1, 21.30, 9.5.82

The use of the word 'edge' by ITN (a frequent occurrence on both channels) implies an unwillingness to acknowledge that the cruiser was outside the exclusion zone. There is also still a reticence to use 'hard' terms to refer to the death toll on the *Belgrano*. This is well illustrated by the BBC's use of the official casualty figures for the *Belgrano* nearly two weeks after the sinking:

> *Newscaster:* Argentina has also issued the casualty figures for the *General Belgrano*, sunk by a Royal Navy submarine two weeks ago. They say that out of a crew of 1,100, 300 are still missing and 20 bodies have been recovered.
>
> BBC2, 19.00, 15.5.82

The statistics below show the terminology used when referring to the fate of the crew of the *General Belgrano*.*

Casualty statements on the **Belgrano**
3–15 May 1982

	Total	BBC	ITN
Lives lost/loss of life	32	18	14
Lost/loss	16	9	7
Casualties	11	6	5
Missing	6	5	1
Perished	4	2	2
Killing and trapping	3	3	—
Missing presumed dead	3	—	3
Drowning Argentinians	2	—	2
Death toll	2	1	1
Victims	2		2
Human disaster	2	2	—
Belgrano disaster	1	—	1
Naval disaster	1	1	—
Missing bodies recovered	1	1	—
Not accounted for	1	1	—
Lost or injured	1	1	—
Sad news	1	1	—
Sad fellow fighting for life	1	—	1
Costing lives	1	—	1
Dwindling hopes	1	—	1
Blood of hundreds of their men	1	—	1
Bottom of the ocean	1	—	1
Grieved over the loss	1	—	1
Funerals when established how many went down	1	1	—

---

*A fuller breakdown of the news language used in these themes is given in Appendix 3.

Survival statements on the **Belgrano** 3–15 May 1982

	Total	BBC	ITN
Survivors/survived	77	47	30
Rescued	18	14	4
They/them (survivors)	12	12	—
Picked up	9	6	3
Safe	9	3	6
Saved	7	6	1
Many thought husbands killed	3	3	—
Men alive	3	3	—
(A rescue ship was) lifesaver of 100	3	—	3
Men looked well	2	—	2
Got off/away/in	2	2	—
Many thought husbands dead	1	1	—
Adrift	1	1	—
Could exist easily	1	1	—
Taken to lifeboat	1	1	—
Scores of sailors reunited	1	—	1
All looked well	1	—	1
Came home	1	—	1
Without killing people	1	—	1
Moving with that aim (not killing)	1	—	1

As these tables show, journalists did not use the term 'killed' when referring to those who died on the *Belgrano*. The only occasion the term 'killing' was used to refer to casualties on the *Belgrano* came during coverage of an Argentine news conference attended by the ship's captain:

> *Journalist:* Captain Bonzo gave a graphic account of how two torpedoes struck the warship, one exploding in the engine room. The decks, he said, became red hot. *Two decks collapsed, killing and trapping crew members resting below. But others did not survive the battles at sea.* Eight crew members of another Argentine warship attacked last Monday were killed.
>
> BBC1, 18.00, 8.5.82

However, even this solitary example of the use of the word 'killing' in reporting Captain Bonzo's remarks is reduced in emphasis. For without a pause we leave the *Belgrano* story and go into another film report about Argentine casualties in a separate incident. The same journalist does the voice-over in both stories. The linking statement is significant: 'But others did not *survive* the battles at sea'. It is unusual in that it joins two separate film reports which are essentially about Argentine deaths. The 'survivability' theme on the *Belgrano* was, in fact, well established by 8 May.

Broadcasters *did*, however, use the term 'killed' when referring to other casualties of British action. Notably this is where British action is seen as unquestionably legitimate in their terms – for example, when a ship was sunk 'inside' the exclusion zone. But 'hard' terminology on the *Belgrano* casualties was softened in context. The phrase 'drowning Argentinians' was used, but in fact related to a story about the rescue of these people. Thus the full sentence read: 'Now the naval dockyard here has seen the gathering up of medical and food supplies to go to the rescue of drowning Argentinians in the South Atlantic.' In a similar fashion, the remark 'Many had thought their sons and husbands had been killed' comes from a film account of *Belgrano survivors* returning home. The phrase 'without killing people' occurs in the question put by ITN (3.5.82) on the possibility of there being no deaths in the Falklands War, which we noted above.

In the tables, of the two references to 'death toll', one is a reported statement by the Pope which refers to deaths on both sides, the other a reference on *Newsnight*; 'Both sides are counting the death toll of the naval battle' BBC2, 2.5.82). A *Newsnight* presenter also qualified one of the two references to the *Belgrano's* 'human disaster' by continuing, 'but there is a good chance that a lot of them will have been saved. (BBC2, 3.5.82). ITN exhibited the same tendency to modify the term on the only occasion the words *'Belgrano disaster'* were used: 'Four days after the *Belgrano* disaster, the South Atlantic and most of the Beagle Channel were calm, ensuring *the best conditions for the survivors*' (ITN, 13.00, 6.5.82).

Alternative accounts which mentioned the death toll were few and usually part of a package of information from British correspondents in Argentina. For example, on 4 May, ITN cited as one of its *headlines* the numbers rescued from the *Belgrano* and then included in the bulletin a statement that 300 sailors had 'perished'.

> So far the Argentinian government has issued no official communiqué on the attack on the *Sheffield*. High placed sources say the ship was hit by an Exocet missile fired from a land-based plane . . . Meanwhile, though the search continues *for survivors likely that more than 300 Argentinian sailors perished*.
>
> ITN, 22.00, 4.5.82

The fact that figures were not immediately available from Argentina on the number of casualties does not explain the broadcaster's emphasis on 'survivors' and the more frequent use of 'soft' terms to refer to the dead. For whatever reason, there appears to have been systematic underplaying of the harmful effects of this British action.

The Sheffield and the casualty theme

The reporting of the destruction of the British destroyer *Sheffield* contrasted sharply with the coverage of the *Belgrano*. It is to be expected that the British media would stress casualties and the seriousness of the events, given that the *Sheffield* was the first major British loss. But the quality of this coverage highlights by contrast the extremely underplayed reporting of the *Belgrano*. It also seems that the military authorities did not wish the media to focus on the *Sheffield* sinking as a major disaster – in which case the reports do show a 'break' with official wishes.

During the period under study the Ministry of Defence had monopolised announcements relating to military engagements and their outcome on the television news. Broadcasts and statements by the Whitehall defence spokesman Ian McDonald frequently punctuated news programmes. Yet given that the media personnel worked within this structural dependence, the language of news did not wholly result from this reliance on MoD sources. This can be most clearly seen on the BBC1 9.00 bulletin on 4 May. This bulletin was interrupted by the Defence Ministry with the news of the attack on HMS *Sheffield*, and the bulletin is therefore of particular interest, as newscaster and specialist correspondents had only minutes to adjust their script and comment upon the MoD announcement:

> In the course of its duties within the total exclusion zone around the Falkland Islands, HMS *Sheffield*, a type-42 destroyer, was attacked and hit late this afternoon by an Argentine missile. The ship caught fire which spread out of control. When there was no longer any hope of saving the ship, the ship's company abandoned ship. All those who abandoned her were picked up. It is feared there has been a number of casualties, but we have no details of them as yet. Next of kin will be informed first as soon as details are received.

This excerpt from the ministerial statement which refers to the *Sheffield* mentions implicitly that the crew fought the blaze and when forced to abandon ship all who did so were 'picked up'. However, the immediate reaction of journalists on this bulletin and those which followed it was to emphasise casualties:

> *Defence correspondent:* That announcement is going to come as a devastating blow to the Task Force commander and to the Navy, and indeed to Mrs Thatcher. The loss HMS *Sheffield*, one of our newest ships in the fleet, is an astonshing loss to have to admit. It is likely she was hit by an Exocet missile which is a very dangerous type of weapon and, as the statement said, the fire spread beyond control. As a result of that the ship had to be abandoned and *undoubtedly there have been quite considerable casualties.*
>
> *Newscaster:* Of course if we get any developments on that *particularly grave* incident we will be bringing them to you in the course of the programme.
>
> *Reporter:* . . . There is no indication here yet at the MoD about the *number of casualties*, but to recap on what the Ministry spokesman said a few minutes ago all those who abandoned her were picked up but it is *feared there have been a number of casualties*. From *a very, very sombre Ministry of Defence* in Whitehall back to the studio.
>
> BBC1, 21.10, 4.5.82

> *Presenter:* And in view of *tonight's terrible news* . . .
>
> *Presenter:* Lets leave tonight, just for the moment the *dreadful news* of the sinking of the *Sheffield*.
>
> *Newsnight*, BBC2, 4.5.82

> *Journalist:* Out of all the polls so far, they have shown that while people are fairly massively behind the government as regards the sending of the Task Force, support falls away very sharply indeed once we talk about the loss of British life, *and that loss, probably on a serious scale*, has now happened.
>
> ITN, 22.10, 4.5.82

From the onset, then, the broadcasting media stress the casualties following the attack on the *Sheffield*, and the human tragedy involved. Such terminology, 'normal' in the BBC's coverage of the *Sheffield*, was consciously censored in the scripting of information on the *Belgrano*. While a report from Brian Barron had been cut to take out a statement by him referring to the 'tragic incident of the *Belgrano*', 'harder' terms are used to describe those who lost their lives aboard the *Sheffield*:

> *Newscaster:* Wednesday's headlines are of course dominated by the attack on HMS *Sheffield with the loss of about thirty British lives.*
>
> *Reporter:* . . . The number of sailors *who perished* still stands at about thirty . . . Next-of-kin are being informed and we expect a list of those who *perished* later this afternoon.
>
> BBC1, 12.30, 5.5.82

Newscaster: About thirty British seamen were *killed* in the attack on the *Sheffield* by an Argentine missile. The Ministry of Defence say that 87 *are either dead or missing or wounded.*

Newscaster: . . . It's still not known how many British sailors were *killed* in the attack on the destroyer *Sheffield*; Mr Nott told the commons the figure is still about thirty. The Ministry of Defence say they are contacting 87 families of men who *are either dead or missing or wounded.*

ITN, 17.45, 5.5.82

A number of 'emotive' links were developed by the television channels through reporting on personal grief and the loss of the ship at a community level. ITN's one o'clock bulletin on 5 May reports troop reaction aboard the *Canberra*. We hear that 'they were stunned and pained. Men have died; men on the same side have died and as professionals they are keen to get on with it.' We go to a 'stunned' city of Portsmouth where families wait for the news of the survivors. Two Navy ratings are interviewed. One says, 'The *Shiny Sheff* was a great ship; the élite of the fleet.' Another says, 'Everyone wants to get down there and get our own back.' The report sums up the reaction: 'The shock of losing their destroyer and as many as thirty men has left an emptiness not witnessed here since the last war.' The coverage continued recording the 'stunning blow' in Scotland. A Scottish mother interviewed was 'shattered', and Londoners were 'shocked', 'stunned' and 'shattered'. The report ended with shots of Nelson's Column in London.

This saturation coverage stressing the desolation felt at the *Sheffield's* loss accords with the news' maximum stress on the fatalities aboard the ship. Significance is given in terms of a national loss during war. It is assumed that the audience has a common heritage vested in the knowledge of its 'Naval hero' Nelson and British naval traditions. This is made explicit in a visual statement in ITN's *News at Ten* on 6 May. Here the newscaster introduces the full list of the dead aboard *Sheffield* with every name individually subtitled on screen against the background of the Royal Ensign fluttering in the wind. At the end of this TV obituary the *Sheffield's* badge fills the screen in silent tribute.

The stress upon casualties was maintained through the coverage of the emotional reactions of those affected and by descriptions of the ship itself:

HMS *Sheffield* has been associated with the city of Sheffield for almost sixty years. Three vessels in the British fleet have borne that name since the First World War. Today the city was in mourning. Flags flew at half mast . . . Children from this orphanage adopted the *Sheffield* as their ship. Today they wept at the news. The *Sheffield's* officers and crew were often at civil functions. The ship was even loaned pictures from the council's art galleries. Local councillors meeting this afternoon offered condolences to the families of the crewmen killed or injured with the possibility that a disaster fund will now be started.

ITN, 17.45, 5.5.82

By 9 May film from the Task Force reporters was available to accompany the graphic narrative:

Newscaster: "Uppermost in most minds is the loss of HMS *Sheffield* and the men who died in her. She is still afloat . . .
Task Force reporter: For the last few days the Task Force helicopters have been keeping a watch on her. She made an eerie sight, drifting in and out of the mist banks; steam still rising from hatches on the foredeck. On the starboard there was huge hole where the missile had struck. Around it black patches where the paint was blistered off by the fire within. The deck was burned and twisted by the heat. The helicopter standing on the stern full of ash.

BBC1, 21.30, 9.5.82

In the same bulletin the filmed account of the memorial service held in Sheffield Cathedral ended thus:

It was a highly emotional occasion, most of those who had suffered direct loss and for the citizens of Sheffield, many of whom can't believe *that their ship is gone.*

BBC1, 21.30, 9.5.82

The tables below show how the treatment given to the destruction of the *Sheffield* was largely defined in terms of casualties, with a predominance of 'harder' terminology:

Casualty statements on the **Sheffield**

	Total	BBC	ITN
Casualties	62	45	17
Loss/es/ing	32	12	20
Die	23	13	10
Missing	20	15	5
Dead, missing and wounded	10	2	8
Killed	8	—	8
Dead	7	3	4
Presumed dead and injured/ies	7	4	3
Perished	5	3	2

continued

continuation

	Total	BBC	ITN
Lives lost	13	3	10
Killed, missing and wounded	2	2	—
Deaths	2	—	2
Dead and injured	2	2	—
Missing and seriously injured	2	2	—
Seriously injured	2	1	1
Mourning	2	1	1
Death toll	2	1	1
Gave their lives	2	—	2
Grave and tragic	1	—	1
Loss of life	2	1	1
Grave for the men	2	2	—
Agony	1	1	—
British blood spilled	1	1	—
Victims	1	—	1
Fatalities	1	—	1
Sank to her grave	1	—	1
Claimed twenty lives	1	1	—
Tragic loss	1	1	—
Tragic confirmation	1	1	—
Tragic incident	1	1	—
Tragic news	1	1	—
Grim news	1	1	—
Dreadful news	1	1	—
Survived the tragedy	1	1	—
Grave incident	1	1	—
Terrible news	1	1	—

Survival statements on the **Sheffield**

	Total	BBC	ITN
Survived survivor(s)	31	26	5
Picked up	16	9	7
Safe saved	13	8	5
Rescued	3	3	—
Crew abandoned ship	3	2	1
Alive	3	3	—
Coming home	2	—	2
Saved themselves	2	2	—
Nearly all accounted for	1	1	—

continued

continuation

	Total	BBC	ITN
They get back	1	1	—
Survived the tragedy	1	1	—
Other men transferred	1	1	—
Getting off	1	—	1
Good news	1	—	1
Unhurt	1	—	1

Certain logistical and pratical differences might also account for some of the divergence in the reporting of the *Belgrano* and the *Sheffield*. The fact that over 300 Argentine sailors who died on the *Belgrano* sank along with the vessel, and that rescue operations were prolonged, inhibited accurate numbers of those killed. The rescue operation itself was a major news item which, it may be contended, merited full coverage in its own right.

However, it seems unlikely that these arguments in themselves explain the major difference in language and visuals between the two events. The television news placed great stress on *Belgrano* 'survivors', when other sources did not; and this form of description was underplayed with the *Sheffield*, although the grounds for it were more secure: 'Nearly all the ship's company and the captain are accounted for . . . initial indications are that twelve men are missing and there are likely to be other casualties' (John Nott to House of Commons, BBC2, *Newsnight*, 4.5.82.)

Another *Newsnight* reference highlights the difference in the reporting of the *Belgrano* and the later sinking of the *Sheffield*:

> *From HMS Sheffield thirty men dead and missing* but 87 families have been contacted by the Defence Ministry in connection with relatives *killed*, missing or wounded. And as for the crew of the *General Belgrano* the Argentinians say they have *rescued* 800 and there could still be another 300 to account for.
>
> *Newsnight*, BBC2, 5.5.82

Why the *Belgrano* was sunk

> For Britain the torpedoing of an enemy ship, with its consequent loss of life, would mean a disastrous setback in the propaganda war . . . For Argentina to shoot first would simply be foolhardy. Her warships are intensely vulnerable to submarine attack.
>
> *Sunday Times*, 11.4.82

The first major engagements of the Falklands fighting came with the bombing of Port Stanley airfield on 1st May and the sinking of the *Belgrano* the following day. The latter accounted for almost a third of the deaths in the conflict.

On 5 May in reply to a question in the House of Commons regarding the distance and the time involved separating the *Belgrano* and the Task Force, Britain's Defence Minister, John Nott, replied: 'I see no reason why we should not be able to provide that information within a few days. There is no reason to conceal it.' This information was not provided till 1st May when it was confirmed that the cruiser was 200 nautical miles away from the Task Force, well outside the exclusion zone. Whatever threat the *Belgrano* posed, therefore, she was clearly, when sunk, not an immediate threat to British ships. The government was reported at the time as stating that the cruiser was sunk on the initiative of the submarine captain. Months later it was revealed in the US and British press that the order to torpedo the *Belgrano* had come direct from the war cabinet. According to the *Guardian* in October, the rules of engagement were 'promptly changed' to permit the attack.

At the time, the sinking was criticised on the basis that the cruiser was not an immediate threat. On 8 May, ITN reported the captain of the *Belgrano's* 'claim' that his ship was headed towards the Argentine mainland. In December the Ministry of Defence finally acknowledged in response to parliamentary questions that it was heading away from the Falklands Islands. Some journalists had doubts as to whether the pre-Second World War cruiser was a serious threat. It was known that, in terms of range and speed, the *Belgrano* was no match for Britain's modern frigates and destroyers or nuclear submarines. Dr Paul Rogers of Bradford University, for example, noted that the armaments were listed in all the major reference books and that even a Task Force frigate could outrange the *Belgrano* using its own missile system. An examination of the *Belgrano* and *Sheffield* sinkings as portrayed on television news shows an explanatory framework which stressed that the Argentines posed a 'threat' to which the British 'responded'.

The 'official' accounts were emphasised within the context of providing explanations of the latest developments, and access to critics was restricted. For example, the Ministry of Defence's explanation of why the *Belgrano* was sunk was developed by journalists as a paradigm for explaining the action:

> *Task Force reporter:* The cruiser had been operating outside Britain's 200 mile exclusion zone for several days . . . The attack was

selective and the cruiser's escorts were allowed to escape.* The Task Force has now dealt heavy blows at the Argentine Navy and Air Force as well as bombing and damaging the airport at Port Stanley.

So far it has shown it can enforce the sea and air blockade that Admiral Woodward said he intended to establish.

BBC1, 18.00, 3.5.82

Journalist: The *attack* on the *General Belgrano* was said to be *fully in accordance with the rules of engagement* issued to the British forces in the South Atlantic. *We now know those rules of engagement are wide ranging and allow the Task Force to attack any ship or aircraft that comes close to the fleet. What happened yesterday was that the Belgrano* along with its two escort vessels, *came close to the edge of the exclusion zone.*

ITN, 22.20, 3.5.82

Newscaster: The Ministry of Defence in London *says the General Belgrano had been manoeuvring in and out of the maritime exclusion zone.*

ITN, 22.20, 3.5.82

Journalist: What seems to have happened in the past 24 hours is that *there have been two separate attempts by the Argentine Navy to close on the British fleet* . . . A British submarine moved in on the Argentine warships *just outside* the 200 mile blockade zone. *The British say,* even though the Argentines were outside the zone, *they were still a threat to the Task Force.*

Newsnight, BBC2, 3.5.82

Journalist: The General Belgrano, as we know, was skirting the edge of the total exclusion zone, and certainly within the sights of its fifteen *guns there could have been* British forces, so the Task Force commander took the decision that *it was justified to attack* the cruiser.

BBC1, 12.30, 4.5.82

Ministry spokesman: As for the cruiser *Belgrano*, she for some time had been in the general area in which she was attacked. *She may have been going in and out of the total exclusion zone or perhaps skirting it . . . This force* because of its position relative to our Task Force and because of its weapon capability overall *posed a major threat* to our ships.

MoD broadcast, ITN, 13.00, 4.5.82

This stress on the cruiser as a 'threat' was emphasised on ITN by including explicit 'threat' references in the introduction or summary of news bulletins. On both channels the assumption of the imminent

---

*It was later suggested the British submarine had hit one of the escorts with a torpedo which failed to explode, though this was not known at the time by journalists.

Argentine attack provided the rationale for extended commentary by television journalists on what this 'threat' really meant – for example, 'is it a pincer movement' or a 'combined attack'? A numerical account of these references is given in the tables below:

Statements that the **Belgrano** was a threat and justifying the sinking

	Total	BBC	ITN
Threat (**including**: major threat, significant threat, very real threat, very obvious threat, serious threat)	28	13	15
Exclusion zone (implied threat) (**including**: not so far from dodging in and out, on edge of near, nosed in and out, maneouvring in and out, just outside, skirting it, around)	28	14	14
Defends (sinking of **Belgrano**)	7	4	3
Protect/ion (**Belgrano** sunk to protect British lives)	7	4	3
Justified (attack on cruiser)	6	5	1
Hours away (**Belgrano** from Task Force)	5	3	2
Rules of engagement (sunk in accordance with)	4	—	4
Self-defence (reason **Belgrano** attacked)	4	2	2
Warning given (to keep away from zone and Task Force)	4	2	2
Any later it would have been too late (**Belgrano** sinking)	4	2	2
Worry that the Argentines forces may attack	4	2	2
May get through to ours (i.e. Argentine attack)	4	2	2
At risk (British lives)	3	1	2
Necessary (attack on **Belgrano**)	3	3	—
Clos/ing (**Belgrano** on Task Force)	3	2	1
Our first duty is to our own forces (i.e. British)	3	1	2

continued

continuation

	Total	BBC	ITN
(Argentines may) sink our ships	3	2	1
No option (but to attack cruiser)	2	2	—
Can enforce sea and air blockade (i.e. **Belgrano** sinking)	2	2	—
Declared zone (defensive zone extended to cover Task Force movements)	2	2	—
Position relative to Task Force (**Belgrano** proximity a threat)	2	1	1
Because of its weapon capability	2	1	1
We must look after their safety (i.e. Task Force)	2	—	2
(Pym hopes) Argentines will now respect exclusion zone	2	—	2
Using minimum force	2	—	2
Aggressive intent (by Argentines)	1	—	1
Argentines were attempting pincer movement	1	1	—
Need to know what that cruiser doing so far south	1	1	—
Was it surprise attack?	1	1	—
Argentines planning combined attack?	1	1	—
If the need arises as commanders decided it did last night	1	1	—
Correct that she was attacked	1	1	—
(**Belgrano**) was trying to see if the British force on its way	1	—	1
Compelled to use force (against **Belgrano**)	1	1	—
Within sights of (**Belgrano's**) guns could have been British forces	1	1	—
(**Belgrano**) not alone with 15 guns	1	—	1
(**Belgrano** with) escorts with Exocet	1	—	1
Exocet is very potent missile	1	—	1
(**Belgrano** if allowed) perhaps fire those missiles	1	—	1
Insisted the cruiser's big guns dangerous	1	—	1
We are not apologising (for **Belgrano** sinking)	1	—	1
No one should be surprised when when Britain uses that force	1	—	1

continued

continuation

	Total	BBC	ITN
Keep clear of the British fleet (Argentines warned)	1	—	1
Became a positive menace (i.e. **Belgrano** group)	1	—	1
Only reason we would have taken out that cruiser (i.e. it could have have fired missiles)	1	—	1
Armaments cruiser and escorts carried (were threat)	1	1	—
The cruiser had substantial firepower	1	1	—
There may be further attacks on our forces (following **Belgrano** sinking)	1	1	—
Protected from fierce attack (i.e. **Belgrano** involved in such attack)	1	1	—
There were no regrets at the action (sinking)	1	1	—
Ignored it at his peril (i.e. **Belgrano**)	1	1	—
In fighting back they've done what they said they would do	1	1	—
An attack which was right to (make)	1	1	—
Exclusion zone (doesn't come into) this argument	1	1	—
Exclusion zone was a moral exclusion zone	1	1	—
An exclusion zone round the (British) forces	1	1	—
The fact that (**Belgrano**) was 35 miles outside is neither here nor there	1	1	—
(Sinking wrong?) No: the imposition of pressures necessitated the exclusion zone	1	1	—
(Necessary action) in order to save lives	1	1	—
pre-emptive action of that kind (necessary)	1	1	—
Responsive action is necessary	1	1	—
That is part of the function of Task Force	1	1	—
Many factors into account (in decision) to attack	1	1	—

continued

continuation

	Total	BBC	ITN
Keep out of the zones declared by us	1	1	—
Cease threatening and attacking our forces	1	1	—
Reluctantly compelled (military objectives)	1	—	1
Duty to defend ships, aircraft and men	1	—	1
(Aggressive intent) seen first in the claims	1	1	—
(Argentines) claimed sunk **Exeter**, **Hermes**, (downed) Harriers	1	1	—
Persistent attacks repelled by our our people	1	1	—

Statements and questions suggesting that the **Belgrano** was not a threat and criticising the British attack

	Total	BBC	ITN
(Cruise) outside exclusion zone*	13	10	3
Sinking uncalled for and treacherous aggression	6	3	3
Irish defence minister . . . Britain as the aggressor	6	2	4
(Task Force) used in a way (which) makes negotiations less likely	5	3	2
Labour leaders like Mr Healey concerned (sinking) bound to weaken world support	5	—	5
English/British muderers	4	4	—
Mrs Thatcher a crazy killer compared with Hitler	4	3	1
(Argentina) accuses Britain of sharply escalating the fighting (denounces escalation)	3	—	3
Outraged at the sinking	2	2	—
Least worrying of serious threats	2	2	—
In violation of UN charter	2	—	2

continued

---

*In addition, four statements noted that the cruiser was outside the zone but did not develop the implications either for or against the action.

continuation

	Total	BBC	ITN
Denied **Belgrano** posed a threat	1	—	1
Cruiser going towards mainland	1	—	1
Junta's version contradicts British (threat report)	1	1	—
Not clear British Task Force was at risk	1	1	—
Outside total exclusion zone and not defying blockade	1	—	1
Gunboat diplomacy	1	—	1
Violation of rules of war	1	1	—
Totally unlawful and cruel	1	—	1
Government has failed to justify attack	1	1	—
A crazy decision	1	—	1
Why was such a level of force used?	1	1	—
How can we be sure it was a threat?	1	1	—
Just how close was she to British ships?	1	1	—
Why didn't British wait to let cruiser get within the zone?	1	1	—
Hours (away) could mean 300 miles?	1	1	—
Was this the minimum use of force?	1	1	—
Do you think that the sinking of the **Belgrano** was really necessary?	1	—	1
(EEC countries) did not mean to back the use of so much military force	1	—	1
Argentina had limited herself to defensive action against British attack	1	—	1
Do you think the government has taken a wrong decision? (on airport, on cruiser)	1	1	—
Shadow Foreign Secretary concerned about Britain losing international support after the sinking	1	1	—
Are you concerned that there's a danger Britain will lose international support?	1	1	—
International support jeopardised if felt we had been responsible for needles loss of life	1	1	—
Not clear there was a political control when cruiser was attacked	1	1	—
Bound to strengthen Argentine desire for revenge	1	1	—

continued

continuation

	Total	BBC	ITN
Ship was torpedoed without declaration of war	1	—	1
We can't have young Argentinians sent to the bottom of the ocean	1	—	1

In these tables we have counted statements that the *Belgrano* was a threat and which justified or implied the necessity of the British action, plus statements which questioned these views or criticised the sinking. A number of more marginal statements were reported on television news, as in the treatment of European reaction. Thus we hear on BBC1 that 'West Germany has expressed concern at the fighting', and that the French have expressed 'consternation'. We hear also that 'Italy is said to be worried about supporting Britain if the violence escalates' (BBC1, 17.40, 21.10, 4.5.82), and that the 'Irish want a meeting of the UN Security Council' (BBC2, 18.35, 4.5.82). On ITN we hear that the Irish are 'appalled at the open warfare between Argentina and Britain' and that in West Germany the Chancellor's office is 'alarmed at the level of force being used'. We hear again that 'Paris has noted with consternation the sinking of the cruiser' (ITN, 13.00, 17.45, 4.5.82). On the main news we are told that West Germany has called the sinking 'a dangerous development' and the French have 'expressed consternation'. In these bulletins the most critical comment reported is the Irish Defence Minister's view that the British are 'the aggressors' (noted in the above tables) which is reported twice each on BBC1 and ITN. As we show in the next section even this criticism is downgraded by reporting that the 'Irish have an interest in portraying Britain as a colonialist aggressor' (BBC1, 21.10, 4.5.82). On ITN we are told that 'It's certain that many governments in Europe will backtrack a little now that the casualties don't seem to be as high as feared' (ITN, 22.10, 4.5.82).

What stands out in these references is the manner in which they are reported. They appear as emotional reactions to the new and dangerous developments but they are not seen as implying outright criticism of Britain (with the exception of the Irish Defence Minister). The other European sources are not spoken of as attacking or condemning Britain. This contrasts with reports elsewhere. The *Sunday Times*, for example, notes that the Irish 'were only saying openly what the others were thinking'. The more critical reactions in the European press were also not reported in the television news, such as the comment in *le Monde* that 'the fact that the cruiser was sunk outside the exclusion zone was judged particularly shocking'. The *Sunday Times* also reported that 'even the pro-Thatcher *Frankfurter Allgemeine Zeitung* referred to the "universal astonishment" at the scale of the British effort to recover "remote and barely inhabited islands"'.

Significantly in the television news references the core of such criticism is often weakened and not reported as being directed at Britain. Thus it remains unclear whether the 'dismay' and 'consternation' are because of the level of force used by Britain, or simply at the increase in the military conflict as such. By contrast the BBC's *Nationwide** on the evening of 4 May developed the rationale of these European responses as direct criticisms:

> *Coming on top of escalation of British military operations* in the South Atlantic in recent days, *the sinking of the Argentine cruiser has shocked European public opinion.* The Irish government has already said that it will demand an end to the EEC-supported trade sanctions against Argentina and will seek a United Nations Security Council meeting to secure a ceasefire and a withdrawal of the forces on both sides. The Danish, Italian and West German governments have also not disguised their concern that Mrs Thatcher has, *in the words of one of them, allowed war-making to apparently, supersede peacemaking* . . . The other European governments totally condemn the Argentine invasion of the Falklands and demand the withdrawal of Argentine troops, but as one European diplomat put it to me today, *'How can anyone justify an action which may cost the lives of half as many Argentinians as there are people on the entire Falkland Islands?' Everyone knows British policy for some years has been to hand over the islands to the sovereignty of Buenos Aires. This kind of force seems out of all proportion.*
>
> *Nationwide*, BBC1, 4.5.82

An important feature of the European responses is that they are subsequently taken up by the political opposition within Britain. Where this leads to criticism being directed at the British government's action, we have recorded it in the tables above, as with Dennis Healey's statement that the sinking 'would lose Britain's support around the world' (ITN, 17.45, 4.5.82). But on other occasions such political arguments are referred to in more marginal terms, as when an ITN journalist notes that 'Mrs Thatcher is fully

---

*Since *Nationwide* was not classified as a news programme we did not count it as part of our sample. We used it along with other current affairs material for comparative purposes.

aware that she is going to be criticised heavily for the sinking of the *Belgrano*. But she is apparently still taking a very tough attitude' (ITN, 13.00, 4.5.82).

On other occasions Conservative politicians such as Mr Pym or Mr Nott make long statements defending Britain's position in the general context of the *Belgrano*. Mr Pym is reported as saying:

> I want to make it clear that the British are not undertaking these military engagements, by choice. We are there to defence British soil and British people . . . They started the aggression . . . They invaded the island first.
>
> BBC1, 21.35, 3.5.82

John Nott:

> We mustn't forget that the islands are British and are settled by people of British descent and they have been invaded by an aggressor who must now withdraw. But there is also a wider purpose in our endeavours; it is to ensure that aggression must not pay.
>
> *Newsnight*, BBC2, 3.5.82

We did not include such general statements in the tables since they were at one level removed from arguments about the justification of the sinking. Peripheral references were also made in reports from the UN about possible effects on diplomacy. Thus we hear: 'If there is a great flap now about Argentine lives being lost then a lot of countries are going to say this has created a totally new situation' (*Newsnight*, BBC2, 3.5.82.)

Despite the considerable criticism of Britain's action at home and abroad, the predominant theme on the television news was that the sinking was justified. Statements on this outnumber criticisms by well over two to one, and occupy a more dominating position in the coverage. Such statements on the *Belgrano* provided hooks onto which news accounts were hung by journalists and problems debated.

By contrast, statements critical of the British action are rarely pursued. One exception to this is an interview by Peter Snow of Admiral Roxburgh on BBC2. This provides the occasion for five of the above critical questions (see table) on 'Why was such a level of force used?', 'How can we be sure it was a threat?', 'Just how close was she to British ships?', 'Why didn't the British wait to let the cruiser get within the zone?' and the suggestion that 'Hours (away) "could mean 300 miles?' (*Newsnight*, BBC2, 4.5.82). This is almost the only occasion when such sustained questioning occurs on this issue. It probably adds to the difference in perception of the BBC and ITN. Compare the above with an ITN interview of Rear Admiral Wemyss earlier the same day. Here the questions raised by the journalist invite an explanation of the British position, and the second one is in fact an endorsement of it:

[1] How was the *Belgrano* such a threat to the lives of British servicemen?

[2] So they could, if they had been allowed to move into the zone and perhaps fire those missiles, *it could have resulted in serious loss of life of British servicemen?*

[3] And would the British forces be satisfied that the cruiser was about to embark on hostile action?

ITN, 13.00, 4.5.82

Another salient feature of the coverage was that in the initial stage journalists often used terms like 'just' outside or 'edge of' when referring to the *Belgrano's* proximity to the exclusion zone. This indicates a reluctance to recognise that the ship was outside. The picture opposite shows the contrast between the news dialogue on ITN, stating that the *Belgrano* came 'close to the edge' of the zone, and the graphic showing it to be inside. However, on 3 May, John Nott

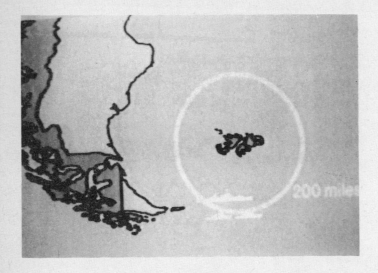

"What happened yesterday was that the *Belgrano* along with its two escort vessels came close to the edge of the 200 mile total exclusion zone."

ITN 22.20 3.5.82

gave a news conference and stated that the *Belgrano* was sunk because it was a 'threat' irrespective of its distance from the fixed 200 mile blockade zone. This is subsequently taken up by broadcasters in their own explanations of events.

Statements that the *Belgrano* was outside the exclusion zone were consequently made by both sides in the argument over the sinking. While some argued that it was outside and therefore should not have been sunk, the British government and its supporters acknowledged that it was outside but insisted that it was 'near to' the zone and/or had violated a 'moral exclusion zone'. Hence we examined the status of each reference (in the sense of whether it was for or against the sinking) in terms of its specific context and who had made it.

Criticisms of the *Belgrano's* destruction were subordinate in the coverage as a whole. Indeed such alternative accounts were undermined by failing to follow them to their conclusion and by going off at tangents:

> *Journalist in Argentina: The military junta's version of the submarine attack contradicts British reports that the Argentine cruiser posed a significant threat to the fleet.* A communiqué tells that the *General Belgrano* was torpedoed outside the zone declared by both countries around the Falkland Islands. When the Argentine people are being told about hostilities either on television or on radio, or in the newspapers, it differs vastly from the accounts in Britain, dismissed here as propaganda. The official communiqués continue to claim, after Saturday's attacks, a complete victory for the Argentine forces, with the shooting down of 11 Harrier jets and two helicopters and severe damage cause to the aircraft carrier *Hermes* and four frigates also hit. Newspapers tell of the triumph of the Argentine forces and other headlines speak of the withdrawal of the enemy. *The Argentine press*, during war emergency, *is subject to certain censorships*, with journalists facing sanctions for reports undermining national morale. Today, however, *details of the submarine attack on the Argentine cruiser was covered*, but on inside pages *with little prominence*. Just how many Argentine soldiers have been killed in the fighting has not been officially disclosed, but this was the first military funeral to be held in Buenos Aires since the British attacks. There were full military honours for the 53-year-old army colonel, one of ten soldiers killed in a helicopter crash near the Argentine naval headquarters on the South Atlantic coast.
>
> BBC1, 18.00, 3.5.82

The journalist begins by reporting the Argentine claim that the *Belgrano* was not a threat but moves rapidly into his next story about Argentine censorship.

ITN's format the same evening parallels the BBC's:

Newscaster: Argentina called the torpedo attack on the cruiser '*a new aggression*' by the British government and said it was a reason why they wouldn't change their stand on the Falklands. *Argentine news is censored.* Ken Rees reports from Buenos Aires on what the Argentines believe about the fighting and what they are being told now.

Reporter: For the first time, today the people of Argentina were being told something other than good news about the battle, after days of stories of victory. Magazines are still on sale detailing stories about the exploits of their forces and there are even some cartoons showing the British in disarray. But the *bad news is there too,* with a report of the Argentine cruiser being torpedoed, *but few details are given and people believe it's all victory.*

                                                        ITN, 22.20, 3.5.82

In these examples, by linking a brief account of the Argentine view of the *Belgrano* incident to the disreputable claims of Argentinian propaganda, the status and credibility of sources of information in Argentina are rendered suspect. At no time do either BBC or ITN state that their accounts are subject to censorship.

On 8 May, BBC and ITN covered a press conference in Argentina which the captain of the *Belgrano* attended. On two occasions the view of the *Belgrano* being 'not a threat' is stated as such. One of these is given here on ITN raising the question of the direction in which the *Belgrano* was sailing. It is not then taken up or developed by journalists:

Reporter in Argentina: The captain claimed the cruiser was well outside Britain's 200 mile exclusion zone when the submarine attacked. Captain Bonzo gave a graphic account of how two torpedoes hit the warship.

                                                        BBC2, 18.55, 8.5.82

Reporter in Argentina: Captain Bonzo denied that the *Belgrano* had posed a threat to the British fleet when it was attacked. He claimed his cruiser was steaming at a slow ten knots towards the Argentine mainland when it was hit by two torpedoes. Captain Bonzo said the cruiser went to the bottom within an hour of being struck, and he declined to express any sympathy for the captain of HMS *Sheffield.* Argentine journalists at the conference burst into applause.
                                                        ITN, 21.45, 8.5.82

The emphasis on the *Belgrano* as a 'threat' supported the view of the Argentines as initiating large-scale military action which in the words of the British authorities 'received the appropriate response'. In this view British military action and the casualties inflicted on the *Belgrano* and at the Port Stanley bombing are not seen as providing a 'reason' for an Argentine military reaction – even though the British suffered no fatalities until the *Sheffield* was sunk. It was, however, possible to see Argentine action as a 'response', as when Jackson Deihl reported in the *Washington Post* on May 5: 'Government sources said the military command and in particular the Argentine navy was determined to exact revenge – " for the torpedoing of the *Belgrano*".' But this link between British military action and its possible consequences in escalating the war was not normally made by journalists in British television coverage of these events.*

The international reaction to the destruction of the *Belgrano* had been one of shock, as it was for the opposition parties in Britain. In the television news the controversy centred on the related questions of why the *Belgrano* had been sunk and who took the decision to engage the vessel. Had the *Belgrano* been sunk following a direct order from London explicitly given by the Prime Minister or had the captain of the British submarine operated according to 'rules of engagement' laid down by the government and taken the decision on his own initiative? The rules of engagement had three main points. Firstly, any Argentine forces infringing the 200 mile total exclusion zone were subject to attack. Secondly, the little-mentioned warning given on 23 April permitted the fleet to attack whenever an immediate threat was posed even outside the zone. Thirdly, an additional rider stated that minimum force was to be used and minimum casualties inflicted.

In the press and broadcasting media, conflicting statements were made about who had authorised the attack. These were partly the result of the ambiguous statements by the government and military personnel on the issue. The Prime Minister was noncommital in the House on 4 May:

> *Tam Dalyell MP:* When the Prime Minister referred to political control, did she herself personally and explicitly authorise the firing of the torpedoes on the *General Belgrano?*

---

*The link is made by Dennis Healey on BBC2's *Newsnight* on 4 May after the sinking of the *Sheffield*. He quotes Alexander Haig as saying that the attack on the *Belgrano* was bound to strengthen the Argentine desire for revenge and make negotiation less possible. Immediately after this the *Newsnight* presenter asks a reporter in Argentina if there is evidence of 'a mood of revenge'. The reporter replies that he has seen no evidence of it. (He presumably does not count the *Sheffield*.)

Prime Minister's reply: I can assure the right honourable gentleman that the Task Force is, and was, under full political control.

Hansard

Criticism by David Steel the Liberal leader on *Nationwide* on 4 May and by Dennis Healey of the Labour Party on BBC2's *Newsnight* on the same date stemmed from the belief that the submarine captain had taken the decision to sink the *Belgrano* on his own initiative within rules laid down prior to the engagement. ITN had evidently much less trouble than the BBC in interpreting statements in the House of Commons, since one of their bulletins was very clear on the issue:

The opposition was also worried that the Task Force commanders may not be under great enough political control. *Mr Nott revealed today that it was the submarine commander who decided to fire the torpedo which sunk the General Belgrano;* that he did so, said Mr Nott, within rules approved by the cabinet.

ITN, 22.05, 5.5.82

This report contradicted ITN's early news on the issue:

The attack on the *General Belgrano* took place in the late afternoon and was said to be fully in accordance with the rules of engagement of the British forces in the South Atlantic. *But it is thought the submarine attack came following a direct order from London,* rather than from the Task Force commander Sandy Woodward.

ITN, 17.00, 3.5.82

The BBC did not report the 5 May interpretation of John Nott's statement. The issue came up again in one of their bulletins on 7 May. During an interview, Admiral of the Fleet Sir Terence Lewin was asked about the political circumstances surrounding the decision which led to the sinking of the *General Belgrano:*

Journalist: Can you tell us whether the sinking of the *General Belgrano* was done on a political initiative or whether it was done purely on the initiative of the commander of the submarine who sank her?

Lewin: Of course it was done by ministerial rules of engagement which were approved by ministers. We don't go around sinking ships without ministerial approval.

BBC1, 21.00, 7.5.82

The non-specific replies of those in authority and the failure of the British media to pursue this crucial issue led in October to a United States journalist revealing that the Prime Minister herself had been consulted prior to the attack on the *Belgrano* and had given the command to attack her. It was revealed in the *Daily Mirror* of 4 October 1982 that Sir Terence Lewin had gone to the war cabinet with the news that the *General Belgrano* had been traced by the submarine *Conqueror* outside the exclusion zone. The *Mirror* continued: 'Sir Terence said the *Belgrano* posed a major threat to the Task Force, *but he pointed out that the Navy's rules of engagement did not allow Conqueror to open fire. The war cabinet decided to change the rules and Conqueror was ordered to fire on the Belgrano*' This account was also substantiated in the *Guardian* the following day and in the *Sunday Times* on 17 October 1982.

During the period of this study the military decision to sink the *Belgrano* had, for television news, occurred in a political vacuum without an individual political figure to account for it. In the *Sunday Times* on 9 May, Sir Nicholas Henderson, Britain's ambassador to the United States, was reported to have been 'shattered' by the news; Glynn Mathias stated that when he asked John Nott at the Ministry on 3 May at 8.30 a.m. to confirm that the *Belgrano* had now sunk. 'He was taken aback by my question. I was convinced he had no idea the ship had gone down.' Instead of exploring the political ambiguities of this action, television news, with some exceptions, predominantly fell back on MoD statements that the *Belgrano* was a 'threat' and was sunk within the rules of engagement. The narrowing consequences of adopting such a view and failing to explore alternatives became apparent when the British ship HMS *Sheffield* was destroyed on 4 May. An article in the *Washington Post* on 5 May and subsequent reports of the Argentine media and public opinion make it clear that one explanation of why the *Sheffield* was attacked was that it was a 'reprisal' for the destruction of the *General Belgrano* and the bombing of Port Stanley airfield. However, TV news personnel did not develop the view that the sinking of the *Sheffield* was a reprisal in their explanations of the attack. Arguably, had they done so it would have reopened a hornet's nest of question on who had ordered the attack on the *Belgrano* and why. More crucially it raised the issue of whether the British were escalating the military conflict, rather than simply using the minimum of force to back up diplomacy, as they claimed.

Reporting world reaction

We have commented above on how European reaction was reported in relation to political debates within Britain. Here we develop the question of how the news featured 'foreign' opinion as such. In highlighting some views, downgrading and omitting others, journalists distinguished between what was regarded by them as 'fair comment' and what was not. Following the sinking of the cruiser an extensive series of reports on foreign reaction commenced on 4 May, but it is largely confined to *Western* reaction, i.e. the NATO allies and those EEC member states which had backed economic sanctions against Argentina:

> Meanwhile there is growing concern among MPs *as there is in friendly countries* about the situation . . . . None of *our European allies* have actually deserted us yet.
>
> ITN, 13.00, 4.5.82

Other reaction, notably Latin American opinion, was dismissed as 'predictable', on the rare occasions it was referred to:

> *Newscaster:* The sinking of a capital warship . . . . is likely to affect the view that other countries take of Britain's stand on the Falklands issue. *The reaction of the Soviet Union was predictable enough, as was that of the Latin American countries.* But some European allies have shown signs of unwillingness to continue active support for Britain, and of course there's Ireland's call for a UN Security Council debate. But what of our most powerful and influential ally – the United States?
> *Journalist:* South America and Soviet reaction has been *predictable*.
>
> BBC1, 21.10, 4.5.82

World reaction was identified in this way as falling into two camps: firstly, acceptable criticisms and legitimate apprehensions among nations supporting Britain over the Falklands; secondly, 'predictable' responses from countries perceived to have an axe to grind against Britain.

The underplaying of foreign reaction to the sinking was sometimes extended to even relatively close allies. The Irish Republic (which was taking economic sanctions against Argentina as part of the Common Market countries' response) was widely reported as having changed its stand on the Falklands issue. Following the attack on the cruiser the Irish now saw Britain as the 'aggressor':

> Ireland has called for an emergency meeting of the UN Security Council following the sinking of the *General Belgrano*. The *Irish government said it was appalled* at what amounts to *open warfare* between Argentina and Britain.
>
> ITN, 17.45, 4.5.82

The Irish Defence Minister said his government now regarded *Britain as the agressor* and Ireland wants a meeting of the UN Security Council to call for a ceasefire.

BBC1, 17.40 4.5.82

In the BBC's later bulletin Irish reaction and its motives are made suspect:

And the Irish Defence Minister . . . now regarded Britain as the aggressor. Whitehall sources were quick to point out that *Ireland has an interest in portraying Britain as a colonialist aggressor.* And the Irish government *quickly announced that the Defence Minister's view was his own.*

BBC1, 21.10, 4.5.82

In Paris, a Foreign Ministry spokesman said: 'We have noted with consternation the sinking of the Argentine cruiser', while in Copenhagen, a Danish government official spoke of the sinking as a 'tragic development':

Well, it's certain that many governments in Europe will backtrack a little now that the casualties don't seem to be as high as feared.

ITN, 17.45, 4.5.82

As for political opinion, today [in the US] . . . the dispute came to the floor of one of the Houses of Congress and *the Belgrano was not even mentioned.*

BBC, 21.10, 4.5.82

From the same bulletin following the rundown on European reaction, Argentina was even cited as taking a mild response to the sinking: '*Another relatively mild reaction* has come from a very unexpected quarter, Argentine Foreign Minister Costa Mendez' (BBC1, 21.10, 4.5.82). After this introduction the report cuts to film of Costa Mendez saying that 'this event' will have an impact on world reaction and might possibly ease the way to peace. In fact, as ITN reported on the 17.45 news the same day, Costa Mendez spoke of the sinking as 'a treacherous act of aggression in violation of the United Nations charter'.

Accounts of critical reaction by Britain's allies were normally viewed in terms of its implications for support for Britain. Foreign reaction was linked to British *justifications* of the attack:

Both Mr Pym and Mrs Thatcher do realise that sinking the Belgrano may alienate world opinion, but the government's attitude to criticism both at home and abroad is that *if it was right to send the Task Force, no one should be surprised when Britain uses that force.*

ITN, 13.00, 4,5,82

Mr Nott told MPs that the Task Force *commander would have ignored the threat from the cruiser at his peril* and Ireland *wants the Security Council* to call for hostilities to end.

BBC1, 17.40, 4.5.82

Journalist: Mrs Thatcher... amid *growing international concern* over the actions in the South Atlantic... told MPs she regretted the loss of life, but she went on:
Mrs Thatcher: Our first duty is to our own forces who are there on our orders with our support.

ITN, 17.45, 4.5.82

The government is said to be *worried about reaction from other countries* too, but when Mrs Thatcher answered questions in the House she insisted that *the attack had been fully justified.*

BBC1, 21.10, 4.5.82

Why the **Sheffield** was sunk

Part of the power of the media to determine how events are to be understood is their ability to isolate problems and present solutions within the context of an established theme. Two such themes in the Falklands coverage were the need to defend both national interests and the Task Force itself. Thus the initial response to the *Sheffield's* destruction in the media was to ask where was the weak link in our defence. From the outset, the political questions that surrounded the relationship between British military action and the sinking of the *Sheffield* were largely ignored. Instead the topic was understood in terms of 'technical' military problems requiring a solution within that definition. To avoid 'Exocets' we need 'Sea Wolfs':

Built by Vickers at Barrow, HMS *Sheffield* was commissioned in 1975. She carried one Lynx helicopter fitted with Sea Skewer missiles and the ship herself was armed with Sea Dart missiles. The Sea Darts were very sophisticated and *in order to combat Argentine Exocet missiles the Sheffield would have needed the short-wave Sea Wolf system.*

ITN, 22.10, 4.5.82

HMS *Sheffield* was the first of the Royal Navy type-42 destroyers and didn't have the *anti-missile weapon* that was fitted to the later types of warship. *This might have saved her from attack by a modern French-built*

Super Etendard fighter bomber equipped with the Exocet missile only fairly recently delivered to the Argentine by the French...

She was a handsome ship and the class is popular with the sailors drafted to the type-42s. *But in naval terms she was under-equipped.* She carried only one Lynx helicopter, only one 4.5 inch gun and only one missile system, the Sea Dart, which is intended to be able to hit other warships out of sight over the horizon or, more importantly, attacking aircraft. So Sea Dart should have been able to deal with the Argentine Super Etendard naval strike planes as they approached *Sheffield* yesterday. But it's possible either that the aircraft weren't detected or that they simply weren't in range. But the *Sheffield* was in range of Exocets.

...It has a devastating impact when it strikes the target. *The loss of the Sheffield might have been avoided if she had been provided with Sea Wolf missiles.* These are so accurate they can hit artillery shells in mid air. *The type-42s don't have Sea Wolf. Money is limited and it would have cost a great deal to provide; though not as much as replacing a warship.*

BBC1, 12.30, 5.5.82

Newscaster: HMS *Sheffield,* built in the early seventies, *fell victim to more advanced weapon technology:* a French-built Super Etendard plane firing the Exocet missile only recently delivered to Argentina. *The Sea Wolf anti-missile weapon* fitted to newer types of British warships *might have saved her.*

Defence correspondent: ...And the action proves that critics of the type-42 design were right.

BBC1, 17.00 5.5.82

The correspondent above then repeats his earlier report in the evening bulletins using libary film shown on the afternoon news.

Meanwhile on ITN we hear:

HMS *Sheffield* was hit shortly after three o'clock yesterday afternoon our time. The exact circumstances of the attack *and just how the Argentine missile penetrated the Task Force's defences is still being analysed.*

ITN, 17.45, 5.5.82

Following this introduction ITN's defence correspondent comes in and gives a description using graphics of how the defensive screen operates using Harrier jet air cover. He explains that since the Harrier defence system failed, the ground-level internal defensive screen of the *Sheffield* had to deal with the incoming attack. He continues:

Sheffield's defences against missiles were limited. Her Sea Darts can shoot down some missiles but not the Exocet.... One weapon *that might have saved Sheffield is the Sea Wolf anti-missile missile.* But it's so new, only two ships in the Task Force have it.

ITN, 17.45, 5.5.82

On all of ITN's bulletins on 5 May, ITN's defence correspondent, like the BBC's repeats his analysis using library film and graphics. On both channels there are minor changes in the words spoken but not in the analysis. Introductions to these items also changed in phrasing but not in meaning. The change in introduction from ITN's 17.45 bulletin to the 22.05 news was particularly significant, however:

> *Newscaster:* HMS *Sheffield* was playing a key role in the defence of the Task Force when she was hit by the Argentine missile shortly after three o'clock yesterday afternoon London time. *Defence chiefs are still investigating how the defender became the victim.* Our defence correspondent Geoffrey Archer *explains why she was so vulnerable.*
>
> ITN, 22.05, 5.5.82

The theme therefore develops from one mention of a technical detail on 4 May into preoccupation with a weapon that 'might have saved HMS *Sheffield*'. By the following evening the topic begins to assume greater proportions. Defining the issue as 'how the defender became the victim' conflates the military capability of the *Sheffield* and its role as a 'forward picket' in the Task Force with the political reasons given by the authorities for sending the fleet to the Falklands. Defenders in 'rule-governed wars' are again essentially passive, and only responsive, to 'threats'. The explanatory framework adopted by newscasters and correspondents in the case of the *Belgrano* and the *Sheffield* thus adhered to the interpretation that the British were not the precipitators of aggression.

That HMS *Sheffield* was one of the most modern ships in the Navy according to the media reports of 4 and 5 May was not incompatible with portraying her as impotent in the face of 'sophisticated weapons'. This theme was developed throughout the period by the questions the media posed and the access they provided for military experts:

> *Journalist:* There were questions this afternoon about the loss of *Sheffield*. The Ministry of Defence spokesman was asked whether there were any plans to bring forth the scheme to equip British vessels *with the Sea Wolf missile. That's the weapon which can shoot down enemy missiles and which might have saved HMS Sheffield had she been equipped with Sea Wolf.* Mr McDonald said that this was *now a priority* which had been *underlined and re-emphasised by recent events.*
>
> BBC1, 21.00, 6.5.82

> *Journalist's question:* Sir Patrick, *we known you can't tell us anything* about what when on in the committee this morning, but it does seem that *your pressure over seven years has been vindicated so far as this anti-missile system is concerned.*

Journalist's question: Had HMS *Sheffield*, for example, been fitted with either the lighter or the heavyweight *Sea Wolf*, would it in fact have been saved?

Journalist's question: Finally, Sir Patrick, can I put it to you, do you think now, and does your committee think, *that the government feel that this whole defence* policy will have to be drastically reviewed?

BBC, 13.00, 12.5.82

And on ITN:

Newscaster's question: It does seem surprising that we knew that the Argentines had the Exocet missile and yet *we apparently did not take the steps,* at that particular time, *to defend our ships from it?*

Newscaster's question: Air Marshal, *do you think that it could have been* avoidable if, for example, *we had had Sea Wolf missiles?*

ITN, 13.00, 5.5.82

Newscaster's question: Vice Marshal [Stuart Menaul], *the American defence experts seem to be shocked how easy it was to knock out the Sheffield.* Does that mean we have to examine at least part of the strategy for the defence of the rest?

ITN morning news, 6.5.82

Newscaster: One weapon... thought to *provide some protection against it is Sea Wolf ....*

Air Vice Marshal Stuart Menaul: As you say, *only two frigates have the Sea Wolf* missiles on board, and they can't be everywhere at the same time.

ITN, 17.45, 7.5.82

Television news defined the problem surrounding the *Sheffield* as a lack of Sea Wolf in thirteen bulletins. This view which emerges from a reliance on 'official sources' is compounded by the number of military and Conservative spokesmen who appear in 'live' interviews. In addition only six interviews were conducted with four political figures critical of the government's military policy, as against seventeen interviews conducted with political spokesmen who were generally supportive of it. (See Appendix 3 for a full list).

A different explanation why the *Sheffield* was hit was occasionally present in new accounts. Broadcasters referred to Argentine reaction which saw it as a reprisal for Britain's attacks on Port Stanley and the *Belgrano*.* Media personnel did not explore this in their own accounts.

---

*Later, outside the period of this sample, and when the immediate debates about these military actions were over, we noticed other references. At the end of the war, for example, on BBC1 news on 14 June, a brief resumé of the conflict was given. The destruction of the *Sheffield* was then referred to as a 'reprisal'.

To have adopted such an approach would have severely strained or challenged the military logic which characterised most explanations of the attack on the *Sheffield*. In short, to have accepted an explanation that the *Sheffield* was destroyed as a response to Britain's strike against Port Stanley or the *Belgrano* might have implied that the British were aggressive and brought into focus the decision taken by the war cabinet to change promptly the rules of engagement. The tendency to avoid an explanation which linked the destruction of HMS *Sheffield* to Britain's pre-emptive strikes was illustrated by the defence correspondent's reports on BBC1 a day prior to the news of Argentine reaction to the attack on the *Sheffield*. This reference mentions in passing the possibility of Argentine 'revenge' – but the British action connected to it is the sinking of a tugboat:

> *Defence correspondent:* HMS *Sheffield* had a ship's company of 270 officers and men. She was a type-42 destroyer reckoned to be one of the most modern warships in the Royal Navy. *It's quite possible that it was one of her Lynx helicopters which sank the Argentine tug* near the same spot two nights ago. *If so, the Argentine navy has taken massive revenge.* In naval terms it more than offsets the loss of the cruiser *General Belgrano,* and in human terms it's possible the casualties may be high.
>
> BBC1, 21.10, 4.5.82

On 5 May, BBC1 exclusively refers to an official Argentine communiqué in two of its bulletins. The report originates in BBC1's afternoon bulletin and also refers to Argentine press reaction which regards HMS *Sheffield's* destruction as retribution for the sinking of the *Belgrano*. Other bulletins on BBC1 and BBC2 do not mention the communiqué, and ITN does not refer to it. On BBC1 it is reported as follows:

> A *communiqué* by the military junta described the attack as *a response to the bombing of Port Stanley airport. Argentine papers, however, refer to the score being evened after the sinking* of the Argentine's cruiser the *General Belgrano,* in which 800 crew members *have now been rescued.*
>
> BBC1, 12.30, 5.5.82

The crippling of the *Sheffield* is officially described here as a big morale booster for the Argentine forces, but after the loss of their own cruiser the *General Belgrano* 24 hours earlier there's no real sense of gloating. *It's said the score has been evened* but, at the same time, the prospects of the cessation of any hostilities are further away than ever....

Argentine newspapers today described the Super Etendard as the avenger of the Belgrano. A communiqué by the military junta referring to the sinking of the *Sheffield said it was a response to the bombing of the island's airport* and a photograph just released, following Saturday's first raid by a Vulcan bomber, purports to show only minimal damage... war fever grips the nation since the British submarine attack.

BBC1, 21.05, 5.5.82

The Argentine military have still not acknowledged their successful attack against Sheffield in any official communiqué, although *details* have been *widely published in newspapers and on television....*

After the loss of their own cruiser there is no sense of gloating. *It's said the score has been evened* but at the same time the prospects for a cessation of hostilities are further away than ever. [Report extended in 9.00 bulletin.]

BBC1, 17.00, 5.5.82

In Argentina the military junta still haven't spoken of yesterday's attacks, but the news has been widely publicised in the Argentine media.

BBC2, 19.35, 5.5.82

Officially there has been no official confirmation from the high command here *about the attack on the Sheffield,* but the newspapers are full of the details of the successful action by the Argentine armed forces. There's still a feeling that the sinking of the *Sheffield* coupled with the news of 800 sailors rescued from the *Belgrano* has restored Argentine pride.... Late last night the Plaza Britanica with its replica of Big Ben in the middle was renamed. It's now called the Plaza Belgrano.

ITN, 13.00, 5.5.82

So far, the high command here has not confirmed the sinking of the *Sheffield,* but the newspapers have no doubts.

ITN, 17.45, 5.5.82

Apart from these short references neither channel placed much credence in any 'revenge' motive at a time when the *Sheffield's* destruction began to dominate the news. The alternative view, that British attacks resulted in a reprisal attack on *Sheffield,* was restricted to just six references on one day. But even here only two on BBC1 report the official communiqué, while two state there was no 'official' response. ITN did not report any 'official' connection between the attack on *Sheffield* and Britain's previous military actions; crucially this theme is not taken up and pursued in the news.

The television news, then, in the main followed a simple military logic. Why had the *Belgrano* been sunk? Answer: because it posed a threat to the Task Force. But when it is asked why *Sheffield* had been sunk, the main answer is because it was incapable of defending itself against Exocets, without Sea Wolf. Questions and answers depend on perspective. The question 'How could we have saved the *Sheffield?* does not receive the answer 'By not bombing Port Stanley airport; by not sinking the *Belgrano;* by Britain promoting a ceasefire, etc.' We do not wish to obscure the argument that the Argentines precipitated the problem by landing on the Falklands in April 1982. But what was largely absent from television news was the possibility that the British were initiating military action leading to a major escalation of the conflict. The dominant account which emanated from Whitehall was so powerful that the sinking of the *Belgrano* could be 'justified' on ITN by referring to the *Sheffield:*

> Ministers do feel there is one consolation in the distress they all feel about the attack on *Sheffield.* When it became clear that the Task Force had sunk the Argentine cruiser *General Belgrano,* there was some feeling, both in Britain and abroad, *that Britain was using more than the minimum force necessary, according to our stated policy. But the loss of Sheffield, it is felt, puts the loss of the Belgrano in a different light. The Task Force clearly had to do what it did for its own protection* and there's no guarantee now that the British won't take further military action.
>
> ITN, 13.00, 5.5.82

The bombing of Port Stanley

The conflict in the South Atlantic became a major shooting war on 1 May. British aircraft launched a full-scale attack on the airfield at Port Stanley in the early hours of that morning. The purpose was to put the runway out of action and render the airfield unusable for Argentine aircraft. The destruction of the runway as well as a smaller airstrip at Goose Green would cut the Argentine garrison's air link to the mainland and make it almost impossible to fly in reinforcements and supplies.

The operation began at 4.23 a.m. when a single Vulcan bomber dropped twenty-one 1,000 lb bombs on to the airfield. The result of the air strike was to put one crater in one side of the runway. The other twenty bombs landed either side of the tarmac where the damage was minimal. One crater made it difficult for Argentine supersonic fighters to use the airstrip but did not deny the runway to Argentine transport plans or smaller ground attack planes. A Hercules CI30 transport plane, a small Pucara and Aermacchi aircraft would have no difficulty using a shortened runway.

The Vulcan raid was followed four hours later by air strikes by Royal

Navy Sea Harriers from the Task Force. Some of the Harriers' bombs caused minor damage to the surface of the runway and damaged or destroyed aircraft at the side of the airstrip. The 1 May attack was concluded with a heavy bombardment from Royal Navy ships.

On 4 May a second sortie was carried out by an RAF Vulcan and RN Sea Harriers. This time the Vulcan failed to get any of its twenty-one bombs on the runway. Again the raids were followed by a naval bombardment. The Royal Navy futher shelled the aircraft with its 4.5 inch guns on 9, 10 and 11 May. There were further Harrier raids on 15, 16, 24, 25, 26 and 30 May and almost continuously thereafter as the final push on Port Stanley commenced. On 12 June, a third Vulcan attack on the runway occurred. None of its bomb managed to hit the runway. There are, however, some doubts about the purpose of this raid. Some reports[1] suggested that the Vulcan was dropping fragmentation bombs which exploded fifty feet above the ground and are designed to hit men and planes on the ground, not to damage airstrips. During the period of the fighting there were two other Vulcan raids on Port Stanley. The purpose of these raids was to destroy radar sites and installations. The anti-radar missiles dropped by the Vulcan appear to have inflicted no significant damage to Argentine search radar around the airfield.

Max Hastings, the first British reporter into Port Stanley, reported that 'civilians told me that they'd [the Argentines] been running Hercules on to the runway at Port Stanley despite all our efforts with naval gunnery, with vulcans, with Harriers, right up to and including the last night'.[2] Sir Frank Cooper, the Ministry of Defence's top official during the conflict, was later to confirm that there was no doubt that 'some use was made by the Argentinians virtually throughout the whole operation'.[3] Brigadier David Ramsbotham, head of Army public relations, confirmed that "the runway itself was possible right throughout"[4] the conflict. British officers in the Falklands did not hide their opinion that the performance of the early Vulcan raids had been extremely disappointing.[5]

The runway at Port Stanley remained operable throughout the conflict and Argentine forces on the islands were being regularly supplied by air from the mainland throughout the period of the fighting.

TV news and the bombing of the airfield
The announcement of the raids of 1 May was reported on ITN lunchtime news bulletin:

Early this morning British aircraft took action to enforce the total exclusion zone and to deny the Argentinians the use of the airstrip at Port Stanley. We are not yet able to give you details but will do so as soon as we have authoritative information.

ITN, 13.15, 1.5.82

The bulletin carried a report from Buenos Aires which had confirmation of the attack from Argentina's chiefs of staff and speculated on how the raid was mounted. The report qualified the speculation, however: 'Until a further statement from the Defence Ministry we shan't know' (ITN, 13.15, 1.5.82).

As a result of the lack of 'authoritative information' ITN was cautious in its speculation about how much damage may have been done to the airfield. The statement from the Ministry of Defence emphasised that the debriefing of the air crews had yet to be completed. Despite the lack of information concerning the effect of the raids on the airfield the BBC defence correspondent's assessment of the raids was less cautious:

The destruction of the airfield will come as a psychological as well as military blow to the Argentines. It means even if a transport plane were to break the blockade it wouldn't have anywhere to land. It means the only communication with Argentina now open to the Argentinians is by ship. It also means that Admiral Woodward has now effectively gained local air supremacy.

BBC1, 12.50, 1.5.82

The defence correspondent's assertions in the absence of hard information are surprising. Following his report, a military expert is interviewed on the objectives of the raids. The expert in reply to the first question states: 'We've given far greater effect to the blockade in that you can't now get aircraft on to the runway if that runway has been cut' (BBC1, 12.50, 1.5.82). The military expert makes a qualification as to whether the attack has been successful in destroying the airfield and achieving its objective, which is reported as 'to stop [the runway] being used by Argentine transport planes and also Argentine Pucara counter-insurgency planes'. The same inhibition is not felt by the interviewer, who proceeds to ask the following questions:

By taking out the runway the Task Force is obviously less vulnerable now from the air, but you've still presumably have got to look over their shoulders so to speak? . . . *The fact that we've knocked out the airfield* — is that likely to affect our own movements when we take the islands?

BBC1, 12.50, 1.5.82

At 15.00 hours the Ministry releases further details of the attack. It is announced that 'Vulcan aircraft attacked the Port Stanley airfield during the night. Subsequently at dawn Sea Harriers carried out further attacks. Both operations were successful.' With the first official statement of the success of the attack, ITN still reports with caution:

> Judging by the little information we have, it could have been a very heavy raid . . . The Defence Ministry says the raids were successful and that presumably means the runway has been wrecked and Argentine troops will hve no further chance of flying in supplies.
>
> ITN, 17.05, 1.5.82

The BBC is far more confident in its reporting. The Argentine junta announced that afternoon that the 'attack by the English seaborne airforce resulted in damage only to buildings surrounding the Malvinas military airbase. The runway remains undamaged although a fire was started but rapidly extinguished when a fuel drum was hit by a bomb.' Faced with contradictory claims from Britain and Argentina, this is how the BBC defence correspondent reports the raids:

> The Vulcan's main target was the runway which they cratered with 1000lb bombs. Each crater will be roughly twenty feet deep and thirty feet across. It's likely that the runway has been *pitted with thirty such craters*.
>
> BBC1, 17.30, 1.5.82

In reporting the 'details' of the attack the defence correspondent gives the strong impression that the damage to the runway has been extensive. Later in the bulletin a further statement from the Ministry of Defence is reported live:

> I can now give you some further information about the raids carried out by our aircraft last night and this morning on military targets on Port Stanley airfield and Goose Green airfield. I can now confirm that runways and aircraft on the ground were hit, in particular the runway at Port Stanley was severely cratered. A full damage assessment is still awaited.
>
> BBC1, 17.30, 1.5.82

Both Ministry and BBC-in spite of the lack of a full damage report—arrive at the same conclusion.

The official statement gives a green light for TV news. Subsequent reporting, despite the discrepancy between the British and Argentine accounts of the events, reinforces the image of a severely cratered and inoperable runway and of Argentine forces cut off from the mainland:

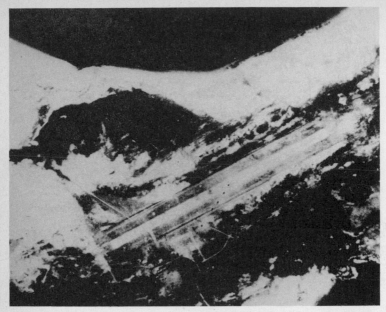

Actual bomb pattern shown on *The Friday Alternative*

Channel 4 7.1.83

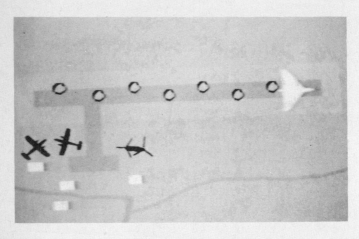

"The Vulcan's task was to pockmark the runway at Port Stanley Airport and it did it with thousand pound bombs: ten tons of explosive."

ITN 21.55 1.5.82

Destroying the Port Stanley runway has cut off the Argentine garrison's life support system. President Galtieri can either order his navy to break the blockade or hope that the troops on the Falklands can somehow hang on.

BBC2, 19.35, 1.5.82

The Vulcan's task was to pockmark the runway and it did it with 1000 lb bombs, ten tons of explosives.

ITN, 21.55, 1.5.82

The report by the ITN defence correspondent is accompanied by strong visual graphics which show a clear line of explosions going along the length of the runway. The impression given is of a 'severely cratered' runway, confirmed by ITN's reporter with the Task Force:

The Harrier pilots confirmed that the Vulcan bomber attack had been successful and following the Harriers' bombing the two airstrips and the surrounding buildings at Darwin and Port Stanley have been severely damaged.

ITN, 21.55, 1.5.82

In response to questions concerning the difficulty for the Vulcan in such an operation, ITN's resident military expert is clear: 'I don't think the crew would have had any difficulty at all with the equipment they've got in finding the Falklands, finding the airfield and bombing it accurately' (ITN, 21.55, 1.5.82). The BBC reporter with the Task Force also confirms the success of the operation: 'After studying the reconnaissance photograph the Admiral's staff pronounced both raids a success, with aircraft damaged and airfields cratered' (BBC1, 22.30, 1.5.82).

At the end of the first day of military action around the Falkland Islands, British television news presented a clear picture of the fighting. In spite of the doubts arising from the contradictory accounts of events emanating from London and Buenos Aires, and because the Ministry of Defence was still awaiting a 'full damage assessment', TV news gave the viewer an unambiguous picture of an inoperable runway and isolated Argentine garrison.

At twelve noon on 2 May the Ministry of Defence issued another statement:

As you know yesterday before dawn Vulcan aircraft attacked Port Stanley airfield. Subsequently there was a follow-up raid by a substantial number of Sea Harriers. The result was a severely damaged runway at Port Stanley airfield and considerable damage to surrounding military installations and stores . . . In the late afternoon of the same day elements of the Task Force situated within the total exclusion zone bombarded Port Stanley airfield to reinforce the effects of the bombing and deter repair work.

BBC TV news, after introducing news of the fighting, followed the official Ministry account of events with its fullest report yet from the Argentine capital. The report made reference to film of the airfield shown on Argentine television:

> The damage from the British bombs on the airfield is described as minor. It only broke the windows in the control tower. This is how Argentine television showed the airfield in their news bulletin yesterday evening. These pictures the correspondent said were taken at twenty past four in the afternoon, twelve hours after the first British attack. The airport was as busy as it had been before. The reason, the report went on: the British bombs had missed their target. Instead they had fallen on spongy soil besides the airstrip digging huge craters but leaving the runway intact.
>
> BBC1, 17.50, 2.5.82

The BBC does not offer any comment on the Argentine version of events. ITN, however, expressed some doubts:

> News bulletins have been showing this film which the Argentine government says was taken at Port Stanley airbase during yesterday's fighting. Despite the strike by Vulcan bombs and Harrier jets the runway is shown to be completely clear. The Argentines admitted damage only to some buildings and a fuel dump. The pictures were broadcast repeatedly during the night and would appear to show that despite the air attack and artillery bombardment the Argentines are able to operate military transport planes in defiance of the British blockade.
>
> ITN, 18.00, 2.5.82

ITN's reaction to this report was to cast doubt on the film used by the Argentines to support their claim that the airfield was not inoperable. These doubts are raised in an interview with an Argentine TV broadcaster:

> *British reporter:* When was this film taken? Today?
> *Argentine:* Today.
> *British reporter:* What time?
> *Argentine:* At 4.00 p.m. 4.30 p.m.
> *British reporter:* It looked very similar to film that we've seen before from there.
> *Argentine:* Well, it is a film from today.
> *British reporter:* Definitely from today?
> *Argentine:* Yes.
>
> ITN, 18.00, 2.5.82

ITN's defence correspondent in his assessment of the fighting which followed the item from Buenos Aires does not seem to have any doubts at all: 'The Argentines know that the Vulcan bomber which wrecked the Port Stanley airstrip can come back and do it again if they repair the airstrip' (ITN, 18.00, 2.5.82). In a later bulletin that evening ITN followed their interview with the Argentine TV broadcaster with a reiteration of the Ministry of Defence's position:

> The Defence Ministry repeated today that the Port Stanley airstrip had been severely damaged. Some defence experts estimate that the Vulcans 1,000lb bombs would have left craters fifteen feet deep even though the runway was built on solid rock.
>
> ITN, 20.45, 2.5.82

This statement appears to reinforce doubts concerning the Argentine claim that the raids were not successful.

BBC TV news that evening is less concerned wth the conflicting claims. Rather than dwell on these it turns to its correspondent with the fleet:

> I've been looking through the reconnaissance photographs, some of which were taken at the time of the attack on Port Stanley airport and some of which were taken afterwards, and they show obviously that a lot of bombs went in where they were intended to go . . . around the runway and around the installations at the end of it, which was the prime reason for attacking the target. There are a number of holes in the runway, some put by the Vulcan in a very clear line of bombs which goes right across and some which go down the middle of the runway which were put there by the Harriers.
>
> BBC2, 22.45, 2.5.82

This report is interesting for a variety of reasons. The reporter states that the prime reason for the raid is to hit not the runway but installations around it. This contradicts what was reported before and what the Ministry of Defence in London announced. The reporter also says that there were a large number of holes in the runway according to his reading of the reconnaissance pictures. On his return to Britain he announced that he was misled concerning these pictures: 'I think we were given the impression that the air raids on Port Stanley had been more successful than they were: that the air blockade was more successful than it was.'[6]

On 26 May film reports from correspondents with the Task Force on the Port Stanley bombing raids were eventually shown on our television screens. The BBC film report again implied that the operation was a success: 'A reconnaissance photograph taken later in the day showed a neat line of bombs from the Vulcan. *It had achieved its object – one bomb on the runway'*[7] (BBC1, 17.40, 26.5.82). The ITN correspondent, despite his optimistic report three weeks earlier, had to admit: 'The reconnaissance photographs showed that the Stanley airport had been damaged but not as seriouly as we'd thought. *Only one of the Vulcan's bombs had hit the strip*' (ITN, 17.45, 26.5.82). The difference in tone is noteworthy. By end of May there was a divergence between ITN and BBC concerning their coverage of the state of the runway at Port Stanley and the effectiveness of the blockade. However, this divergence did not occur until mid-May. During this period that gave most coverage to the airfield both channels, in spite of alternative information, presented the raids as successful.

The BBC summed up the first weekend of military action in the Falklands in its weekly *News Review* programme. The contradictory claims concerning the airfield were not mentioned, though there is perhaps a hint of doubt in this BBC2 report: 'The bombs *were said to have caused* big craters in the airstrips, leaving it in a condition where it cannot now be used,' (BBC2, 18.50, 2.5.82). The BBC correspondent with the Task Force also summed up the first weekend of fighting:

> The Task Force has now dealt a heavy blow to both the Argentine navy and the airforce, as well as bombing and damaging the airport at Port Stanley. So far it's shown it can enforce the sea and air blockade of the islands that Admiral Woodward, the commander, said he intended to establish. This demonstrates to the troops ashore that they cannot expect much in the way of reinforcements or help from the mainland if they decided to resist any British invasion.
>
> BBC1, 21.35, 3.5.82

BBC news then proceeds to devote some time to examining the conficting reports of the fighting:

> The Argentine junta's account of the conflict has been strongly criticised by the Ministry of Defence in London. Their concern is that Argentine claims may worry families of men aboard the Task Force, because it takes time to check the facts. And the Ministry cite four examples of what they call fabrications by Argentina. The Ministry say HMS *Exeter* was not involved in military operations; Argentine resistance on South Georgia is over; all Task Force aircraft are safe and *Port Stanley airfield is out of action*.
>
> BBC1, 21.35, 3.5.82

This report refers to the necessity of taking time to check facts. But much of the reporting and military analysis is based on speculation. Perhaps more important is that British official sources are accepted almost without question. Broadcasters did not normally extend their scepticism of information from Argentina to the official pronouncements of the Ministry of Defence.

On 4 May, Defence Secretary John Nott made a statement to the House of Commons. Referring to the raids of 1 May he stated that 'the runway was cratered and rendered unusable by transport aircraft from the mainland'. He proceeded to announce that more raids had taken place: 'A further sortie was made today to render the airstrip unusable for light supply, communications and ground attack aircraft operating within the Falklands Islands themselves.' It was on 4 May that some doubt was raised on television about the British account of the bombings. BBC2's *Newsnight* reported on Mr Nott's Commons statement:

> What Mr Nott did reveal in the Commons was that there was another attack on Stanley airport last night and I understand that it was once again a Vulcan bomber from Ascension that made almost a precise re-run of last Saturday's raid, dropping twenty-one 1,000 lb bombs in a freefall from over 10,000 feet. So clearly, either the Argentines had managed to do enough repairs to the cratered runway to make another attack necessary, only 72 hours later, or as some American sources suggest, the original raid only shattered part of the runway.
>
> BBC2, 22.45, 4.5.82

This was the *only* reference on television news to reports emanating from the United States that the runway was not destroyed and could still be used by cargo planes.

These reports did emerge in parts of the British press. However, the press in general embraced an interpretation that emphasised the successful execution of the operation. The newspaper headlines on the morning of 3 May illustrate this. 'Raids Cut Off Argentines' read the headline in the *Daily Telegraph*. The articles referred to the Argentine forces as being 'now cut off' and the runway as having been 'pounded'. The newspaper's defence correspondent in another front-page article, 'Airfield "inoperable"', wrote of 'the cratering of the airfield'. The *Daily Mirror* stated the raid 'meant that, with their lifeline airstrip to the mainland ripped to rubble, the 10,000 Argentine troops had become virtual prisoners of the Royal Navy'. The *Daily Mail* reported that the runway had been 'blasted through'. The *Sun* made reference to a 'crater-covered runway' (5 May). *The Times's* editorial of 3 May began assertively: 'With the bombing of Port Stanley airfield the isolation of the Argentine invasion force is now complete. Pressure on the beleaguered garrison must be maintained and, if necessary, increased to secure the ultimate demoralisation of the Argentine forces.'

Doubt about this version of events first emerged in the *Guardian*. In an article, 'Clash of Claims Fills Lull after Port Stanley Bombing', the paper's defence correspondent stated that, in the light of discrepancies between the London and the Buenos Aires version of events, 'there was obviously some room for doubt as to how much damage had been done on the airfield'. The *Times* of 5 May reported: 'American sources had indicated that the runway at the Islands' capital might still be used by aircraft needing only a short, rough runway.' The *Guardian*, reporting the second Vulcan said the attack may have been needed 'because the first left too few craters'. The newspaper's defence correspondent had stated that 'sooner or later the Argentines will have to demonstrate the truth of their claims'. This is what they began to do.

One of the problems that confronted British TV news during the war was that, while very little was coming back from British reporters with the Task Force, Argentina was able to get film back from the islands quickly and fairly regularly despite the blockade. British television had access to this film through Buenos Aires. The problem was how to treat the film. With little new film from the Task Force and sparse accounts of the action coming from the Ministry, this footage was of great value in news terms. Yet TV producers and editors were extremely conscious of the criticisms from the government that the showing of Argentine film on British television handed a propaganda victory to the enemy. The pressure to use Argentine TV film for its news value was in part resolved by using it to demonstrate the 'crudity' of Argentine propaganda.

Argentine TV film of the first raids on Port Stanley began to arrive in London during the second week of May. The *Daily Telegraph* of 11 May carried a report on an eighty-minute film, shown on Argentine TV on 9 May. The film included footage of the 1 May raids and the conditions of the airstrip following the raids. Subsequent raids were also included. The article reported that 'film of the Port Stanley airstrip showed several ruts but as the camera passed along its length it seemed serviceable'. These shots 'would have been hard to fake because they included bomb damage to the buildings, and a crippled Cessna aircraft, owned by Mr Rex Hunt, British Governer of the Falklands, could be seen at the side of the runway'. This film led some of the quality newspapers to call on the Ministry of Defence to provide pictures to support their claim that the runway was out of action.

There was some concern expressed at widespread television coverage of the Argentine pictures. But how did British television respond?

British television established its viewpoint in the initial days within which it reported the bombing raids on Port Stanley. During the period of the fighting there were forty-eight news stories making specific reference to the effects of the raids. Statements that the airfield runway was destroyed/unusable outnumbered those that it was operable/usable by almost three to one. Most of these are official statements reported from the Ministry of Defence or the Argentine junta. Statements directly attributable to journalists indicate that in general they accepted the assertions that the runway had been destroyed. The dominant theme running through the coverage was that the runway was unusable and the Argentine forces were cut off. Argentine TV film, showing an operable runway and little damage, had to be reported against this background.

Television news had some difficulty in admitting that the runway could still be operable. On many occasions when film of Port Stanley was used no reference was made to the condition of the runway. In some cases, in spite of the evidence of their own eyes, they continued to maintain the optimistic line. It appeared as if some broadcasters had difficulty in saying that the Argentines could be telling the truth and the Ministry could be misinforming them.

The first substantial footage from Argentine TV to include pictures of the aftermath of the bombing was shown on British screens on 9 May. The initial reaction was one of scepticism. The first screening was on ITN lunchtime news. The defence correspondent makes no direct reference to the runway although he does comment on the damage around the airfield: 'The bombs have heavily pitted the ground' (ITN, 12.00, 9.5.82). The film is used to illustrate that British claims about the early fighting are generally correct. For example, he states that the film 'suggests that British claims of damaging aircraft and equipment were true' (ITN, 12.00, 9.5.82).

The BBC defence correspondent acknowledges that the film indicates the blockade had been broken:

> Perhaps the most significant thing about the film is that it has arrived in Buenos Aires from the Falklands. Lieutenant Taylor's aircraft was shot down on Tuesday so we know these pictures have come out either by sea or by air. That means the blockade was successfully broken and if aircraft have been able to fly out if follows they can also fly in.
>
> BBC1, 17.50, 9.5.82

The correspondent does not further speculate that, if indeed the air blockade had been broken, where did the planes land? He does, however, refer to this in a later bulletin. His comments follow a report from the BBC's man with the Task Force saying that 'certainly for the past few days some Argentine air and sea traffic had been getting to the Falklands, probably bringing in stores'. This is because 'the thick sea mist has made it difficult for Sea Harriers to operate' (BBC1, 21.30, 9.5.82). It appears that only in such unusual circumstances could the blockade be breached:

> The night attack on Port Stanley airfield is important because it surprised a Hercules escorted by Mirages approaching an airstrip which the Ministry of Defence has claimed was destroyed. Obviously the runway has been repaired; equally obviously it will have to be recratered. The fact that the airfield is usable explains how film of the first Sea Harrier attack last week managed to reach Buenos Aires from the Falklands.
>
> BBC1, 21.30, 8.5.82

An explanation has been given: the film's arrival must be accounted for by the repair of the runway. ITN's defence correspondent also raises the spectre of a repaired runway. He refers to shells 'bursting over the runway to deter attempts to repair it' (ITN, 9.5.82).

The following day ITN begins to ponder the implication of the film. In an item on the nature of the propaganda war being waged by Argentina, the introduction of which mentions the use of film in helping Argentina to 'win the propaganda war', the defence correspondent comments that Argentina viewers

> also saw film of the results of the bombing. The ground and the apartment buildings at Port Stanley looked deeply pitted by the attack and there were several fires. Britain announced that these first raids on the airport were successful and the runway had been cratered but these pictures apparently shot after the raid showed a large section of the runway intact. Several aircraft besides the runway seemed to have been damaged. But apparently this Argentine Hercules transport plane was able to take off again; *Since this film was shot the airport has been bombed and shelled several times*.
>
> ITN, 17.45, 10.5.82

The possible failure of the British attack is raised, albeit in an item on Argentine propaganda. It is not apparently a major matter of concern because of subsequent attacks on the airfield. On BBC news there is a similar reluctance to acknowledge failure:

British reports referred to the airstrip as being severely cratered; but according to the Argentines these pictures taken three days after the attack show it to be intact and fully operational. The rough ground and the strip is pockmarked with bomb craters. *It seems extraordinary that such a heavy bombardment should have missed the 4,000 ft runway.*

BBC1, 17.40, 10.5.82

As the day wears on, the authenticity of the film begins to be called into question. In an analysis of Argentine propaganda a comparison is made between film footage claiming to show an Argentine transport plane landing at Stanley after the bombing, and film shown much earlier:

After the British bombed Stanley airfield, the Argentines produced this film which they claimed showed a Hercules still able to land there. But study the film on the top left-hand corner. As BBC television news showed that night, this film shown days earlier is strikingly similar.

BBC1, 21.50, 10.5.82

In this same bulletin was an item on the intelligence uses of such film:

Those pictures from the Falklands shown on Argentine TV were subject to censorship; nevertheless they revealed quite a lot when analysed. Intelligence experts in London scrutinise every scrap of Argentine news coverage as do their opposite numbers in Buenos Aires. Our defence correspondent has also taken a look.

BBC1, 21.00, 10.5.82

In the report that followed the runway or damage to the airfield is not mentioned.

BBC2's *Newsnight* devoted a great deal of time to assessing TV film of the first few days of military action. The emphasis is again on propaganda:

The reporter said that in the first attack the aircraft must have been damaged. A few seconds later he changed his mind. Several buildings were seen ablaze with no attempt made to extinguish the fires; he claimed that Britain had only hit the area around the airport but the runway itself was still intact. Only one thing was missing from the film – shots of the runway itself.

BBC2, 22.45, 10.5.82

The BBC reporter accuses his Argentine colleague of making contradictory statements, although he appears to contradict himself at the end of his report:

Later the programme returned to Port Stanley showing what it claimed to be an undamaged airport runway. This, said the commentator, disproved BBC reports that the runway has been severely cratered. The marks on the tarmac, he said, were clods of earth thrown up after the raid. While on the face of it even these pictures do not prove anything, the film could have been taken at any time during the last ten days after the runway had been repaired. A heavy transport plane was later shown taking off, apparently on 3 May, unlikely if British claims to have seriously cratered the runway two days before are accurate.

BBC2, 22.45, 10.5.82

The reporter does, however, conclude by saying that the fact that these pictures are being shown on Argentine TV indicates that the blockade has been broken. The newscaster sums up the report by stating that 'the British blockade continues on the whole to be effective' and it is simply that 'the odd Argentine plane is getting through'.

The BBC had a great deal of difficulty accepting the evidence of their own eyes. They continued to doubt Argentine claims concerning the runway at the time when ITN began to acknowledge that there could be something in them. ITN coverage of the film gradually began to focus on the inability of the Ministry of Defence to supply pictures to support their claims:

Mr McDonald faced a series of questions about the photographs of the bombing raids earlier this month on Port Stanley airfield. Asked why the photographs had not been made available to the public, Mr McDonald repeated that they still hadn't reached this country from the South Atlantic. He said the lack of photographic evidence to back British claims that the Port Stanley airfield had been out of action left the government at a public relations disadvantage but could only say that the photographs would be made available as soon as possible.

ITN, 13.00, 11.5.82

ITN looked elsewhere for information concerning the discrepancy between the claims: 'Independent sources from South America suggest a Hercules got through the blockade last Wednesday. Some Argentine planes and some ships have almost certainly beaten the blockade' (ITN, 22.00, 10.5.82). However, ITN was still ambivalent about the runway. On the one hand it reported that aircraft, including Hercules, were breaking the blockade, and on the other it stated: 'our correspondents have seen photos of the craters'. There seemed little attempt to bring together these contradictory pieces of information. Then on 14 May ITN began to carry reports from Ministry sources that light aircraft could still use the runway. This led to a bizarre item on *News at Ten* of 14 May. Over a film of a Hercules transport – the largest cargo plane in the Argentine air force — taxiing along the

"The Ministry of Defence now concedes . . ."

ITN 22.00 14.5.82

". . . that light aircraft can still use the runway . . ."

ITN 22.00 14.5.82

"... even though it has been badly cratered"

ITN 22.00 14.5.82

runway at Port Stanley, the reporter comments: 'As for the airstrip at Port Stanley, well the Ministry of Defence now concedes that light aircraft can still use the runway even though it is badly cratered' (ITN, 22.00, 14.5.82). The gap between the image and the commentary indicates that either the journalist does not believe his own eyes or his comments are tongue in cheek. If the latter, then it is an indication of the increased pressures of the time that journalists cannot point out clearly that the Ministry of Defence's claims are disingenuous.

ITN, did, however, appear to be wrestling with a dilemna. This culminated in the clearest report on the effects of the bombing that appeared on British television during the conflict. Following yet another attack by Sea Harriers on the airfield on 15 May, ITN carried a report 'on the continuing campaign to put Port Stanley airfield out of action' on the main evening bulletin of 15 May:

> It was just over two weeks ago when the Ministry of Defence first said that the Port Stanley airfield would be closed. Since then there've been five major raids. On 1 May, Vulcan bombers and Harrier jets cratered the 4,000 ft runway. The Ministry of Defence described the raid as successful but three days later they agreed that light supply aircraft

could still use the airstrip and further sorties were undertaken. From 9 to 11 May, British ships bombarded targets in and around the airfield but Argentina said the bombardment was having little effect. Two days ago the Harriers once again attacked the airfield and its related installations. Yesterday came the fourth major air attack in just over two weeks. One reason for continuing to attack the airfield could be to deter repair work; another could be to knock out radar installations that represent such a threat to the fleet. But the Ministry of Defence has yet to produce photographs showing just how badly damaged the airfield really is. And if Argentine aircraft are still using it then further raids cannot be ruled out.

ITN, 20.45, 16.5.82

This is the closest ITN comes to accusing the Ministry of misinformation. It is clear that the raids were less successful than the authorities had reported. ITN appears to be aware of this but is cautious in its criticism of the Ministry; it is reluctant to refer to the failure of the raids. However, ITN did attempt to tackle the dilemma raised by the contradictory claims following the arrival of film to support Argentina's claim. Although overall ITN reported that the runway was unusable twice as much as it reported it was usable, there was an attempt to analyse British claims.

At this time, in the middle of May, the BBC was subject to a great volume of complaints from sections of the Conservative Party on its coverage of the conflict. For whatever reason, the BBC news did not seem to want to take on the problems posed by the conflicting claims. It was apparently more willing to accept the success of the raids. In the BBC2 review of the week's news on 16 May-the same night ITN called on the Ministry of Defence to substantiate its claims — there is a round-up on the differing accounts: 'Argentine cameramen filmed first Harrier raid on runway at Port Stanley. Pictures shown on Argentine TV to support junta's *unreal claims* (BBC2, 18.50, 16.5.82). The claims were summed up by the BBC thus: 'Junta said RAF had missed both runway and control tower. Pure propaganda, says MOD-runway was totally unusable *even for light planes*' (BBC2, 18.50, 16.5.82). BBC news exhibited here the tendency to go along with the official British view of events, even in the face of alternative evidence.

As the Falklands conflict escalated to its conclusion, accounts of the invasion, Goose Green and the final push to Stanley inundated our screens. The continuing raids on Stanley were reported amidst the action-packed news bulletins but the reason for them in general remained obscure. If reasons were given they focussed on the need 'to frighten and demoralise the Argentine troops at Port Stanley' (ITN, 17.45, 21.5.82).

BBC news made the most number of reference to the further raids. It persisted in adhering to the image of 'successful' operations and an unusable runway:

> The bombing raid at Port Stanley will have been aimed at military stores, especially fuel but it's also *to keep the runway unusable*. By now, the Argentine commander General Menendez will be dearly wishing he had Task Force jump jets which don't need airfields.
>
> BBC1, 21.00, 25.5.82

BBC news analysis of the raids of 24 May was that they were designed 'to keep the airfields out of action' (BBC1, 18.00, 29.5.82). A few BBC journalists had accommodated themselves to the fact that the runway was operable, but even they felt the need to report 'good' information: 'According to the Argentine TV reporter who witnessed the attack at midday last Saturday, its bombs missed the runway. *However they did go very close*' (BBC2, 22.50, 21.5.82).

In the later stages of the conflict some further attention was paid to the blockade of the islands. This was to some extent sparked off by a statement given to the House of Commons by Defence Secretary John Nott. In his statement of 26 May, Mr Nott reported to his colleagues that 'reinforcement and resupply are virtually denied to the Argentine garrison on the islands'. With speculation mounting concerning the state of the garrison, as British troops came nearer to Stanley, this statement was deemed to be of some importance. The defence correspondents of both channels had no doubt of the condition of the military garrison:

> General Menedez now had had almost a fortnight with virtually no supplies coming through.
>
> BBC1, 21.00, 26.5.82

> The Argentines are getting vocal support from Buenos Aires but precious little else.
>
> BBC1, 21.05, 30.5.82

> . . . . whether the Argentines will be called upon to surrender, knowing they are cut off and without chance of resupply, remains to be seen.
>
> ITN, 13.00, 1.6.82

Even in the late stages of the conflict, defence correspondents continued to assert that the Argentine forces were isolated in Stanley. Again these statements predominate, yet other views do occur at this stage:

Reports from the Task Force say that in spite of the air and sea blockade fresh supplies and ammunition have in fact been reaching the troops in Port Stanley.

BBC1, 17.40, 1.6.82

Argentines are getting a picture of minor skirmishes around Port Stanley with communications to and from the mainland intact.

BBC1, 13.00, 2.6.82

Argentine film was still reaching Buenos Aires from Port Stanley.

One of the last episodes concerning the garrison is the report of special Argentine units being sent to reinforce the troops in Stanley. On 3 June an ITN reporter announced: 'A unit of the Argentine special forces, supposedly equivalent to our SAS and SBS, was flown in from the mainland, fresh and equipped to harass the British positions' (ITN, 22.00, 3.6.82). The statement stands out; the assumption is that the Argentine troops can be moved into Stanley with little difficulty. This report came from a correspondent on the Falklands.

The following day the BBC takes up the story:

Whitehall is dismissing the claims made in Buenos Aires that the Argentine troops in Port Stanley have been reinforced. According to one British official, the only way they would have got there is by swimming.

BBC1, 21.50, 4.6.82

The steady bombardment by the Task Force ships and by land-based artillery makes it difficult for any resupply of the Argentine garrison and this afternoon Ministry of Defence sources dismissed Argentine claims that reinforcements, ammunition and food had been brought by transport planes from the mainland. The Ministry called such claims as belonging to the '*Invincible* class' and said reinforcements could only have come in by swimming.

BBC2, 22.45, 4.6.82

The BBC again emphasised official sources and chose to pass over different accounts from journalists at the front line. *News Review* summed it up: 'Argentina claims its troops reinforced from mainland. UK said troops *could* get there but only if they swam' (BBC2, June 1982).

The BBC did give more coverage to Argentine claims the next day. But perhaps the last word should be left with the ITN reporter in Buenos Aires: 'Special Argentine troops with bad-weather experience are apparently being flown in [to Stanley] from the Andes. How, isn't explained' (ITN, 13.00, 7.6.82).

In spite of alternative sources of information, television news seemed rarely to extend beyond the statements from the Ministry of Defence. When TV news did report on information from other sources such as those in Argentina, it was sceptical of the nature of the material it received. This had extraordinary results in some coverage. On 4 May a Sea Harrier was shot down while attacking the airstrip at Goose Green. Five days later film taken by an Argentine amateur cameraman reached London. It showed the attacks on the airfield on 1 May and wreckage of a plane. ITN was first to get hold of this piece of film which was regarded as a scoop as it was the first film of the hostilities in the Falklands. This is how ITN's defence correspondent reported on the wrecked British plane:

> But the attack had been concentrated on the airfield where it is assumed these pictures of wreckage were taken. This roundel is *not* in the colours carried by the British Harriers and may have come from an Argentine plane destroyed on the ground. The variety and totality of wreckage scattered round the airfield suggest British reports of inflicting severe damage to aircraft and military equipment there *were* true. *One piece of wreckage had the word 'Harrier' on it but was unidentifiable.* Britain says

"One piece of wreckage had the word Harrier written on it but was unidentifiable."

ITN 12.00 9.5.82

she lost no aircraft during this raid though one Harrier was shot down three days later near the other airport at Goose Green. These would seem to be aircraft wheels, although it's not yet clear what type of plane they came from.

ITN, 12.00, 9.5.82

The correspondent has convinced himself that all the film is from 1 May; since the Ministry of Defence said no planes were lost on that day, the wreckage shown could not possibly be of a British plane. He was also keen to point out the damage caused by the British raids. This led him to ignore evidence before his own eyes (see italics). It also showed an apparent ignorance of military equipment. The colours of the roundel *are* unmistakably British and the wheels are clearly from a Harrier since their undercarriage design is unique. A serial number on the plane is also shown. Later in the day the following commentary accompanied the same piece of film, an unacknowledged correction of the original story: 'The cameraman was also taken to the Goose Green airstrip where a British Harrier jet was shot down last Tuesday. The Royal Navy roundel showed through the film of paint.' (ITN, 18.50, 9.5.82).

Once having established a view of the Port Stanley raids – a destroyed runway and cut-off garrison — the news found it difficult to step beyond it. New facts and information were fitted into this framework. The constraint seemed to emanate from the need for broadcasters to maintain their image of purveyors of reliable, balanced and objective information. Journalists found it difficult to admit that they had made mistakes. Following the ceasefire, TV news expressed surprise concerning the condition of the airfield. The subject was not considered in any detail. In *Task Force South*, a BBC production in August, viewers were finally told what British troops had heard before the final push on Port Stanley. In it we see shots of a briefing for troops. A soldier comments:

> The RAF missed the fucking runway . . . bombs all around it but there are thirteen aircraft, some of which are definitely Pucara, parked on the aprons around Stanley airfield. There's also another report that they have managed to reinforce themselves from the mainland.
>
> BBC1, 12.8.82. *Task Force South*, part 8

This piece of film was absent from the pictures of the advances on Stanley which were first shown on British TV on 25 June.

The bombing of the runway at Port Stanley airfield illustrates how television news overestimated the ease with which a military operation could be conducted to re-take the Falklands. The portrayal or the military option as relatively unproblematic was a central factor in legitimising the decision to fight in the South Atlantic.

THREE

The Home Front

Mrs Thatcher said it made us realise we are all really one family.
BBC1, 21.00, 21.5.82

This chapter analyses the image TV news constructed of the nation at war. The bulk of TV news reports on the 'Home front' were about the relatives of the Task Force waiting at home. We look at this coverage in detail, finding that the Task Force families – the women in particular — were mainly presented as models of support for the war but were largely denied the possibility of expressing their own opinions and doubts.

Task Force families

The relatives and friends of those serving on the Task Force had a crucial part to play in reporting the home front. Although the viewing public was assumed to have an insatiable appetite for Falklands news, and the Prime Minister insisted that the Falklands 'were but a heartbeat away', most British people were not directly involved. Few had previously heard of the Falklands; the fighting was invisible, thousands of miles away, and (in the judgement of the *Financial Times* of 7 April, 1982) 'no vital national interest in any material or strategic sense' was at stake. But friends and families of men and women on the Task Force were 'deeply involved in the current events' (BBC2, 22.45, 5.5.82); reports on their plight became a familiar item on the news, appearing three or four times on each channel in the first week of the fighting. Their experiences were part of the national experience of the war; their human reactions and emotions were offered up to the rest of us via the TV, to provide the Falklands story with a 'human interest' angle, allowing us to share a surrogate personal involvement in the distant and confusing campaign. As one serviceman's wife put it: 'Ordinary people with no military involvement felt it was *their* lads out there, fighting for what they believed in' (Sara Jones, *Options* magazine, April 1983).

We analysed a total of 141 items relating to Task Force families from 390 bulletins recorded over the period 1 May to 14 June 1982. Seventy-one dealt with families waiting at home (twenty-three of these concerned the Royal Family), fifty-one with partings and reunions, and eighteen with memorial services. In some cases the views of relations were highlighted, as in these report on the first deaths of British servicemen: 'The father of a Sea Harrier pilot who also died has said, "I'm proud to have a son who died for the country he loved"' (ITN, 13.00, 5.5.82).

When the *Sheffield* sank, one bereaved mother appeared, saying:

I'm proud of him, I'm extremely proud of him, and if he's gone to war and fought for his country, and died for his country, I'd like everybody to feel that it's not in vain.

BBC1, 21.00, 6.5.82

But during the whole period of the fighting we found only one case of a bereaved relative's doubts over the campaign being quoted – in this report on the casualties of HMS *Sheffield*:

Twenty-year-old Neil Goodall had planned to get engaged at Easter. Instead he sailed with the Task Force . . . His mother who lives in Middlesex said, "My son never joined the Navy to die for something as wasteful as this.'

ITN, 22.00, 6.5.82

We found only two interviews with relatives suggesting that the loss of life might not be worth it: in one late-night bulletin on BBC2, a naval wife says:

I didn't want them to go out there . . . I feel now I'd like to see it go to the United Nations . . . I feel there has been too much bloodshed already and I feel that if there is any more the nation is going to turn against the government.

BBC2, 22.45, 5.5.82

While in an interview on a lunchtime bulletin two naval wives give their opinion:

I just think neither of them want to lose face, do they?

Just give it back to them . . . I mean it's our men that's out there, if they can blow up one ship, how many more are going to go? It's ridiculous.

BBC1, 12.30, 5.5.82

In the main bulletins on the same channel later in the same day, these less-than-supportive remarks are edited out and replaced with an interview with the wives of two survivors, in which the only question raised is: 'How did you pass the time?' (BBC1, 17.40, 5.5.82).

Apart from these exceptions in the first days of fighting, the Task Force families appeared only as supporters of the campaign; and as the losses mounted and their suffering increased, they disappeared from our screens, not to be readmitted until afterwards on the return of the survivors, to display what the TV journalists described as 'the indescribable joy of knowing that a loved one is safe' (ITN, 22.00, 11.6.82).

If this was the TV image, what was the true experience of those at home who were close to someone on the Task Force? Obviously it is not possible to measure or summarise all the varied attitudes and reactions of people who lived through the war knowing that someone close to them daily faced death or disablement. It is hard to imagine the full cost of war in human terms, the impact on people's lives when men were killed or injured. The Task Force friends and relatives, however, had no choice but to face up to and bear the human costs – this was precisely what made them such an important group for the TV coverage of the war at home. From this perspective, their views on the war understandably varied. Many remained loyal to the Task Force whatever happened. One bereaved mother said:

> I miss him terribly. Sometimes I would have felt better if I had gone to war. If I could have laid down my life for him I would. I loved him so much. But it was such a worthwhile thing. They went because they were needed. It wasn't a waste. I wouldn't ever accept that.
>
> Pamela Smith, mother of a corporal killed at Mount Harriet,
> *Sunday Times*, 3.5.82

Without denying the strenght of such loyalty and pride, or the personal conviction that the British cause was just and 'it wasn't a waste', it is important to realise that not all relatives reacted in the same way. It would be facile to try to draw a line between 'supporters' and 'critics' of the campaign – relatives could feel both anger and loyalty:

> I'm bitter he went through Ireland and then got killed for an island nobody had ever heard of. They should have blown it out of the sea. But I knew he'd like it this way because he was so proud of his country.
>
> Jean Murdoch, mother of lance-corporal killed on the Falklands,
> *Glasgow Evening Times*, 8.7.82

However, many expressed definite opposition to the war in the light of their own experiences:

> We probably all thought it was worth it at the time . . . but when you finally do lose someone, it makes you wonder then whether it was worth it. I probably would've thought it was if my brother hadn't been lost in it, but it makes you look at it completely differently when you lose someone.
>
> Ben Bullers, brother of a sailor killed on *Sir Galahad*,
> *The Friday Alternative*, (Channel 4, 7.1.83)

> I think it should never have happened – this government virtually invited Argentina in . . . . Throughout this whole crisis the only ones who really feel it are those who have actually lost someone or had someone injured. It just doesn't hit home with the rest of us, and that's the unpleasant reality – that's why they can yell and cheer on the

quayside .... There's no glory to war, and despite what's being said about patriotism really–what's there to be proud to be British about?
Brenda Thomas, wife of a caterer on a Task Force aircraft carrier,
Spare Rib, August 1982

I am proud of my son, but not proud of the fact that he died for his country in a war which was not necessary. I accept that it's a serviceman's duty to fight, but in a futile situation like this, I think it's evil to put men's lives at risk when negotiations around a table can save so much heartbreak.
Mrs Samble, mother of a sailor killed on HMS *Glamorgan*,
Bridport News, 18.6.82

David had to die because of crass error, and weakness disguised as boldness in high places.
Hugh Tinker, father of lieutenant killed on HMS *Glamorgan*,
A Message from the Falklands, Junction Books, 1982

He did not die for his country, he died because of his country. There were men in charge of that strip who were paid to know better.
Mrs Gillian Parsons, mother of a Welsh Guard killed at Bluff Cove,
Week in Week Out, BBC Wales, 25.3.83

So there was a clear current of opinion among the Task Force relatives against the conduct of the campaign. It could have been expressed, and might possibly have had some impact on the views of the 'ordinary people with no military connection' who felt 'it was their lads out there'. But the TV news representation of the Task Force relatives' emotions was carefully controlled. The relatives' support for their loved ones was used to obscure their real thoughts about whether they should have been sent to war at all.

Soon after the sinking of HMS *Sheffield* on 4 May 1982, the BBC Board of Governors issued a firm ruling that the relatives of the dead would not be interviewed at all. The official grounds were those of 'privacy' and 'taste', but the *effect* was to silence those who could have told use most directly about the human costs of the fighting,[1] and to censor any doubts they may have had about whether the fighting was worthwhile. The BBC did make certain special exceptions. At an NCA meeting where fears of 'undermining the national will' were discussed,* the chief of current affairs programmes mentioned that:

Nationwide had shown one [interview with a bereaved relative] which, was impeccable and had given him no concern on any score. He had referred to ADG [the Assistant Director General], had then discussed it

---

*For a fuller account of this see Chapter 1 above.

with DG [the Director General], and had been given the go-ahead.
NCA minutes, 8.6.82

Nationwide's 'impeccable' interview featured a widow who worked for a naval wives' self-help organisation, saying, 'I certainly don't feel bitter', and talking about another woman whose husband was killed on the same ship – 'she's absolutely marvellous . . . coping fantastically' (*Nationwide*, 4.6.82).

A number of assumptions were made by the TV reporters about the role that relatives were to play on the screen. The BBC Assistant Director General's justification of the ban on interviews with the bereaved is interesting here:

> Put brutally, interviewing a widow was an 'easy' story and he was strongly against an opening of the floodgates when restrictions were eased. The answers that the bereaved would give were, after all, largely predictable.   NCA, 8.6.82

The journalistic consideration (an 'easy' story) is put above the right of people directly affected by the war to express their views. He dismisses as 'largely predictable' the whole variety of reactions among people struggling to understand and judge a controversial war in which they had to sacrifice a close relative. Most revealingly, reporting on the bereaved has to mean 'interviewing a widow'.

Wives, mothers and sweethearts

This last assumption reveals one of the main preconceptions structuring the coverage of the Task Force relatives: that those left behind are all women. Although those serving on the Task Force had men and women close to them – fathers, brothers and lovers were left behind as well as wives and mothers — the TV news framework evidently sees that it is *women* who wait while the men go and fight; 'widows' who are left when they die. In a total of forty-eight interviews with relatives at home during the period of the fighting only four men appear: three 'proud' fathers, and Prince Charles who says that Prince Andrew is 'doing the most important job' (ITN, 21.15, 26.5.82).

All the remaining relatives are wives, mothers and fiancées. The conviction that waiting is the *women's* role is so total that 'wives' seems interchangeable the 'families' in the journalists' vocabulary:

> These remarks highlighted a particular problem for the *families* of servicemen, of which reports to believe and which to discount. [Our reporter] has been finding out how naval *wives* in Portsmouth have been coping.   ITN, 17.45, 5.5.82

The calls from distressed *families* for news about their men went on all night. But in the large naval estates around Portsmouth the grief is being shared by all the *wives*. ITN, 17.45, 5.5.82

The company has invited *wives and families* of the crew of the *QE2* to a meeting . . . The *wives and mothers* of merchant seaman have found the waiting war a lonely one. BBC1, 17.40, 3.5.82

A further indication of the way the news treated waiting at home as a 'women's affair' is that women reporter were more visible here than in any other area of the Falklands coverage. Over half the reports on families at home were done by women reporters, who covered only a small minority of the diplomatic, political news, and only one military story (on the Red Cross 'safe' zone in Port Stanley).

It is very unusual for married women in the home to appear on the news. An underlying assumption is that serious news stories should be about public events – government proposals, stock market movements, etc. The lives of women at home are taken as a sort of steady background, only 'newsworthy' in this case because the men are absent, and because the men are making news. Having selected 'ordinary' married women's thoughts and lives as an issue in these extraordinary circumstances, the TV journalists present them in a traditional women's role, which does not include expressing dissident views. Reports on the relatives are approached as 'human interest' items, 'soft' news stories where the issue at stake is how wives and mothers, sitting at home with emotions rather than political opinions, cope with the waiting. Given the rare chance of reports from naval housing estates to present an area of life that the news normally neglects, the TV journalists find themselves falling back on the old-fashioned stereotypes of women's role and family life.

According to the 1980 General Household Survey, conventional family units — couples living with children — make up only 31% of households.* Households where the woman is dependent on the man and stays at home to look after the children are only 13%. Altogether, two thirds of married women have paid jobs outside the home. This is not to cast doubt on the genuine warmth, security and family solidarity that the TV cameras captured, or the depth of joy and relief felt in reunions with survivors after the war. The point is that the TV news

---

*This represents the percentage at a given moment in time but such family arrangements are a stage of life which many people pass through. Consequently at any given moment some people have just left such arrangements and others are about to enter into them.

portrait of the nation at war was *selective*, and that it selected images of unity and families, concealing much of the real conflict and true attitudes within the country. This is as true of the image of family life as the image of broader public opinion.

The news reports present the conventional stereotypes. Women are shown in relation to men, and not at all as individuals in their own right. In the coverage of Task Force wives, mothers and fiancées, we do not hear any details of their jobs, for instance, or any activity at all apart from waiting for their men.[2] These are typical introductions to interviews with two women:

> Karen Murphin's only source of information was on news bulletins. She last saw her husband in November. Since then Kevin, who is a stoker, and his shipmates were in the Mediterranean before going to the Falklands.
>
> ITN, 22.05, 5.5.82

> He was the ship's NAAFI manager, although he had in fact served previously in the Army. His employers, the NAAFI, say they're proud of him; so are his family.
>
> BBC1, 21.00, 24.5.82

In one fairly long interview with a naval wife, the woman is not even named; instead the camera zooms in on her two-year-old son as she feeds him, and the reporter begins:

> Peter Goodfellow's father is a sailor too. He was the engineering officer aboard the frigate HMS *Antelope*. Commander Goodfellow was injured. When the news was first broken to his wife, the Navy still had no idea of the extent of his injuries. She had to wait.
>
> BBC1, 18.00, 4.6.82

He tells us about the man's job, and even the two-year-old boy's name is given, but we hear about the woman.

The women are most commonly interviewed with babies or young children on their knees. Every report from naval married quarters estates includes a shot of women with children, used as 'wallpaper footage', while the reporter's voice-over reminds us, 'But for the women and children life must go on' (ITN, 13.00, 5.5.82). We are shown close-ups of weeping widows at memorial services, but they only kneel and weep, they are given no chance to speak. When they are picked out of the congregation they are identified only in relation to their men:

> Wives of Acting Chef Michael Till and Petty Officer Anthony Norman. Both men died when an Exocet missile hit the *Sheffield*.
>
> ITN, 20.45, 9.5.82

Early arrivals were the widows of two of the men who perished, Petty Officer Anthony Norman and Acting Chef Michael Till.

BBC1, 21.30, 9.5.82

Since so few *male* relatives were featured, it is not possible to make a properly representative comparison with TV's presentation of men left at home in the same position; but one was Prince Charles whose life is detailed elsewhere in the news; another is referred to by name and occupation:

A second man that died as a result of the explosion that destroyed the frigate HMS *Antelope* on Sunday . . . . Today his father Mr Stanley Stevens, who's a miner, said . . . Stevens had died for a good cause.

ITN, 17.45, 27.5.82

A third male relative appeared after his son was awarded a DSC. He is filmed at his radio as the reporter begins, 'At his home in Anglesey, Keith Mill's father Alan, who's a keen amateur radio enthusiast, has already passed the news to radio hams in Montevideo'; and is then interviewed declaring, 'I'm absolutely delighted . . . and obviously very very proud to be his father' (BBC1, 13.00, 4.6.82).

Female relatives, by contrast, are shown without occupations or interests outside the home, waiting anxiously for their men, listening to the news, looking after children and weeping for the dead. This is not confined to women in Britain: a report on a Falkland Islands woman who had escaped to Chile to have her child identifies her husband by his job and shows the woman, as usual, 'waiting':

In spite of worries about the safety of her husband on the Falklands, the birth went beautifully, a fine 8 lb baby girl, Zoe Alexandra, born here in Chile, but nationality British Falkland Islander. And her lucky father is *Alex Betts, an accountant* in Port Stanley . . . . In the next days Rosa will leave hospital to *wait* for her island home's liberation.

BBC1, 17.05, 25.5.82

As well as being shown only within and in relation to their families, women are portrayed, not as active members of society, but more as vessels of emotion. TV reporters seem scarcely interested in what they think or what they do, but only in what they *feel*. There are only two cases in the period when any relatives are invited to speak for themselves about the political implications of the Falklands War:

Now that Ian has been hurt, how do you fell about the Falklands crisis and Britain and Argentina? Do you still support Britain's stance?

ITN, 20.45, 2.5.82

BBC2 22.45 5.5.82

BBC2 22.15 3.5.82

BBC1 17.40 5.5.82

What have been your thoughts since the Task Force left? Have you had any thoughts about what the government should be doing in all this?
BBC2, 22.45, 5.5.82

On both occasions the women showed themselves perfectly able to give cogent answers. There were no intrinsic reasons to stop asking this sort of question, but none the less it is not raised again in the other forty-six interviews. Instead, we endlessly hear the question, 'How do/did you feel?'[3]

Whenever men are interviewed, there is a marked sex difference in the questioning, as if men are *not* expected to have feelings. For example, in a *vox pop.* on Londoners' reactions to the sinking of HMS *Sheffield* (ITN, 13.00, 5.5.82), the interviewer asks seven men in the street what they 'think' or 'believe' – the main question being, 'Do you *think* it was inevitable?' Only one woman appears, and for her the question is, 'Can we just ask you how you *felt* when you heard about HMS *Sheffield*?'

In a 'human interest' end-of-bulletin story about the wedding of a lieutenant commander who was about to leave for the Falklands ('Despite the crisis, wedding celebrations went ahead this afternoon at a country church . . . for all concerned the timing has proved exactly right' – BBC1, 22.10, 8.5.82), the bridegroom is asked whether his marriage is 'going to make things more difficult for you if it comes to action?', while the bride is asked how she *feels* about being separated so soon. Reporters sometimes see the answers as very 'predictable' in this sort of questioning:

> *Reporter:* How were you feeling as the *QE2* came up? Did you glimpse him up on the deck? Did you see him?
> *Woman:*   No, I didn't have my glasses on.
> *Reporter:*   Through tears probably.
>
> ITN, 22.00, 11.6.82

The reporter assumes, even before he asks, that the woman should feel like crying; although in the same report, an interview is broken off in embarrassment when a *man*, the captain of a sunken ship, understandably distressed, bursts into tears.

The same ideas of a woman's role are revealed elsewhere in the Falklands TV coverage, in casual remarks by journalists, treating women as 'sexual interest', marginal to the real business of the news. For instance, a woman at the dockside in black stockings delivering a singing telegram as the troops embark is picked out and described as 'some cheeky light relief' (BBC1, 21.00, 12.5.82); and over close-ups of women dancers a reporter comments: 'Hot Gossip gave the troops something of what they'll no doubt want to see' (ITN, 20.45, 30.5.82). Women actually involved in the campaign can receive the same sort of treatment: the caption given to the MoD photograph of soldiers talking to women in Port Stanley is '42 Commando met the more decorative of the Islanders'; while the commentary for film of nurses working in a military hospital is 'but now it's over and there's time to chat up a nurse' (both ITN, 22.15, 17.6.82).

An interview with the parents of a stewardess on the requisitioned *QE2* concentrates on her being surrounded by 3,500 men, and the journalists suggests that 'she might have got a taste for it by now . . . (*laughs*)' (BBC1, 11.40, 11.6.82). This sort of innuendo is mild and respectful compared to the coverage in the popular press at the same time. 'Sexy Capers on the Ocean Rave! Buxom blonde Jane Broomfield yesterday spilled the beans on saucy antics that turned the *QE2* into a floating love-nest,' began the *Sun's* story on the *QE2* stewardess (12.6.82). But although the TV news is more dignified and restrained, it does share similar, very limited preconceptions about women's roles. When the first woman soldiers were sent out to the Falklands garrison after the British regained the islands, the news story (ITN, 22.00, 19.7.83) was about what *clothes* they would wear (evening dresses for off-duty and wellington boots for the mud).

"42 Commando met the more decorative of the islanders"
ITN 22.15 17.6.82

The waiting war

The basis of these stories is that the families are having a difficult time, and reporters made serious attempts to capture the shock and suffering. For instance, these items on the reaction on naval estates to the sinking of HMS *Sheffield*:

> There was a deep feeling of shared grief.
> BBC1, 12.30, 5.5.82

> Today was the day the reality of the conflict in the South Atlantic came home; the reaction was naturally one of shock.
> BBC1, 17.40, 5.5.82

> There was no mistaking the feeling of desolation here . . . . And the anxious wait goes on, with the fear that tomorrow might bring news of more deaths, more injuries. The war that seemed such a long way off is real enough now.
> ITN, 22.00, 6.5.82

At the same time, reporters seem anxious to point out the positive side, the benefits of the experience, to maintain the picture of high morale instead of exposing any doubts that might have been raised about British policy. In the BBC2 *Newsnight* item on 3.5.82 on how 'naval wives have been getting together to cope with the strain', all the interview questions are upbeat ones about plans for a summer ball on HMS *Invincible* when it comes back. The coverage of families on HMS *Sheffield's* crew focusses on the relief of women hearing their men have survived:

> One Faslane woman described how she at last got good news of her son. Chief Petty Officer Steven Ball is one of the lucky ones, his wife cannot believe he is coming home . . . For Karin Murphin the long wait for information ended suddenly . . . he has been picked up.
>
> ITN, 22.05, 5.5.82

There is an interview with one of the bereaved (newsworthy because 'in the confusion' the MoD told her that her son was missing, then that he was safe, and then that he was lost). The reporter's only comment during the interview is: 'you, if I may say so, seem to be holding up very well indeed' (BBC1, 17.40, 21.00, 6.5.82).

Family and community solidarity in the face of adversity are repeatedly underlined:

> The crisis has brought wives and families together in a way that they've never known before.
>
> BBC2, 22.45, 3.5.82

> The grief is being shared by the families.
>
> ITN, 13.00, 5.5.82

> The grief is being shared by the wives.
>
> ITN, 17.40, 22.05, 5.5.82

> In a community as close as this, their grief is a common one . . . . Many know their men are safe, but everyone helps unreservedly. There is a feeling here that they are all in this together.
>
> ITN, 17.45, 6.5.82

The coverage of meetings for isolated Task Force relatives is again about home-front morale being kept high:

> The launch of a club to help families . . . they'd felt isolated, and this was a way of overcoming it.
>
> BBC1, 13.00 27.5.82

> . . . invited wives and families of the crew of the *QE2* to a meeting to reassure them that the ship was in no danger . . . The morning proved that *a trouble shared is a trouble halved*.
>
> BBC1, 17.40, 3.6.82

The only interview questions in these reports reveal the priority of morale:

Is the meeting a morale-booster do you think?

BBC1, 13.00, 27.5.82

So you're happier now?

BBC1, 13.00, 17.40, 3.6.82

Who speaks?

Every single report on reactions the day the *Sheffield* was hit shows an anxious wife sitting by the radio or zooms in on newspaper billboards or front pages. The BBC reporter opens with: 'The local newspaper calls it the city of anguish', over a close-up picture of the headlines (BBC1, 17.40, 21.05, 5.5.82). 'The copy of the local paper says it all,' commented *Nationwide's* reporter (BBC1, 18.00).

ITN 17.45 26.5.82

The items on Londoners' reactions (ITN, 13.00, 5.5.82) start at a station news-stand, again with the camera scanning the headlines while the reporter tells us how the commuters studied them. Later when HMS *Coventry* sank, the TV turns to the press again showing film of papers piling off the press:

This was how the news was rushed on to the city street.

ITN, 17.45, 26.5.82

Civilians and servicemen's families were once again faced with the grim headlines.

BBC1, 18.00, 26.5.82

Thus the TV news uses other media literally to mediate: we hear of 'anguish' first via the newspaper, instead of direct from the anguished themselves; this sets up a closed circle in which the media refer to one another instead of directly to the public.

This reluctance to give access to the participants (unless they have a very high status) is common–journalists seem happier turning to accredited 'experts' and 'sources', professionals like themselves. This was prevalent in the coverage of the Task Force families, with journalists repeatedly finding someone else to speak for them, since it was assumed that wives and mothers can contribute only individual emotional reactions, and not any objective or political overview. For instance, an ITN evening report, supposedly on the families at a Gosport naval estate, shows film of the estate, a woman pushing a child on a swing, a family at home and a naval chaplain arriving to visit. The reporter's voice-over tells us about how much the families help each other, but she selects just one person to speak about their experiences: the naval chaplain.

Chaplain: It's been marvellous to see the amount of support that these families have had . . . really remarkable, their resilience is superb.

ITN, 17.45, 6.5.82

Or again, a report on a memorial service for the *Sheffield* shows weeping widows at their pews; but the only words we hear are from the Provost, speaking about the men 'who had given their lives for Queen and country'. According to the newscaster, he 'summed up the feeling of the city' (ITN, 20.45, 9.5.82).

By failing to give a voice to the relatives themselves, TV news controlled not only the picture of their opinions about the war, but also the image of the Navy at home. They broadcast the official MoD, news release about information centres for next of kin, assuring us that 'they will be able to provide information for relatives'. This kind of assurance has to be seen against the experiences of many relatives, who reported that the information was grossly mishandled, that the Navy itself made the waiting much harder to bear by consistently being rude and unhelpful, and refusing to give information, and that the emergency lines were rarely obtainable in emergencies. One woman with a husband in the Task Force wrote in July:

> I heard nothing at all from the Navy the whole time . . . . The Navy still haven't contacted me and I have no idea when he will get home, it could be months. And that's so typical. Wives and families – the ones they say it's all for — have never been taken into consideration.
>
>   Brenda Thomas, quoted in *Spare Rib*, August 1982

Such dissatisfaction was never investigated by the TV news until it was forced to their attention by a group of forty Navy wives speaking out publicly on 26 May, demanding that their MP raise with the Navy their complaints about information centres. The women's action presented the TV news with something of a contradiction – it did not fit in with their image of loyal wives waiting quietly at home, nor their image of a super-efficient naval machine.

ITV did not cover the issue at all until the story was given formal legitimacy by being raised in Parliament on 26 May 1982 (when the Secretary of State for Defence himself admitted that he could have been wrong about releasing some information). Even when the relatives' anger and the charges against the naval information service of inefficiency and rudeness are not mentioned. ITV gave us a single sentence:

> Wives of other men serving with the Task Force have also spoken of the distress caused by waiting to hear exactly which ship has been hit.
>
>   ITN, 21.15, 26.5.82

The BBC does cover the complaints sending a film crew down to the meeting between the wives and their MP. On the main news we hear:

> Sailors' wives from Gosport in Hampshire where many naval families live are unhappy about the flow of information from the Task Force.
>
>   BBC1, 21.00, 26.5.82

There are three clips of women speaking, two suggesting to the MP that a list of ships hit could be released after next of kin have been informed. The angry woman mentioned a naval information officer telling her, 'I don't know what's wrong with you wives, you're all hysterical', was edited out after the first lunchtime report; and, ironically for a report of an occasion when women are specifically speaking out for themselves, none is interviewed or given a chance to articulate her complaints. Instead the camera zooms in on the small children in their arms and at their feet, while we hear the authoritative tones of the reporter describing the constituency's connections with the Navy and reminding us of, 'The difficulties facing Ministry spokesmen and the Navy's information service' (BBC1, 17.40, 21.00, 26.5.82). The person who is interviewed to sum up the women's views is the MP who speaks about announcements in the media and says kindly of the women that 'they're grown up and they want to be kept informed'.

The next night the story of relatives' complaints is followed up (BBC1, 21.00, 17.5.82) but by now the mediation of their views is so complete that they are not featured at all. The newscaster introduces the report with:

> The Royal Navy's been answering criticisms that they take too long giving relatives and dependants information after radio and TV broadcast news of sinkings and casualties. The Navy invited the BBC to see for itself the welfare operation it has mounted.

The women's stand in making their complaints has now been written out of the story: 'the Royal Navy's been answering criticism', but it is disembodied criticism, we are not told who it comes from – moreover, it has already been answered, this is established right at the beginning. The nature of the criticisms is limited to the point that the Navy takes too long to contact relatives. The complaints about release of information to the media and about what the women termed the insulting way they were treated have been dropped. Then 'the Navy invited the BBC to see for itself', and it came when invited: the Navy obviously has less trouble getting a platform than the women do.

The report opens at the naval information centre at HMS Nelson in Portsmouth, with film of busy officers at their desks as the reporter explains how they arrange 'for welfare personnel to call on the families of both survivors and casualties'. The starting point then is the naval operation rather than the experience of the families. Next we move out to the naval estate. The camera starts on the playground, then pans up and follows a naval social worker through the door of a flat where two wives are waiting, while the reporter goes on:

> This afternoon Marie Powell, who's a naval social worker, visited two wives who learned last evening that their husbands aboard the HMS *Coventry* were safe. They were very happy about how they were kept informed.

So relatives do appear, but as usual they are female relatives, getting good news, defined only by the name of their husbands' ship. According to the reporter they are 'very happy', with no awkward opinions and, above all, they do not speak. Finally we get to the criticisms, but none of the dissatisfied relatives are introduced to explain the problem themselves; instead the reporter speaks for them – 'They were very happy about how they were kept informed, but a lot of wives are not – and returns to HMS *Nelson*, where a naval captain is shown giving a speech on the problems caused by the Argentines, the media, and 'security'. He fails to address the charges of naval incompetence, secretiveness or rudeness, assuring us: 'What I would say above everything else is that if we have time then we can get in touch with people quickly.'

This 'follow-up' story is no more than the Navy being given a right of reply to the criticisms which surfaced in a very controlled way on the previous night's news. It is a typical case of broadcasting 'balance'. The 'wives express concern' story is formally balanced by the 'Navy welfare service' story, but the Navy speaks from a position of power, has official status, and is granted a preferential direct access.

A disappearing act

That a story about the plight of the families waiting at home should become a story about the problems of the Royal Navy information centres is an effective illustration of how much the coverage changed during the course of the fighting. In the early days, the personal grief and anxiety of those directly affected were at least covered, albeit in the limited framework of 'wives and mothers showing their support' and by presenting them as individual tragedies. When HMS *Sheffield* was lost, there were two days of news items about reactions among families and on the naval estates (thirteen items in all) claiming to show how 'the reality of the conflict in the South Atlantic came home' (BBC1, 17.40, 5.5.82). But as the losses mounted, the suffering families disappeared from our screens. Two weeks later a second ship went down, HMS *Ardent* at San Carlos. Twenty-four men were killed and thirty injured, but their friends and families did not receive the same attention, and the reports of the grieving at home port were brief and impersonal:

In Plymouth, home of HMS *Ardent*, flags were at half mast and there was thirty seconds silence before this year's city marathon got under way.

BBC1, 17.45, 23.5.82

One family at home connected with the *Ardent* was selected by the television news: 'And we go back to the Falklands for our final story, about a remarkable hero from the tragedy of the *Ardent*' (BBC1, 21.00, 24.5.82). He was 'remarkable' because he manned the gun although he was a civilian NAAFI manager. The BBC1 report begins with the newscaster telling his story over a still picture of his face, then moves on to film the women at home. First we see his mother, inevitably asked 'how do you feel?', replying:

> Well, we were ever so proud of him, because well we just didn't know what was happening you see, and we were glad that he'd done something for his country.

Then his fiancée, filmed sitting at the garden gate, is asked:

> If somebody told you that your John was going to be sitting there machine-gunning low-flying jet planes that were attacking his ship, would you have believed them?

She is asked what she *thinks*, not what she thinks about the war, or the loss of the ship, but:

> *Reporter:* What do you think about John now?
> *Fiancée:* I think he's marvellous. I always thought he was marvellous anyway.

ITN carried a similar report. After the newscaster's introduction we see the hero's mother leafing through a family photo album during the reporter's voice-over account of what happened. She is then invited to give a mother's view:

> In a way it surprised me but I can understand it now because he was always a bit of a lad and he liked to scrap, and well I think he's really proved himself.

The reporter gives more details of her son's career, showing still photographs; then the item closes with a shot of the family grouped in front of their house as the reporter concludes:

> Now his fiancée in Plymouth and big family in Birmingham are waiting to give a hero's welcome for the man who forgot he's now a civilian.

ITN, 22.00, 24.5.82

Coverage of the families at home had been reduced from a guarded attempt to capture some of the personal grief involved to upbeat 'human interest' stories of 'remarkable' heroism while mother and fiancée are at the sidelines, 'waiting to give a hero's welcome'.

Following the sinking of HMS *Sheffield*, the direct reporting of the impact of the war on families at home dried up almost completely after 26 May. We found one reported statement of support from a relative:

> Today his father, Mr Stanley Stevens, *who's a miner*, said Stevens had died for a good cause, and he was 100% behind the battle to retake the Falklands.
>
> ITN, 17.45, 27.5.82

Apart from this, their experience is mediated once more by safer, official sources. For example, the 'special problems facing the families of servicemen' are referred to again (BBC1, 21.00, 24.5.82) but the item does not feature any families directly; it reports only Defence Secretary Nott's speech in the House of Commons about the 'tragic loss of life' and the 'deep sympathy of the whole nation to the relatives and friends of those killed and injured'; so that it is Nott's view of the relatives as objects for sympathy and his comments about 'the whole nation' that are covered rather than the families' own opinions or experiences. Similarly both channels' reports on where 'the loss of the *Coventry* is being felt paticularly sharply' (BBC1, 21.00, 26.5.82) turn out to be about the *city* of Coventry rather than the families or friends of the crew, the twenty dead or the twenty seriously injured. For both the initial reaction and the memorial service, those interviewed as 'spokesmen' are the Lord Mayor and a Royal Navy lieutenant commander.

The language of family involvement is still seen as appropriate: the Lord Mayor of Coventry describes the sailors as 'like sons', while the SAS are described as 'one of the families' in Hereford where 'the entire city mourns' eighteen SAS men killed when a helicopter ditched (BBC1, 20.55, 23.5.82). But by now Task Force families themselves are referred to only in passing: 'Apart from leading figures in the community, the cathedral was packed with families of men aboard HMS *Coventry*, and shoppers' (ITN, 22.00, 28.5.82). The city's formal and official mourning rituals – the memorial services and the flags at half mast — are covered, instead of the immediate impact of the deaths and injuries or the relatives' reactions.

Later still, when fifty-one were dead and forty-six injured after the daylight raid at Bluff Cove, or twenty-three killed and forty-seven wounded in the battle for Mount Longdon, there were no news items

about their families or the families or friends of those who were waiting
to hear whether their men would be next.

Partings and reunions

The Task Force families shot back into prominence at the quayside
and on the airport tarmac when the survivors returned from the
Falklands. Suddenly their voices were heard again, with as many as
thirty-eight interviewed on a single programme (*News Afternoon
Special*, BBC1, 11.40, 11.6.82). For the coverage of families waiting at
home, indeed the war itself, was framed by emotional scenes of
families parted and reunited:

> It was an emotional departure.
>
> BBC1, 22.00,
>
> The dockhead swelled with people and emotion.
>
> ITN, 22.00, 12.5.82
>
> . . . these joyful, tearful reunions.
>
> ITN, 22.00, 11.6.82
>
> Then the moment they'd all been waiting for, as fathers, sons and
> husbands poured onto the tarmac.
>
> BBC1, 21.30, 27.5.82

As soon as they pour onto the tarmac, the 'marvellous fighting forces'
are transformed into 'fathers, sons and husbands', instantly integrated
back into the TV's idealised image.

Earlier in the war, on 12 May, ITV had covered the departure of the
QE2. This helps show how this image is built up. The reports from the
Southampton docks concentrate on the soldiers: 'without doubt',
exclaims the reporter, 'it was the troops' day!' She interviews soldiers
embarking on the *QE2*, and in the early report at lunchtime she
interviews two wives as well:

> *Reporter:* How do you feel about him going?
> *Wife:* Well, upset, disappointed, but it's his job, he's got to do it, so it's
> just one of those things really.
> *2nd Wife:* He knows his job, so long as he keeps his head down and one
> hand on the lifeboat, that's good enough for me.
>
> ITN, 13.00, 12.5.82

Then the report finishes with shots of soldiers waving from the ship's
deck. However, by the evening the opening footage of 'the troops' day'

remains, but the interviews with the wives are edited out. Instead of hearing them speak for themselves (and admit to being 'upset, disappointed') the camera focusses on their tearful faces as they wave Union Jacks on the quayside, while we hear the reporter's account of that day's emotions:

> The carnival atmosphere built up both on the quay and on the ship. The dockhead swelled with people and emotion. There was a lot of jollity and some cheeky light relief. As one well-wisher looked on, another's bra was hoisted aboard . . . [The *QE2*] slipped her moorings, leaving the crowd and the razzamataz behind her.
>
> ITN, 22.00, 12.5.82

Comparing the two bulletins, we can see the newsroom's interpretations of the event being constructed. In order to put across the final image of 'the carnival atmosphere . . . jollity . . . razzamatazz', the true feelings of the women left on the quay are excluded, leaving only the image of their tearful faces and brave smiles on the screen as the men sail away. The significance of television's reports did not pass unnoticed at the time: the BBC's NCA meeting of 25 May was told by the Assistant Director General that 'there had been thanks and praise from the MoD for the coverage of the departure of the *QE2* for the South Atlantic'.

While the interviews recommenced when the troops came back, the journalists still limited what should be discussed, asking mainly, 'How do you feel?', 'How would you feel about him going back?' and 'What are you going to do now?': The question of 'Was it worth it?' was put firmly behind us:[4]

> The ordeal is finally over – they're about to be reunited with their families.
>
> BBC1, 13.00, 27.5.82

> This evening the tragedy was all but forgotten – his friends and neighbours were just glad to see him alive.
>
> BBC1, 21.30, 27.5.82

> As the *QE2* approached the quayside, the time for reflection seemed to be over, and the feeling was mostly one of relief at being home, and delight at seeing loved ones.
>
> BBC1, 21.00, 11.6.82

> The memory of those three weeks and more ago, when those three ships were lost, today being *erased by happy family reunions*. The moment for meeting relatives, kind words and smiles, though *not erasing the resolve*.

> Many signs from the *QE2* this morning and on the dockside, slogans
> that read, 'Falklands First, World Cup next!'
>
> BBC1, 11.40, 11.6.82

And there is a deeply conventional image of the return to normality
when the men get home:

> They made their way home to find peace and privacy . . . one man, asked
> what he'd do tonight, said simply, 'I'm going to be waited on'.
>
> BBC1, 21.30, 27.5.82

Although survivors are given some opportunity to talk about their
experiences during the war ('Oh dear, what happened to you?' a
reporter asks a burn victim from HMS *Coventry* – BBC1, 11.40,
11.6.82), what is emphasised in the commentary is the families'
emotions:

> . . . their job at today's reunion.
>
> BBC1, 12.30, 27.5.82

> . . . unconcealed joy.
>
> ITN, 22.00, 29.5.82

> . . . great many emotional hugs and kisses on the tarmac . . . an amazingly
> joyful occasion.
>
> BBC1, 21.00, 7.6.82

The joy is directly tied to the family being brought back together.
'*Back with their families*, the survivors from HMS *Sheffield*', ran the
BBC1, 21.30 news headline on 27 May. When the *QE2* returned, ITN
covered two reunions beyond the quayside: one survivor was filmed at
a street party outside his Plymouth home; another, from HMS
Antelope, was picked out because his wife had given birth while he was
away, and the local TV company had intervened to give him his first
sight of the baby from a studio in Newcastle before he returned home.

It was perfectly accurate to report that the homecomings were very
emotional – the hugs and kisses and street parties were not invented by
TV. The problem is the selection involved: the emotions of the joyous
homecoming are news, whereas the less morale-boosting emotions of
the friends and families waiting anxiously at home or suffering
bereavement are excluded. For example, the excitement of the
survivor returning to his family and seeing the new baby is celebrated
on TV, though nothing was heard at the time about the experience of
his wife who had gone into labour when she heard his ship had been
hit. The Task Force homecomings are treated as major media events,

extensively covered, often rather in the style of the Royal Wedding – the return of the *QE2*, for instance, was the subject of an eighty-minute special news programme on BBC1, using eight on-the-spot reporters, and a fifty-minute special on ITN. It was advertised on five separate occasions during the previous day's ITN bulletins ('Don't forget the *QE2's* return on ITV tomorrow morning!'), probably helping to produce the crowds which TV cameras then arrives to film. This enthusiasm and these resources were never devoted to covering the equally important but unhappier feelings on the home front. As a senior ITN reporter pointed out to us later:

> You compared the return of the *QE2* and the *Canberra*. When we did the *QE2* it was a big megalopolis special. When the *Canberra* came home, with the bodies – what was it? – a minute, twenty-second quickie. In strictly moral and human terms we should have honoured the return of the dead. ·

Instead, we find the experience of the Task Force relatives deployed to include the entire nation in a surge of pride and support.

"Where better than here to catch the mood of the nation"

BBC1 12.30 12.5.82

'Where better than here to catch the mood of the nation?' asked a reporter at Southampton as the *QE2* left, over film of troops holding up an enormous Union Jack (BBC, 12.30, 12.5.82). Then later on its return:

> *Headline:* They waved, they kissed, they talked of heroism, the *QE2* is home.
> *Newscaster:* One banner on the Southampton quayside said it all: 'Welcome home lads,' it said. 'We're so very proud of you.'
> > BBC1, 21.00, 11.6.82

There is one day's outburst of cynicism and irony, one homecoming that is described as a 'carefully organised hero's welcome', (BBC1, 22.45, 6.5.82), an 'elaborately staged welcome' (BBC1, 21.00, 6.5.82); but this was the return of the *Belgrano* survivors to Argentina.

Women at the top

The TV news coverage of Task Force relatives, then, shows a very traditional image of women, and it is interesting that even those women who are already public figures in their own right, specifically the Prime Minister and the Queen, are not totally immune. Some references to the feminine stereotype are made only casually and in passing, for example in this report on the Prime Minister's meeting with the US President at Versailles: 'The President didn't seem to mind one bit that she exercised a lady's privilege and was late' (BBC1, 21.00, 4.6.82).

Looking at these women at the top, the significance of the assumptions about the nation and the family becomes clearer. The Prime Minister has considerable control over her media image, unlike the Task Force relatives, and she also has a special interest in fostering traditional pictures of family life. She frequently describes herself in 'typical housewife' terms; for example, in one interview on how she dealt with the Falklands crisis she says: 'It's like when you have a family crisis. Someone has to stay in control and keep going' (*Women's Own*, 28.8.82). Mrs Thatcher's preferred image of the nation as a whole, and specifically the nation at war, leans heavily on idea of the family as an ordered unit, all pulling together. This was made explicit in her speech at Finchley on the day of the British landings on the Falklands:

> The Prime Minister said today that the courage and skill of the men in

the Task Force had brought a new pride to this country. Mrs Thatcher said it made us realise we are all really one family.

> BBC1, 21.00, 21.5.82

The TV news goes beyond reporting Mrs Thatcher's words: in its own structuring of news from the home front it shares and endorses her views. Thus the nation is seen to be made up of families; within the family women are dependent on men and occupied with the home, the heart, and the children; women in the family are proud of their men fighting for the nation; the nation is united like a family is united; and the nation is united behind the men (and women) of the Task Force. The Queen is also shown as fitting into women's allotted position, as if the national crisis produced an equality overriding the divisions in society, reducing even the Queen to just 'one of thousands':

> The Queen is one of thousands of worried mothers with a son in the fleet.
>
> BBC1, 17.05, 26.5.82

> For a moment, we were not looking at a Pope and a Queen, but rather at a concerned priest and an anxious mother.
>
> ITN, 17.45, 28.5.82

She is also accessible to the 'normal world' of television viewers, as ITN news stressed in their story about the Queen visiting the *Coronation Street* set in Manchester:

> *Headline:* And in the normal world of Coronation Street, the Queen meets the neighbours.
> *Journalist:* An out-of-work school leaver asked the Queen in Manchester today, 'How's Andrew?' and got the answer, 'I hope he's alright.' The actor Peter Adamson also had his thoughts on the Falklands; he told the Queen, 'Our hearts are with you.'
>
> ITN, 22.05, 5.5.82

This suggestion of equality is significant, as the Royal Family is often presented as a model family, a family that represents the nation, in itself a symbol of national unity and social solidarity.

The Royal Family can be seen as offering the viewer 'personal' identification: 'For the Royal Family it's a *personal* anxiety: Prince Andrew is a helicopter pilot with the Task Force' (ITN, 21.15, 26.5.82). Messages from Royalty are used to frame stories about other families, as if to set the appropriate tone. An item on the families of HMS *Sheffield* survivors in Faslane and Portsmouth begins:

> As friends and families connected with six different naval bases waited

for news today, the Queen sent her own message to the Chief of Naval Staff . . . . And the Prince of Wales, whose brother Andrew is a helicopter pilot on HMS *Invincible*, joined the Princess to send 'our very deepest sympathy to the wives and families of those who gave their lives so courageously'.

ITN, 22.05, 5.5.82

(ITN's news that day closed with a piece of film from the archive showing the Queen launching HMS *Sheffield* in 1975.)

There is nothing new in the TV's concern with the words and activities of the Royal Family. As Alastair Burnett put it:

The Royal Family . . . has very many plain people who watch its activities with great affection and interest. It is, I think, something that adds a sense of continuity and coherence in their lives.

Alastair Burnett, *Guardian*, 19.12.83.

In fact their position as a constant background to the turbulence of daily news was underlined during the Falkland crisis: a report on the Queen and Prince Philip at the Chelsea Flower Show began:

Despite what's happening abroad in the South Atlantic the yearly pattern of life here seems to be unchanged . . . . The Royal Family are traditional visitors to the Chelsea Flower Show.

BBC2, 18.50, 23.5.82

There is nothing new either in the TV news pretension to give the viewer access to some sort of personal contact with Royalty. The same tendency can be seen for instance in the advertising for ITV's *National Salute to the Task Force* on 18 July 1982; the *TV Times* cover showed a Union Jack and an engraved card with a picture of Prince Charles below the words, 'Your invitation to join the Prince of Wales', as if watching TV really puts the viewer in his company.

What is remarkable was the unusually explicit political content of the comments of this 'one of thousands of worried mothers', given to us as much more than 'personal anxiety'. Take the use made by BBC1 of the Queen's speech at Keilder Dam on 26 April:

Headline: The Queen speaks for the nation.
Newscaster: The Queen spoke today for the whole nation . . . she said her thoughts were eight thousand miles away and she prayed for the success of the Task Force.

BBC1, 17.05, 26.5.82

Or take ITN's use of her speech during President Reagan's visit, in the prominent positions of the headline and closing summary:

Headline: The Queen says we're standing up for freedom.
Summary: The Queen said that Britain was standing up for freedom in the Falklands. The conflict was thrust on us by naked aggression, she said, and we are naturally proud of the way our fighting men are serving their country.

ITN, 22.00, 8.6.82

British history

Even routine coverage of royal pageantry is drawn into the Falklands net. When the Queen is filmed walking into Westminster Abbey in formal robes, the newscaster points out:

> The Queen looked pensive this morning when she attended a service at Westminster Abbey for the Order of the Bath. Yesterday she said her thoughts and prayers were with the servicemen in the South Atlantic. They of course include Prince Andrew.
>
> ITN, 13.00, 27.5.82

At the Chelsea Pensioners' founders' day ceremony:

> As the Queen arrived to take the salute, nobody needed reminding that once again British servicemen are fighting for their country.
>
> BBC1, 13.00, 10.6.82

And with more royal/military spectacle at the Trooping of the Colour: 'Things weren't totally normal . . . everyone conscious of the situation in the South Atlantic.' (ITN, 21.00, 12.6.82).

When Prince Charles presents new colours to the 15th Scottish V Volunteers battalion of Parachute Regiment, his face appears behind the newscaster under the 'Falklands Conflict' logo, and we are reminded:

> Soon too Falklands may be added to the battle honours . . . . Servicemen, said the Prince, were among the first to make the ultimate sacrifice in defence of principles and values.
>
> BBC1, 17.40, 21.00, 28.5.82

An important part of the Royal Family's role is to keep alive links with British tradition and history, even on the Task Force itself:

> The ships of the Task Force weren't too busy to forget naval tradition when they crossed the Equator on their way south . . . . And who better to play the King of the Sea than Prince Andrew?
>
> ITN, 21.45, 15.5.82

The Queen is always shown surrounded by reminders of her family history and the nation's history, as in this report on President Reagan's visit to Windsor. The news slips into potted history tones:

> She led him through the Waterloo Chamber, pointing out the delights created by her ancestor George IV to commemorate Napoleon's defeat . . . Their cheerful steps led them to St George's Hall, a great chamber built by Edward III . . . . Especially for the occasion, Queen Victoria's dining table had been installed.
>
> ITN, 22.00, 8.6.82

In the Falklands coverage, journalists carried their sense of historical occasion beyond the Royalty stories, slipping historical references into reports about ordinary mortals as if to heighten awareness of Britain's historical traditions at a time when the armed forces were defending them. For instance, interviews with commuters crossing London Bridge include shots of a naval relic – 'In the Thames sat the old seadog HMS *Belfast* looking sombre' – and refer to older victories too: 'above the tourists towered Britain's greatest naval hero, Lord Nelson' (ITN, 13.00, 5.5.82). Reports from Portsmouth naval estates seize on street signs as an opportunity to make historical link (Normandy Road, etc.), as the reporter intones: 'The people are not strangers to famous sea battles' (ITN, 13.00, 17.45, 22.05, 5.5.82).

A common historical parallel is 'people haven't known anything like it since World War II' (BBC1, 19.40, 5.5.82). It is debatable whether the Falklands were actually like the Second World War at all, since national security was not threatened, and most people were not directly involved. But it is as if an attempt is made to incorporate the Falklands into the flow of British history and legend, by injecting historical references wherever possible and appealing to selected folk-memories of the last war – Vera Lynn, for instance, who did actually release a record during the Falklands campaign. The BBC not only treated this as news, but also gave us an historical intoduction, an interview with Vera Lynn, and extracts from her song accompanied by wartime stills of the 'forces sweetheart' and current film of her wandering through an English country garden:

> *Newscaster:* Dame Vera Lynn has recorded a patriotic song for the men of the Falklands Task Force. Dame Vera became the forces' sweetheart in the Second World War, with songs like 'We'll Meet Again' and 'The White Cliffs of Dover'. Her new record, on sale shortly, is called 'I Love this Land' . . . .
> *Song:* I love this land,
> I love her hills and rivers and trees . . . .

Dame Vera: . . . I was very happy to be able to do something . . . .
Song: These memories of home, when my memories roam,
   Bring England near at hand.
   It will stay that way for ever.
   Which is why I love this land.

BBC1, 18.00, BBC2, 19.15, 29.5.82

Meanwhile, other popular songs released especially for the Falklands War such as Crass's 'How does it feel (to be the mother of 1,000 dead?)', which lack the patriotic element of 'Love This Land', do not make news in quite the same way.

When British military action began with the bombing of the Port Stanley runway, it was given a place in Britain's record by being compared to Second World War air attacks. A reporter "interviews" Second World War hero Sir Arthur Harris:

Newscaster: The man who organised Britain's air offences during the Second World War, ninety-year-old Marshal of the RAF Sir Arthur Harris, attended a special service for the Air Crew Association . . . . Afterwards he gave his own views on the Falklands conflct.
Reporter: Although this was a dedication service, there was a discernible spirit of buoyancy among the congregation, typified by Sir Arthur 'Bomber' Harris, Marshal of the RAF. After the service I asked Sir Arthur about the air assault on the Falklands . . . . What sort of action would you be recommending should be taken now if you were involved?
Sir Arthur: Exactly that, keep the runways out of order so that our enemy, if he's worth calling that, can't use them.

BBC1, 17.50, 2.5.82

On another occasion, a Harrier pilot on the Task Force is asked in an interview: 'Do the dogfights compare with those in the Second World War?' (ITN, 18.15, 14.6.82).

The ships of the Task Force itself are also wreathed in history. On the day of the *QE2's* departure ('the biggest single troop embarkation since World War II' – BBC1, 21.00, 12.5.82), ITN's main bulletin shows a long sequence of archive film of the *Queen Mary* leaving New York in 1943:

The *Queen Mary*, Cunard's former flagship, was also requisitioned for the war, in 1943 . . . . Churchill later said the use of the *Queen Elizabeth* and *Mary* shortened the war by nearly a year.

ITN, 22.00, 12.5.82

Churchill appears again later, in a comparison with the present Prime Minister:

Mrs Thatcher has to go on saying it's business as usual in Downing Street . . . . In war, a real war, a Prime Minister is protected, as Churchill was.

> ITN, 21.00, 19.5.82

Another favoured memory was D-Day. Before the British landing on the Falklands, a defence correspondent suggests the parallel:

Now to what extent would an operation like this be a re-enactment in minature of the day that changed the course of the last world war?

> BBC2, 22.55, 19.5.82

The bulletin goes on to show lengthy clips of film from 1944, complete with the original commentry ('Then we hit the beach, and we were there!'), only to follow it with the current MoD account: 'Now the re-invasion of the Falklands, if it does happen, will look very different.' The reports from San Carlos return to the theme: '4,000 men of the 5th Infantry Brigade have now completed the second Falklands D-Day landing', evidently assuming a common stock of memories and images: '*it would have reminded anybody* of British Tommies landing on D-Day in 1944' (BBC2, 23.25, 6.6.82) – as if all generations of viewers would be keeping alive these memories of forty years ago, although none of the harsher memories are rekindled, nothing is said for instance about the victims of the war or those left to mourn for them.

Instead our thoughts are directed to moments such as the liberation of Jersey from the Nazis. Both the BBC and ITN take the opportunity of Jersey's donation to the Falklands campaign to show film of crowds lining the streets and women kissing soldiers as the British march in. The link is made explicit:

Jersey is planning to give the British government £5 million to help free the Falklands and re-establish the islanders in their homes . . . . The Channel Islanders may well know better than any Britons how the Falklanders are feeling, as British troops bring about their liberation.

> BBC1, 21.00, 4.6.82

The sense of historical occasion can be seen at its height in the BBC coverage of the Falklands remembrance service, sweeping beyond the Second World War to embrace 'more than 1,000 years of fire and pestilence':

And so on so many occasions of joy and sadness, a thanksgiving and remembrance, through more than a thousand years of fire and pestilence, peace and war, the nation turns again to London's cathedral church, with its golden cross lifted high above the City and Ludgate

Hill . . . . Not for today the pageantry that brought Nelson home to St Paul's or Wellington to his marble tomb.

BBC1, 26.7.82

The national interest and dissent

The TV news reference to British history finds a close parallel in government speeches which appeal to our history and heritage in order to justify, interpret and celebrate the campaign. For example, Mrs Thatcher's famous speech at Cheltenham on 3 July presents Britain as:

> the nation that had built an Empire and ruled a quarter of the world . . . . We rejoice that British has rekindled *that spirit which has fired her for generations past* and which today has begun to burn as brightly as before. Britain has found herself again in the South Atlantic and will not look back from the victory she has won.

She comments in an ITV documentary:

> I was very upset at the people who lost their lives in the Falklands and then I thought of Wellington after the battle of Waterloo.
>
> *PM. The Woman at No. 10*, ITV, 29.3.82

And to the *Daily Express*:

> I had the winter at the back of my mind. The winter . . . down in South Georgia, the ice, what will it do? It beat Napoleon at Moscow.
>
> *Daily Express*, 26.7.82

The TV news broadcasters would rarely use such openly partisan rhetoric as the Prime Minister's. The question of their independence from the government was hotly debated at the time of the Falklands, and the broadcasters were self-consciously defending their integrity. They apparently believed that they were successful. A BBC managing director insisted:

> Our contribution to national morale relies on telling the truth. We are not in the game of patriotism. We are dealing with the job of finding out facts.
>
> Richard Francis, speech at International Press Institute, May 1982

The BBC in particular took great pride in presenting 'all sides' of the story in a 'balanced' way. One journalist asked in a news interview:

> Is it not a vindication of the way in which broadly the media, and God knows the range of opinion has been broad enough, has treated it that

when the public are faced with such a wide range of opinion, they still say 'yes we have seen it all' – and *I think they probably have seen it all* – 'and still we back the government'? Now isn't that an enormous source of strength?

Newscaster interview question, BBC2, 22.45, 12.5.82

However, as we have seen, the coverage was not 'neutral' and the viewers did not exactly 'see it all'. The problem here was not simply direct government manipulation, but that by basing justification of their policy on appeals to national unity and the 'rekindled' national spirit, the government hit broadcasting neutrality in a very weak spot.

In this case the government managed to define the national interest as the prosecution of its own policy against Argentina. This put the broadcasters in a painful position: while the liberal, centrist values of many journalists and their loyalty to the national 'consensus' were probably not in sympathy with the government's radical conservatism, they did share a view of the nation, a belief in national interests which can override the divisions and conflicts in our society. As one reporter put it:

> The broadcasting authorities have themselves felt as though they're on a desert island which the sea is gradually eating away, and have moved more and more to the centre of the island . . . . At precisely the time when the conflicts in our society demand a greater degree of courage to interpret the realities of what is going on . . . it's very easy to get caught in the web of the Establishment's perception – I find it happening to me.

Jonathan Dimbleby, *Stills* magazine, November 1982

The broadcasters' idea of 'national consensus' can lead to a blindness to social conflict – leaving the coverage open to the government's use of the concepts of 'national unity' and the 'national interest'.

The routines of 'balance' were not enough to produce impartial coverage. In fact it can help to *create* the very national unity and consensus of opinion that it relies on to establish its supposedly impartial position. The Annan Report on the future of broadcasting recognised:

> At a time when many people feel that society is fragmenting, broadcasting welds it together. It links people, gives the mass audience common topics of conversation, makes them realise that, in experiencing similar emotions, they all belong to the same nation.

Oddly enough, the British broadcasters seem to recognise the role of the media in creating national unity in Argentina more readily than in their own case:

Argentine President General Galtieri has also been preparing his people for war through the medium of broadcasters and newspapers . . . . The newspaper headlines sum it all up in Buenos Aires as the military junta prepares the nation for war and drums up patriotism.

BBC2, 18.50, 2.5.82

Newscaster: Argentine television has been rallying the country's 27 million people for war using rather bizzare methods . . . .
Correspondent: Argentine television presents a lunchtime magazine of pure propoganda.

Untranslated clips from the Argentine programme are shown, then the newscaster comments at the end: 'You'll have noticed the British television's approach is rather different' (ITN, 13.00, 5.5.82).

This is not to suggest that the British government or British TV are the *same* as those in Argentina,[5] but the free criticism of Galtieri's junta for 'drumming up patriotism' by manipulating the media underlines the British broadcasters' own uncritical assumption of 'national unity' at home. During the Falklands War the general problems of broadcasting independence were sharpened, because keeping public morale on the home front high was seen as part of the war effort, so the 'national interest' demand that the TV news should paint a picture of national support, and isolate opposition to the war. Too much questioning of the government's policy and the precise interests it served was thought by some to be unpatriotic.

The most specular case of the limits put on acceptable expression of dissent on TV was not about the news but about the *Panorama* programme *Can We Avoid War?* on 10 May 1982. It led to immediate outbursts in the House of Commons the following day, with Conservative front-bencher Sally Oppenheim branding it

'An odious subversive travesty in which Michael Cockerell and other BBC reporters dishonoured the right of freedom of speech in this country.

House of Commons, 11.5.82

This opened a bitter debate on TV coverage of the crisis in general and *Panorama* in particular. The BBC's Chairman had to reassure the Prime Minister that 'the BBC is not neutral' (BBC press statement, 11.5.82), and he and the Director General Designate were summoned to a stormy meeting of the Conservative backbench Media Committee to face calls for their resignation. *Panorama's* presenter Robert Kee first publicly disowned the controversial programme, then left the BBC. The press soon joined in the row, with cries of 'traitors' – the *Sun* commenting:

> The *British* Broadcasting Corporation needs a shake-up. Too many of its studios are infested with arrogant little know-alls ready to serve up their loaded version of 'truth' to viewers.
>
> *Sun* leader, 15.5.82

It was an impassioned episode, important if for nothing else in reminding us how self-conscious the BBC is of its degree of independence, and how mistrustful the Conservative right wing is of the BBC's liberal centrist 'neutrality'. As one MP who spoke out against the programme reflected:

> The Conservative Party has long been suspicious of the BBC because of the undeniable fact that its trainees always seem to be recruited from those with extreme left-wing motivation.
>
> Alan Clark, MP, *Washington Post*, 27.5.82

Our own analysis of the programme shows that it contained more statements in support of government policy than against. None the less it was probably the clearest articulation on television at that time of alternative views. Its effect on the rest of programming was probably to make it more difficult than usual to feature these views.

In *Panorama* the following week there was a report from the constituency of David Crouch, one of the dissenting MPs, using interviews at his Conservative Club which showed that he did not represent local views. The *Panorama* team then went to the Yarrow shipyard in Glasgow to interview workers who supported the Task Force and were stepping up work on frigates for the South Atlantic. This interviewing was carried out on a Sunday afternoon and did not feature the Yarrow workers who were rejecting overtime. (40% had voted *against* lifting an overtime ban for the sake of the Task Force frigates.)

In news programmes there was some coverage of dissent within the Labour movement, but it was mainly in the traditional mould of coverage of internal disputes between MPs:

> Mr Dennis Healey had launched a thinly veiled attack on Mr Tony Benn for breaking away from the party in his views on the Falklands crisis.
>
> ITN, 17.45, 12.5.82

Attacks on the breakaway views rather than the views themselves often make the news:

Barnsley's Labour MP Mr Roy Mason has criticised his local party and the miner's president Mr Arthur Scargill, who voted to recall the Task Force. Mr Mason said, 'I can't think it right that we should give in to a damnable military junta.'

ITN, 22.00, 17.5.82

Roy Mason's words about not 'giving in' are put on the screen with his picture – his local party and the miner's president appear only as objects of his criticism, and not with their own views in their own right. This is the nearest we get to coverage of 'grassroots' Labour views, though of 66 resolutions on the Falklands from constituency Labour Parties, 6 backed the front-bench line of support for the Task Force, and 60 dissented. There were no news items on dissension in the ranks of the Conservative Party, for instance the splits discussed on *Panorama*, or the Prime Minister's policy adviser Ferdinand Mount's call for a ceasefire in the *Spectator* on 6 May. Doubts about the military escalation came from various quarters but did not receive much TV news coverage, and were not offered the same treatment as official policy.

Access

If some views are less acceptable on TV than others, who *did* appear on the news about the Falklands? Our breakdown of studio interviews reveals a rather limited choice.

Studio interviews — 'Falklands' items, all TV news, 1 May to 14 June 1982 (390 bulletins)

Politicians	Conservative MPs	74
	Labour MPs	22
	Alliance MPs	15
'Experts'	Military	72
	Academic	9
	Industry	6
	Other	4
Falkland Islanders		22
Media	British	16
	USA	3
Diplomats	British	15
	Argentine	13

continued

continuation

Britain	Serving military officers	8
	Church leaders	6
	Shipping industry	5
Argentina	Civilian	7
	Military	1
World	Chile	2
	USA	1
	Commonwealth	1
	International Red Cross	3

Figures for interviews given in the TV studios do not reveal everything about who appeared on the screen. We exclude some familiar faces like the 'family' interviews in the home and on the quay, the 53 MoD statements (featuring the new screen personality Ian McDonald, who *never* gave televised interviews), the 43 appearances of the UN Secretary-General on his way in and out of meetings of the UN, and even 52 of the Prime Minister's own appearances (at news conferences, in recorded reports from Parliament, interviews outside No. 10, etc.). But since studio interviews are a prestigious form of appearance, and normally provide the best opportunity for putting across a point of view, these figures give an important indication of whose views are given the best airing on TV news. They show a clear 'hierarchy of access' which it would be hard to justify as 'balanced'.

The single highest-scoring group is Conservative MPs with 74. Of these, 50 interviews are with the four members of the 'war cabinet', and none featured the most extreme 'hawks' or 'wets', ensuring that the official government view was dominant. This compares with only 22 studio interviews for Labour, almost half of them with Dennis Healey, and a total of 3 for the Parliamentary 'Peace Party' (out of the 73 who signed the Early Day Motion on 4 May 1982 calling for an immediate truce in the South Atlantic). The only other group to appear in anything like these numbers is the military 'experts'–at 72—who mainly discussed possible military tactics and analysed past military exploits. It is noticeable that taken together 'our experts here in the studio' make up the second biggest group after MPs, reflecting once again TV news' tendency to pull away from people immediately involved in events and giving pride of place to the 'expert' who can make 'authoritative' comments as if s/he (usually he) was outside and above the action. This is part of the ritual of TV 'balance and impartiality'; but in fact the experts are *not* always impartial or disinterested. The military experts were almost all retired military officers, in general retaining their military outlook. No other groups were as fully represented: a glaring example is the very low figures for world opinion – a touchy subject for the government (since world support declined as British action was thought to escalate).

The Falkland Islanders themselves (whose views or interests were said to be 'paramount') receive a respectable 22 appearances. Seventeen of these interviews were with a single member of the Falkland Islands Council; but the broadcasters could hardly give access to a wide range of Falklanders in the circumstances. It is interesting to note that the islanders get roughly the same total number of studio interviews as the Argentines (21 including the diplomats). Allowing for this, the general picture given by the studio interview figures remains one of strictly controlled access, with overwhelming preference given to the government and the military, and a TV voice for only a very narrow range of views.

'Revoluntionary Communists Supporting Argentina' (BBC1, 23.5.82, 17.45). Although we argue that public attitudes to developments in the South Atlantic were more complex and flexible than the 'pro-war'/'anti-war' caricatures, there was a section of the population which clearly opposed the military operation and when the fighting started called for a ceasefire and serious peaceful negotiations. It is hard to judge the size of this minority, especially without putting too much trust in opinion polls – although there are polls taken *after* the British victory showing 22% against the war 'given the cost in lives and money' (*Economist*, 22.6.82) and 25% seeing it as Britain's 'greatest mistake' of the year (*Observer*, 2.1.83). Furthermore, the anit-war minority was not an isolated fringe; many of those in the 'middle' who did not condemn the war outright did not give it unconditional support either. While backing the troops, they shared much with the anti-war group, as can be seen in the unwillingness to sacrifice life and the support for UN administration (see the polls analysis above). This was uncovered again much later in a Gallup poll commissioned by the *Daily Telegraph* in which two thirds of those questioned thought the war was not inevitable:

> The government should have done more to prevent a war over the Falklands.
>
> | | |
> |---|---|
> | Agree | 67% |
> | Disagree | 25% |
> | Neither, don't know | 8% |
>
> *Daily Telegraph*, 4.2.83

During the days of the fighting, there was a network of active groups throughout Britain demonstrating their opposition. Activities included a Saturday morning leafleting campaign by a Plymouth women's group:

> There was some hostility of the 'what a cheek, giving out such a leaflet in Plymouth of all places' type, plus the usual shouts of 'you could't do this in Argentina/Russia'. But there was quite a lot of positive response too – many people coming up and asking for one when they realised what it was about, saying that they agreed. And we noticed that many older women supported us, recalling the horrors of previous wars, and their loss of friends and relatives.
>
> Plymouth Women's Centre report, *Spare Rib*, August 1982

There were also marches, meetings, pickets, fasts and vigils organised by forty-nine different *ad hoc* Falklands peace committees up and down the country. One local committee reported:

> More than 500 people sent letters of protest to the government protesting at the escalation of the conflict in the sinking of the *General Belgrano*, and urging an immediate ceasefire . . . . This activity was followed by a hastily convened public meeting on May 15th. Over 200 people representing a broad cross-section of the community attended, clearly united in their concern . . . on 21st May a 24 hour vigil and fast started, calling for peace, which was maintained by 20 people and supported by several hundred others . . . . It was decided to maintain a presence for peace from 1.00 to 2.00 p.m. each day until the war ends . . . the response to the Bangor Ad Hoc Campaign suggests that in this part of Britain at least, the military 'solution' commands much less than the 80% claimed by the media.
>
> *Output*, local Bangor paper, June 1982

The forty-nine local committees linked to a National Peace Committee in London – which had the formal backing of eight MPs and some thirty national bodies (mainly peace groups and churches) presented the Foreign Secretary, Francis Pym, with a ceasefire petition bearing 26,000 signatures on 8 June.

In other words there was a small but active movement opposed to the war, demanding a ceasefire and the reopening of negotiations, supported by perhaps one in four of the population, with many more apparently open to its arguments. How was this reflected on TV news? None of the activities outlined above was mentioned. There was some coverage of the three rallies and marches in London, although the BBC ignored the 3,000 people marching down Fleet Street on 16 May protesting about media coverage of the crisis.

Another interpretation does surface: the late-night BBC2 news item on a Falklands peace march on 23 May reports that the march attracted five to ten thousand people and that:

> they represented many and varied political and religious views. As well as MPs, trade unionists and Church leaders the groups ranged from the Milton Keynes Peace Movement to the Ecology Party and the Latin America Bureau.
>
> BBC2, 22.40, 23.5.82

But the picture on the main bulletins is rather different, giving lower numbers for the turn-out and stressing the 'revoluntionary communist' and 'left-wing' participation:

> several thousand people . . . among them revolutionary communists supporting Argentina . . . speakers including left-wing Labour MPs Tony Benn and Dame Judith Hart.
>
> BBC1, 17.45, 20.55, 23.5.82

> 4,000 people were there, including Mr Tony Benn.
>
> ITN, 18.30, 20.45, 23.5.82

Only one interview is shown in the reports – and it is put to Benn rather than to any of the other speakers at the rally (who included a bishop, a Social Democrat, and an Argentine ex-political prisoner). The question is:

> As news of the landing by the Task Force dominated people's thoughts today I asked Mr Benn whether the rally was not inopportune?
>
> ITN, 18.30, 20.45, 23.5.82

The marchers were introduced with suspicion – '*it was called* a march for peace' (ITN, 18.30, 20.45) — and as a potential source of trouble. The BBC1 report opened with film of police vans — 'a substantial police *task force* gave protective cover to the demonstration' (BBC1, 17.45) — although it did not tell us about the police threat to ban the demonstration altogether (lifted only at the last minute after MPs appealed to the Home Secretary). In this report counter-demonstrators, from the anti-CND pressure group the Coalition For Peace Through Security, were described as 'pro-Falklanders', as if by proposing a ceasefire and negotiations the peace marchers were 'anti-Falklanders'. In fact it is not clear that all of the Falklands Islanders believed that the best solution was to send the Task Force. As early as 27 April, 1982 a very senior BBC editor is recorded at the confidential NCA meeting as saying that he had received a call from a Falkland Islander 'to the effect that Tony Benn was the first politican to have talked sense about the crisis'.

"Pro Falklanders"

BBC1 19.45 23.5.82

"There'll always be an England"

BBC1 21.00 12.5.82

We can compare the above coverage to that of 'pro war' mobilisation. This is the end-of-bulletin item in a main BBC1 news, accompanied by shots of the small crowd waving Union Jacks:

> And finally, a display of patriotism on Merseyside tonight, where more than 500 people gathered to sing songs as a sign of their support for the British troops out in the South Atlantic. The idea was the brainchild of a Liverpool mother of three, and she advertised it in a local paper. The response was so enthusiastic, she cancelled plans to hold the rally at a local park, and arranged it at the Bier Head, where ships sailed past to join the transatlantic convoys of the last war. The people went on singing for over an hour (*Singing*): 'There'll always be an England, And England shall be free.'
>
> BBC1, 21.00, 12.5.82

The 'display of patriotism' organised by a 'mother of three' in support of the Task Force is presented as good news – 'the response was so enthusiastic' — in contrast with the guarded and stereotyped approach to the displays of the peace marchers.

'*Things in Their Aircraft Factory Will Never Be Quite the Same Again*' (ITN, 13.00, 29.6.83). The war in the Falklands ended on 14 June 1982. But the spirit of the Falklands was to live on. The Prime Minister's initial reaction to the Argentine surrender was: 'It's *Great* Britain . . . it's been everyone together and that's what matters.' Her speech on 3 July 1982 – 'We have found a new confidence, born of the economic battles at home and tested and found true 8,000 miles away' – and Nigel Lawson's proclamation on 22 June 1982

> Nothing could have signalled more clearly that the long years of retreat and self-doubt are over . . . it's the rebirth of Britain . . .

– these show how the government was determined to carry the carefully fostered spirit of national unity and hard-working values beyond the fighting in the South Atlantic and into the everyday battles of domestic politics and industrial relations.

The link between the military victory and industrial relations was taken up by the media. The BBC's industrial correspondent asked David Howell: 'Is the government going to meet this strike with the same resolve it showed over the Falklands?' (BBC1, 18.00, 27.6.82). In fact the link had already been established on the news, with reports on how productivity shot up in the British companies supplying the Task Force:

> The company making the special apparatus has been working seven days a week since the Navy placed the order last month. An order had

been expected, but five days after the attack on the *Sheffield*, the signal came – send them now. Production leapt from 50 a month to nearly 2,000 a week, and suppliers cut through red tape to deliver parts in record time.

BBC1, 11.40, 11.6.82

It was clear that the image of national unity on the home front was not a special case confined to the Falklands War itself and the constraints imposed by the fighting. It is equally useful in peacetime:

> Only now is one of the engineering success stories of the Falklands War becoming apparent . . . . The speed with which the conversion work was carried out, in days rather than months, is being hailed in Whitehall as a shining example of what can be achieved by British industry when the chips are down . . . . In the vast British Aerospace assembly plant hangar, a long-forgotten wartime spirit was rekindled. They built forty Lancaster bombers a week here during the nation's darkest hours, and now a job which in peacetime might have taken a year or more was completed in just eighteen days . . . . The company hope it'll prove to be an important lesson for the future, and that things in their aircraft factory will never be quite the same again.

ITN, 13.00, 29.6.82

Public Opinion*

The issue of public opinion on the war was rarely analysed in television news coverage. In the seven-week sample period we found the BBC and ITN each carrying news items on only three of the numerous opinion polls. Public opinion was not treated as controversial or particularly newsworthy, on the grounds that it was taken to be largely in support of the military campaign. As Patricia Holland writes about the press:

> The popular papers, indeed, construct 'public opinion' as one of the characters in their drama. It becomes a kind of affirmative Greek chorus, a crowd which occasionally troops onto stage to offer patriotic support to 'the nation' and 'our boys'.[6]

Since it was the backbone of the newsrooms' framework for understanding the war, the belief in massive public support was rarely stated explicitly. More often it was revealed indirectly, for example in

---

*For an account of some of the theoretical issues raised by opinion polling see Appendix 1.

the way interviewees' claims were treated. Contrast two interviews on one bulletin. When Tony Benn says:

> We must stop the killing now. That's the way world opinion has been going, that's the way British opinion has been clearly expressed . . .

the interviewer immediately challenges him: 'What evidence do you have for saying that?' (ITN, 13.00, 5.5.82). (In reply Benn quotes the *Sunday Times* poll, which was not reported on the TV news, in which 60% said the return of the Falklands was not worth a single serviceman's life.) However, when the chairman of the Conservative Defence Committee, Anthony Buck, appears a few minutes later and says:

> I think that the rightness of the British cause and the clear wishes of the Falkland Islanders will cause there to be a vast majority of reasonable and sensible people seeing that our cause is right, and that it as I say does not pay to appease fascist dictators . . .

the same interviewer lets his claim about 'the vast majority' pass unchallenged.

The broadcasters can of course, like Benn, point to public opinion polls in their defence. The various polls show a consistent majority 'satisfied with the government's handling of the crisis', which can be used to justify the assumption that the public is supporting the war. But this needs to be looked at more carefully. One of the problems with opinion polls is that they are used to reduce complicated issues, about which people may have a range of opinions or none at all, to flat 'yes-or-no', 'for-or-against' results. This packaging of people into camps seriously distorts and misrepresents actual opinion. Take the *Sunday Times* poll that Benn quoted: 60% say the Falklands are not worth a single life, and yet in the same poll 70% say they are satisfied with the government's handling of the crisis, with only 23% dissatisfied. The point is that although the polls went on showing support for the government at around 70%, this cannot be straightforwardly read as 70% support for the military option (any more than 23% dissatisfaction can be read as 23% anti-war feeling). Many obviously agreed with the sending of the Task Force, wanted to see Britain take some decisive action against the Argentine 'aggression' but did not want a shooting war. The Task Force was, after all, portrayed as a 'back-up' for the diplomatic effort. Their opinion on British policy would depend on what options seemed open. Another of the problems with opinion polls is the assumption that every individual has a fixed attitude to every question at any one time, without allowing for uncertainty or discussion. Since the country did not divide neatly into pro-war and anti-war factions the pollsters' results depend very much on the questions they choose to ask, and therefore need to be interpreted carefully.

ITN's *Weekend World* commissioned a poll for their programme on 9 May 1982. It is a crucial example since it is the only poll in the rather thin coverage of public opinion that was taken up on all three channels' news. It was presented on all the bulletins as a reaffirmation of high and rising public support for government policy and military escalation. The reports began:

> The latest opinion poll suggests that most people in Britain still back the government's handling of the Falklands crisis.
>
> BBC1, 17.50, 21.00, BBC2, 20.05, 9.5.82

> A new opinion poll shows that more people are now prepared to accept British casualties in the Falklands.
>
> ITN, 18.30, 9.5.82

Later on ITN this interpretation was strengthened:

> Public opinion here seems to be hardening in favour of decisive action to retake the Falklands, even if it means more British casualties.
>
> ITN, 20.45, 9.5.82

After these introductions the newscasters go on to present results from two of the questions in the poll, although, as the illustrations show, they give a confusing variety of questions and percentages.

For instance, BBC1 at 17.40 shows 55% 'for invasion' (interestingly the BBC graphic for public opinion is two soldiers), while ITN has 70% wanting 'to launch an invasion', and by 20.05 the BBC has 70% 'for invasion if "no other alternative"'. If we go back to the original poll, the question on the possibility of an invasion was:

> If the Argentine government refuses to compromise and the British government decides that a long-term blockade of the island is too risky, what should the British government do?
>
> Should they:
> –launch an invasion of the Islands?   70%
> or
> –abandon their claim to the Islands?   18%
> Don't know   11%

The full question – never read out on the news — is a very limiting one.

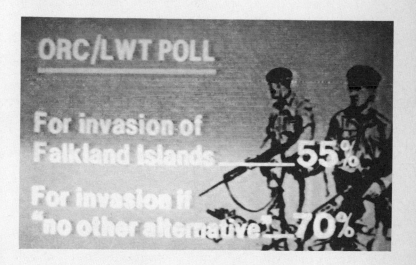

It asks about support for an invasion *after* ruling out the other options, *after* negotiations have failed,[7] and a long-term blockade is ruled out. Any other options, like economic sanctions or UN administration, are excluded: the choice is to invade or abandon Britain's claim. It is a typical case of the way opinion polls on complex subjects often remove all the doubts and reservations that make up people's opinions so that they can reduce the question to a simple statistic. It might be interesting to know that, when 1,000 people are offered this narrow choice, 70% opt for invasion once everything else has been ruled out, while 18% (nearly one in five) are prepared to abandon the British claim altogether if invasion is the only way to pursue it. But since it does not tell us what people think of the *true* situation – in which there was still a possibility of a negotiated settlement, and (according to the Defence Secretary, who was interviewed on the same news bulletins) the British were in a position to maintain a long blockade — it does not justify the TV news interpretation, particularly not ITN's claim that public opinion 'seems to be hardening in favour of decisive action to retake the Falklands', or the bald 'launch an invasion . . . . 70%' on the screen, which implies that 70% want an invasion *now*, without making it clear that the opinion was given in the hypothetical situation that an invasion was the *only* way to defend the Falklands.

The second opinion poll question that the news chose to tell us about was the one on loss of life. The question was:

Do you think that the recovery of the Falkland Islands is worth the loss of more British servicemen's lives if that should prove to be necessary?

Yes	55%
No	38%
Don't know	7%

Once again the wording of the question is by no means neutral; it asks if the loss of British lives is worth it *if* it proves to be 'necessary'. Apart from the documented tendency of people to reply 'yes' to yes-or-no pollsters' questions, the question assumes that loss of life *will* be necessary. Previous polls by the same same organisation, ORC, had asked a different question:

How many British soldiers' and sailors' lives would you be prepared to see lost in order to regain the Falkland Islands?

A majority had always replied 'none'. No doubt ORC had to change their question after some British lives were lost; but it is impossible to tell if the new result represented a real 'hardening' of opinion to accept casualties, or reflected only the change of wording to 'necessary' casualties. Television news did not consider these points. The BBC rewrote the question altogether picking out the 55% figure and presenting it as 55% 'for invasion', which is odd since there was another question specifically about invasion. ITN introduced the whole item with the claim that *'more people are now prepared to accept* British casualties . . . public opinion seems to be hardening', latching onto the change from previous polls when most people opposed any casualties, but without telling us that the question had been changed, and without giving the full question.

This careless interpretation on the news represents the reporting of the public opinion poll to fit a newsroom viewpoint. This is clear if we look at the missing results, the questions that were left out of the reports. A striking case is the question on UN administration and negotiations:

> Do you support or oppose the idea that the United Nations should administer the Falkland Islands for an interim period during which Britain and Argentina negotiate about the future of the Islands?

Support	76%
Oppose	19%
Don't know	8%

The 76% majority in favour of handing the Falklands over to the UN while the British and Argentine governments hold more talks was a significant rise on the 63% majority when the same question was asked in the previous ORC poll (before there were any British casualties), showing widespread and rising agreement with what was in effect the 'Peace Party' argument for UN administration and more negotiations. Like all poll questions, it avoids the complications (with no mention of Argentine withdrawal for instance, or the brief for negotiations), so it cannot be used as evidence for a straightforward 76% support for UN administration on any terms; but it does help clarify the context of the more hawkish results that the news *did* tell us about. It means that neither the 76% paper majority for the UN and talks nor the 70% paper majority for invasion represented blind determination for any one course, that there was no unqualified 'pro-war' landslide and that opinion depended, quite sensibly, on the options presented. But the news told us about only one side.

The poll question on support for government policy is also instructive. The BBC reports on the poll introduce it as more evidence that 'most people in Britain still back the government's handling of the

Falklands crisis'. This was true; but the reports go on to present support for an *invasion* as if the government policy that most people backed was a policy of invasion. This is misleading on two counts: first, official policy at that time at least as far as the public were told was to keep all options open, including the peace talks, economic sanctions, and the military blockade. Secondly, the question that produced the usual result of majority backing for the government was:

How do you feel about the government's policy of trying to regain the Falkland Islands by *diplomatic means* [our italics] backed by the threat of the use of force?

Strongly support it	59%
Quite strongly support it	17%
Neither support nor oppose/don't know	10%
Quite strongly oppose it	5%
Strongly oppose it	6%

The question can be criticised for ruling out any uncertainty about what government policy was (for instance, any doubts about the British government's good faith in diplomatic negotiations); but as it stands it shows once again that there was support for a 'policy of trying to regain the Falkland Islands by diplomatic means', and that public opinion was not demanding the use of force (invasion, for instance) for its own sake – force was presented as a 'threat' to 'back' peaceful negotiations. The high support for this very specific policy as it is put in the poll question is not the same as a public mandate for *any* government or military policy in the Falklands with indiscriminate loyalty.

One more result which did not appear on the news was the sex difference in the answers. Women gave noticeably less support than men to military options and the sacrifice of life. This raises questions from what 'public opinion' really is. Quite apart from the way opinion polls can be selected, manipulated and abused, it is not clear exactly what the most scrupulously reported poll is supposed to measure. Polls add together the views of different individuals, as if all opinions were equal; but that does not necessarily mean that they uncover an underlying 'national will' of 'the people'. For one thing, the people are not an undivided mass (thus men's and women's opinions differ). Also, everyone's individual opinions are not held with the same force or passion, so what does it mean to add them together? One of the major influences on opinion is the mass media themselves – especially since opinion about the war was so dependent on the information the public had about what the war meant and what other options were open. We have here a situation in which television selectively informs people's attitudes, then selectively reports on what those attitudes are, and finally, as we have seen, uses this version of public opinion to justify its own approach to reporting.

FOUR

Diplomacy

Here, we look at two key phases in the diplomatic efforts to end the war. The first is Peruvian peace plan of May 1982 and the second is the United Nations ceasefire plan of June that year. What links them both is that on television their failure was largely attributed to Argentina.

The Peruvian peace plan

The President of Peru, Belaunde Terry, launched his initiative to bring about a peaceful settlement to the Falklands conflict immediately following the collapse of Haig's shuttle diplomacy at the end of April 1982. The details of the conception, negotiation and collapse of the initiative are confused and even contradictory. Even with hindsight it is far from easy to obtain a clear picture of the events surrounding the initiative. However, from a detailed study of the world press of the time, and the material published subsequently, it is possible to reconstruct some of the circumstances surrounding the initiative.

The initiative appears to have gone through two phases. The first phase took in the events of the weekend of 1 May. The President of Peru played a prominent role in these events and announced to the press the imminent success of his mediation on 2 May. He was in contact throughout the weekend with the junta in Buenos Aires and Secretary of State Haig in Washington who had the ear of the British government. On 3 May this phase and the initiative ended with the issuing of a communiqué in Buenos Aires, rejecting the seven-point plan.* The sinking of the *Belgrano* and the similarity with the Haig

*See Appendix 2 for details.

144

proposals were cited as aggravating factors.

The second phase of the Peruvian initiative involved the events of 4 to 6 May. The prime mover at this time is the US Secretary of State, Haig. The British government appeared more serious about these efforts than those of the previous weekend. Ministers, while never being overly optimistic about the chances, did state that some hope existed. On 6 May the Foreign Office announced the collapse of the initiative. It blamed Argentina's intransigence.

How, then, were the negotiations on Peru's plan reported by British TV news? We show in this section that TV news presented Argentina as the intransigent partner in the negotiations while Britain was portrayed as willing to achieve a diplomatic settlement. We also show how the collapse of the initiative was reported very largely in terms of Argentina's intransigent negotiating stance. These are certainly not the views taken by everyone at the time. Rather they represent a particular interpretation of the negotiations. A variety of views existed on the parties' attitudes and the reasons for the failure of the initiative. TV news organised its reporting around a certain view of the negotiations and this view broadly coincided with the official view of the British government. Doubts about the official view are occasionally expressed – mainly in the BBC2 programme *Newsnight*.* But the mass of TV news chose simply to relay the official view, without serious questioning, and at the expense of other opinions. This reinforced the belief that Argentina was not willing to negotiate seriously, and presented what appeared to be a considerable diplomatic effort by Britain.

How the parties were presented

In the early evening of 6 May the Foreign Office issued a statement announcing the failure of the Peruvian peace initiative. In this statement the Foreign Secretary said:

> I am deeply disappointed that Argentine intransigence has once again frustrated a constructive initiative. Had they genuinely wanted peace they could have accepted the latest proposals put to them and could have had a ceasefire in place by 5.00 p.m. tomorrow.

---

*TV news coverage does in certain respects differ from that of *Newsnight*. For example, *Newsnight*, despite reference to Argentine intransigence and its rejection on 6 May, entertains the possibility that not all the fault lay on Argentina's side: 'Now taken at face value those ideas might have yielded results but all day both sides have in fact been laying down preconditions' (*Newsnight*, BBC2, 6.5.82).

The following morning the Foreign Secretary made a fuller statement to the House of Commons. He again blamed Argentina for the collapse of the initiative: 'Argentine intransigence has again led it to reject proposals for a diplomatic solution.' He proceeded to compare the efforts of Britain and Argentina to achieve a peaceful solution: 'We have worked, and will continue to work, positively and constructively for a peaceful solution. I wish I could say that the Argentine junta had been working in a similar spirit; clearly it was not.' Mr Pym referred to Argentina's 'diplomatic obstructionism' and outlined what he saw as the stumbling block: 'They appear to be asking for a ceasefire without any clear link with a withdrawal of their invasion force.' He pointed out that 'the Argentines so far have insisted that a transfer of sovereignty to them should be a precondition of negotiations on a final settlement'. However, Mr Pym stated that 'although one phase of the diplomatic effort has been brought to an end by Argentine intransigence, another phase is already under way in New York'. Britain had responded in a 'positive and substantial' manner to the UN Secretary General's initiative. Doubt was cast on a report that Argentina had accepted the initiative: 'Indeed it is difficult to believe that Argentina, having rejected ideas devised by Mr Haig and the President of Peru, can now accept the Secretary General's ideas, which have a similar basis.' Mr Pym concluded his statement with an appeal to the junta: 'I hope the Argentines will henceforth show that readiness and desire to achieve a peaceful settlement which so far has been evident only on our side.'

The message of Mr Pym's remarks are clear. Argentina was intransigent and unwilling to compromise to attain a peaceful settlement. The junta was not (unlike Britain) intent on negotiating seriously.

The Foreign Secretary's view was not shared by others. In reporting the collapse of the latest round of negotiations, the *Guardian* carried a report, from its correspondent in Washington and at the UN, entitled 'Inflexible attitudes thwart diplomacy'. The article began:

> Another effort to find a peaceful solution to the Falklands seemed to have come full circle last night. Despite protestations from Britain and Argentina of their readiness to seek ways to end the fighting, neither seemed ready to shift position sufficiently to allow progress.

The *New York Times* stated:

> the apparent consensus of informed diplomats and American officials here [the UN] today was that there has been no significant movement

toward resolving the Falkland Islands crisis. Rather, there is an assumption that both Argentina and Britain, by their public statements and actions, are trying to position themselves to lessen international and domestic criticism if major fighting resumes by the end of this weekend, as many officials believe it will.

This echoed news expressed elsewhere in the US media. Joe Kraft in the *Washington Post* reiterated this theme in an article examining the problems confronting each side in negotiating a peaceful solution. He referred to the 'spur of necessity' under which the British government had put itself: 'Conditions in the South Atlantic dictate that military action be taken swiftly, not long postponed.' He also spoke of the inability of Argentina's decision-making apparatus to handle negotiations. Kraft saw *both* sides as having locked themselves into a military confrontation which they were unable to avoid. An ABC TV diplomatic correspondent expressed this opinion most succinctly in a an assessment of the chances for a peaceful settlement on the 5 May edition of *Nightline*:

> The fact of the matter is that both Britain and Argentina recognise that they are under very strong pressures in terms of world opinion to give the impression that they are willing to recognise the other side's point of view and willing to come to terms. But the fact of the matter is that the positions they are taking diplomatically haven't changed from before the time that all the trouble started.
>
> *Nightline*, ABC, 5.5.82

Doubts *were* cast on Britain's position in the negotiation by elements of the British press. For example, Geoffrey Parkhouse in the *Glasgow Herald* referred to the government's insistence that Argentina respond first to any diplomatic proposals and stated, 'the result was that the junta was diplomatically wrong-footed as part of a sustained campaign by the new British diplomacy to cast Argentina in world opinion as the intransigent party in the dispute'.

Britain's role in the negotiations was subject to a great deal more scrutiny following the end of the conflict. Hugo Young reported a conversation he had with a member of the cabinet. According to the Minister:

> The purpose of the war cabinet's apparently intense search for peace had been, as he saw it, to make the British understand why they had to go to war; in other words to maximise the chances that they would face and tolerate the casualties that were sure to come. From this it was hard to avoid the conclusion that the peace efforts were in part a charade.
>
> *Sunday Times*, 4.7.82

Alexander Haig was, however, to maintain his view that the Argentines were 'intransigent' and 'unwilling to negotiate'. It has been argued that Haig had an interest in portraying Argentina in the most unfavourable light. Gavashon and Rice in their book, *The Sinking of the Belgrano*, described Haig's briefing on his diplomatic efforts to the US Senate: 'Instead of their contributing positive proposals, they [the Argentines] were shown as rejecting Haig's. Instead of negotiating they were shown as intransigent.' In the authors view Haig had to be careful about too close an identification with Britain. They describe US policy in this respect thus:

> Their reputation for throwing their own weight around had been inhibiting their foreign policy ever since the wars in Indo-China. Before they could back the British preparations for a massive counterstrike, they needed some moral ground for action. Argentina's 'intransigence' provided it.

Haig also had to convince the 'Latino lobby' in the Reagan administration of the correctness of siding with Britain. Thus it can be argued that Haig concurred with a British policy of portraying Argentina as unwilling to negotiate.

There is, then, evidence to suggest that at this time *both* sides were unwilling to compromise and negotiate seriously. Despite the variety of possible interpetations, TV news focussed primarily on Argentina as the intransigent party. In the days surrounding the collapse of the Peruvian intitiative, the Argentine position was described thus:

> It's easy to see why the Argentines would prefer to use the UN. A debate in the Security Council would give the Russians, who desperately need Argentine meat and wheat, the power of veto, and the UN is a lumbering machine. Nothing happens there very quickly, and time is not on Britain's side. The Argentines, on the other hand, can afford to *string this crisis out,* as Michael Buerk tells us from Buenos Aires.
>
> BBC1, 21.00, 6.5.82

> There's been *no real shift* in the Argentine position over the Falklands. The UN peace proposals are so vague that Argentina can accept them without compromising on any of the basic issues. That acceptance does not mean the government here is prepared to withdraw any of its troops, or accept a UN peace-keeping force, without explicit assurances on its ultimate sovereignty over the Islands. And sovereignty is not even mentioned in the peace plan. The general terms of the UN proposals have been accepted here because it is felt that time is on Argentina's side.
>
> BBC1, 21.00, 6.5.82

It's all very vague and therefore probably acceptable to Buenos Aires, who can afford to *sit it out* for a while.

BBC1, 17.40, 6.5.82

Argentina's decision to work through the UN and not with the Haig/Peruvian peace initiative strongly suggests that the military junta at home *is playing for time*.

ITN, 17.45, 7.5.82

Some reports from Buenos Aires say the junta have accepted the UN framework. Whitehall doubts this, pointing out that *junta members speak with different voices*, and as far as Whitehall is concerned, *with forked tongues*. They are, the feeling is, *playing for time*, and time is on their side. Britain's weapon for enforcing a diplomatic solution is of course the Task Force, but what about the approach and the morale of the men who control the Force?

BBC1, 21.00, 7.5.82

But for now another diplomatic heave, this time through the UN. Something Mr Pym is not approaching with any under optimism. The Secretary General's ideas, although acceptable to Great Britain, are still very sketchy. 'And,' said Mr Pym, 'the Argentine attitude is *obstructive.*'

ITN, 22.00, 7.5.82

Argentina's intransigent stance is contrasted with Britain's 'flexibility' and desire to achieve a peaceful solution:

A peace plan put forward by the South American country of Peru has been turned down by Argentina. Britain's Foreign Secretary, Mr Pym said that if it had been accepted by them, fighting could have stopped this afternoon. He said he wished the Argentines would work as hard as Britain for a peaceful solution.

Newsround, BBC1, 7.5.82

Mr Pym said that it had failed despite *British flexibility*, because of *Argentina's intransigence* about withdrawing from the Falklands after a ceasefire came into effect.

ITN, 13.00, 7.5.82

In London the Foreign Secretary Mr Pym told the Commons today that the main diplomatic effort is now centred on the UN. He said the government *was working urgently* and constructively with the UN Secretary General, Señor Perez de Cuellar.

ITN, 22.00, 7.5.82

Today Mr Pym carried the House of Commons with him, with his *undertaking to work tirelessly and constructively for a peaceful solution.* The changing events in the South Atlantic mean that MPs are in a volatile mood.

BBC1, 21.05, 5.5.82

He pledged that Britain would work *positively and constructively* for a peaceful solution.

BBC1, 21.00, 7.5.82

The position adopted by TV news in its presentation of the parties is nowhere more clearly indicated than in an interview with the Shadow Foreign Secretary on 7 May. This interview takes place following Mr Pym's statement to the House on the collapse of the plan. The journalist asked these questions:

> Mr Healey, do you think there's any hope of a peaceful settlement through the UN, given the Argentines' intransigence?.
> But do you think that the Argentines might just be deliberately dragging things out? . . .
> How long will the government's patience, in trying to secure a diplomatic settlement, last?

BBC1, 12.20, 7.5.82

There is a peculiar example, which indicates the care broadcasters were taking in their reporting of Argentina's position: on 5 May BBC TV news carried a report from its diplomatic correspondent which appeared on both its early and its main evening news bulletins. The report concentrated on the state of the negotiations and the possibility of a ceasefire. A significant phrase is omitted in the second report:

> Although the Foreign Office will not confirm it, it appears that American Secretary of State Haig suggested to Britain an unconditional forty-eight hour ceasefire before, as the State Department put it, 'things really get out of hand.' *Well, that would have been acceptable to the Argentines* but Britain's line is no ceasefire without withdrawal of Argentine troops from the Islands and unprejudiced negotiations about their future. On those crucial points, London and Buenos Aires are as far apart as ever.

BBC1, 17.40, 5.5.82

But in the next news the phrase on Argentina is omitted:

> Although the Foreign Office won't confirm it, it appears that American Secretary of State Haig suggested to Britain an unconditional forty-eight hour ceasefire before, as the State Department put it, 'things really get out of hand'. But Britain's line is no ceasefire without withdrawal of Argentine troops from the Islands and unprejudiced negotiations about their future. And on those crucial points London and Buenos Aires are as far apart as ever.

BBC1, 21.00, 5.5.82

Doubts are sometimes expressed about Britain's negotiating position. Some of these are from Argentine sources. For example, an

Argentine representative to the UN referred to 'gunboat diplomacy' (ITN, 22.00, 3.5.82). Such references can be easily dismissed given the nature of the source. Likewise the questions from an Irish jounralist to Mr Pym during a press conference on 7 May:

> And at a news conference Mr Pym was clearly angered by a question from an Irish journalist, whose government wants European sanctions against Argentina to be lifted. The journalist was asking Mr Pym if he was demanding too many concessions from President Galtieri.
>
> BBC, 21.00, 7.5.82

The reporting concentrated on the Foreign Secretary's anger and his very strong response. Viewers had also been informed earlier that 'Whitehall sources were quick to point out that Ireland had an interest in portraying Britain as a colonialist aggressor' (BBC1, 21.00, 4.5.82).

More significant doubts are occasionally expressed. For example, on 3 May a BBC reporter at the UN referred to the 'uncompromising British view that Argentina must make the first move if there is to be peace' (BBC1, 21.35, 3.5.82); or the ITN parliamentary correspondent who states that 'the British government have always said their aim was a peaceful solution but it has seemed to many so far that they have sought peace on terms that could never be acceptable to the Argentines' (ITN, 22.00, 5.5.82). This reference is made more 'safe' by the correspondent proceeding to note that 'now . . . the words have changed slightly but perhaps significantly'. The following exchange occurs between Mr Pym and a BBC reporter at the 7 May news conference:

> *Reporter:* We stand by our basic demands, withdrawal and open negotiations with no preconditions?
> *Pym:* That must be so.
> *Reporter:* You're not going to give us the details of the UN framework but can we assume that it meets all our basic requirements or you wouldn't have given it a positive response?
> *Pym:* I think so, I mean I think we have made the position clear and I don't think I can really add more to it, to what we've been saying in all the debates and so on, that what I have said already.
> *Reporter:* But that framework is acceptable to us on questions like sovereignty, the wishes of the Islanders, the withdrawal, the cease-fire, it meets all our basic requirements?
> *Pym:* Yes, that's right.
> *Reporter:* So it can't be acceptable to the Argentines?
>
> BBC1, 17.40, 7.5.82

These exchanges in the news raise some doubts about the nature of the negotiations. Yet nothing is spelled out. They remain as isolated counter-examples in a framework which largely features the view that Argentina is unwilling to negotiate while Britain is anxious to do so.

On the Peruvian peace plan just one reference draws clear attention to the fact that Argentina was actively entering into negotiations. In the second week of May the Peruvian government put out their version of events. This account was published in both *The Times* (10 May) and the *Guardian* (13 May). The process of negotiation around the plan is outlined. The initial proposals submitted by the Peruvians were:

1. Immediate cessation of hostilities.
2. Mutual withdrawal of armed forces.
3. The installation of representatives from countries other than the parties involved in the conflict to govern the islands temporarily.
4. The British and Argentine governments would recognise the existence of differing and conflicting claims over the Falkland Islands.
5. The two governments would recognise that the viewpoint and interests of the islanders must be taken into account in seeking a peaceful solution to the problem.
6. The contact group which would immediately intervene in the negotiations to put this agreement into effect would consist of Brazil, Peru, West Germany, and the United States.
7. Before 30 April next year a definite agreement would have been reached under the responsibility of the above four countries.

Guardian, 13.5.82

According to the Peruvians the Argentina junta put forward three amendments to proposals 4, 5 and 6 respectively:

4. The two governments recognise the existence of differing and conflicting claims over the Falkland Islands, and will take account of the resolutions on the islands approved by various international bodies.
5. The two governments recognise that the aspirations and interests of the local inhabitants must be taken into account in the definitive solution to the problem.
6. The contact group which would intervene immediately in the negotiations to implement this agreement would be composed of various countries to be designated by common agreement

On the day of the publication of this version of events in the *Guardian*, former Prime Minister Edward Heath was interviewed in ITN *Falklands Extra*. In the middle of the interview Heath said:

Now here the government has something to explain. As I said in the House of Commons tonight, what we were told was that the Argentine government had rejected the Peruvian peace proposals. It is now appearing quite plainly in a statement from the Peruvian government that what the Argentines did was to suggest three amendments to the Peruvian proposals. Now this is negotiation. Personally looking at these three amendments I find it very difficult to see how we can have rejected them. There was only one possible point which may have irritated people and that is that they asked that major resolutions passed by international organisations should be recalled. That's perfectly natural. The government now has to explain why it said Argentina rejected the Peruvian proposals when we're told by the Peruvians that Argentina put forward three amendments.

ITN, 22.00, 13.5.82

The subject was not pursued by the interviewer and Heath's criticism of the government's handling of the negotiations was not taken up. Heath's statement that Argentina was negotiating stands in sharp contrast to the view adopted by TV news that Argentina' intransigence resulted in the failure of the Peruvian peace plan.

There were, then, doubts concerning both sides' position on the plan. In the current affairs programme *TV Eye*, doubts on Britain's position are raised by Dennis Healey:

> I think we really should make our own position a little more clear and not wait for them and I think we would gain a good deal if we were known to accept the proposal – particularly if they turned it down. So far of course we've had really no clear indication of what the British government's view is on any of these proposals.

ITV, *TV Eye*, 21.00, 6.5.82

These doubts did not emerge in the TV news coverage which reported that Argentina had rejected the Peruvian plan that Britain had accepted. The fault lay with the junta. This line entered the conventional wisdom and was clearly enunciated in Robert Kee's introduction to the controversial *Panorama* of 10 May:

> So far attempts at a diplomatic solution, which our Task Force was sent to the South Atlantic to support, have failed, *through no fault of our own*. Both Mr Haig's plan and the Peruvian plan, which we accepted, have been turned down by Argentina. It looks as if Mrs Thatcher's options have become increasingly restricted to military options.

Panorama, BBC1, 10.5.82

The reasons for failure

The Foreign Office's account of the failure of the plan dominated the TV news coverage:

> A statement issued just a few minutes ago by the Foreign Secretary, Mr

Pym, said that he was deeply disappointed that Argentine intransigence had again frustrated a constructive initiative.

BBC2, 19.10, 6.5.82

Argentina has rejected a peace plan which could have produced a ceasefire in the South Atlantic at five o'clock tomorrow afternoon.

BBC1, 21.00, 6.5.82

Mr Pym said Argentina has rejected peace. The Foreign Secretary, Mr Pym, said tonight that there could have been a ceasefire by five o'clock tomorrow evening on Peru's plan but Argentine intransigence, he said, had stopped it.

ITN, 22.00, 6.5.82

The Foreign Secretary, Mr Pym, said that once again the Argentines had frustrated a constructive initiative.

ITN, 22.00, 6.5.82

In the Commons he repeated that the ceasefire could have been enforced by five o'clock tomorrow afternoon if Argentina had accepted the Peru initiative.

BBC1, 12.30, 7.5.82

My Pym went out of his way to stress to MPs and world opinion that Britain had worked tirelessly for a settlement and, but for Argentines intransigence, we could have had an interim agreement.

BBC1, 12.30, 7.5.82

A peace plan put forward by the South American country of Peru has been turned down by Argentina.

BBC1, 17.05, 7.5.82

In the House of Commons he again blamed Argentine intransigence for the collapse of the joint Peruvian and American peace plan.

BBC2, 19.10, 7.5.82

This is not to say TV news was unaware of other possible factors in the failure. The Peruvians claimed that the sinking of the *Belgrano* was a contributory factor. The Peruvians expressed the opinion that every time their mediation effort showed signs of success, Britain would escalate military action.* In this account it is the British government that stymied the talks. On TV news there is one reference to this link:

A government spokesman has again insisted that Argentine sovereignty over the Falklands is outside any discussion. He said the junta almost accepted the failed Peruvian proposals which didn't mention

---

* *Guardian*, 13.5.82.

sovereignty but the talks were broken off when the Task Force sank the cruiser the *General Belgrano*.

ITN, 22.00, 10.5.82

During the whole coverage of the Peruvian initiative this link is never taken up or elaborated on. It remained an isolated reference despite the fact that senior political figures publically expressed anxiety and doubt.

The Peruvian account also raises other doubts. On the news we are told that Argentina had 'rejected' or 'turned down' peace; it had 'frustrated' a constructive initiative'. However, the Peruvians stated that they did not formally put any proposals to the junta after 3 May. This confirmed in some of the newspaper reports of the time.* The ITN diplomatic correspondent gives fleeting support to the view when he stated that 'the whole exercise was called off by the Peruvians' (ITN, 22.00, 6.5.82).

The bulk of TV news coverage of Peruvian mediation efforts came after 5 May, at the time when the British government was seeking to highlight its concern with the initiative. British TV news, however, made no reference to the events of the previous weekend – when serious negotiations had apparently ended.

On the evening of 2 May the Associated Press Agency man in Lima had attended a press conference given by the Peruvian President, Belaunde Terry. Following the conference he sent this telex to his New York headquarters:

> President Fernando Belaunde Terry said today that Great Britain and Argentina would tonight announce the end of all hostilities in their dispute over the Falklands.
>
> The basic document was drawn up by the US Secretary of State, Alexander Haig, and transmitted to the Argentine government by the Peruvian President.
>
> He said that long and continuous contact between the two sides began yesterday, continued last night and early this morning and will be published tonight.
>
> Belaunde said that he was unable to make known the terms of the agreement in advance except for the first about which there is no discussion: immediate ceasefire.

President Belaunde's statement, along with the Argentine communiqué the following day, was reported in the British quality papers. TV news did not devote any coverage to these events. It did indicate

---

* However, the *N Y Times* records Haig as saying that they did.

that it was aware – albeit obliquely — of some Peruvian involvement in the peace process. On 2 May an ITN correspondent at the UN reported the latest UN attempt to put together a mediation initiative:

> The plan is a modification of a Peruvian idea but it is known that the Secretary General himself believes it is worth pursuing.
>
> ITN, 18.00, 2.5.82

The reporter concluded his assessment of the initiative's chances of success by saying, 'the fact that the plan is a Peruvian idea might commend it to Argentina' (ITN, 18.00, 2.5.82). Apart from acknowledging the possibility of Peruvian involvement in diplomatic negotiations no other reference was made to the Peruvian initiative. What then was TV news interested in that weekend? It was preoccupied with the military events in the South Atlantic. On 1 May, British forces started their bombardment of Port Stanley airfield. News bulletins were specially extended to cover the flurry of activity. Yet in spite of this the four longest news bulletins that weekend devoted just 14 minutes out of nearly 70 minutes of Falklands news to diplomatic events. The diplomacy stories covered included the visit of the Foreign Secretary to Washington, the nature of support for Britain, the implications of the Port Stanley bombing for a diplomatic settlement and an assessment of the pressures on Argentina. The tone of the reporting of these stories was upbeat:

> There are several battles being waged at the moment far away from the Falklands and Britain appears to be winning them all.
>
> BBC1, 12.50, 1.5.82

> Even Concorde could not prevent Mr Pym falling behind in the latest developments, so fast were things happening in the South Atlantic but already he was able to say Britain was on top.
>
> ITN, 18.00, 2.5.82

Mr Pym's visit to Washington and the United Nations was seen as the major diplomatic story that weekend. The tone for the reporting of the visit was set down before the Foreign Secretary's departure for New York:

> And Mr Pym the Foreign Secretary goes to the United States tonight in the knowledge that there is overwhelming support for Britain's case there and that unlike his visit a week ago when the Reagan administration distanced itself from him to avoid being accused of taking sides, this time he goes as the representative of a nation fighting to uphold democratic freedom. That's how the Americans see it now.

And instead of trying to find ways of bringing the two sides together through compromise Mr Haig will this time be discussing practical help for Britain in her campaign to shift the Argentines from the islands.

> BBC1, 12.50, 1.5.82

The Foreign Secretary, Mr Pym, is due in New York about now. He'll be talking to top US officials about America's offer of material support for British forces.

> ITN, 21.55, 1.5.82

On his arrival in the United States the change in Mr Pym's status is reiterated:

As one member of Mr Pym's delegation neatly put it: when Mr Pym was here a week ago, he was here to negotiate with a mediator; now he's here to consult with an ally.

> ITN, 18.00, 2.5.82

However, both the BBC and ITN used the opportunity of Mr Pym's visit to the United States to reassess Britain' strategy to regain the islands in light of the military activity in the South Atlantic. The Foreign Secretary restated Britain's position on his arrival in New York:

Britain's strategy all through has been to apply inexorable pressure upon Argentina . . . Our Task Force is there to back up our diplomatic efforts.

> ITN, 18.00, 2.5.82

It is interesting that the BBC and ITN emphasised different points in the reassessment. The BBC diplomatic correspondent sees the military action as compatible with Britain's declared policy:

This is phase three of the government's strategy. First came the political pressure in the form of the United Nations resolution calling on Argentina to get out of the Falklands. Then the economic pressure starting with the EEC sanctions and building up to the United States announcement yesterday. And now the military options comes into play.

> BBC2, 19.25, 1.5.82

The correspondent also stated:

If as looks likely the casualties during the Port Stanley airport operation are negligible, hopefully non-existent, Britain's use of force is not likely to damage our cause.

> BBC1, 12.50, 1.5.82

Another BBC reporter makes this assessment:

> It is being stressed that although force is being used this is no change in
> British policy. Armed diplomacy has been on the cards from the outset.
>
> BBC1, 13.50, 2.5.82

Neither correspondent examines in any detail the impact of military
action on the diplomatic efforts. One BBC correspondent who did
explore the relationship between military and diplomatic efforts came
to a particular conclusion:

> But most of all the British are exuding an air of determination,
> diplomatically as well as military – the line is, we are in the process of
> reclaiming the islands; we shall do it peacefully if possible and by force if
> necessary. *Force is obviously necessary.*
>
> BBC1, 13.50, 2.5.82

> . . . and the British, both publicly and privately, are showing a great air
> of determination here that they will negotiate if they can, that they'll
> fight if they must and for the present it seems that they must.
>
> BBC1, 17.50, 2.5.82

Thus BBC reports of diplomatic activities include references to the
necessity of the use of military force.

ITN expressed more concern about the impact of the escalation of
military action on the diplomatic effort to find a negotiated settlement.
ITN's diplomatic correspondent began his assessment thus:

> There is now a very real danger of military pressure against Argentina
> running too far ahead of the diplomatic efforts.
>
> ITN, 18.00, 2.5.82

The correspondent stated that the 'diplomatic front badly needs
reviving' but concentrated solely on the UN and its merits as an
institution to bring about a settlement. There was no reference to Peru
acting as a mediator. On this occasion ITN still questioned the nature
of the link between the diplomatic process and military operation more
than the BBC.

TV news presumably focussed on military events that weekend
because war is more newsworthy than diplomacy. It could also be seen
as a result of the lack of official government information on the latest
mediation effort. The British government, at least publicly, was not
interested in the intervention of the President of Peru. This changed
on 4 May and it is around this time that British TV news took up its
coverage of the plan. On 5 May BBC TV made a reference to a
Peruvian plan:

> Under consideration here [at Whitehall] are several ideas. A Peruvian
> plan is being backed by the Americans but does not at the moment
> appear to be making headway.
>
> BBC1, 12.30, 5.5.82

That afternoon the Foreign Secretary made a statement to the House
of Commons:

> In the House of Commons, Mr Pym said among plans for peace is an
> important one from the South American country of Peru, a close friend
> of Argentina.
>
> BBC1, 17.05, 5.5.82

The early evening news bulletins took up a Foreign Office
announcement that 'there has been intense diplomatic activity today to
try to find a solution to the crisis' (BBC1, 17.40, 5.5.82).

Examining 'the chances for peace' BBC's diplomatic correspondent
stated that what hope there is 'rests on a Peruvian plan backed by the
US' (BBC1, 17.40, 5.5.82). ITN confirmed that 'the plan now being
considered was a mixture of the revised US peace plan and the
proposals put forward by Peru' (ITN, 17.45, 5.5.82).

In its assessment of the chances of the prospects of this mediation
TV news is relatively pessimistic. For example, the BBC's political
correspondent reported that in spite of the new diplomatic moves
'MPs don't have a great hope' of a negotiated settlement. The
diplomatic correspondent was more blunt: 'There are no signs that
diplomacy is going to solve this crisis.' However, TV news did report
on a change in Britain's attitude to the negotiations. The BBC reported
that MPs detected 'signs of flexibility in Mr Pym's approach over
negotiating a ceasefire and an Argentine withdrawal' (BBC1, 21.05,
5.5.82). ITN noted that despite government sources claiming there is
no change, Britain does 'seem to be pursuing the new initiative from
Mr Haig and the President of Peru with more urgency than they have
shown in the past' (ITN, 22.05, 5.5.82). The reporter surmised that
'apparently the ceasefire could come with a commitment to withdraw
rather than immediate withdrawal'. The BBC's man in Washington
also raised hopes: 'The British were giving their answer, and they
thought it a constructive one, to the Peruvian plan'. (BBC1, 17.40,
5.5.82).

Both ITN and the BBC noted a change in Britain's negotiating
position and implied this flexibility could assist the negotiations. This
theme is continued on 6 May up until the collapse of the plan was
finally announced:

The difference is the fact that there has been a shift in the British position which, it is felt, Argentina might just find more accommodating.

ITN, 13.00, 6.5.82

There is absolutely nothing to suggest that Argentina will respond to the package that Britain has now accepted but President Galtieri's junta, divided though it is, must collectively realise that this must be their last chance of avoiding a devastating conflict.

ITN, 13.00, 6.5.82

He's [Mr Haig] in touch with the government of Peru which might be able to persuade Argentina to agree to the plan.

Newsround, BBC1, 17.05, 6.5.82

TV news, although not too optimistic, saw the Peruvian initiative as the best hope for a settlement:

My Pym believes that the Peruvian initiative with very strong American support represents the most likely way of getting negotiations going.

ITN, 22.05, 5.5.82

What diplomatic hope there is seems to rest on the Peruvian plan being backed by the United States.

BBC1, 21.05, 5.5.82

It is not so much that TV news is cautious about the prospects for the initiative but the fact that it emphasised the initiative at all that is interesting.

If we compare this coverage to that of ABC news in the United States a different emphasis is apparent. On ABC TV the chief diplomatic correspondent made this assessment:

If the British and Secretary Haig are still pursuing the Peruvian initiative, which is really an American initiative, they'd better forget [it] because the Argentinians rejected it on Sunday.

Nightline, ABC, 5.5.82

The correspondent then outlined the stumbling block:

The initiative at first interested them because it talked about the aspirations and future of the Islanders ... Then on Sunday, through the US Ambassador in Lima, Secretary Haig changed it to read 'the wishes of the Falklanders' which is absolute red flag to the Argentinians.

Nightline, ABC, 5.5.82

The clear impression given was that the latest initiative involving Peru and Haig was a no-goer. The negotiations had broken down over wording, and military escalation had intervened. In examining Argentina's position, ABC news is more interested in another peace plan put forward by the UN Secretary General. In an interview with an Argentine diplomat the newscaster says:

> . . . we are really talking about two totally different plans – one which seems to be acceptable to your government and one which seems to be acceptable to Whitehall – and those two plans seem, at least on the surface, to be inconsistent with one another.
>
> *Nightline*, ABC, 5.5.82

British TV news did take up the two peace plans but chose, unlike ABC, to emphasise the Peruvian initiative:

> It's [the UN plan] all very vague and therefore probably acceptable to Buenos Aires *who can afford to sit it out*. The government seems to be giving a nod to these ideas . . . but its real support goes to the Peruvian plan.
>
> BBC1, 17.40, 6.5.82

The state of the Peruvian initiative was confused during this period from 3 to 6 May. Who was making the running? Haig or the Peruvians? To what extent was the junta involved? What, if any, was the relationship between the UN and Peruvian plan? Did Britain accept the plan? This confusion is indicated in TV news coverage by the variety of terms used to describe the initiative:

> Britain seems to prefer Washington's plan.
>
> BBC1, 17.05, 6.5.82

> A Peruvian plan is being backed by the Americans.
>
> BBC1, 12.30, 5.5.82

> The plan now being considered was a mixture of the revised peace plan and proposals put forward by Peru.
>
> ITN, 17.45, 5.5.82

> . . . the plan being put forward by the Peruvian government jointly with the Secretary of State, Mr Haig.
>
> BBC1, 12.30, 6.5.82

> . . . are the vital ingredients of the new peace ideas of the American Secretary of State, Mr Alexander Haig.
>
> ITN, 22.05, 5.5.82

> . . . the main efforts go into what is really the Haig plan Mk II.
>
> ITN, 22.05, 5.5.82

Despite this confusion in the coverage, and the doubt surrounding the plan and status of the parties, TV news was in no doubt as to who was to blame for the collapse of Peru's mediation. When in doubt, its main answer was to rely on government sources and blame Argentina. This is not to say that the Argentines were blameless or that they did not indeed wish for prolonged negotiations. But if the Argentines preferred to 'string things out', then the British could be seen as seeking a swift settlement and perhaps for this reason as instigating a major military escalation. This of course differs from the British government's preferred view of itself as 'urgently and constructively pursuing peace'. In the confusion of the time and given the normal reliance of television news on official sources, it is perhaps not surprising that the government view predominated. But it is important to note the ease with which the government publicised its own apparently intense search for peace in the few days after the sinking of the *Belgrano* and *Sheffield* at a time when according to some commentators these very actions had made impossible.*

The UN ceasefire plan

> Let me say at once that we all hope that the Argentines will obey Resolution 502, that they will undertake to cease fire, and to withdraw, immediately, or within a very few hours, so that no further lives can be lost.

These are the words of Francis Pym, speaking at a news conference shown on ITN's *News at Ten* on 4 June 1982. It is a familiar statement of the government view. Britain sees herself as forced by Argentine refusals into a position where lives must be lost, specifically by Argentina's refusal to obey Resolution 502. The British presented Resolution 502 to the United Nations Security Council immediately after the Argentine invasion. It demanded a ceasefire, immediate withdrawal of Argentine forces, and a diplomatic solution. Ten of the

---

*As when Dennis Healey stated in the House of Commons on 4.5.82 (and later on *Newsnight*) that military action such as the *Belgrano* sinking could destroy the possibility of negotiations. The Commons statement was featured briefly on ITN (22.00, 4.5.82) but was not developed by journalists as a possible way of understanding the subsequent military or diplomatic activity at this time. We noted one reference by a journalist taking up the issue of Britain 'escalating military action' in a question to Mr Pym, who is asked whether this will force the Argentines to the negotiating table (ITN, 22.00, 3.5.82).

fifteen nations in the Security Council voted in favour, and '502' became established as the central plank in Britain's diplomatic campaign, and was invoked frequently in defence of Britain's position.

On 1 June 1982, with British forces advancing towards the Argentine garrison at Port Stanley, two Argentine negotiators left for New York in another attempt to settle the dispute through the UN Security Council. Through the Spanish and Panamanian delegates (Argentina is not a Security Council member), General Miret and Admiral Moya put forward a fresh ceasefire proposal. For three days Security Council members debated and amended the proposal to try to find a formula that would be acceptable to the British. Miret told the *Washington Post*:

> We have softened our position to the maximum . . . we have given up or are giving up everything that is prudent in order to achieve an honourable peace.
>
> *Washington Post*, 3.6.82

The *Washington Post* also quotes another Buenos Aires sources saying that the junta, in particular Lami Dozo, the air force commander, were prepared to make almost any concessions to obtain a ceasefire and save face. The following day the UN correspondent comments:

> One Western diplomat who backs the British position interpreted the Argentine concession to mean that Buenos Aires is *desperate to achieve a ceasefire, even on British terms*, before the British launch their drive on Stanley, the Islands' capital.
>
> *Washington Post*, 4.6.82

The Argentine concession was to introduce Britain's Resolution 502 into the ceasefire call. The final version was presented to the Security Council for voting on 4 June:

> 1. Requests the parties to the dispute to cease fire immediately in the region of the Falkland Islands (Islas Malvinas), and to initiate, simultaneously with the ceasefire, the implementation of Resolutions 502 (1982) and 505 (1982)* in their entirety.
>
> Text, UN ceasefire resolution point 1

(Points 2 and 3 of the ceasefire call provide for verification and report-back.) There is still room for dispute about how exactly to interpret the ceasefire call and what to expect from the Argentines, but the *Washington Post* tells us that a deputy in the Argentine UN mission

---

*Resolution 505 was passed on 26 May and urges a ceasefire and a settlement through the UN.

accepted the interpretation that the Spanish–Panamanian resolution would require Argentina to commence unilateral withdrawal of its troops simultaneous with the ceasefire.

Washington Post, 4.6.82

The Times in London judged:

> The text was being tailored almost exclusively to try to meet Britain's specifications . . . . It was assumed that Argentina was prepared to accept a resolution tying a truce with the removal of its troops from the Islands.
>
> *The Times*, 5.6.82

By the afternoon of 4 June when the vote on the ceasefire resolution was approaching, it looked to some as if there was a chance of stopping the fighting and getting the Argentines to withdraw from the Falklands. But what were TV news viewers told about it? The answer is that in spite of the huge volume of coverage of the Falklands conflict this ceasefire proposal received very little attention. At first it is presented as a story about how Britain may have to veto the resolution. At the close of the late-night news on BBC2 on 2 June there is an unusual mention of Argentine concessions – but the possibility is raised only to be quashed:

> . . . and just a bit of news in from our colleague Ian Smith at the United Nations in New York. He heard from Hugh O'Shaunassy of the *Financial Times* that perhaps there was some willingness on the Argentine part of the UN to make new concessions at this eleventh hour. However, Ian tells us that the British delegate to the UN Sir Anthony Parsons has told the UN Security Council that a ceasefire resolution proposed by Spain and Panama tonight is unacceptable to Her Majesty's government. Sir Anthony said it failed to link a cessation of hostilities with Argentine withdrawal as required by Security Council Resolution 502. This effectively means that the British will veto the resolution if it comes to a vote. That's all from us tonight.
>
> BBC2, 22.55, 2.6.82

The following day the references to possible Argentine concessions disappear. Nothing is said about the fact that Argentines are involved in writing and rewriting the resolution, or about the suggestion that Argentina is 'desperate to achieve a ceasefire, even on British terms'. Instead we hear a reiteration of the view that nothing will ever come of peace talks. At lunchtime on ITN:

> *Newscaster:* Let's come back to what's left of the peace process. With me now is our diplomatic correspondent who spent many weeks in New York watching it collapse.

Correspondent: What has been very clear is that whatever has happened in New York or whatever has been happening in New York has had no relation at all to what's going on in the South Atlantic . . . . I would be very surprised if anything happens of consequence before the battle for Port Stanley.

ITN, 13.00, 3.8.82

And on BBC1:

One more go round at the Security Council . . . out of a back room came the text of a new ceasefire resolution . . . . There can be no settlement nor hope of a settlement until the last Argentine soldier is ousted from the islands.

BBC1, 13.00, 3.6.82

As the day progresses the items get shorter but the message remains the same: the British will be 'obliged to use their veto' (BBC1, 17.40, 3.6.82).

On ITN's early evening bulletin a military report concludes, 'It seems today there's very little doubt that a major offensive on Port Stanley is now certain' (ITN, 18.50, 3.6.82), immediately before the newsreader gives the report on the UN discussion.

The story changes in the evening when the ceasefire resolution is finally amended to include Britain's Resolution 502. We are still not given the text of the amended resolution on the news, or precise details of its content, and nothing is heard about Argentina's involvement or her changing stance; but in the period between the resolution being amended on 3 June and the voting late on 4 June, five out of the seven bulletins which cover the resolution make it plain that it now links the ceasefire with Argentine withdrawal. On ITN's *News at Ten*, for instance, the headline before the break is: 'Britain is thinking hard about an amended resolution calling for a ceasefire in the Falklands and an Argentine withdrawal' (ITN, 22.00, 3.6.82). After the break the newscaster states that the resolution 'links a ceasefire with a simultaneous implementation of Resolution 502, which means a withdrawal of Argentine troops' (ITN, 22.00, 3.6.82).

The strongest words come from *Newsnight's* correspondent, who goes so far as to imply that, now that Britain's Resolution 502 is included, Britain perhaps ought to agree to stop the fighting: 'Sir Anthony's [the British UN delegate] point appeared to be answered . . [Britain] can't afford to be brutal in rejecting calls for a ceasefire' (BBC2, 22.45, 3.6.82). However, such a comment is very much the exception. On 4 June, the day of the crucial vote, four out of the eight bulletins before the voting did not mention the resolution at all. In one of these, an interview with the Prime Minister is actually *cut* just as a journalist begins the question, 'Can you say anything about the ceasefire moves at—[*Cut*]' (ITN, 17.45, 4.6.82).

When the resolution does appear it is only in brief items read by the newscaster, without receiving the time and resources devoted to a major story. And in every case in this period, when we are told about the Argentine commitment to withdraw, we are also given warnings that the commitment should not be trusted:

> But even now, the wording may not be specific enough to satisfy the British . . . . Britain must now decide whether to go along with the new resolution for a ceasefire, or to veto it on the grounds that it's just another Security Council piece of paper that Argentina can ignore. A difficult decision to make.
>
> > BBC1, 21.00, 3.6.82

> *Newscaster:* There could still be a stumbling block . . .
> *Correspondent:* Even if this amended resolution is passed, Argentina could treat it exactly as she treated 502, she could ignore it.
>
> > ITN, 22.00, 3.6.82

> However, this most recently amended version is sloppily drafted and in trying to please both sides contains ambiguities which the British will be unwilling to endorse simply because they may be insufficiently sure signals to the Argentines that they must withdraw.
>
> > BBC2, 22.45, 3.6.82

> Our political correspondent says it's clear that no resolution will be acceptable to Britain unless it contains a watertight guarantee of withdrawal.
>
> > BBC1, 13.00, 17.40, 4.6.82

> Mrs Thatcher says there's no question of holding back the military action while the diplomats talk.
>
> > BBC1, 21.00, 4.6.82

Of course the TV journalists are right to point out that Argentina had not previously obeyed Resolution 502, and to show some healthy scepticism about Argentine promises and the workings of UN diplomacy. But by ignoring the evidence that the Argentine position had changed, and sometimes ignoring the ceasefire call altogether, TV news gave support to the view that the military 'final thrust' was necessary, and obscured important doubts about the way the British government was handling the crisis.

At the UN Security Council, the ceasefire resolution – 'tailored al-

most exclusively to try to meet Britain's specifications' as *The Times*
said — eventually came to the vote on the afternoon of 4 June. Nine
members voted in favour of the ceasefire, and this made the resolution
mandatory. Four abstained. The USA first voted against the
resolution, but minutes later a delayed message arrived from the
Secretary of State instructing the American delegate to abstain, and
she immediately announced that she would withdraw the 'no' vote if it
were possible. The only country voting 'no' finally was Britain.

The TV viewers that night might not have been too surprised at this
outcome: we had been told that 'Britain is thinking hard' (ITN, 22.00,
3.6.82), but the British government's eventual position had been
predicted and justified, ('obliged to use their veto . . . no settlement nor
hope of a settlement . . . not specific enough . . . sloppily drafted', etc).
The very fact that the resolution received so little attention on TV
before it came to a vote gives the impression that it was never a very
urgent or hopeful possibility.

From outside the narrow framework of the news, Britain's veto can
be seen as extraordinary and certainly in need of explanation. Britain
had been insisting on 502 from the beginning 'so that no further lives
can be lost' as Pym put it – so why veto a resolution committing
Argentina to 502? The official answer was that the ceasefire resolution
was never worded strongly enough to make sure Argentina withdrew
as planned; but nine nations were prepared to vote for it, the resolution
included provision for the UN Secretary General to 'use such means as
he may deem necessary to verify compliance' and, as we have seen,
reports from Buenos Aires indicate that the junta was searching for a
way out. Even the USA delegate, who technically voted with Britain,
said: 'It became clear to her that Britain was refusing to accept certain
amendments that she considered reasonable' Jeanne Kirkpatrick, US
UN Ambassador, quoted in the *Washington Post*, 5.6.82.

The ceasefire resolution had included a reference to Resolution 505
(an earlier attempt by the Security Council to call a ceasefire), which in
turn refers to existing UN policy on the Falklands. Unfortunately for
the British government, the UN policy since 1965 (with Resolution
2065) has been that British administration of the islands is a 'colonial
problem' and that Britain and Argentina should hold negotiations on
sovereignty. This policy was reiterated by the UN General Assembly
after the conflict in November 1982, with a 90–12 vote majority
supporting an Argentine resolution on sovereignty. The whole
question of Argentina's claim, colonialism, and the idea of negotiable
sovereignty threatened to undermine Britain's self-image as the

legitimate protector of the Falklands. A commentary in *The Times* linked the question of the British veto to the problem (for Britian) of UN involvement:

> An additional problem with the draft resolution had its roots in the complex political power struggle within the British inner cabinet over the prospect of future negotiations with the Argentine military junta over the islands. The Spanish–Panamanian text invokes Resolution 505, which envisages a United Nations role in a negotiated settlement.
>
> *The Times*, 5.6.82

However, all of these awkward questions can be avoided – British isolation, British unwillingness to settle peacefully, British unwillingness to negotiate on sovereignty — if the blame for the fall of the resolution is put solely on the shoulders of Argentina for being intransigent about withdrawal; and this was the message that came across on the TV news.

The one explanation for Britain's veto of the ceasefire resolution appearing on the news was that Argentina would not withdraw her forces:

> *UN correspondent:* The final text, in the British view, was not strong enough to get the Argentine occupation forces off the islands.
>
> BBC1, 17.55, BBC2, 19.05, 5.6.82

> *Dip. correspondent:* A Foreign Office spokesman said . . . 'We know it would have left the Argentines on the Falklands, worded as it was.'
>
> BBC1, 17.55, 21.15, BBC2, 19.05, 5.6.82

> *Newscaster:* A resolution put forward on Friday for a ceasefire was vetoed by Britain as there were no guarantee from Argentina. Britain says Argentine forces must be withdrawn from the islands within a set time before this country accepts a ceasefire.
>
> *News Review*, BBC2, 18.30, 6.6.82

An ITN correspondent even went so far as to state: 'The UN resolution was in their view not at all close to being acceptable, as Mr Haig had suggested, because *it didn't link a ceasefire to withdrawal*' (ITN, 21.45, 5.6.82). This is an extraordinary reversal: it is one thing to follow the government view that the link was not firm enough, but none of the parties involved had claimed that there was *no link at all*. On the same programme two days earlier the newscaster had explained that the resolution 'links a ceasefire with a simultaneous implementation of Resolution 502, which means a withdrawal of Argentine troops' (ITN, 22.00, 3.6.82).

Resolution 502 itself, having held pride of place in the British diplomatic effort for so long, drops back out of view after the veto, at least as far as the TV news is concerned. On one occasion it resurfaces, but in a typical example of formal 'balance' its significance is referred to and then immediately downgraded:

> The Americans say because 502 was mentioned in last night's resolution, British interests were protected. The British claim that even though 502 was mentioned last night, it did not make that resolution acceptable.
>
> BBC2, 23.10, 5.6.82

The TV news reported without question the official view that it was Argentina's refusal to withdraw that forced Britain to block this move to stop the fighting. However, what was most remarkable about this coverage of the Security Council vote was that the British veto is not the focus of the news story at all. Here are the headlines on the day the failure is reported:

> As the final battle lincs are drawn on the Falklands we hear from our man with the British forces: 'Artillery units are preparing to fire the biggest barrage fired by British guns since the Korean War, or possibly even the Second World War.' . . .
>   Mrs Thatcher is angry with America for faltering over the Falklands, but Mr Reagan didn't know of the mix-up.
>
> BBC1, 17.55, BBC2, 19.05, 5.6.82

> The Falklands: on standby for the final push. First stories of how the SAS dared to win. The American turnabout: Haig says 'It was my fault.'
>
> ITN, 21.45, 5.6.82

Two points stand out here: first that the prospect of more military action is given higher priority than news of peace talks; and second that the Security Council vote is treated as a story about United States 'faltering' and 'turnabout'. This tendency to concentrate only on the US position was established before the 'turnabout' as soon as the first news of the vote came through. The newscaster's only comment as he replaces the telephone receiver after hearing that the chances of a ceasefire have collapsed is:

> That report from [our correspondent] seems to bear out what was said earlier in the programme by Mrs Thatcher in Paris about President Reagan maintaining his full-hearted support for Britian's position on the conflict.
>
> BBC2, 22.45, 4.6.82

By focussing on the USA's changed vote, the news excludes any analysis of the British veto. The references to Argentine withdrawal quoted above are passing mentions in reports which focus for the most part on Mrs Kirkpatrick's embarrassment, Mrs Thatcher's 'dismay', President Reagan's having slept through 'the drama', and details of phone messages between Haig and Kirkpatrick. Our screens are filled with pictures of newsmen jostling around Mrs Thatcher and President Reagan sitting side by side at a banquet during the Versailles summit, while we hear about 'the painful and embarrassing hangover after last night's extraordinary sequence of changed minds and hurt feelings' (BBC2, 23.10, 5.7.82).

The *reasons* for the US preferring not to oppose the ceasefire resolution are discussed only in terms of US loyalty as an ally. On the news any possibility of stopping the fighting did not seem to be the issue – since Britain had come out against the resolution, opposing it became a test of loyalty:

> President Reagan's administration have been trying to portray last nights voting mix-up at the UN as a simple disagreement over the wording of a document, and not a retreat from its support for Britain. But the British, while remaining officially silent, have let it be known that Mrs Thatcher was dismayed and angry.
>
> BBC1, 21.15, 5.6.82

This approach to moves for peace ('three days of finessing, reworking and adjusting resolutions came to a sudden and quite predictable end: they got nowhere' – BBC, 17.55, 5.6.82) went hand in hand with an enthusiastic approach to military developments. ITN's headlines on the night of the collapse of the peace plan are an example of this. The peace initiative comes third – before we hear 'On standby for the final push' and 'How the SAS dared to win'.

Peace negotiations were not only misrepresented, they were squeezed out, in this case by the SAS 'daring to win'. This referred to a story about the taking of South Georgia. In one incident a group of SAS soldiers had landed on a glacier in terrible weather conditions and then had to be rescued. It is ironic that ITN should have focussed on this, since by some accounts the operation was near to a fiasco and could have led to the Task Force being called home. But ITN introduced the story as 'primarily one of an incredible ability to survive in conditions which would finish off normal mortals'. This lapse into the imagery of *Boy's Own Paper* betrays a fascination with the fighting which in part explains the failure to report more peaceful avenues. While the contents and prospects of the ceasefire call were never properly explored, every military engagement was anticipated and recreated in the studio. Military speculation was divorced from the 'diplomatic front', so that it was easy for journalists to concentrate on military advances without having to consider whether they had to be made. The opening of this bulletin just after the failure of the UN ceasefire plan betrays no trace of concern that any peace moves could have interrupted the military thrusts:

> Good evening. By tonight everything is ready for the British assault on Port Stanley. The build-up of men and equipment is thought to be complete, and the one thing that had been delaying the final assault, *the weather*, has improved.
>
> BBC1, 21.15, 5.6.82

Conclusion

From the above analysis there emerges a possible scenario for the relation between television news and public opinion. It is clear from our work on diplomacy that whatever was blamed for the failure of negotiations, it did not normally include the actions of the British.* This country's government was very largely reported as 'urgently pursuing peace' and as using the Task Force as a 'back-up' for diplomatic efforts.

Yet there are fleeting moments in media coverage when journalists acknowledge a different version of events and suggest that British policy was to seek a military victory. Here is a diplomatic correspondent on BBC speaking three days *before* the UN ceasefire plan of 4 June:

> Before the British Task Force set foot on the islands ten days ago, the Argentines could have possessed them legally in a matter of months, but now that set of proposals is no longer on the table . . . . There can be no question of the islands being handed over to Argentina in the foreseeable future and certainly not to the present military junta. One Whitehall source put it this way: 'There are a number of widows and orphans – there will undoubtedly be more. If they were to see the Argentine flag flying in a year or two, they would ask quite rightly, "Why did our men die?"'
>
> BBC1, 21.30, 31.5.82

The implication is that rather than diplomacy being 'backed up' by military force, in fact the use of military force had made negotiation

---

*We do not suggest here that the Argentines were all for negotiation while the British prevaricated. It is possible that Argentina saw negotiations as a way of gaining time. The point is that when diplomacy failed the blame was largely attributed to only one side.

impossible, or indeed redundant, except perhaps as a 'ritual' through which television viewers were persistently taken. In retrospect there is evidence to suggest that even before there were any British losses it was government policy to escalate military action. But it seems likely, that at the time, journalists knew that there was no real hope for diplomatic proposals such as the United Nations plan for a ceasefire on 4 June. When the Peruvian peace plan was presented on the news, we were told largely that the reason for failure was Argentine 'intransigence', but not 'British military escalation'. The UN ceasefire was vetoed by Britain because 'it would have left the Argentines on the Falklands', rather than because the British could not negotiate since they had to justify losses already incurred. If journalists really believed that the British were not serious in negotiation, then it might explain in part their sometimes dismissive attitude to peace proposals. Journalists could refer to such initiatives as coming to 'a predictable end'. In a sense they were correct in that the failure may have been predictable but not perhaps for the reasons given.

A very limited account *was* given of who was 'refusing to compromise'. When the news reports public attitudes, it relies on opinion-poll questions which reflect such knowledge about who is to blame, and who has made the fighting 'necessary'. There is a knowledge derivable from the news that diplomacy is difficult, while British military operations are being accomplished with apparent ease. Military action by Britain is seen as a necessary 'response' and its human consequences are muted. Questions in opinion polls can specifically presume such ways of understanding events. In the crucial poll on whether Britain should invade the Falklands, people were asked if they agreed with this as long as the Argentine government 'refused to compromise'.* Under such conditions it is possible to have a majority of the population accepting an invasion, if they believe there is little alternative. A version of these results, saying 'Launch an invasion . . . 70%', was then highlighted on the news. What we are not told is that in the same poll, when people are asked what other alternatives they favour, a total of 76% wished the Falklands to be administered by the United Nations while Britain and Argentina negotiated.

The final irony is that broadcasters should use their own versions of what public opinion was to justify their approach to reporting. ITN

---

*It is interesting that the opinion poll which referred to Argentina refusing to compromise was taken on 7 May 1982 while the Television News items reporting the failure of the Peruvian peace plan and Argentina's 'intransigence' began the day before.

used its assumption of 'majority support for Task Force action' to justify its intended policy of giving a 'nightly offering of interesting, positive and heart-warming stories of achievement and collaboration born out of a sense of national purpose'.* By contrast, our analysis suggests it is not clear that a majority of the population desired the escalation of military conflict, and it is even less certain that they would have supported 'government policy' on this, if they had been better informed as to what that policy was.

---

*ITN evidence to Parliamentary Defence Committee, quoted above in Chapter 1.

Section T[wo]

Defence an[d]
Disarmamen[t]
Peace Contests

Section Two

Defence and Disarmament: Peace Contests

FIVE

The Propaganda War

What in the name of God is strategic superiority? What is the significance of it politically, militarily, operationally at these levels of number? What do you do with it?

Henry Kissinger[1]

The paradox of security is not only that in the nuclear world those habits of mind and expressions of power to which we are accustomed are no longer consistent with security, even in its restricted form of defence. Were it merely so, the situation would be only unfortunate rather than grave, and it would be stable. The paradox is bitter because the relationship between nuclear weapons is volatile and corrosive. It is an inverse relationship: the more that people and states seek to increase their security by the old methods, but with the new atomic power, the less security they have; and the more that heightened insecurity is sensed, the faster the arms race becomes, the heavier its economic burden, and the more hateful, aggressive, expansionist and devious the enemy appears. In this way the spiralling accelerates viciously and the hope of escape recedes as the nuclear presence spreads over the whole political landscape.

Gwyn Prins[2]

Deterrence doctrine is full of paradoxes. One side tends to judge its own stance by its intentions (peaceable), and the stance of the other side by its military capabilities (excessive). Military preparations which are seen by one side as wholly defensive may increase tension if the most rational response of the other side is to improve its offensive capability. The possession of nuclear weapons may deter the other side from attacking, but it is extremely difficult to use nuclear weapons to compel or coerce. The more explicit the declaratory policy for deterrence, the less room for manoeuvre for the deterrer in a crisis. To attack non-combatants directly is contrary to both international law and ethics . . . but a conditional intention to attack enemy non-combatants is thought by some to be less provacative than to intend to attack missile silos, which have to be struck first because they may be empty if stuck second. To improve the accuracy of nuclear delivery systems enables them to be used more discriminately, but may be perceived as provocative by the other side because accuracy is more important for the first strike attacks on military targets than for second strike attacks on cities.[3]

These quotations represent some of the concerns and perplexities which surround discussion about the place of nuclear weapons in the world today. Such discussions, apart from being conducted, literally, in different languages with the potential for misunderstanding to which that can give rise, also draw upon different specialist modes of discourse: ethics, philosophy, politics, science and technology, theology, military, international relations. In practice these may be segregated or mixed up in various combinations. How is our information about these matters structured and organised? Given the global significance of the issue – we now have the capacity to destroy ourselves and our planet – the responsibilities facing those in the mass media are awesome. Journalists themselves face considerable difficulties in getting information, understanding its significance and presenting it to us in a comprehensible way. We are not interested in making debating points about bias or distortion but rather in trying to explore in an illustrative way some of the things that happen in practice, the problems that this points up and, by implication, possible alternatives.

The media are at the centre of a struggle to define and influence public opinion. Media coverage of the peace movement, for example, can be seen in the context of a propaganda war which surrounds the nuclear debate. The superpowers are engaged in a battle to influence public opinion. The government in the UK wages a campaign to defuse the message and impact of growing peace movement. For their part, organisations like CND try to use the media to convey their message to the British public.

Where did the Regan administration stand on arms control, peace initiatives and nuclear policy? Critics could point to ambiguities, uncertainties and contradictions. In October 1981, President Reagan said: 'I could see where you could have the exchange of tactical weapons against troops in the field without bringing either one of the major powers to pushing the button' (*Financial Times*, 22.10.81). Did this mean that the USA would consider fighting a nuclear war at Europe's expense? The President later said that such a view was an 'outright deception'. What then was the thinking on limited nuclear war? In November 1981, the controversy between Alexander Haig and Caspter Weinberger over whether there was a NATO contingency plan to fire a demonstration nuclear shot to warn the Soviet Union against pressing a conventional attack on Western Europe was reported in the *Sunday Times* (8.11.81) and elsewhere. At the level of stragetic weapons, there was the question of whether the Reagan administration were really looking for parity or for superiority against the Soviet Union. This was linked to the possibility that the USA was developing a policy of winning a nuclear war, rather than a policy of deterrence based on the notion that a nuclear war is inherently unwinnable. One relevant text from the Department of Defense, *Fiscal 1984–88 Defense Guidance*, was leaked to the press in June 1982:

> United States nuclear capabilities must prevail even under the condition of a prolonged war.... Should deterrence fail and strategic nuclear war with the USSR occur, the United States must prevail and be able to force the Soviet Union to seek earliest termination of hostilities on terms favourable to the United States.... US strategic nuclear forces and their command and control links should be capable of supporting controlled nuclear counterattacks over a protracted period while maintaining a reserve of nuclear forces sufficient for trans- and post-attack protection and coercion.[4]

All this bears upon the development of counter-force and first strike weapons. Mr Weinberger, for his part, argued that there was no contradiction between the view that there could be no winners in a nuclear war and planning to prevail, if war occurs, by denying victory to the Soviet Union. Not everyone followed his logic.

There were other doubts. Was President Reagan serious about arms control? At his first presidential press conference he said that one can never trust Soviet leaders who 'reserve unto themselves the right to commit any crime, to lie, to cheat, in order to obtain objective'. In March 1983 he was telling an evangelical conference in Florida that the Russians had the aggressive impulses of an evil empire and described them as the focus of evil in the modern world. As early as the 1960s Mr Reagan had said:

> We are being told that we can sit down and negotiate with this enemy of ours, and that there's a little right and a little wrong on both sides. How do you compromise between good and evil? How do you say to this enemy that we can compromise our belief in God and his dialetical determinism?[5]

This kind of perspective with its faith, later conveyed in his speech to the British Parliament in June 1982, that Marxism–Leninism would be consigned to the ash-bin of history, provides grounds for doubting the President's sincerity about arms control. The doubts were further fuelled by the delays in getting to the bargaining table with the Soviet Union, some eighteen months in fact. The fate of the Arms Control and Disarmament Agency in the United States has also been commented upon. There were cuts in funding key activities of the agency, which among other things meant that it had to rely upon the Pentagon for classified research it used to do itself. Eugene Rostow, widely regarded as a 'hawk' on arms control matters, was appointed director, but proved to be too liberal for the administration's taste and was replaced by Kenneth Adelman. In 1981 Adelman had commented that arms control was a sham and that the real value of arms control negotiations was as an aid to managing public opinion. But, as Jeff McMahan has pointed out:

> Despite its evident hostility to all forms of arms control, the Reagan administration was eventually forced by public pressure and in particular by the emergence of the peace movements in both Europe and the US to open negotiations with the Russians on the control of both strategic and theatre nuclear weapons. In both cases the administration's strategy has been to play to the world audience, cultivating the image of a government deeply committed to the reduction of nuclear arms, while at the same time assiduously avoiding an agreement with the Russians.[6]

In his recent book *Deadly Gambits*, Strobe Talbott has shown how Paul Nitze's attempts to accomplish something on arms control at the INF talks were blocked by Casper Weinberger and Richard Perle. Nitze's famous 'walk in the woods' with his Soviet counterpart was aimed at exploring the possibility that the US would install only Cruise and not Pershing II missiles if the Soviets would cut back to an agreed number on their SS-20s. This was stopped in its tracks and, as he expected, the Soviets subsequently walked out on the negotiations in November 1983.[7]

Certainly, when President Reagan called a press conference to announce his 'zero option' on 18 November, 1981, television news interpreted what he was doing as part of a propaganda campaign. It was, said the ITN correspondent, 'aimed at calming the growing European peace movement protesting at the risk of nuclear war' (ITN, 13.00). In the evening bulletin the same correspondent said that the main reason for the statement was to try to counter the growing anti-nuclear movement in Europe which had tended to portray the USA as the bad guy. The careful management of the event was also wryly commented upon: 'It was interesting to note that since Mr Reagan's recent *faux pas* have usually been in response to journalists' questions, today he wasn't allowed to answer any.' The BBC correspondent described the occasion as the President's 'peace offensive'. It was intended, he said, 'to demonstrate to his European allies that the administration is serious in its search for arms control'. It wanted to remove the confusion that had arisen as a result of the conflicting signals that had been sent out. The correspondent also registered that 'the administration had become deeply concerned about the growth of the peace movement in Europe' (BBC1, 17.40).

The awareness of the propaganda war also comes through on television news in June 1982, when the START talks were announced, and subsequently during the President's European tour, which included a NATO summit conference. On 31 May, the BBC's correspondent, Martin Bell, referring to the President's statement on START, said:

> President Reagan's audience were . . . . were the servicemen, veterans and their families gathered in the Arlington amphitheatre, but it was a speech also directed at a wider audience, in Western Europe particularly, and intended to show the President to them in the role of a friend of the alliance and a spokesman for peace. There are deep concerns in the White House that what should be an easy popularity-building trip for the President may be soured by the anti-nuclear movement in Europe, by suspicions of US defence policy, by existing strains within the alliance and, of course, by the Falklands War.
>
> BBC1, 21.30

On the lunchtime bulletin next day ITN used a report from America's ABC news. This was briefer but the reporter commented: 'trying to defuse some of the critics of the anti-nuclear movement, the President said his goal was peace'.

On 9 June, the BBC's lunchtime news has a report from its correspondent in West Germany, Keith Graves:

> President Reagan comes to the NATO summit meeting at a time when the alliance is filled with self-doubts. Dispelling those is the main aim of this tour. For him the next two days will be decisive because nowhere more than in Germany is he regarded as a man of war: a right winger who has indicated that a limited nuclear conflict with the Warsaw Pact is an acceptable scenario, and that war would, in the first instance, be fought on German soil. His message will be negotiation with the Kremlin rather than confrontation. The indications here, though, are

that the majority of his allies will be sceptical, under pressure, as many of them are, from mounting anti-nuclear movements back home.

On BBC2's *Newsnight*, another correspondent, Charles Wheeler, explained that Mr Reagan had not originally intended visiting West Germany, but Chancellor Schmidt had indicated that this would have sent West German/American relations into a complete decline and had lobbied hard and successfully to get the NATO summit meeting transferred from Brussels to Bonn: 'So here Mr Reagan is – undeniably the least widely admired American President ever to tread on German soil, but determined to make a good impression on a people who were once proud to be called America's most uncritical friends in Europe.' The correspondent shows his awareness of the management of public opinion which underlines the visit:

> President Reagan's courtship of his European allies has been well prepared in a series of speeches and political moves towards arms control. These have been received here with relief. But to many West Germans his conversion from re-armer to disarmer has been too sudden and too slick to be convincing. There was a vivid example of President Reagan's over-anxiety to please in his speech today at the Bundestag, the lower house of the German Parliament. There he came close to aligning himself to a German peace movement which only four months ago he was condemning as financed by the Kremlin.

One further example from the same correspondent: on 28 June he contexualised the START talks by running back over Reagan's record and attitudes towards arms control, arguing that, according to Reagan, 'the rules of détente have allowed the Soviet Union to achieve clear nuclear superiority, an imbalance he was determined to reverse'. The correspondent illustrated from Reagan's speeches what he called 'the President's implacable anti-Soviet line' and suggested that this had led to great strains in the Atlantic alliance. But this had also spilled out into more general public expressions of discontent:

> Meanwhile public agitation against the nuclear arms build-up had spread from Europe to America where the campaign took the form of a demand for an immediate freeze of strategic nuclear weapons at existing levels to be followed by negotiated reductions. Broadly based and supported by the churches and a powerful minority in the Congress, the campaign attracted even greater support than the anti-war movement of the sixties and seventies. The Reagan administration argued that a freeze would simply perpetuate Moscow's present nuclear advantage, but by now the demand for comprehensive talks on arms limitations was too strong to be resisted.

Later in his account the correspondent concluded:

> The President's critics here in Washington simply don't believe in his conversion to the cause of arms control. They say he was acting under pressures, both domestic and foreign . . . . But it's one thing to be willing to sit down with the Russians and quite another to make the concessions necessary, if there's ever to be an arms control agreement.

We can see from these examples that television journalists did display an awareness of the propaganda war which the United States was waging, and we see below that this was also true in 1983. It was made clear that there was an uneasy relationship between the US and Europe and that the US leadership of the alliance was held in low esteem.

The concern within NATO to defuse the peace movement and to mobilise, or rebuild, support for NATO policy was also reflected in articles published in *NATO Review*. In December 1982, John Palmer reported in the *Guardian*, 'NATO set for battle with the peace movement'. He wrote:

> NATO foreign ministers left here yesterday prepared for an unprecedented public relations battle with the peace movement... However, they recognised that they still had a long way to go to convince public opinion in Europe about missile deployment. The Foreign Secretary, Mr Pym, made it clear that British ministers plan an all-out offensive next year against the supporters of unilateral disarmament.
>
> *Guardian,* 11.12.82

NATO Review Nos. 3/4, 1983, has a cover cartoon of a peace demonstration with two placarded slogans: 'No to Pershing II in Europe' and 'Join the Passivists'. The demonstration merges in the front into columns of SS-20 missiles. Inside is an article by a member of the Norwegian Parliament, Grethe Vaerno, on 'Public Opinion Strategy'. His expressed view is that there is a need to struggle with public opinion, to analyse why the peace movement has gained such widespread support and to develop a strategy designed to regain public support for the alliance. This means reinforcing the view that there is a Soviet threat – military and political. He suggested that a mental barrier had been constructed in people's minds by expectations of peaceful co-operation and goodwill, which did not take account of the Soviet military build-up. This had enabled what he called the anti-NATO campaign to criticise NATO nuclear doctrines and the low nuclear threshold in battlefield weapons. Vaerno argued that there is a leadership crisis in the NATO countries which has been the most serious obstacle to consensus over security. The essence of his diagnosis and prescription was as follows:

> The mood of the day is *distrust*. Leaders have been proved wrong, everybody's opinion is equal to the next man's. Nobody accepts authority and nobody is believed, particularly not the elected politicians, establishment figures and the military. There is a marked desire for direct influence and paticipation even outside the normal political system. This is hard to change, perhaps impossible. It may be countered by creating a more informed public. It is, however, paramount that political leaders should not abdicate responsibility for taking the lead in shaping public opinion. When they stop insisting on what they feel is right; when they start to follow what they perceive as a popular trend; when they refrain from using their position to explain; and deprive those who still believe in them of a positive lead, then they have started a vicious circle of dwindling support both for themselves and their policies.[8]

The call for an informed public certainly strikes a democratic note, although the assumption that members of the peace movement are not well informed is more questionable, given the burgeoning literature to which they have contributed. Indeed, later in the same article, Vaerno makes two points which find an echo in statements from the peace movement. The alliance has to demonstrate that its long-term goal is a peaceful relationship, not confrontation, superiority or an offensive capability, otherwise it will get no popular support for its defence plans. This is precisely what debates about Trident, Pershing II, Cruise, MX and first use are all about. Secondly, the alliance has to show that it is genuine in its attempts to lessen the dangers of nuclear war. Vaerno points out that it is not enough simply to assert that NATO's policy of deterrence has kept the peace for more than three decades:

> The fear will always be there – fear of deterrence failing, of being a target for nuclear weapons. Other questions cause confusion – those concerning a moral refusal to be the first to use such weapons; theological discussions about deterrence as a means of righteous defence; logical questions about the credibility of a suicidal strategy (for both sides by the way). These are serious dilemmas for quite a lot of people. We should not be afraid of a more open discussion about nuclear doctrine. It would be meaningless to pretend that the problems are not there.[9]

The enthusiasm displayed for a public opinion strategy of this sort appear in the wake of well-known dissent to the dual-track decision of 1979, is expressed in public opinion polls and the growth of the peace movement. Before that, however, in the 1970's debate had not been pronounced, nor had it obviously been encouraged, despite the great increase in nuclear stockpiles during that period. A study by the Stanford Institute – *An Assessment of European Attitudes on tactical Nuclear Force Modernisation*, commissioned by the US Department of Defense – counselled that on such matters general public debate was to be avoided:

> As the history of the 'Carte Blanche', the ADM, the 'mini-nuke', and even the 'neutron bomb' controversies shows, the process of issue formation in public debates tends to result in a vast oversimplification of complex problems, and in the presentation to the public of highly technical issues in sensationalistic terms. If proposals for modernisation of NATO's tactical nuclear force should prematurely catch the attention of wide public audiences on both sides of the Atlantic, the very options which should result from the reform effort may be foreclosed.[10]

Here we have a classic example of the 'expert knows best' tendency with accompanying resonances of keeping it within the secret recesses of privileged bureaucracies. This can have anti-democratic consequences. When dissent does occur, as in the instance of the growth of the peace movements of Europe and the United States, the governments concerned have a repertoire of responses which they can draw on. They can present such movements as naive, subversive, knowingly or unknowingly controlled by 'the enemy'. They can also claim that peace campaigners are emotional as compared to reasonable and knowledgeable politicians and officials. In slightly more conciliatory – though sometimes patronising – tones, they can say that they, like the peace movements, are seriously concerned for peace and that the only differences are over the means to achieve it. As President Reagan said in the West German Parliament in June 1982:

> To those who march for peace, my heart is with you. I would be at the head of your parade if I believed marching alone would bring about a more secure world. And to the 2,800 women in Fielderstadt who sent a petition for peace to President Brezhnev and to me, let me say that I myself would sign your petition if I thought it would bring about harmony. I understand your genuine concerns. The women of Fielderstadt and I share the same goal.
>
> BBC2, 23.00, 9.6.82

This repertoire was widely called upon by the British government in its response to the peace movement. The government was and remains a strong supporter of the NATO alliance. It believes in the validity and necessity of the nuclear deterrent. The doctrine is inextricably linked with a concept of the Soviet threat. Thus the government pamphlet *The Policy of Deterrence* begins:

> The threat of conflict in Europe springs from the fact tht the Soviet Union continues to maintain massive military forces in Europe, conventional, chemical and nuclear, well in excess of those required for its own defence. These forces are being constantly improved, particularly in their mobility and firepower.[11]

It spells out the view of deterrence as follows:

> The essence of deterrence if that, to prevent war, or use of the threat of war, a country must itself maintain the instruments of war and make it clear to any potential aggressor that it is willing to retaliate against aggression. It must create in the mind of a potential aggressor an unambiguous recognition of both its capability and its willingness to use military means to resist an attack and to restore peace.[12]

In the Statement on the Defence Estimates 1981, a formal note on 'Nuclear Weapons and Preventing War' is included. Deterrence is defined in terms of seeking to ensure that 'whatever military aggression or political bullying a future Soviet leader might contemplate, he could not foresee any likely situation in which the West would be left with no realistic alternative to surrender'.[13] The contribution to NATO's deterrent nuclear strategy is said to operate at three main levels:

> First, we endorse it fully as helping to guarantee our security, and we share in the protection it gives to all Alliance members. Second, we co-operate directly, like several other members, in the United States power which is the main component of the nuclear armoury, by making bases available and providing certain delivery systems to carry United States warhead. Third, we commit to the Alliance nuclear forces of various kinds – strategic and theatre – our independent control.[14]

The deterrence policy of the British government also includes reference to the independent deterrent. The rationale for this is given in another government pamphlet, *Trident: Britain's Strategic Deterrent*. The argument start from the premise that 'It would be an enormously grave decision for the United States to use nuclear weapons in defence of Europe with all the risks that this would involve for the US homeland.' This thought may enter into the adversary's calculations:

> It is possible that the Soviet Union – perhaps under a different leadership with a different outlook, perhaps facing internal or external problems – might at some stage in the future believe that it could impose

its will on British and Europe by military force without becoming involved in strategic nuclear war with the United States.

An independent nuclear force under British control, as Polaris is and Trident will be, means that in those circumstances the Soviet Union would have to consider our reaction as well as that of the United States – and it would know that our survival would be more directly threatened by aggression in Europe. This would enormously complicate Soviet planning, and in the view of successive British governments and of our NATO allies it strengthens deterrence and reduces the danger of an attack.[15]

In support of this position and against its critics in the peace movement and beyond, the government has conducted its own propaganda war. We have already referred to the NATO foreign ministers' meeting in December 1982 and its declared intention to do battle with the peace movement. At the beginning of 1983 the government considered the idea of launching a campaign against CND. In justifying the campaign – which did not formally go ahead – a government minister spoke of the need to combat 'the immense amount of misinformation floating around'.[16] In the months leading up to the 1983 General Election much of the government's anti-CND comments focussed on the political unreliability of the organisation. References to the CND as being 'dupes of the Kremlin' or 'communist-manipulated' or 'naive and misguided idealists' or 'subversive' or 'tools of the Soviet Union' were commonplace.[17]

There was no reason to suppose that the Soviet Union was not also engaged in a propaganda war. Everybody else was. Since it was opposed to the deployment of Cruise and Pershing II missiles in Western Europe it had its own reasons for supporting the peace movement in Europe. Given that from the government's point of view – with its rooted assumption about the Soviet threat – this could be viewed as a form of ideological warfare designed to subvert the democratic process in the West, one can see how this coincidence of interests could be interpreted. At its worst it is revealed in the anti-CND slogans—'communist', 'neutralist', 'defeatist'—with the close-to-the-surface suggestion of treachery. CND, for its part, has always made clear its opposition to SS-20s as well as to Cruise and Pershing II and has taken the view that it is the structures supporting the cold war which must themselves be dismantled. Consequently, when the Soviets talk about negotiating from strength or maintaining rough parity, the peace movement contests this position. The peace movement in the West sees itself as a third force challenging the militaristic stances of both East and West. This may have been an unwelcome discovery to the Soviets on occasion, particularly since the peace movement is also likely to raise human rights issues and draw attention to unofficial peace movements in the East. This has indeed led to some notable peace campaigners in Britain, such as E. Thompson, being labelled by the Russians as 'anti-Soviet'.

Built into any deterrence theory is the notion of an adversary, a potential enemy. Unmistakably in the thinking of the US, the UK, and NATO, that adversary is the Soviet Union. One problem, however, is that while the existence of something called 'the Soviet threat' is widely adhered to in the West, if it is expressed in a vague or general way it is not clear what particular threats deterrence theory is supposed to be nullifying. If our imagination knows no bounds so that the adversary comes to be viewed as all-powerful and therefore a continuing menacing presence, we run the risk of giving a blank cheque to anything done in the name of deterrence. When that is incorporated into our thinking we will tend to operate on the principle of 'worst case' analysis. Hence new weapon technologies, modernisation programmes and increased spending on defence can be justified on the elastic assumptions relating to deterrence and the nature of the threat.

It is not our purpose to contend that the Soviet Union does not constitute any kind of threat and that the mass media are wrong to suggest otherwise. Indeed, within the peace movement itself there is a developed awareness of the role which the military play in Soviet society. Mary Kaldor, for example, whilst suggesting that Casper Weinberger is on a 'threat-inflation trip' designed to justify his own arms build-up, goes on to state:

> Clearly, there is a threat to peace and stability which stems from the presence of so many immensely destructive instruments of war in both East and West. This is why we need to consider the ways in which the Soviet Union contributes to the risk of war and inquire into the source of Soviet arms build-up.[18]

If there are different understandings of the phenomenon, then there might well be different assessments of its significance.

This point can be illustrated by reference to the Report of the Alternative Defence Commission, *Defence Without the Bomb*. There a general distinction is made between the risks to war which the present situation gives rise to and the question of Soviet intentions:

> In practice, pursuit of parity promotes a nuclear arms race, and the Soviet Union can be criticised by the disarmament movement for

accepting the military logic of nuclear build-up at the risk of world peace, but this does not prove any aggressive design.[19]

The authors then go on to distinguish six different ways in which the Soviet state might be characterised, which may lead to different interpretations of the concept of threat, and of course by extension what should be done about it. These are:

1. The USSR is a Marxist – Leninist regime committed to its original goal of worldwide communist revolution.
2. The USSR is dominated by the military and this is expressed both in domestic organisation and in military aggression abroad.
3. The Soviet Union has inherited the mantle of Russian nationalism and is aggressively imperialistic in its policies.
4. The Soviet Union is internally a conservative regime but wants to prove its great power status on the international stage.
5. The internal weakness in the USSR may result in adventures abroad.
6. Soviet military and foreign policy is essentially defensive shaped by an awareness of economic and military weakness in relation to the West and rooted in memories of the Second World War.

The authors find the fourth and sixth propositions the most compelling. That, of course is their assessment. But unless these elements are unpacked and evaluated we cannot really know what it is we are supposed to be defending against. It could be argued that there are risks attached to choosing one interpretation rather than another, but by the same token there are risks attached to any policy and any political judgement. It is not a basis for excluding them from careful consideration. We readily concede that more research needs to be done on the way the Soviet threat is conceptualised in the media, but we think there are clues as to what is happening.

Panorama did a feature on the Soviet threat entitled *Feeling Misunderstood*, (25.1.82). While it was somewhat hostile to the Soviet Union in its opening statement, making great play with the term 'propaganda', within the film there is an interesting exposition of the encirclement thesis as perceived by the Soviets. Thus the opening announcement contextualises what is to follow:

The success that Soviet propaganda has in making many of its own people feel that they are misunderstood by the West derives very largely from exploiting this very proper human disgust with war and, if separating propaganda from fact on both sides is often difficult, it's particularly difficult in the Soviet Union where the only fact allowed is propaganda – so much so that you could say propaganda doesn't exist.

Panorama 25.11.82

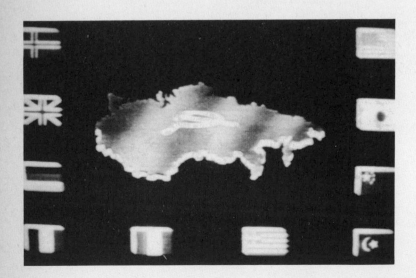

The film is then presented and although the introduction has heavily qualified it, the alternative statement on how the Soviets see things, as compared to common Western views, is of interest. The use of a map of the Soviet Union, with all the flags of the nations mentioned in the following quote surrounding it, is a strong visual accompaniment:

> The West perceives the Soviet Union as always trying to expand its borders, always looking for new spheres of influence, but it is possible to look at the world map in a different way and most Russians do. In the frozen north, Norway neighbours Russia's sea lanes. On the western borders or the Warsaw Pact is Europe with American and local NATO forces. With bases in Italy the West has better control of the Mediterranean. On the desolate border between Turkey and the Soviet Union, America has installed radar so sensitive that it can detect rocket tests deep within Russia. To the south the smouldering and hostile mass of navy and air force heavily committed. Looked at this way the Russians could argue that they are encircled.

If the encirclement thesis is dismissed as propaganda then it will be treated as inherently suspect. It does, howe ver, surface from time to time in the West. In September 1982, Dusko Doder wrote on the 'New Moscow Fear of Encirclement' for the *Washington Post*.[20] He suggested that what the Russians see as an emerging alliance between China, Japan and the United States gives them a new sense of strategic vulnerability. The argument is deployed at book length by Jonathan Steele in *World Power: Soviet Foreign Policy under Brezhnev and Andropov*.[21] This book became the occassion for a discussion on BBC2's *Newsnight* (18.10.83) in which it was shown that conventional Western views about the Soviet threat were challenged from this perspective. A map which put the Soviet Union in the centre of the perspective, as in the *Panorama* programme, was used to illustrate the thesis. The general position was endorsed by Professor John Erickson on the programme. Elsewhere, when he reviewed the book in the *Guardian*, Erickson reflected that it had appeared in the midst of a maelstrom in East- West relations, and commented:

> Let me say at once that given this particular context, one of unpleasant, dangerous and distorted exchanges, it is reassuring to take up a cool and judicious analysis, neither an apologia for the Soviet Union nor a polemical bludgeoning of the Western powers.
>
> *Guardian*, 6.10.83

The *Newsnight* programme regards itself as explicitly atypical. We have not found any evidence that seriously contradicts that view. This suggests that television news, even when it is aware that a propaganda war is being carried on over issues of arms control and disarmament, typically operates within limited perspectives.

If there is a generalised, undifferentiated image of 'the Soviet threat', this can lead to linguistic usages in the coverage of news about the Soviet Union which carry overtones of adversarial menace and danger. A good working illustration of this was provided when the President of the Soviet Union, Leonid Brezhnev, died on 10 November 1982. In the reports of his death, on 11 November, the emphasis is placed on the Soviet military build-up:

> A second arms limitation treaty(SALT II) was only signed after five long years of haggling and Russia's military might grew alarmingly.
>
> Channel 4, 19.00, 11.11.82

> In Brezhnev's final years the Soviet military build-up continued, outstripping NATO in a number of areas.
>
> BBC1, 11.11.82

On Brezhnev himself the same bulletin tells us:

> President Brezhnev's place in history is assured. The man advocated disarmament yet presided over the biggest military build-up the world has ever seen.

The military emphasis is repeated on the day of the funeral: 'Marshall Ustinov as Defence Minister has presided over an unprecedented military build-up', (BBC1, 15.11.82). Without discussion of the context in which the arms race has taken place, this not only makes assumptions as to whether the Soviet build-up is bigger than that of the USA, it also identifies the Soviets as the threat to world stability. Yet there are, of course, other views on the matter:

> America's oldest President, *who has put through the most gigantic peace-time defence build-up in this country's history* [our italics] has formed an amazing alliance with the nation's young warriors.
>
> *Mail on Sunday*, 29.1.84

Brezhnev himself was an exponent of the encirclment thesis. In an interview given in 1981 he had said:

> Imagine yourself in our position. Could we indifferently regard how they were besieging us on all sides with military bases, how increasing numbers of carriers of nuclear death, irrespective of what form – missiles from the sea or land, air bombs, etc. – were targeted from various areas of Europe on Soviet cities and factories.[22]

Prins and his colleagues of the Cambridge University Disarmament Seminar, in noting this, ask whether this should be treated as propagandist rhetoric or a genuine perception of the Soviet position, and they conclude:

> The fact is that the Soviet Union and its allies confront a Western alliance with far greater economic power, with superior technology, and with a greater and more varied deployment of military force around the world.[23]

This fact, if such it be, does not surface on television news at this time. Room is made to comment on the economic ills of the system in the USSR, combined with an emphasis on its military might. ITN put it this way: In a flagging economy there's zero economic growth, lagging technology, and 15% of production spent on defence' (ITN, 22.00, 15.11.82).

One of the reasons given for low economic growth in the Soviet Union might be its military spending. But if the premise of technological backwardness is also endorsed there must be limits as to what the Soviet Union is achieving. The argument of military superiority does not flow easily. Is the Soviet Union superior in computer technology, for example, upon which so much of modern weaponry depends? Again Channel 4 news told us:

> the crisis which erupted in Poland in 1980 leading to the emergence of Solidarity revealed the chronic economic ills of the entire Soviet system.
>
> Channel 4, 19.00, 11.11.82

So the occasion of Mr Brezhnev's death becomes an opportunity to castigate the entire Soviet system. If Soviet television were to report that the debt crisis of Mexico (which is considerably worse than Poland's) reveals the chronic economic ills of the entire capitalist system many in the West would dismiss it as cheap propaganda. This reminds us that facts and observations are routinely put in an interpretative framework; by such means attempts are made to render the world intelligible to us. The perspective of a Soviet empire, ruled by a dictator, emerges in the accounts:

> Leonid Ilyich Brezhnev, arguably the most powerful man in the world, is dead. He'd ruled Russia for eighteen years. For most of that time he was undisputed leader of 260 million people in the Soviet Union and controlled the destiny of 120 million others in Russia's Eastern empire.
>
> BBC1, 21.00, 11.11.82

And later, on the day of the funeral: 'Leonid Brezhnev, ruler of the Soviet empire for nearly two decades, has been buried,' (BBC1, 21.00, 15.11.82).

These sentiments, attitudes and images were deployed to their fullest extent on ITN's description of the funeral, as the following transcript reveals:

> They came to Red Square today to bury Brezhnev and not particularly to praise him. All who were there were there by official invitation. So it is when dictators die. Others were there by orders. They carried him out from the House of Unions where he had lain in state. They mourned him because for eighteen years he had kept the Soviet system intact. The military funeral was meant to confirm his system. A small armoured car drew the gun carriage with his coffin. It was a better ordered funeral than Stalin's and such grief as there was was probably genuine. And the military carried the medals he loved so much. So he came into Red Square, where so often he had been the man of power, only the third Soviet leader to be buried there. The lid was taken off his coffin and he lay, looking up, almost symbolically, at the new rulers who had succeeded him on Lenin's tomb, where he had been eight days before.
> His old friends had come: Indira Gandhi, who spoke her mind, and the clients who didn't: Jaruzelski from Poland, Castro from Cuba and Yasser Arafat. And Andropov spoke. Andropov and the Prime Minister . . . carried the coffin and his widow Victoria, his daughter and his son said goodbye in an older ritual than the atheistic state allowed . . . . It may be that the future will say that Brezhnev's chief achievement was to create nothing but a Soviet navy.
>
> ITN, 22.00, 15.11.82

Besides the account of the funeral itself, we had already been told of the reception at the Kremlin:

> Intent on being there were the Polish puppet, General Jaruzelski . . . and also Cuba's bearded Fidel Castro. Their new master was holding a party. One of the few non-communist faces Soviet viewers would recognise was Mrs Gandhi, with Afghanistan on her mind, and she bowed to Brezhnev's picture.
>
> ITN, 22.00, 15.11.82

The newscaster's description brought together in one passage a mixture of indictment, negative judgements, amateur anthropology, speculative attribution of motives and, in the end, contradiction. The 'older ritual than the state allowed' was manifestly performed at the state funeral. Yet all of this is offered as a direct media statement and leaves any concept of impartiality in shreds. To its credit Channel 4's *The Friday Alternative* gave a sharp critique of this coverage, questioning the use of terms like 'puppet', 'dictator' and 'empire'. It was pointed out that when General Franco died ITN had used language rather differently: 'Franco gave Spaniards the stability that they needed' (quoted on *The Friday Alternative*, 18.11.82).

The Friday Alternative's report appeared to have its effect. When Mr Andropov died in 1984, words like 'puppet' and 'dictator' no longer are used. Instead of 'clients' the news talks of 'allies'. Instead of juxtaposing atheism against religion we are simply told that 'Mr Andropov's wife, dressed in black, followed Russian tradition and kissed her husband for the last time.' In the great volume of words that pours out of news programmes day by day such linguistic changes may seem small. Nevertheless there is some reason to think that they signify a growing debate within news rooms and a commitment by some journalists to reporting news events in a way which does not reinforce the cold war. We will see in the following chapters how this problem is addressed not only by those who make the news but also by those who report it.

SIX

Breaching the peace at Greenham Common

TV news coverage of Greenham Common and the women's peace movement

The women-only peace groups throughout the country, and particularly the women's peace camp at Greenham Common air force, base, form a distinctive part of the British peace movement. We have taken them as a key example not because we believed they were particularly badly treated but because they provide the media as a whole with a reason to feature a series of stories. At the same time they are outside the main stream of sources for news journalism and do not 'fit' well into the routine way in which stories are assembled. In addition the women's movement has its own press which runs parallel to the rest of the media and offers its own account of events. There are also statements issued from other sources such as the police. As such it was important to lay out the range of perspectives which were available on the Greenham issue, to examine how each was treated in news accounts and to suggest why the coverage was as it was.

By the end of 1983 the women's peace movement had become highly visible in the media, the Greenham women in their woolly hats a familiar sight on our screens. BBC1's evening news on Christmas Eve 1983, for example, carried a film report about the women celebrating their third Christmas at the peace camp. We hear about donations arriving at the camp, about the women giving excess Christmas puddings to local children's homes, and a woman describing a campaign of attacks by local vigilantes: by now Greenham Common is well enough established to provide a seasonal news story without a mass demonstration or any arrests. The women even have the status of their own logo appearing behind the newscaster. Although the forms

196

of protest varied, the television reporters seem to become quickly accustomed to them:

> Such scenes have become a familiar sight outside this particular court building.
>
> BBC1, 21.00, 15.2.83

> . . . members of the women's peace camp staging their now familiar demonstration outside all seven of the entrances to the base.
>
> BBC1, 21.00, 31.3.83

> Then they did what they often do: they sat down and started to sing.
>
> BBC1, 17.40, 8.7.83

Greenham Common was not always so well covered on the news. It came out of relative obscurity in December 1982, when 30,000 women were seen on television 'embracing the base'; by then the camp had already been in existence for over sixteen months, virtually ignored by the media (although the fact that it attracted large numbers of women *before* it attracted much media coverage indicates that the camp and the national women's peace movement were already very active). In the earlier days, Greenham Common was not treated so seriously. In a brief report on BBC news of an incident not covered at all by ITN, it was dismissed as a 'so-called peace camp':

> Four women campaigning against nuclear weapons were arrested this afternoon after bailiffs arrived to demolish their *so-called peace camp* at Greenham Common near Newbury in Berkshire.
>
> BBC1, 21.30, 25.5.82

After the first sixteen months the Greenham Common camp did start to receive more coverage, but many events still were unreported. For example, on 25 June 1983, a large number of women arrived and put together a four-mile banner made up of embroidered sections from all over the world. Participants claimed that over 300 women entered the base but this was not covered on TV. Nor did the news report the regular break-ins, with small groups of women breaching security and entering the base, which continued on a daily or weekly basis throughout 1983. Another example of editorial selection was the treatment of International Women's Day for Disarmament on 24 May 1983. As the main BBC1 news reported:

> Thousands of women in Britain have been holding anti-nuclear demonstrations, they've been marking International Women's Day for Disarmament with protests in city centres and outside military bases . . . the organisers claiming that up to one million women had taken part nationwide.
>
> BBC1, 21.00, 24.5.83

Women were shown linking hands around the Ministry of Defence in London, protesting in a Kingston-upon-Thames supermarket, rallying in Glasgow, being dragged out of a military base in Devonport, and lying down in the main road in Bristol. The BBC report, lasting 1 minute 15 seconds, did not invite any of the women involved to explain their protest, and did not tell us about the full number of demonstrations across Britain (over 100) or about the simultaneous action in fourteen other countries; but it at least recognised that thousands of women participating in over 100 co-ordinated anti-nuclear and anit-military protests are making news.

By contrast, the Channel 4 and ITV news bulletins on the same night did not mention the women's actions at all. The absence of coverage of International Women's Day for Disarmament is even more striking since both ITN evening bulletins led with long items on defence and disarmament (discussing Labour's plans to scrap Polaris and the MX vote in Washington). Channel 4 news even appeared to run out of stories for its hour-long bulletin. Before the final item the newscaster is reduced to asking, 'Is there anything else out there?' The reply is a two-minute 'light' report on summer, beginning;

> It was just one of those great ideas that news editors sometimes pass on to reporters: has summer finally arrived?...

> before the closing news summary, 'and that's Channel 4 news tonight, a day when the election campaign was dominated by defence' (Channel 4, 19.00, 24.5.83). ITN and Channel 4 chose to feature only debates within political parties or in the US Congress. So however 'familiar' Greenham Common's songs have become, the TV news can still leave out the women's peace movement.

We analysed the coverage of six women's peace demonstrations that appeared on the news between December 1982 and December 1983, in a total of thirty eight bulletins; and compared it with other reports including some from the women who participated. We found that many features central to the camp were not covered in the news. First, why is the camp all-women? This is a fairly obvious question, asked by many visitors to the camp except apparently TV journalists; it does not seem to be prevalent in news reports and was not explained or raised in any of the coverage in our sample.[1] How is the camp run? The women's peace movement has developed its own form of organising, based on collective decision-making and individual responsibility, run without leaders or any formal structure of bureaucracy. It's an exceptional method, quite distinct from the way CND, for example, or any political party works; but again the TV did not tell us about it. Instead, it gave the impression that the women's peace camp is run by the better-known disarmers of CND:

> At Greenham Common today women peace protesters have started a five-day attempted blockade. It's one of a number of events organised by CND to coincide with US 4th of July celebrations.
>
> BBC2, 19.35, 4.7.83

> Once again demonstrators from all over Britain converged on Greenham Common, and CND's hopes of a big turnout were fully realised.
>
> BBC1, 22.15, 11.12.83

The camp has always been independent from CND, and there are many differences between the two.

A further question is, what exactly is the political protest the camp is making? The broadcasters have grasped the fundamental idea that the camp is opposed to Cruise missiles – although even this is not always made clear. Coverage on the two ITV evening bulletins and BBC2's *Newsnight* of the opening of the five-day blockade at Greenham Common avoided giving any reason at all for the women's action. The full BBC2 report ran:

> Women peace compaigners have been trying without success to prevent workers entering or leaving Greenham Common air base. Police were there is strength and cleared a passage to allow workers in and out. There was one arrest. The protest began today on American Independence Day and is expected to continue until Friday.
>
> BBC2, 22.25, 4.7.83

On ITN the newscaster began: 'At Greenham Common police broke up an attempted blockade by women peace protesters' (ITN, 17.45, 4.7.83); and the correspondent concentrated on how the women were dragged away rather than why they were there. The BBC1 news did state that the protest was against Cruise. This is the full text of a BBC1 report:

> American Independence Day has been marked by more protests *against the siting of Cruise missiles* in Britain. The largest demonstration was at Greenham Common air base. Several dozen women tried to block coaches carrying base workers into the compound. There have been no reports of arrests.
>
> *Correspondent:* There are fewer protestors than previously at Greenham. Too few to succeed in their aim of blockading the base. A large force of police is apparently prepared if many more arrive

> as the five-day protest goes on. The main aim is publicity which helps
> explain the choice of today, American Independence Day.
>
> BBC1, 17.45, 4.7.83

Note the claim that 'the main aim is publicity'. The same point was
made on International Women's Day for Disarmament: 'The women
were more interested in putting across their anti-nuclear message than
in inconveniencing the public'. (BBC1, 21.00, 24.5.83).

The news does not give any publicity to the women's *case*.
Opposition to Cruise is mentioned, and some 'anti-nuclear message' is
referred to, but the women have no chance to explain exactly *why* they
oppose Cruise, *why* they are anti-nuclear. In particular, the broader
anti-militarism of the women's peace movement, and the links they
make between male supremacy, male violence, and nuclear weapons,
are buried. Of course 'putting across their anti-nuclear message' is not
the broadcaster' job; but they are falling down on the job of providing
informative reporting if they cover the demonstrations without
explaining (or allowing the demonstrators to explain) what they are
trying to say.

Moreover the broadcasters *do* find space to give a full and proper
explanation of the official pro-Cruise message. The BBC2 news story
Countdown to Cruise on 9 November 1983 reports on:

1. (50 secs.) Mrs Thatcher's speech in Bonn urging the Soviet Union to
   accept the 'zero option'.
2. (18 secs.) The 24-hour peace camps set up at all the 102 US bases in
   Britain (though the newscaster adds that 'the government says they
   got their sums wrong and there are only 74').
3. (27 secs.) 'The effort of a group of Greenham women to take their
   action to the other side of the Atlantic' with their court case against
   President Reagan for acting illegally in deploying Cruise.
4. (30 secs.) The visit of fourteen Labour MPs to the Greenham peace
   camp "to show solidarity";
5. (10 secs.) The government announcement that policing Greenham
   had cost £1.5 million over the past year;
6. (12 mins. 25 secs.) The correspondent's own story of how 'this
   morning I went down to Greenham to look as it were behind the
   wire'.

This is the background he gives to the decision to site Cruise in
Europe:

> These missiles, planned for Britain, Holland, Belgium, Germany and
> Italy, are intended to tell the Russians: Just in case you are tempted to
> try any attack, the West can now strike back from European soil, at
> selected military targets as far away as Kiev and Minsk, without having

to risk certain annihilation by calling in America's intercontinental strategic system.

So the argument runs, these new Cruise missiles here at Greenham Common will actually make war *less* likely, by demonstrating to the Russians that if they attempted to lop off Western Europe from America, there would actually be a credible and still very demanding Western nuclear response.

Well, there's debate about the cogency of that nuclear strategy.

BBC2, 23.00, 9.11.83

At this point the reporter goes into the technical details of deployment: the training and organisation of missile crews, the composition of missile convoys, the construction of missiles, the timetable for deployment:

> If all goes well, and all these tests are successfully passed, then the 501st will be awarded its Initial Operational Capability, its IOC. By the end of the year, Greenham will be a fully active nuclear weapons base.
>
> BBC2, 23.00, 9.11.83

This is follwed by the use of the silos, and the programme for convoy dispersal. Finally, he interviews a military specialist in a wood – 'an extremely good dispersal area' — about how the missiles would be fired. The official justification for Cruise – resting on the assumption of a Soviet threat ('to tell the Russians: 'Just in case you're tempted to try any attack'), and the deterrence arguements ('these new Cruise missiles here at Greenham will make war *less* likely') – presented in detail as 'news'.

This is scarcely in neutral terms, using such phrases as *'if all goes well* . . . Greenham will be a fully active nuclear weapons base'. Meanwhile, the case *against* Cruise is reduced to the single sentence: 'Well, there's debate about the cogency of that nuclear strategy' – even though the whole item is based on reports of active *opposition* to Cruise. In all, 1 minute and 15 seconds are devoted to the protest, and 12 minutes and 25 seconds to the 'technical background'. If it were not for the peace camp, the Greenham Common base would probably not be news at all, yet the political reasoning of the camp is virtually silenced.

The broadcasters sometimes argue that the business of TV news is to tell us about each day's events, and that 'background' issues and 'in-depth' explanations are properly left to current affairs programmes. However, it could be countered that the huge growth of a women-only movement, its unusual form of organisation, and the developing arguments against Cruise are all integral parts of the news about particular events, essential for allowing the viewers to come to an understanding of them. It is untrue to say that the news always confines itself to reporting merely 'what happened'; it does attempt to explain the background to *some* issues. Consider, for instance, not only the 'in-depth' justification for Cruise missiles on BBC-2 quoted above, but also the normal reporting of Westminster politics, with political correspondents offering their analysis of the arguments and the internal working of the parties.[2] The problem is neither lack of space nor the news/current-affairs split – it is the journalists' assumption that Westminster politics are more important than the politics of grassroots opposition movements like the peace movement. (Which perhaps explains why BBC1 and BBC2's evening reports from Greenham Common on 9 November 1983 both carry an interview with a visiting, male MP, rather than with any of the peace women.) This may seem a 'natural' value judgement to the broadcasters, but it is a value judgement none the less.

Perhaps one of the reasons why the news captures so little of this innovative work is the women's refusal to tailor their activities to the needs of the media. A film about the camp[3] records an incident of a TV journalist having difficulty coping with their obvious lack of respect for professional journalistic practices:

> *Journalist:* For God's sake, I'm doing a piece to camera to put your protest in a logical – in a way that people will understand – and make out that you're making some sense, and you go and clown around in the background and that doesn't do your case any good at all .... The bloody thing won't be used if you're doing cartwheels in the background because it will be distracting.
> *Peace camper:* But why should it be distracting? We're doing all kinds of things here.
> *Journalist:* I know you are, and when we film you doing them that's fine but when I'm doing a piece to camera ... You were deliberately doing cartwheels in the background and you must know – all right I'm sorry I called you a tit.
> *Peace camper:* But there's a way of speaking to people ...
> *Journalist:* I know there's a way of speaking to people – I've got a job to do and my job is completely messed up.

Public opinion and support

Another aspect of the Greenham Common peace camp not really dealt with in the news is the question of how much public support it has for its call that Cruise missiles should not be sited in Britain. There are hints given that, although the peace women themselves are sincere and confident, the television journalists from their position can see that they ought to pay more attention to 'criticism of their cause' and the fact that there is 'no hope':

> They left tonight having spent two days somewhat detached from dispute about and criticism of their cause, but full of confidence in it.
>
> BBC1, 21.00, 13.12.82

> [*Interview question*] Are you surprised by the level of support, given that there seems to be really no hope now of stopping the Cruise missiles?
>
> Channel 4, 19.00, 8.7.83

From this point of view, support would indeed be a surprise. On a BBC World Service radio programme answering listeners' letters, we hear that:

> Our news editor's view is that it's obvious that the Greenham Common women are protesting against the views of the established majority. After all, if the Greenham Common women were supported by the majority, they'd have nothing to protest about, would they?
>
> BBC World Service, 25.11.83

In fact, though, as a range of public opinion polls over a period of time consistently show, more people are opposed to Cruise than in favour of it; and most polls show an absolute majority against Cruise. Here are the results:

Siting Cruise in Britain

	% against	% for	Don't know
April 1981 Marplan for *Guardian*	50	41	9
December 1982 Gallup for *Sanity*	58	31	11
January 1983 Marplan for *Guardian*	61	27	12
January 1983 MORI for *Sunday Times*	54	36	10
February 1983 Gallup for *Daily Telegraph*	54	36	10
May 1983 Marplan for *Guardian*	54	34	12
May 1983 Harris for *Observer*	55	32	13
October 1983 Marplan for *Guardian*	48	37	15
October 1983 MORI for *Sunday Times*	51	43	6
November 1983 NOP for *Daily Mail*	47	37	16
November 1983 Marplan for *Guardian* and *Panorama*	47	42	11

continued

continuation	% against	% for	Don't know
November 1983 Gallup for *Daily Telegraph*	48	41	11
December 1983 Marplan for *Weekend World**	66	28	6

*This poll question was about deployment rather than sitting, as Cruise missiles had arrived by December 1983.

Note Some of the variations in results are attributable to variations in the sampling techniques and in the wording of poll questions, but the underlying trend is clear.

In other words, the repeated demonstrations at Greenham which the TV news (sometimes) covers are in some respects voicing majority opinion, and not the lost cause of a 'detached' few. The fact that the cause commands such widespread support could well be important in the viewers' perception of the Greenham demonstrations, but the TV news almost always fails to mention it.

We found only two cases in our sample when the TV news mentioned public opinion in conjunction with women's peace protests. One was on 9 November 1983, in the coverage on Channel 4 news of the Greenham women's court case and the 102 peace camps across Britain. It was a straightforward report on the latest poll, backed up with animated block graphs on the screen:

> An NOP poll published in this morning's *Daily Mail* shows that 94% of people want dual key control of Cruise missiles and an increasing number of people are against Cruise being deployed at all here. Now only 37% of people favour the deployment of Cruise, while 47% oppose it.
>
> Channel 4, 19.00, 9.11.83

However, none of the ITV or BBC bulletins that evening mentioned the poll. Why was it relevant news at seven o'clock but not at nine, ten or eleven?

The second case was on 11 December 1983, the day following screening of the nuclear war film *The Day After*, and the day that 20–40,000 women encircled the base at Greenham Common. Both ITN evening bulletins used the Marplan poll commissioned by ITV's current affairs programme *Weekend World*, as a link between the opening item on Greenham Common and the item on reactions to the film *The Day After*: 'An opinion poll shows just under two thirds of people in Britain think a nuclear war is becoming more likely' (ITN, 18.30, 21.45, 11.12.83). Public opinion on the likelihood of nuclear war is picked out as the only relevant question. There were other results from the same poll, showing clear majorities against the deployment of Cruise and disapproving of the government's handling of the issue, which were screened on *Weekend World*:

Do you approve of the government's handling of the Cruise missile issue?

Yes   36%
No   52%
Don't know   12%

Should deployment of Cruise missiles go ahead even without arms negotiations talks in progress?

[Arms negotiations talks were *not* in progress at this time.]

Yes   28%
No   66%
Don't know   6%

Weekend World, ITV, 12.00, 11.12.83

These results were not given on the news, although the reports on the poll immediately followed items on the demonstration against Cruise.

So in spite of readily available evidence, TV news here failed to make clear the extent of public support for the campaign against Cruise missiles. It also seems to be confused about the support given to individual demonstrations. During the blockades in July 1983 covering all eight entrances to the base for five days, the peace camp estimated that several thousand women participated altogether, with over 1,000 on the first day (4 July) and over 2,000 on the last day (8 July). There were about 100 women already living at the camp at that time. These are the numbers given on the television news:

4 July			8 July		
ITN	13.00 –	less than 150 70 at one gate*	ITN	13.00 –	no figure
			ITN	17.40 –	about 600
ITN	17.45 –	less than 300	ITN	22.00 –	about 600
ITN	22.00 –	less than 300	C4	19.00 –	a few hundred
C4	19.00 –	about 40 at one gate*	BBC-1	13.00	
				17.40 –	no figures
BBC-1	13.00 –	several dozen	BBC-1	21.00 –	about 600
BBC-1	17.40 –	several dozen	BBC-2	22.50 –	about 600

continued

*These two numbers were given over the same piece of film of the same gate.

continuation

```
BBC-1 21.00- 'too few to
              succeed
              against a
              highly
              organised
              force of
              police'
BBC-2 19.35
       22.25- no figures
```

Even with some cynicism about the participants' own count, the TV news figures, as well as being inconsistent, seem rather low. Even the highest TV figure for 4 July-'less than 300'-would scarcely be enough to maintain the eight blockades; and the BBC's 'several dozen' would be accounted for by the permanent peace campers alone, without the coachloads of supporters. Three of these came from Glasgow alone.

The TV figures also compared oddly with those given in the press. The *Daily Telegraph* (5.7.83) gives no overall total but says that 150 had assembled at a single gate by 6.00 a.m.; and the *Daily Express* says 'only 500 supporters attended', which is over 200 more than the very highest TV figures. Neither paper is particularly supportive of the peace camp.

On 12 December 1983, the nine-mile perimeter fence was ringed with women; the camp estimated over 40,000. The majority of newspapers said 30,000. The BBC conceded 'nearly 30,000', while ITN gave 'some 20,000', differing from the camp's estimate by over 20,000 and once more undercutting even the *Daily Telegraph*, which gave the lowest newspaper figure of 25,000.

Violence

The coverage of violence at Greenham Common is crucial as there are at least two very different perspectives at stake. From the official perspective of the police and military, they do have to use force, but only the minimum necessary to maintain public order; and the military need to keep nuclear weapons in order to deter their use. The 'trouble' therefore stems from demonstrators, particularly the hard core of troublemakers amongst them, many of whom have overstepped their democratic right to protest and have had to be convicted and imprisoned for breaching the peace and other offences. From the women's peace movement's perspective, on the other hand, the camp exists to oppose state violence, specifically the nuclear defence policy, but increasingly drawing in the less extreme levels of 'normal' state use of violence in the military, police and prisons.

One of the camp's own central principles is its commitment to *non-violence*, which the women feel is the basis of their demonstrations. For instance, when the police break up a blockade, the women say that they resist passively instead of struggling physically, to make it clear that the force or violence originates from the police. Here is a typical news description of such an occasion:

> The police returned as more men and supplies turned up and had to get inside. Again the women linked arms and were dragged away, this time encountering slightly rougher handling from the police. But again there were no injuries and no arrests. The road clear, the convoy rushed inside, and the police dispersed at speed to avoid any further confrontation.
>
> ITN, 22.00, 4.7.82

This is very different from the accounts given to us by the women involved in this blockade. They all stress police use of force. According to the participants, 'slightly rougher handling' included women being pulled by the hair or by the neck, having their arms twisted up their backs, and being thrown on top of one another into a ditch. On other occasions women say they have suffered concussion and broken bones at the hands of the police and soldiers. The TV report, while acknowledging the rougher handling, is more from the police point of view: the men and supplies 'had to get inside' (the women felt they 'had to' stop them); there were 'no injuries' reported by the police (the TV journalists did not ask the women if they had been injured); and the police were 'avoiding confrontation'.

The women's non-violence in the face of this is sometimes referred to on the news – 'For the Greenham Common women, it is what they term non-violent direct action' (BBC1, 13.00, 8.7.83) – but their approach is neither explained nor compared with that of the police. There is a contradiction in the coverage here: although the words are deadpan, as in the example above, or the caption below, the *film* shows women being treated roughly, having their hands battered by soldiers with sticks, and mounted police galloping straight for them; so such violence does get some TV exposure. The women at the peace camp have reported other forms of harassment which don't appear on the news, such as soldiers throwing stones through the fence and slashing

"There were scuffles as women were dragged from the roof of one of their vans."   BBC1 21.00 8.7.83

their tents, and strip-searches in police custody. But still the TV news tends to play down the authorities' use of force to counter the women's protest.

The arrival of soldiers to back up police, an important escalation which was headlined in *The Times* ('Greenham Women Face Army', *The Times*, 5.7.83), was not commented on by the TV. The five BBC bulletins and Channel 4 news that day do not mention the Army at all, while on ITN they appear only in passing:

> This Independence Day blockade started forming up long before dawn but not in strong enough numbers to worry a heavy police and Army presence.

> ITN, 17.45, 22.00, 4.7.83

The only time the question of the use of force against the women made a big splash on TV news was when Mr Heseltine announced in Parliament on 1 November 1983 that they could be shot by US servicemen if they ventured inside the final fence around the silos housing the missiles. The stir this caused only underlined the media's general lack of awareness about violence used against peace protesters: the risk of getting shot near nuclear weapons stores had been common knowledge in the peace movement for years. It had even been mentioned in press reports earlier in the year ('Two Greenham women who claimed they got into the base on Wednesday night said they saw notices warning that people went in at their own risk of being shot' –*Guardian*, 26.6.83).

The TV news appears to assumed that a nuclear weapons base is on the whole a peaceful place, disturbed only when crowds of protesters arrive. Thus two reports close with:

> As the demonstrators headed for home, local residents were hoping for some peace and quiet.
>
> BBC1, 21.00, 8.7.83

> Tonight the day of action ended . . . and peace returned to Greenham Common.
>
> BBC1, 22.15, 11.12.83

Violence against women and accusations against the police do not seem to make news; but the story was different when a policeman was injured and the women could be accused. On 11 December 1983 some of the women standing at the Greenham perimeter fence started to rock it rhythmically with their hands, and the fence posts swayed. One of these post hits an unfortunate policeman, who was knocked unconscious. This incident (and three other 'slight injuries') became the focus of the TV reports:

> *Headline:* The Greenham women attack the camp's perimeter fence, nearly sixty are arrested and four policeman are hurt.
> *Reporter:* . . . There were fewer police on the side nearer the missile bunkers, and it was here that the women launched an assault. Inspector Michael Page from Reading was hit on the head by a concrete post. He was unconscious for half and hour, and the crowds delayed an ambulance taking him to hospital. Three other policemen were slightly hurt.
>
> BBC2, 20.35, 11.12.83

> *Newscaster:* Good evening. The Greenham Common peace women today pulled down the perimeter fence at the Berkshire air base during the biggest demonstration since American Cruise missiles arrived last month. 20,000 or more joined the protest, forty-two were arrested. A police inspector was knocked unconscious by a toppling fence post. He is in hospital. Three other police were hurt . . . .
> *Reporter:* The peace protestors came from all over the country . . . . At a gate on the east of the camp, words changed to action as the women made concerted attacks on the perimeter fence. Concrete posts wobbled under the weight. The police inspector was knocked out when one hit him.
>
> ITN, 21.45, 11.12.83

Headline: Greenham under attack again – seventy arrests and policemen are hurt.

Newscaster: A peaceful day of protest by nearly 30,000 demonstrators at the Greenham Common air base in Berkshire turned to violence just before dark . . . . Just after three o'clock the nine-mile perimeter fence was attacked at several points. There were seventy arrests and four policemen were hurt.

Reporter: . . . Elsewhere women protesters were doing their best to tear down the airfield's perimeter fence with their bare hands, and in one or two places almost succeeding. Four policemen were hurt. One, Inspector Michael Page, was knocked out when a concrete post fell on him.

BBC1, 22.15, 11.12.83

BBC1 and 2 did report the women's statement that they regretted the accident; BBC2 added that they 'claimed that one of them had her fingers broken by soldiers', and ITN said that 'two peace women were injured'; but the stress was firmly on the police injuries, which were blamed on violence from the women. The language used to describe the women's actions shows the perspective of the news:

'attack... assault... concerted attacks... attack... turned to violence... tear down'.

This is not how the participants saw their rocking of the fence. Compare the accounts in the women's press:

GREENHAM WOMEN FACE VIOLENT ATTACK
... Soldiers, armed with huge wooden sticks and metal bars reached out across the barbed wire and started bashing women's hands, some had their fingers crippled. A women got entangled in the barbed wire, soldiers pulled her through without allowing her to disentangle herself.

Outwrite, January 1984

The Changing Face Of Greenham
... Hundreds of women were injured by police wrenching women's hands from the fence or soldiers hitting their hands with sticks... women got into the base and were wrapped in barbed wire and beaten up. The soldiers then tied the women to concrete fence posts and masturbated in front of them before letting them go.

Spare Rib, February 1984

Women at the camp reported that seventeen demonstrators were treated in hospital in Newbury that night. They also stated that one of a group of thirty who entered the base was 'kicked unconscious' by MoD police. The TV news did not ask if any women got into the base or if any were hurt. If the broadcasters faced a choice of perspectives on the responsibility for violence at Greenham Common, it is fairly clear which one they adopted.

Balance

> Two very eloquent groups of campaigners.
>
> > BBC1, 21.00, 4.7.83

One of the things that stands out in the expanding TV news coverage of the women's peace movement is the ingenuity of the broadcasters' attempts to find 'balancing' stories, i.e. stories putting the other side of the argument. Sometimes they are provided by straightforward government statements (which may be timed specifically to counter disarmament demonstrations.) On 9 November 1983, when the Greenham women started their case against Reagan in the US courts, and peace camps were set up at all US bases in Britain, the Prime Minister made a speech in Bonn urging the Soviet Union to accept the 'zero option'. All the evening news bulletins linked the two stories together. BBC1's headlines ran:

> No to Cruise – Greenham women go to court in America.
>
> No to the SS-20s — that's my Christmas wish, says Mrs Thatcher.
>
> > BBC1, 21.00, 9.11.83

Announcements by other public figures have also been used. On 4 July 1983, the day of a series of anti-nuclear protests at Greenham Common and elsewhere, a group of trade union leaders held a press conference on the question of the Labour leadership contest, at which Frank Chapple and Terry Duffy underlined their rejection of Labour's policy of unilateral nuclear disarmament. The main ITN news reported this before their item on Greenham Common:

> Electrical and engineering trade union leaders formally rejected unilateral disarmament today . . . . On the other side, the Greenham demonstrators marked American Independence Day with what they called the start of a four-day blockade.

The Greenham report proceeds, without any interviews or statements from the women. At the end we return to Frank Chapple and Terry Duffy, who make speeches to the camera. The framing is complete:

> The supplies and personnel to get this Cruise missile base operational before the end of the year are still getting through. Trade union leaders

who do not support the Labour Party's stance on disarmament declared
their hand.

> ITN, 22.00, 4.7.83

The BBC news also links the two:

> There was criticism too for the Greenham Common anti-nuclear
> protestors. Electricians' leader Frank Chapple said they should thank
> their lucky stars they're living in a society which allows them to
> demonstrate without being put in gaol. American Independence Day
> has been marked by more protests against the siting of Cruise missiles.
>
> BBC1, 17.45

> A group of trade union leaders has said Labour should move away from
> its unilateralist policies . . . . And the electricians' leader Frank Chapple
> had criticism for the Greenham Common protesters. He said they
> should be glad they lived in a society which didn't gaol its dissenters.
> And at Greenham Common today, women peace protesters have
> started a five-day attempted blockade.
>
> BBC2, 19.35

On days when there were no press conferences putting the other side,
the news proved itself able to generate its own balancing stories. For
example, on 15 February 1983, forty-four women went on trial in
Newbury for breaking into the base, while a further sixty broke in but
were not arrested. ITN followed its report on these events at
Greenham Common with a report on another Cruise missile base in
the United States, beginning 'It's easy to love your local missile base',
and using interviews with local residents to show that they were not
worried by Cruise. This was the newscaster's link in the first bulletin:

> Well, one missile base where there's no problem with demonstrators
> and trespassers is Griffiths air base near the town of Rome in New York
> State. Even the proximity of Cruise missiles doesn't worry the local
> population, as John Suchet reports.
>
> ITN, 13.00, 15.3.83

By the evening it was:

> In the United States some communities have learned to live with Cruise
> missiles, at a profit. People in the town of Rome, in New York State, say
> their local missile base has helped the economy.
>
> ITN, 22.00

There was no 'news' in the normal sense in the report from the USA;
the apparent reason for showing it was to 'balance' the women's
protests.

Lady Olga Maitland's organisation, Women and Families for Defence, seems tailor-made for supplying copy to 'balance' news from Greenham Common with a firm pro-Cruise line. It was set up in March 1983 with mainly this in mind – 'We do a lot of counter-activities,' as a spokeswoman in their London office told us. The spokeswoman said it was 'hard to calculate' how many members they have, but quoted 'up to 300' as the largest attendance at any of their rallies. They concentrate their energies on 'being the other point of view' and countering what they perceive as a bias towards CND in the media, particularly television.

The startling success of Women and Families for Defence can be shown by looking at the BBC1 coverage of the blockades at Greenham Common on 4 July. The lunchtime bulletin concentrated straightforwardly on the blockades themselves. This was the newscaster's introduction summarising the film report:

> Women peace protesters have begun a five-day blockade of the Greenham Common air base in Berkshire. They're demonstrating against plans to site American Cruise missiles there. At daybreak several dozen women tried to block coaches carrying base workers into the compound, but police dragged them away.
>
> BBC1, 13.00, 4.7.83

During the afternoon Lady Olga Maitland visited the camp, and after that the whole focus of the news coverage changed. The headline was: 'The nuclear debate in full cry at Greenham Common,' with a short clip showing Lady Olga speaking in front of a singing crowd of peace protesters blockading a gate: 'With American aid NATO has acquired a strength which has made it imperative . . . '). When we come to the item itself, the 180-word description of the blockades given at lunch-time is cut down to 100 words, and the correspondent now continues:

> *Correspondent:* But not all the women at Greenham today were against Cruise missiles in Britain. Lady Olga Maitland and the women for defence were there to make sure of their fair share of the attention and to try and make themselves heard arguing in support of NATO policy.
> *Lady Olga Maitland:* With American aid NATO has acquired a strength which has made it imperative . . . .
> *Correspondent:* There was real dialogue. The discussion was ordered and peaceful.
> *Demonstrator:* As an American I have to say that it is my country that has taken every step in the arms race, and Russia has played catch-up, and historically please get your facts right.

Lady Olga Maitland: It is the Russians all the way have led the arms race.

Demonstrator: That's not true.

Correspondent: But at the end of a long hot day, no sign that two very eloquent groups of campaigners had narrowed the difference between them in the nuclear debate.

BBC1, 21.00, 4.7.83

A story about a mass protest has been transformed into an 'ordered dialogue' between 'two very eloquent groups of campaigners', with the small pressure group Women and Families for Defence presented as equivalent to the women's peace movement. The concept of 'balance' is operated within a structure of power and access, which the broadcasters accede to in practice, but are unwilling to acknowledge.

SEVEN

Say it with Figures: Zero Option and START

How did television news deal with the 'numbers game', in relation to the announcements of zero option and START? We suggest that, although there was an awareness of a propaganda battle being waged between the superpowers (just as this was recognised later in relation to the interim zero option), there are certain matters which remain relatively unexamined. There is a sense in which journalists are at risk by trying to work through frames of reference which others have set for them.

There are of course basic problems as to the reliability of data. Given the security and propaganda elements involved, getting at the facts is by no means a straightforward matter. In practice we are dealing with estimates and approximations. Behind the apparently objective facts are a variety of assumptions and evaluations. In this sense the figures are a social construction. It can help to know something about the sources from which the figures are derived. In the main these sources are not given on television news, although, as we shall see, some attempt is made to indicte that there are different points of view.

Built into the presentation of arms control formulations such as 'zero option' or START is the notion that parity is a prerequisite for effective agreements and indeed by extension, once that can be agreed, the superpowers can 'build down'. In practice this concept of parity does not turn out to be strictly defined in nuclear terms. The assumption that the Soviet Union has a superiority in conventional weapons can also be used for NATO to claim the need for nuclear weapons to offset this alleged disadvantage. This is an assumption which merits investigation in its own right but it does not really surface in the television news accounts. It does of course link in with a more general assumption of the Soviet threat, with its scenario of an invasion

215

of Western Europe, and also lies behind NATO's doctrine of willingness to be the first to use nuclear weapons in circumstances which have never been made entirely clear.

Parity, then, cannot strictly mean comparing like with like. Moreover even when we turn to nuclear weapons, not only are there different force dispostitions between the Soviet Union and the United States, as between land, sea and air-based weapons systems, but distinctions such as strategic significance for the Soviet Union, even if the West chooses to label them intermediate weapons.

There is, however, an even more fundamental point. There are authoritative statements which question the connection between arms control, leading to arms reductions, and the principle of parity. Daniel Frei's recent study, *Risks of Unintentional Nuclear War*, argues that the assessment of strategic balance is open to many interpretations because the respective forces contain a variety of weapons with different characteristics and performance parameters. Moreover, there are inherent uncertainties as to how the command, control and communications systems of each side would perform in time of war. Consequently, he suggests, conclusions about parity or relative superiority are impossible to make with any degree of confidence. Given that discussions about superiority, parity or equivalence do not rest upon any kind of generally acknowledged measure for strategic forces, Frei notes that in practice selective information can be presented to an audience as 'proof' of one's own inferiority in order to stimulate a build-up. But if both sides accuse the other of aspiring to superiority that will become the occasion for modernisation and adding to the existing stockpile.[1]

The point was made, if anything more strongly, in the Report of the Secretary General of the United Nations: *Nuclear Weapons*. Instead of the principle of parity serving as a basis for stability in arms control, it is argued that the reverse is the case. We quote from this report since it is a point of view not recognised in any developed way by television news reports:

> Peace resting on the system of deterrence has been said to require approximate parity or balance between the forces of the States involved. The view is held that parity ceases to exist if one side acquires a 'first-strike' capability, i.e. the capacity to deliver a nuclear strike against the other without risking an intolerable reprisal. In these conditions the general fear is that deterrence can or may fail. Yet the concept of parity rests on a situation which is inherently difficult to evaluate. Each super-power's nuclear arsenal consists of many components of different size,

function and importance. Since each of these components may be subject to constant technological development on both sides, but not always simultaneously, parity is a process whose equilibrium must continuously be re-established. Hence, the notion of balance is then, by definition, almost unstable. In addition, one cannot ignore the psychological factors in the assessment of mutual destruction capabilities. The problems connected with establishing parity are illustrated by the introduction of the broader concept of 'essential equivalence', which allows for asymmetries in the respective strategic arsenals.[2]

We can see that the above quotation draws attention to the connection made between the principle of parity and the concept of deterrence. In *Defended to Death,* Gwyn Prins and his colleagues argue that this has several consequences. It assumes that balance of force should be interpreted as balance of numbers. This is not so since deterrence in essence calls for a sufficient threat of unacceptable damage and that can lead to concepts of minimum deterrence not parity. More nuclear weapons do not therefore mean more security. In addition it leaves out of the discussion any questioning of the nature of deterrence theory itself. So, by concentrating on technical questions of numbers, the perspectives of the politicians are correspondingly reduced, with very unfortunate consequences:

> ... crucially, it made accurate and detailed assessment of the adversary's capabilities of central importance: analysis on the assumption of the 'worst case' weakened the incentive to understand Soviet intentions, and in the situation of the Cold War it was not difficult to assume that these were as horrendous as required. 'Intentions' were conflated with 'capabilities' and were taken for all practical purposes to be the same.[3]

If we read the following account of what was covered by television news concerning zero option and START, we will observe that the questions and assumptions raised in this introduction are scarcely identified. Consequently the news, whilst showing some awareness of the propaganda battle, found it difficult to contextualise the issues in a way that was both comprehensible and sceptical.

TV news and President Reagan's zero option

On 18th November 1981, President Reagan gave a press conference to announce his zero option proposal. This preceded the Geneva arms control talks on what are variously called intermediate or theatre nuclear weapons. These began on 30 November 1981. On both these days news programmes on BBC and ITN dealt with aspects of these proposals. We want to look particularly at the numbers which were utilised.

On the day of the press conference, ITN anticipated the announcement with a piece to camera by the defence correspondent. He cites the United States view that there are now 250 *missiles* with a total of 750 *warheads* targeted on Western Europe. The US claimed this represented a dramatic build-up on the Soviet side. Under a picture of President Reagan is the message: 'No SS-20s/No Cruise'. This of course is an oversimplification of the zero option since it doesn't mention Soviet SS-4s and -5s nor Pershing II missiles on the US side, although they are referred to in the correspondent's statement. He then refers to the Russian claim, based on a statement attributed to President Brezhnev, that the Soviets have 975 nuclear *weapons* aimed at Western Europe as against NATO's 986 targeted on Eastern Europe. This is set out on a map of Europe and naturally gives the impression of rough parity. The NATO figure here is said to include British and French submarine-launched missiles, American F111 bombers and British Vulcan bombers. He notes the Soviet argument that the deployment of 500 *Cruise missiles* (no mentione here of Pershing II's) would tilt the balance very much against them. Against this, says the correspondent, is the US view that this doesn't include Soviet bombers like the Backfire. After that 'the argument becomes desperately complicated'. He suggests that the Soviets are unlikely to talk about *missiles* in isolation.

We can see in this account an awareness of the difference between the Soviets and the Americans, and the correspondent conveys the Soviet view that parity already exists at this level of weaponry. The numbers are presented in a context which makes inferences about Soviet and US intentions. The US, we are told, wants to calm growing fears in Europe about the risks of nuclear war and in particular the protests of the European peace movement. The Russians, it is suggested, may want to spin the talks out in the hope that the democratic processes in Western Europe objecting to deployment will give them what they want. At the same time we can see that the numbers cited move from missiles to warheads to weapons without any discussion of the significance of these categories to the wider debate. Nor is there any mention of the issues of first use NATO doctrine, the counter-force capabilities of the Cruise and Pershing II or the Soviet view that these are strategic weapons since they can hit the Soviet Union.

On the same day *News at Ten* reported the press conference and the fact that the Russians had dismissed the offer as a propaganda exercise. The colour chart used by President Reagan, entitled 'Balance of Comparable US and Soviet Intermediate Range Nuclear Forces' was shown in close-up.

The comparison given is between the United States and the Soviet Union using the years 1975 and 1981 as the data base; the unit of counting is *delivery vehicles*. The intended effect of this chart, borne out by the President's words, is that the Soviets have an overwhelming superiority and the US simply wishes to redress the balance. A TASS news agency report is quoted. 'To the Russians,' says the correspondent, 'it seems that President Reagan is asking them to remove about 1,000 *warheads* while NATO keeps its forces as they are.' This figure, one presumes, is referencing the 975 nuclear *weapons* cited on *News at One*.

On 30 November *News at Ten* came back to the matter when the Geneva talks opened. This time we are told, with illustrative maps, that there are 5,000 intercontinental *missiles* based on land or sea. How

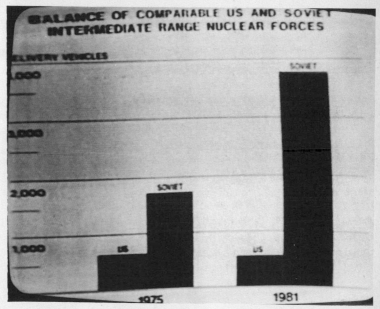

ITN 22.00 18.11.81

many belong to the Soviet Union and how many to the USA is not made clear. We are then told there are 10,000 nuclear *weapons* in Europe which are not controlled by any treaties. These are said to consist of shells at the lowest level, aircraft at the next level up and at the highest level land-based *long-range missiles* which are 'nearly all Russian'. The accompanying map with this information naturally conveys an imbalance.

There is then claimed to be an imbalance at the top of the hierarchy. These missiles, it is said, are more likely to reach their targets than any aircraft. So the US proposal is to install 572 new Cruise *missiles* 'to balance the Russian threat,' to be placed in five NATO countries including Britain, but to seek a new treaty based on the US offer sloganised under a picture of President Reagan: 'No Cruise if Russia dismantles 600 *missiles*'. This is followed by a picture of President Brezhnev with the caption: 'Wants eradication of 100s of *weapons*. The point is then made that the US wants to talk about *missiles* only, whilst the Soviet Union will want to discuss European-based bombers. General Haig is then filmed saying that the deployment of the *missiles* will offset the Soviet advantage.

Where did the figure of 600 *missiles* come from? In the earlier bulletin a figure of 250 *missiles* was cited, as we have seen.

Again, we can see that the correspondent does reference differences between the United States and the Soviet Union as to what should be included. None the less, we are given an account of a weapons heirarchy from intercontinental through to land-based long-range *missiles,* to *aircraft* and down to nuclear *shells.* The inference is that there should be balance at each level in order to ensure security. This is the taken-for-granted assumption, even while it is recognised tht there might be some argument over what to count.

There are, of course, those who question whether such a concept of balance is necessary to ensure security. In addition there is another feature which the Soviets see as asymmetrical and working to their disadvantge. The Soviet Union's intermediate-range missiles (called long-range on the ITN bulletin) cannot reach the USA, whereas all forward-based United States nuclear systems have direct strategic meaning for the Soviet Union since they are capable of striking its territory. In the Soviet view this already gives the United States an important strategic advantage.[4]

Let us turn now to BBC coverage. The Reagan press conference was reported on the early evening bulletin on BBC1. The Americans, it was reported, would cancel their intended deployment of 572 Cruise and

Pershing 11 *missiles* in Western Europe if the Soviet Union removed its
SS-4, SS-5 and SS-20 *missiles*. Martin Bell reported that 'the
President countered the Soviet claim that a rough equivalence in their
weapons exist'. Here the chart comparing the two countries' *delivery
systems* was shown, as on the ITN bulletin. This, said the reporter, was
'the President's peace offensive'. This was followed by a report from
the Moscow correspondent who said, 'Bearing in mind its assiduously
cultivated Soviet peacemaking image, they can't afford a peremptory
dismissal of the proposal.' This did not sit easily with the TASS report
cited by ITN. However, whilst the diplomatic and political aspects of
the proposal were discussed on the bulletin no other figures were used.
Hence there was no discussion of the significance, capabilities or
purposes of the weapons as such.

However, a *Nationwide* programme followed the matter up. Zero
option was described as 'one way of solving the worrying imbalance
between Soviet and Western medium range missiles' by the presenter.
The distinction was drawn between strategic, theatre and tactical
nuclear weapons. The issue was presented as dealing solely with
theatre weapons. Strategic weapons are defined as intercontinental –
those which can reach the Soviet Union and the USA respectively,
which again misses the point that the Soviets regard US forward-
based systems as strategic. We are then given a run-down of the
European theatre, which reads as follows:

West		East	
Cruise	464	SS20	350+
Pershing	108	SS4/5	380

This gives a total of 572 *missiles* for the West and 730+ for the East.
However, the 350 figure is speculative since a voice-over tells us that
the actual figure is 250, which would give a total of 630 *missiles*. So on
the Soviet side of the account we are now in receipt of four different
missile figures, from three news bulletins and *Nationwide:* 250, 600,
630, 730+. There was a discussion between Dr G. Treverton, an
American, at the International Institute of Strategic Studies, and
Vladimir Pozner, a Moscow commentator. In the course of
this, Pozner claimed that the adoption of zero option would leave
NATO with a two-to-one advantage.

The most detailed attempt to deal with the arithmetic of zero option
was on *Newsnight,* 30 November. The point was made at the beginning
that the issue was 'frighteningly complex'. The complexity was like
that of a chess game but with each side trying to play be different rules.

The matter was pursued by looking first at the US view, then the Soviet view and finally the US reply. The maps and graphics were accompanied by running totals as additional weapons or warheads were noted. It proceeds as follows.

The US view. There are 175 SS-20s facing Europe (this is a new figure for us). There are 'hundreds more' older SS-4s and -5s also facing Europe, making a total, with the SS-20s, of 525. (Compare this with the 250, 600, 630, 730 noted above.) Therefore the Americans will introduce 572 missiles into Europe. However, as the older SS-4s and -5s begin to be phased out over the next eight years it is expected that the number will go down from 525 to 400. But what should actually be counted are *warheads* not *missiles*, which would bring the Soviet total to 1,200 against 572 missiles with one warhead each on the US side. Therefore go for zero option and remove all of these on both sides, or in the US case don't go ahead with deployment if the Soviet missiles are removed.

The Soviet view. We are told that they don't dispute the 528 *missiles* on their side. This is mildly surprising since the number cited above was 525. Nor do they dispute the 400 figure after phasing out older systems. However, on the West's side they count 170 FIII bombers based in Britain and West Germany and 530 missiles based on carriers and land capable of reaching the USSR. This makes 700. To this running total is added 120 missiles based on Polaris submarines and British Vulcan bombers. Finally, to the 820 is added 135 French missiles based on air, land and sea and 72 missiles already in West Germany with dual key arrangements. *Newsnight* gives total as 1,000 although it is actually 1,007. If to our 400 you add in Soviet long-range bombers, the Russians say, this still comes to only 920 and therefore the West has an advantage before the deployment of the new missiles.

The US Reply. Against the soviet figure of 920 the appropriate figure on the West side is 693. (This figure comes out of nowhere in relation to what has gone before and one assumes it is an adjustment to the 700.) However, if the Soviets put a figure of 1,000 on the West side then the 920 is no longer the correct figure. If all comparable medium-range missiles are added the Soviet total is 2,500 according to the US. This advantage attributed to the Soviets is not spelled out. But the final stage in the argument is to suggest that both sides go back to

BBC2 *Newsnight* 30.11.81

counting land-based intermediate missiles only.

As this count proceeded it became very difficult to tell whether missiles, warheads, weapon systems or delivery vehicles were being counted. A Soviet contributor to the programme, Vitalay Kobysh, said that he didn't know how many years it would take to agree to the same figures. The American, Paul Warnke, a former arms control negotiator, suggested that the 'entire concept of a Euro-strategic balance makes no logical sense to me. We now have 10.000 warheads with which we can destroy every Soviet target several times.' This calls into question the whole issue of the significance of what was being counted. Figures can give a spurious concreteness to what is at issue. We can easily forget that any one of these warheads, whether called intermediate or strategic, carries a bomb many times more destructive than the Hiroshima bomb. Hence, unless the question is raised as to the circumstances in which we would actually use such weapons, the preoccupation with arithmetic may obscure rather than clarify what is at stake.

Figures, then, are not 'hard facts' which, as it were, speak for themselves. Thomas J. Hirschfield, a former US arms control official, made the point very well in his comment on the INF talks:

> Both parties differ on what is to be negotiated away, and therefore what the balance is. The United States says that the Soviets lead six to one – in intermediate range launchers. By adding systems of Allies to the US count and dropping certain systems from their own side, the Soviets try to show balance – 986 US versus 975 Soviet. Depending on what weapons are counted, and whose, one perceives superiority or rough balance. These are of course essentially political calculations.[5]

TV news and President Reagan's START proposals

> The START negotiations opened in June 1982 with a US proposal to reduce missile warheads to 5,000 for each side (from current levels of about 7,000) with a distinct ceiling of 850 for ICBM and SLBM launchers (which would require a cut of two thirds for the Soviet Union and about one half for the United States). A further limitation provided for only half (2,500) of the total warheads being placed on land-based missiles. This position was widely viewed as being patently one-sided, in terms of cutting Soviet numbers more than the United States, shifting the emphasis on to sea-based systems with which the Soviet Union feels less comfortable, and excluding areas of US advantage such as bombers and air- and sea-launched missiles.[6]

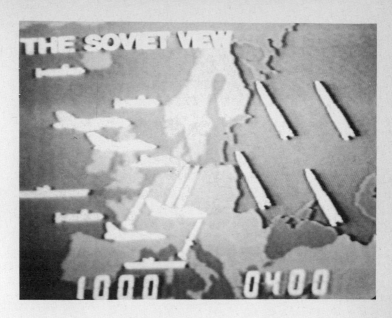

BBC2 *Newsnight* 30.11.81

ITN reported the opening of START (Strategic Arms Reduction Talks) in Geneva on 29 June. It was explained that these had to do with heavyweight nuclear weapons, which the superpowers had aimed at each other, and not the shorter-range weapons, which were the subject of separate negotiations. In a sequence of three world maps we were told that (1) both sides had thousands of missiles, (2) thousands based on land, thousands on submarines and hundreds carried by aircrafts and (3) very roughly each side had 7,500 *warheads*.

No source was given for these figures but we were reminded that each warhead is bigger than that used at Hiroshima. It is suggested that counting missiles now means less than counting warheads. The exposition then proceeds with the aid of two unnumbered bar charts. These suggest that the USA has an advantage in land-based missiles. It is said that land-based missiles are more accurate whereas sea-based missiles are less vulnerable. The second chart then depicts a 'strategic missile balance' in which the relative advantages are traded to make for equality across the board.

We are then told that Russia has 70% of its warheads based on land and 20% in submarines. The US, it is said, have 20% based on land and

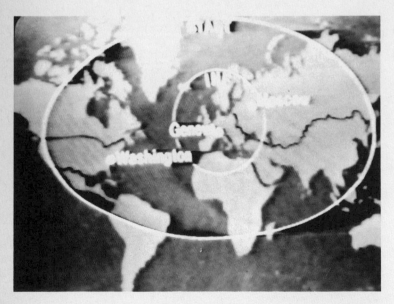

BBC1 21.00 29.6.82

50% based on submarines. The US proposal is for each side to reduce it's arsenal by a third to 5,000 each with only a half of these being based on land. By way of a comment it is reported that Russia thinks the land cutback is unfair and has called for a freeze on all new developments, but the USA thinks a freeze would preserve a Russian advantage. Clearly Russia's 70% and the US's 20% for land-based warheads are relevant here if we are working from a figure of 7,500 to begin with on each side. What is not said is that only 10% of the Russian total is unaccounted for, whereas 30% of the US total is not labelled. These figures must refer to air-based missiles, which effectively are not discussed. A similar presentation is later made on *News at Ten* except that the reference to hundreds and thousands of missiles is left out from the exposition accompanying the maps, and an additional diagram is introduced to illustrate the fact that some missiles can have as many as ten warheads. The reference to the Soviet objection that the proposal is unfair since it emphasises land-based missiles is edited out. This means that the inferences from the tabulated data are harder to draw.

The account on BBC1 begins with a map that differentiates between INF and START negotiations. The long-range weapons are those which can reach the homelands of each superpower from the other's country. Medium-range weapons are those which are targeted on Europe. This fails to identify the ambiguity of the distinction between theatre and strategic weapons. Asymmetry exists, as we have seen, because medium-range weapons can reach Russia but not the United States.

We are then given the following illustrated comparison of ICBM warheads:

1972	USA	1,500	1982	USA	2,100
	USSR	1,300		USSR	5,960

No source is given for these figures but we should note that they are land-based missiles. From this the conclusion is drawn that the Soviets have a three-to-one advantage. One reason for this is said to be that whereas the US Minuteman has only three warheads, missiles like the SS-18 can carry up to thirty. The US proposal is said to be that there should be a reduction of at least a third below current levels. This is rather untidily put since this seems to refer to ICBM warheads which are land-based. Yet we are then told that this would still leave 5,000 strategic warheads on each side – 'enough to destroy the world many times over'. This of course refers to air- and sea-based systems as well as land-based and no appreciation is given of the differential force structures between East and West. Neither is any account given of the theory of deterrence which lies behind the numbers discussed. That is taken for granted.

ITN and BBC then present somewhat different sets of figures. ITN by mentioning 7,500 warheads on each side suggests an existing parity, whilst partially admitting the different force compositions as between land, sea and air of the two sides. BBC with its focus on ICBMs tends to present the matter in terms of a Soviet advantage. There is more to be said about the 7,500 figure, which was in fact put forward by the US. McMahan has noted:

> This was curious, since official sources had previously cited a figure of 9,000 strategic warheads for the US and between 7,000 and 8,000 for the Soviet Union. The explanation behind this discrepancy is that the Administration's proposal, and therefore its figure for the total number of warheads, covered only ballistic-missile warheads, and excluded warheads carried by strategic bombers–though, echoing official pronouncements, the press often reported that the proposal called for reductions in 'strategic warheads'. The fact that the proposal simply ignored warheads carried by strategic bombers is significant: for that is an area in which the US enjoys a large advantage over the Soviet Union – one which is increasing and will continue to increase as the US equips more of its B52s with Cruise missiles, and begins to deploy B-1 and stealth bombers also armed with Cruise missiles.[7]

This is presumable why the ITN correspondent had difficulty locating the air-based missiles in the exposition and why, in effect, he left the out.

The figures cited by McMahan for strategic warheads are roughly approximated in the *SIPRI Yearbook* (1983):

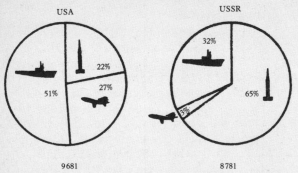

At the same time, the percentages given as between land, sea and air forces' warheads call for some adjustment to the figures used by ITN, but they are of the same order of magnitude. As the SIPRI account properly reminds us:

> The composition and characteristics of the strategic nuclear forces of the United States and the Soviet Union differ widely, reflecting the divergent historical, technological and geostrategic factors that have influenced their development.[8]

EIGHT

Talking of Peace: UN Special Session on Disarmament 1982

In 1978, at the end of the first UN Special Session on Disarmament (SSDI), a Final Document was agreed by the General Assembly. Among its clauses in the Declaration we find the following:

> Enduring international peace and security cannot be built on the accumulation of weaponry by military alliances nor be sustained by a precarious balance of deterrence or doctrines of strategic superiority. Genuine and lasting peace can only be created through the effective implementation of the security system provided for in the Charter of the United Nations and the speedy and substantial reduction of arms and armed forces, by internationl agreement and mutual example, leading ultimately to general and complete disarmament under effective international control. At the same time, the causes of the arms race and threats to peace must be reduced and to this end effective action should be taken to elimate tensions and disputes by peaceful means.[1]

Later, in two stark sentences, the Declaration states:

> Removing the threat of a world war – a nuclear war – is the most acute and urgent task of the present day. Mankind is confronted with a choice: we must halt the arms race and proceed to disarmament or face annihilation.[2]

Since the British government approved this document it is reasonable to suggest that it should be of more than passing interest to the British people, as it no doubt should be to the peoples of other nations who likewise endorsed it. When the 1982 Special Session on Disarmament (SSD2) began, this could have been an occasion for considering how far governments have adhered to this view and what has been done constructively in the field of disarmament, given the sense of urgency and crisis that pervaded the 1978 session. In the case of Britian, for example, we might legitimately enquire why it has held on to its doctrine of deterrence despite its declaration. Why has it extended its nuclear weapons programme notably with its commitment to install the Trident weapons system? In other words, 1982 with the advent of SSD2 could have been viewed as a time of evaluation and critique in Britain and of course in other countries, notably the nuclear powers.

An alternative perspective would be to draw attention to the gap between words and actions on the part of the international community and effectively write the event off as a waste of time. This is what tended to happen on British television news. The report of the opening of the session given on BBC1 on 7 June told us that 'on past performances its expectations of success are not good'. The reporter in New York says: 'The first session was held four years ago and resulted in nothing but a lot of speeches. It will be the same this time.' He points to the impotence of the UN to achieve ceasefires in the Lebanon and the Falklands and concludes: 'If the last session was anything to go by world leaders will stand and make their pleas for arms control and their governments will continue to rearm.' If we happen to agree with this judgement we might describe it as reporting without illusions. As far as news values are concerned, however, it still leaves a choice. The media could use its influence to put world leaders under close scrutiny in an attempt to make them more accountable for the gap between their words and actions. This could raise the level of public awareness of what is going on and what is at stake. Or the event could be dismissed with a metaphorical shrug of the shoulders. This is what tended to happen.

The low expectations at the outset were followed at the end of the session with a statement that emphasised disappointments:

> The Special UN Session on Disarmament has ended – with an admission of defeat after failing to produce a comprehensive programme for arms reduction and control. Delegates agreed no progress had been made since the last special session four years ago – and they made no effort to hide their disappointment at failure.
>
> BBC1, 10.6.82

This statement makes no reference to the inauguration of a world disarmament campaign which, however modest, was a positive outcome. Moreover, since, as we shall show, coverage was so sparse, there was no basis for evaluating what had taken place, what the problems were and what the crucial areas of disagreement were. Given the overwhelming importance of the topic it could be argued that we need to know the reasons for failure (if such was the case) as well as the success stories.

ITN, whose coverage of the event was more sparse than the BBC's, adopted a similar position. On the lunchtime bulletin of 17 June, in what was only the channel's second reference to the event, the newscaster introduces the subject in an oddly casual fashion, involving the use of slang: 'In New York, a special session at the United Nations General Assembly on nuclear disarmament, *known, I kid you not, as SOD,* is now in its second week.' The use of the acronym to convey a swear word is a trivialising gesture. Since the initials for the conference were SSD2 it is unnecessarily confusing, indeed misleading. The diplomatic correspondent takes up the story and concludes:

> The theatre and publicity generated by these events encourage high expectations of dramatic results. That's unfortunate because there won't be. There's been a lot of rhetoric here but the real work about arms control is not going on at the United Nations at this time. And long after President Reagan has come and gone the dimension of the intensive public debate about disarmament and arms limitations will have changed very little if at all.

There was some difference in coverage between the BBC and ITN. In particular the BBC covered the peace demonstrations. On the opening day of the session there was a parade past the UN building and then on to a rally in Central Park, New York. With hundreds of thousands participating it provided evidence of the growth of the peace movement in the United States and was described by the organisers as the biggest rally ever in the history of the United States. It was not featured at all on ITN. The BBC also covered the subsequent anti-nuclear protest which attempted to blockade the diplomatic missions of the five nuclear powers. Given that hundreds of demonstrators were arrested (numbers given on bulletins varied) and that the then West German Chancellor, Helmut Schmidt, had said in his speech that day that governments could not brush aside the worldwide groundswell in support of disarmament, but should think of it as a motivating force, ITN's lack of coverage is noteworthy. The BBC's correspondent in New York gave a sympathetic account of both events:

> From early this morning in tens of thousands the demonstrators were coiled around the streets near the United Nations on the east side of Manhattan. New York loves a parade and this was a parade. Led by some spectacular street theatre, masks, costumes, floats and streamers and the symbols of peace on stilts. Not everyone was in favour but the small group of counter-demonstrators supporting a strong nuclear

defence for the United States was in a very small minority. The 5,000 police on duty have had little to do so far but watch the passing show. The marchers are on their way to Central Park for a gathering of up to half a million people intended to show to the administration and to the world the strength of the anti-nuclear movement in the United States. This rally was billed as the biggest ever in the history of the United States. With the final figures not yet in it is hard to know whether it has achieved that. But it is huge. It is also peaceful, even downright good humoured, and has taken this city by storm.

BBC1, 19.10, 12.6,82

1500 New York City policemen stood between the demonstrators and the diplomatic missions they were trying to blockade. The scene outside the British mission was typical. The warnings were followed by arrests. A hundred of them here and eight hundred altogether in the first two hours of the protest. By far the largest number, more than four hundred, had volunteered for the blockade of the American mission across the road from the main UN building. Mostly their protest was non-violent. Aside from a few misunderstandings the police also used as little force as possible. Attempts to storm the barricades and get through to the American mission were bound to fail and did so. Against appearances there were no serious injuries. The demonstrators did not succeed in their primary objective of stopping the work of the diplomatic missions but it did draw attention to itself as a serious political protest and many of the people taking part made it clear they will be back to try again just as soon as they are at liberty to do so.

BBC1, 17.40, 14.6.82

Three days later ITN does make a retrospective reference to the peace movement. Indeed, together with the pledge on the part of the Soviet Union at the UN session not to be the first to use nuclear weapons in any war, it was cited by the correspondent as a factor that President Reagan would be compelled to take into consideration in giving his speech. Despite this the overall mood of the commentator is pessimistic as we have noted. ITN did not report, as the BBC did, that on the same day as President Reagan delivered his speech, Senator Edward Kennedy called for a nuclear weapons freeze:

> But people everywhere are speaking out against a nuclear arms race that could threaten the survival of the human race. In 1982 the Earth itself is an endangered species. Let no one doubt the futility of this fateful competition. Neither the United States nor the Soviet Union will ever permit the other to secure nuclear superiority. Each nation wil match the other bomb for bomb, missile for missile, step for step on an accelerating treadmill that will finally carry us across the nuclear brink. Balanced precariously at the edge of that brink, with the stark choice, may be existence or extinction. The two great powers at long last must

spend less time preparing for a nuclear war and more time for preventing one.

This statement appeared on a lunchtime bulletin but not on the main evening bulletins where the attention was given to the Reagan speech.

Given the prevailing news attitude that 'it won't change anything', we can more readily understand that from 7 June–10 June, coverage on all three channels occurred only on 15, 17, 18 and 23 June. After 23 June, when the British Prime Minister spoke at the session, apart from a *News Review* programme which referred back to that speech on 27 June, there was no further coverage of the event until the final statement about how disappointing it had all been.

As far as the speeches to the Special Session were concerned, only five were reported on British television: Herr Schmidt, West Germany; Mr Gromyko, Soviet Union; Mr Begin, Israel; President Reagan, USA; and Mrs Thatcher, United Kingdom. Only the last three were quoted, not Mr Gromyko's own speech which, incidentally, was one of the longest given to the conference.

This means that none of the seventy-six representatives of Third World or non-aligned countries were heard; the heads of state of Denmark, Finland, Eire, Japan, Norway, Sweden, Italy and Yugoslavia went unreported; not one of the speeches from non-governmental organisations, e.g. CND and WCC, was mentioned. Consequently speeches by figures of international stature such as Helder Camara, Sean McBride, Lord Noel Baker, Philip Potter and Rear Admiral Gene La Rocque were thought not to be newsworthy. The significant absences tell us as much about news values sometimes as the content.

If we look at the way the reported speeches were handled on television, we can see something about the editing process. The Begin speech was delivered in the midst of the Lebanon crisis and the film of the speech drew attention to the large number of delegates who stayed away or walked out when he spoke. In the case of the Reagan speech, first note the lead into the speech:

President Reagan has accused the Soviet Union of pursuing policies of tyranny and repression and repression backed up by the biggest arms build-up in history.

BBC1, 17.40, 17.6.82

President Reagan has accused Russia of pursuing a programme of aggression, repression and atrocities backed up by the biggest arms build-up in history.

ITN, 17.45, 17.6.82

> President Reagan has accused Russia of aggression, repression, tyranny and atrocities in its actions round the world.... President Reagan said the Soviet Union had embarked on violence supported by the biggest arms build-up in history.
>
> ITN, 22.15, 17.6.82

These sledgehammer openings compete with each other as to how many hostile words they can pump out. Only one late-night bulletin indicated another possible way into the story: President Reagan ignored a Soviet challenge to renounce the first use of nuclear weapons' (*Newsnight*, BBC2, 22.25).

The second point is this. Although there is some variation on the cutting and length of the extract, the direct quotes all include the following:

> Soviet aggression and support for violence around the world have eroded the confidence needed for arms negotiations. While we exercise unilateral restraints they've forged ahead and today possess nuclear and conventional forces far in excess of an adequate deterrent capability. Soviet oppression is not limited to the countries they invade. At the very time the Soviet Union is trying to manipulate the peace movement in the West it is stifling a budding peace movement at home.

Apart from one or two commentators indicating that the speech was rather hawkish, that is all we heard. This means that we were offered a series of disputable assertions and no indication at all as to what the USA was constructively proposing to do about world disarmament. Yet for all the rhetoric of the above passage there were parts of the speech in which proposals were made. The President mentioned four points as an agenda for peace: the elimination of land-based intermediate missiles, a one-third reduction in strategic ballistic missile warheads, a substantial reduction in NATO and Warsaw Pact ground and air forces, and new safeguards to reduce the risk of accidental war. Whatever the merits or prospects for such proposals, they were made. But they were not reported. Since we heard none of this nor one word of Mr Gromyko's speech we were in no position to judge how far the two great powers had found any point of meeting at all beyond the rhetoric.

If we turn now to the British Prime Minister's speech it is to note first of all that while a good deal of attention was given to the visit, the quoted speech itself was edited down to versions of between three and seven sentences on the bulletin. In order to show something of the editing process, we give two examples in parallel:

BBC, 17.40

Thatcher Mr President, the message I bring is practical and realistic. It's the message of a country determined to preserve and spread the values by which we live. It contains not much comfort for those who seek a a quiet life for themselves at the expense of the freedom of others. Nor to those who wish to impose their will by force. We believe that wars are caused not by armaments but by the ambitions of aggressors and that what tempts them is the prospect of easy advantage and quick victory. We believe that the best safeguard of peace lies not only in a just cause but in secure defence. We believe we have a right and duty to defend our people whenever and wherever their liberty is chal-lenged.

ITN, 17.45

Thatcher We believe that wars are not caused by armaments but by the ambitions of aggres-sors and that what tempts them is the prospect of easy advan-tage and quick victory. We believe that the purpose of nuclear armouries should be to prevent war and that can be achieved by smaller armouries. We believe that a balanced reduction in conventional weapons could create greater stability. We believe we have a right and duty to defend our own people whenever and wherever their liberty is chal-lenged.

These sentences are taken from the end of the speech. The sentence with which all bulletins ended the quoted speech was always the same. The overall framing of the speech was in relation to the Falklands conflict. Our attention is drawn to empty Argentine seats at the session. As one BBC correspondent put it: 'She was here for a speech on disarmament but the visit inevitably had a strong Falklands flavour to it.' (BBC1, 21.00).

This appeared to control the use of quotations, since both channels prefaced the extracts in similar ways:

> Not once did she mention Argentina though her closing words were aimed directly at Argentina's empty seats.
>
> ITN, 17.45

> The speech didn't directly mention the Falklands but the references were clear. War, she said, is not caused by the arms race but by the ambitions of aggressive nations. The delegation from Argentina was not in place to hear her.
>
> BBC1, 21.00

Consequently on British television news we heard nothing in detail about what the British government was proposing on the disarmament question. Instead another element of the so-called 'Falklands effect' was on display.

This leads us to a final comment in this section. Although most coverage was given to the Reagan and Thatcher speeches, even that, as we have seen, was in some respects slim and selective. Much of the news time surrounding the events was taken up with ritual activities. So we have Mrs Thatcher shaking hands with the Secretary General of the UN and later with her entourage walking up a UN building corridor. The point about news as ritual is that we, as an audience, are given the impression that we are in on the event, yet the public performance we see is often very thin on content. When this happens despite its immediacy, news is less than informative.

Journalists and policians understand well that the routines of public life call for ritual performances which are sometimes consciously stage-managed to the satisfaction of both sides. Occasionally the social collusion which this entails is drawn to our attention. For example, during the period of SSD2 President Reagan was on a European tour, which is possibly another reason why the coverage of the session was so sparse on British television – there were many visual treatments of ceremonies, parades, state banquets and such-like. The artificial non-informative character of this kind of news was candidly stated by the BBC's Charles Wheeler, whilst President Reagan was in West Germany:

> To catch a glimpse of their American visitor Germans must turn to television with its narrow view of a few carefully controlled events and non-events like arrivals and departures of the glamorous and the great.
> BBC2, 23.00, 9.6.82

News as ritual may be regarded as something of a spectator sport. We may judge it according to taste or entertainment value but not as an aid to rational understanding of great public issues. We are not employing a reductionist argument here and implying that all news is simply to be understood as ritual. Rather, we suggest that news is a selective combination of ritual, rhetoric, factual claims and statements, informed (sometimes misinformed) speculations and interpretative comment. We find it difficult, indeed unhelpful, to assign labels like 'objective', 'impartial' or 'neutral' to such a manufactured product. The beginning of wisdom is to recognise news for what it is and not what it claims for itself.

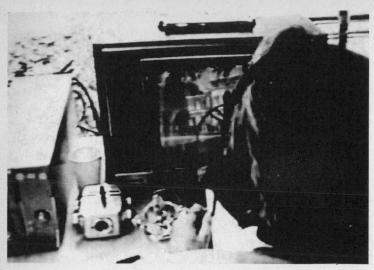

"To catch a glimpse of their American visitor Germans must turn to television with its narrow view of a few carefully controlled events and non-events like arrivals of the glamorous and the great."

BBC *Newsnight* 9.6.82

What the quality papers said

By way of comparison we looked at the coverage given to the UN Special Session by the British quality press. The similarities and differences can be indicated by showing what stories were covered and, where there was overlap, if the news angle varied. In chronological order they can be enumerated and summarised as follows.

1. *The opening of the special session*
Both *The Times* (3.6.82, 7.6.82) and the *Guardian* (3.6.82, 8.6.82) carried stories on this topic. The *Financial Times* had one report (7.6.82).

The *Financial Times* provided a brief report from 'our UN correspondent': UN bid to end 'rush to destruction'. This was a quote from the Secretary General of the UN, Perez de Cueller. The main purpose of the five-week session was defined: 'to focus world attention on the problem, not negotiate solutions – they must await the attention of diplomats and arms experts in smaller groups than the 157 nation

Assembly'. It referred back to the 1978 Special Session and cited Jan Martenson, head of the UN Disarmament Centre, who in a pre-session press conference said that the situation was far worse than in 1978.

The Times' opening story from Zoriana Pysarwisky in New York was headed: 'Cynicism at peace session'. After drawing attention to the backdrop of conflicts in the South Atlantic and Lebanon she wrote: 'The mood of the delegates of the 157 governments was notably cynical in sharp contrast to the sense of mission that has inspired tens of thousands of peace demonstrators to flock to New York.' The second report – 'UN tries again to halt the arms race' – also pointed to the 'anti-war movements from all over the world [which] are expected to bring their campaign to full force to counter the momentum of the spiralling arms race'. It also referred to the Palme Report[3] and noted its call for the elimination of tactical nuclear weapons from central Europe by the end of 1983. The Palme Report was not mentioned on television news during the period of the Second Session, although it was briefly mentioned on 2 June (BBC2, 22.55). It was not specifically linked with the Special Session. Nevertheless, Dr David Owen, a member of the Independent Commission on Disarmament and Security Issues which produced the report, was quoted as saying that the proposed ban on nuclear weapons in Europe would reduce the risk of so-called limited war.

The *Guardian's* 8 June report of the opening session also cited Perez de Cuellar's 'rush to destruction' phrase and Jan Martenson's press conference. Martenson – who did not appear on television news – told the press that £335 billion was the annual global arms bill for all types of weapons and military equipment. The end of the article touched on a matter that had been dealt with at greater length on 3 June, namely the denial of visas to intending members of the conference in New York by the US Justice Department. The earlier article had focused on two British citizens, members of the Labour Party and CND; it also suggested that representatives from Japan and the USSR were experiencing difficulties. The second article noted a claim from a Tokyo disarmament organisation that 222 Japanese had been refused visas. This was not reported on television news. It was certainly no secret. The *International Herald Tribune* reported on 9 June:

> More than 300 foreign peace activists, most of them from Japan, have been denied visas to attend a United Nations disarmament conference that opened on Monday in New York because they are affiliated with organisations that have Communist links.

This was done under the provisions of the 1952 McCarran–Walter Act and led to a good deal of activity in the US courts in an attempt to change the decisions. The *Economist* also took the story up on 12 June – 'Peaceniks or pinkos?' - and noted that more than 350 of the 1,400 invited to the conference had been refused visas. These included General Francisco da Costa Gomes, former President of Portugal, General Nini Pasti of Italy, a former NATO officer, and the British Labour MP, James Lamond. The *Economist* reported that the ban was maintained against all but 42 people.

2. *Japanese arms*

On 11 June, the *Daily Telegraph* ran a report by Ian Bell that Japan was to spend more on arms. It was not reported elsewhere or on television news. 'The Japanese philosophy,' wrote the *Telegraph,*' outlined in a speech by Mr Suzuki, the Prime Minister, is consistent with the Reagan administration's view that arms reductions are best achieved by first building up military forces and then negotiating cuts.' As the only country to have experienced nuclear war, as victim, this admission was thought to be somewhat embarrassing and was the subject of a press conference convened by the Japanese after the speech.

3. *The second week of the special session*

In *The Times* 14, June, Zoriana Pysariwsky anticipated the speeches for the second week – Gromyko, Schmidt and Reagan - and gave a general appraisal of the conference: 'Rhetoric and reality at UN session'.This article suggested that the West had been reluctant to convene the Second Session, but had been pressurised into it by Third World countries and the anti-nuclear movement. She referred to a Third World disarmament proposal which looked to total disarmament in the next twenty year period and noted the West's preference for bilateral negotiations. This point of difference was not elaborated nor was it covered at all on television news. She also contrasted the enthusiasm of the peace demonstration to the official debate which 'has been conducted in an almost empty General Assembly hall'.

4. *Peace demonstrations and the nuclear freeze movement*

The 12 June peace demonstration which paraded past the UN building and rallied in Central Park was covered by *The Times* (14.6.82) – '"Freeze" call unites protestors'. The *Telegraph* (15.6.82) –

'1,200 arrested at US peace demo' – focussed on the 14 June attempts to block the UN missions of the five nuclear powers. Both of these reports agreed with the BBC that there had been no serious incidents and that the protest was mostly non-violent. As the *Telegraph* put it, 'not a single truncheon had to wielded or a canister of tear gas fired'.

5. *Schmidt speech*

This was reported on 15 June in *The Times*, the *Financial Times* and the *Guardian*. On television the speech was mentioned only on ITN's lunchtime bulletin in two sentences, which linked it with the peace demonstrations:

> If these peaceful protesters were looking for an acknowledgement of their concern about the nuclear arms race they found it in Monday's speech by Chancellor Helmut Schmidt. He pointedly warned the General Assembly that anti-nuclear protesters were not all starry-eyed fanatics and urged his colleagues not to ignore what he called the positive moral force in the anti-nuclear campaign.

The quality press reports were longer. Two of them, the *Guardian* and the *Financial Times*, also referenced his comments on the peace movement, albeit with different emphasis: 'Schmidt salutes the peace movement' (*Guardian*) and 'Schmidt qualifies support for N-protests' (*Financial Times*). This last report quoted the following passage from his speech:

> We must be conscious of the danger that our citizens, frightened of the terrors of a nuclear holocaust, may soon be no longer able or willing to understand why negotiations concerning practical stages towards disarmament go on and on for years; why, as they see it, the idea of national prestige has a greater effect on the decisions of governments than do the necessities of mutual security.

Was this the Helmut Schimdt who had promoted NATO's twin track 1979 decision and, in the event, led to the deployment of Cruise and Pershing 11 missiles in Western Europe? The fact that it was could be glimpsed from *The Times* report where we learn that the speech gave strong support to President Reagan's proposals – START, zero option and mutual balanced force reductions in central Europe.

6. *Brezhnev statement*

On 16 June the story was carried with similar headlines in all four quality papers:

'Brezhnev pledge on first-use weapons ban' – *Financial Times*.
'Russians pledge not to be first' – *Guardian*.
'Brezhnev vows "no first strike" ' – *Times*.
'USSR "will not start atomic war" ' – *Telegraph*.

The reports noted that the pledge was greeted with applause. The *Guardian* and *The Times* both pointed out that this pledge was at variance with NATO's doctrine of flexible response. The *Guardian* suggested that this was being interpreted by NATO as 'a propaganda move in the battle in the General Assembly to convince the Non-aligned group and the Third World of the nuclear powers' commitment to peace and disarmament'.

The television reports did not mention the applause given to this speech and were much shorter: two sentences for ITN, three for BBC1 and four for BBC2. ITN contrived an interesting juxtaposition of items:

> President Brezhnev has told that the Soviet Union will not be the first to use nuclear weapons. The promise was read out for him at the Special Session of the United Nations on disarmament by the Soviet Foreign Minister, Mr Andrei Gromyko. From Afghanistan, though there are reports of a big Soviet victory against guerilla forces in the Panshar valley, sixty miles northeast of the capital Kabul. The Panshar has long been the centre of resistance to Soviet occupation.
>
> ITN, 22.00, 16 June, 1982.

The following day, 17 June, the *Telegraph* followed the speech up with a report from the House of Lords: 'Peers welcome Brezhnev promise of no first N-strike'. This was an extended account of a number of speeches. Lord Brockway urged the British government to reconsider its attitude on no-first-use and argued that the acceptance of verification of arms treaties by the Communist countries was 'extraordinarily important'. Lord Mayhew thought that very high priority should be given by Western governments to Mr Brezhnev's challenge and hoped that it would not be treated as 'just propaganda'. He argued that the strategy of flexible response was losing credibility as a deterrent. Lord Kennet, the SDP defence spokesperson, profoundly hoped the government would seize the Brezhnev declaration with both hands and welcome it. He maintained that Soviet proposals to put its nuclear installations under international controls were a tremendous advance after years of resistance. These speeches were not reported on television news, nor was the information they contained about Soviet proposals on verification conveyed.

7. *Kennedy speech*
Senator Edward Kennedy spoke to a special gathering at the UN commemorating the centenary of President Franklin Roosevelt's birth. We have seen that this was briefly itemised on a BBC lunchtime bulletin. It was also the subject of a brief report in *The Times* on 18 June. Kennedy called for a nuclear freeze with full and effective verification and rejected the concept that a further nuclear arms build-up must be a prelude to a freeze.

8. *Reagan speech*
This was reported on 18 June by *The Times* – Deeds not words, call by Reagan – and the *Telegraph* – Russia told to show sincerity over arms cuts. In addition, *The Times* printed a partial text of his address. Only there do we read about the four points constituting his agenda for peace. The press reports, as with television news, concentrated on his attacks on the Soviet Union with his references to its tyranny, repression and violation of human rights. *The Times* notes: 'Diplomatic observers were struck by the harshness of his remarks which sought to underscore the differences between the two sides.'

9. *Thatcher speech*
The British Prime Minister's speech to the UN Special Session was signalled as early as 16 June in the *Telegraph* – 'Premier to tell the UN of unilateral arms cut risk. This dealt with an exchange between herself, Mr Foot and Mr Cryer in the House of Commons. In reply to Cryer's observation that 'millions of people were sick and tired of government representatives talking about disarmament at the United Nations and building up stockpiles of weapons as the Tory government was doing', she replied that the two major nuclear powers had not gone to war against one another. Nuclear weapons were achieving their purpose. They were a deterrent which made the prospect of war too horrifying.

Mrs Thatcher's UN speech was delivered on 23 June and reported in the *Telegraph* on 24 June – 'Thatcher tells UN "Arms control cannot stop war"'. The speech was extensively quoted, and James Wightman reported that she was well received by a well-filled conference hall and applauded at the end. The Prime Minister later drew attention to this when Dr David Owen criticised the speech as one in which she wanted 'to beat ploughshares into arms'. She replied: 'You will be extremely disappointed to know it received more applause than any other speech made there for three years' (*Daily Telegraph*, 25.6.82). Extracts from the speech were given without comment in *The Times* on 29 June – 'Good intentions do not ensure peace'.

10. *Report from Moscow*

The Times printed a report from Richard Owen in Moscow, on 19 June, headed 'Reagan scores for Russia'. This alluded to satisfaction in the Soviet Union because they had scored a point in the propaganda war with the United States by proposing no-first-use of nuclear weapons. Mr Reagan's speech had failed to respond to this, it was said. The thrust of the report was that the Soviet Union was prepared for a long propaganda campaign to support its views on arms control and was mobilising its considerable resources, including the Russian Orthodox Church, to impress world opinion.

11. *Gromyko New York press conference*

This was covered by the *Guardian* – Gromyko criticises US "cold war" policy – on 22 June. Much of the conference was concerned, according to the *Guardian*, to convey the Soviet view that the US was going into strategic arms talks with unacceptable positions. Mr Gromyko said that the US position would imply a very drastic change in the correlation of forces to the advantage of the United States and the detriment of the Soviet Union'. This press conference was not reported on television news.

12. *The end of the Special Session*

At the end of the conference there were reports in the *Telegraph* and *The Times*:

> 'UN fails to agree on arms plan' – *Telegraph* (12.7.82)
> 'Nitpicking makes farce of UN arms conference' – *The Times* (9.7.82)
> 'Bitterness at failure of UN arms control' – *The Times* (12.7.82)

These reflect the sombre tone that also characterised television news. The *Telegraph* cited the Assembly's President Ismat Kittani's view that the conference was 'a sorry record of failure'. According to the New York correspondent of *The Times,* Western diplomats saw the problem as one of Soviet intransigence. They were referring to its insistence on no-first-use and its call for a nuclear freeze. In its final report *The Times* commented:

> The most striking irony about the failure of the session was that it met at a time of intense political awareness and activity, whereas members of the public had remained generally oblivious to the first session, which had been termed a success.

The *Financial Times* also recorded its verdict: 'UN arms talks end in discord' (12.7.82)

While there may have been incidental passing references to other stories, these twelve consitute an account of the main contours of coverage. It is fuller and more extensive than television news. However, the coverage of speeches is much the same with the emphasis on Reagan and Thatcher, together with some attention paid to the Brezhnev statement. This means that again there was no coverage of non-governmental organisations. They are given a final word, courtesy of *The Times*, on 12 July: 'But it was the private groups which expressed particular outrage at the assembly's failure and 76 of them issued a statement accusing governments of betraying public confidence and the aims of grass roots movements.'

NINE

The Church and the Bomb: Framing and Reporting a Debate

The bishop's move

> The way forward which the report took was to say that if nuclear weapons are not morally acceptable, then it is of the first urgency to get rid of them. What would be the safest way of doing that, and the one most likely to succeed? Contrary to the popular impression given by the media and never eradicated, we did not advocate unilateral nuclear disarmament. The report recommended a modest unilateral reduction by the West, which would not in any way endanger security. We accepted that the nuclear deterrent had played a part in keeping the peace since 1945. What we urged strongly was that new developments were eroding the stability of the present equilibrium and that it could not last for ever. Balanced force reduction had not so far delivered the goods. Had not the time come for independent initiatives which were carefully calculated not to tempt anyone to the gamble of war? I still firmly believe that this idea has not been defeated by argument. It has only been distorted by misrepresentation.[1]
>
> John Austin Baker, Bishop of Salisbury

The Church and the Bomb, subtitled 'Nuclear Weapons and Christian Conscience', was published on 18 October 1982. As part of its continuing concern about the issue of war and disarmament, the Church of England Synod in 1979 asked its Board of Social Responsibility to set up a working party. Its brief was to study the implications for Christian discipleship of the acceptance by the major military powers of a role for nuclear weapons in their strategy and to consider the bearing of this on the adequacy of past Christian teaching and ethical analysis regarding the conduct of war. The working party was ecumenical in composition. Its members were mainly theologians, including pacifists and non-pacifists, but also included a lecturer in War Studies from Kings College, London. It was chaired by John Baker, who in 1982 had become Bishop of Salisbury. From 1978 to

1982 he had served as Rector of St Margaret's, Westminster, and Speaker's Chaplain.

The report, a substantial document, was published in book form. In succeeding chapters it looked at the technological, strategic, political, legal, moral and theological aspects of the possession and use of nuclear weapons. It went on to analyse the principal policy options which nuclear states might, or do, pursue to maintain peace: negotiation from strength, balanced force reductions, multilateral disarmament with unilateral stages and unilateral renunciation. It concluded that 'there are fundamental objections on the basis of ethics and faith both to the use of and the conditional intention to use nuclear weapons'.[2] The final chapter contained twenty-two recommendations based on its conclusion that 'the nuclear element in deterrence is no longer a reliable or morally acceptable approach to the future of the world'.[3]

The working party advocated discriminating support for the United Nations in its work for peace. It thought that pressure should be brought to bear on the British government to ensure that the debate on defence and disarmament is a real one and commented:

> We welcome the recent increase in the availability of information. It must be said, however, that the government's counter-offensive against the peace movements, however understandable, has often not improved upon the level of some peace movement propaganda.[4]

The role and responsibilities of the media were also explicitly commented upon, including the need for an informed understanding and an appreciation of how other nations see the issues of defence and disarmament. The need for constant vigilance in the use of language was noted:

> Commentators need also to warn us again and again about the vague terminology that springs from woolly thinking and begs questions – for example, the constant tendency to use bland expressions like 'take out' when what is meant is the destruction of a city and its inhabitants, or words like 'strength' or 'power' to mean more and better nuclear weapons, thus predetermining the outcome of the argument.[5]

More specifically, the report recommended the cancelling of the Trident programme and the phasing out of Polaris and Chevaline; the phasing out of other nuclear weapons in Britain including US air and submarine bases and the refusal to accept Cruise missiles in Britain.

Even before it was published there were press accounts of what the report was proposing. David Fairhall and Martyn Halsall, respectively defence and religious affairs correspondents, wrote the lead story in

the *Guardian* under the headline: 'Whitehall salvo at Church arms
plan' (15.10.82). They refer to the alarm bells which the report set
ringing in Whitehall:

> Officials have reacted by reiterating the official view that successful
> multilateral negotiations to reduce nuclear arms are only likely to be
> achieved from a position of nuclear strength; an 'independent' deterrent
> is an asset to NATO as well as to Britain if she were ever on her own; and
> that we cannot honestly shelter under the American nuclear umbrella
> while refusing to take the risk of having American nuclear bases on our
> soil.

Conservative MPs were reported as fearing that the Church of
England was falling into the hands of 'trendies'.

The next day Winston Churchill MP described the report as
representing

> the workings of a narrow activist group, inspired in some quarters with a
> political motivation. There could be nothing more immoral than if the
> government of this country were fecklessly to pursue the unilateralist
> policies advocated by this report and CND.
>
> *Guardian*, 16.10.82

This was interpreted as the opening of a government campaign against
the report in which the Prime Minister was expected to get involved.
In the House of Commons on 19 October she rejected the report's
advocacy of a non-nuclear policy for Britain: 'Nuclear weapons are an
essential part of our security. If there was any suggestion of unilateral
disarmament it would threaten the peace and security we have enjoyed
in this country for the past thirty seven years' (*Guardian* 20.10.82).
This followed the accusation in the House from the Tory MP Robert
Atkins who referred to the group 'supposedly eminent and certainly
unrepresenative clerics [who] seek to undermine the defence of the
United Kingdom' (*Guardian* 20.10.82). This comment came the day
after London Weekend Television reported a survey finding that 40%
of the Church of England clergy thought Britain should abandon its
nuclear deterrent.

The *Guardian* did take up the issues raised by *The Church and the
Bomb* with some vigour. The publication date, 18 October, was the
occasion for a long editorial–'Which path back from the brink?'–and
was linked to a sympathetic reference to Jonathan Schell's *The Fate of
the Earth:* 'For if there is even a chance that Schell's glimpse of
Armageddon is right, then the framework of strategy and doctrine that
locks together conventional and nuclear war is shot to pieces'
(*Guardian* 18.10.82). Mrs Thatcher's often repeated statement that

nuclear weapons have kept the world at peace for thirty seven years (she said it again the next day, as we have seen) was put in an alternative perspective: 'That is a pimple on the face of history. Can they so work for millenniums to come? If human frailty, miscalculation or dementia puts the logic at risk, then how can that risk be diminished?' The failure of multilateral disarmament to make progress in the light of the continuing escalation of the arms race was noted and a call to the West to pursue more actively nuclear disarmament policies was made.

On the same day the Bishop of Durham, John Habgood (now Archbishop of York), wrote about the report on the Agenda page: 'Morals of the Bomb'. His comments and intervention are of particular interest since he had chaired a World Council of Churches Hearing in November 1981 on Nuclear Weapons and Disarmament. This was subsequently published under the title *Before It's Too Late*. Habgood commended the report as an example of Anglican sanity at its best. However, while he took the view that the moral argument against nuclear weapons is unanswerable, he was not happy with the way this was connected in the report to what he saw as pragmatic political arguments:

> I am not at all sure that the Church as a corporate body would be wise to identify itself too closely with a particular political programme. It is not that churches have no right to make political judgements. Sometimes they have to. In a case of this complexity the problem is that decision-making must depend on a host of subtle factors which those not directly engaged in the business of politics have difficulty in estimating.

He argued, therefore, that the role of the Church here is to set a moral direction and put pressure on the political process, whilst recognising the imponderables surrounding the process which make movement in the desired direction difficult to accomplish.

The following week, Peter Jenkins, one of the *Guardian's* senior writers, used the report as a springboard for further thoughts: 'Widening the constituency of concern' (27.10.82). He also commended the report as exemplifying the enquiring spirit of the times so far as the nuclear issue is concerned. He set this alongside other challenges to nuclear orthodoxy.

These include Robert McNamara, McGeorge Bundy, Gerard Smith and George Kennan's challenge to NATO's strategy of 'flexible response'; Lord Carver and Lord Zuckerman's disbelief in the feasibility of 'limited nuclear war' and the Palme Commission's call for a zone free of battlefield nuclear weapons. Received nuclear wisdom is losing its sway over the public mind:

> The paradox of deterrence becomes too paradoxical for sensible minds when it reaches the point at which war-fighting and *'war-winning'* capability is deemed necessary for the credibility of deterrence. This is not thinking about the unthinkable but double-thinking about the unthinkable.

Following a strong critique of the Reagan administration Jenkins suggested that unilateral nuclear disarmament in Britain is too parochial a solution and offered a threefold list of priorities: first, a verifiable nuclear freeze; second, a no-early-use NATO strategy involving the use of battlefield nuclear weapons; and third, political policies of détente or managed coexistence backed up by simple deterrence.

Elsewhere in the media the report also gained attention. Professor John Vincent examined the arguments in his piece – 'Church against Bomb' – in the *Sunday Times* (24.10.82):

> It can be recommended with confidence to anyone new to the study of the question. It is not . . . a unilateralist tract and anyone who denounces it as such without having read it will come badly unstuck . . . . The sentences are crisp, intelligent and unemotional. The Church has taken a lurch towards reality.

His main reservation was that the effects on Western Europe of creating a nuclear-free Britain within NATO were problematical. Moreover, in order to make war less likely, we need to know more about the behaviour of the two superpowers. This, in Vincent's view, the report did not do with sufficient thoroughness, although he readily admits it is a difficult task.

In the *Observer*, Conor Cruise O'Brien wrote two articles on successive weeks, which prompted a response from the Bishop of Salisbury (24.10.82, 31.10.82 and 7.11.82). According to O'Brien, what's wrong with the report was that

> Its political conclusions are incompatible with its central, ethical contention, which does point in the direction of withdrawal from a military alliance based on the concept of nuclear deterrence. You can't be against nuclear deterrence and in favour of NATO.

Nevertheless, O'Brien went on to suggest:

> because of its ethics and irrespective of its comparatively Mickey Mouse political conclusions, *The Church and the Bomb* is a profoundly

subversive work. Mrs Thatcher is said to be very angry about this report, and from her point of view she is right to be angry. If the Church of England adopts this report, it will be saying that the strategic thinking of the Western alliance is ethically intolerable.

The Bishop's reply was one which also had relevance for the Habgood argument already cited. It was to stress the importance of going beyond ethical principles to practical recommendations on the grounds that this was an appropriate way of stimulating debate not pre-empting eventual conclusions. He was looking for discussion that could have real consequences. This form of pragmatism was seen as necessary in the light of the fact that orthodox claims for the realistic (that is, peacekeeping) character of mutual balanced force deterrents were themselves highly disputable: 'Mutual balanced force deterrence is said to be "stable" while suggestions of even modest unilateral reductions are dismissed as "seriously destabilising". This is almost the exact reverse of the truth' ('The freedom not to be afraid', *Observer*, 7.11.82).

The importance of the Church and the Bomb debate to which the report gave rise was, then, clearly recognised by the quality press. The potential rift between Church and state was identified. But in addition, the internal differences between bishops of the Church provided another element in the story. 'Bishops will clash in debate on Bomb' was the title of Judith Judd's piece in the *Observer* (6.3.83). She outlined the varying positions of the Archbishop of Canterbury and the Bishops of London, Salisbury, Durham and Birmingham. The piquancy of Salisbury's position was savoured: a Thatcher appointment to the Bishopric, he had been converted, as he saw it, by the reasonableness of the arguments of his colleagues on the working party. He had, suggested Judd, 'startled everybody, including himself, by becoming the strong man and extremist of the Church of England'. This put him directly in conflict with the Bishop of London, who was chairing the Board of Social Responsibility, to which the working party had first to report. He, said Judd, 'has shocked Christian nuclear disarmers by saying that nuclear weapons are morally acceptable'. For the record, the Bishop of London outlined his position in an address that was later published:

> While recognising the utterly appalling prospect of the use of nuclear weapons, I believe that their possession and use can be morally acceptable as a way of exercising our moral responsibility in a fallen world. I do not believe that we can ever say that their possession or use can be morally good. At best we can say that they may be morally acceptable.[7]

As for Archibishop Runcie, he was described by Judd as a
multilateralist opposed to the conclusion of *The Church and the Bomb*:
'The Archibishop, holder of the Military Cross, will weigh his words
with customary care.'

Framing and linking the debate: two illustrations

We give now two illustrations from the quality press of the way the
'Church and the bomb' debate was contextualised. The examples are
drawn from the *Sunday Times* and the *Guardian* and form something
of a constant with TV news coverage, which we examine later.

On consecutive Sundays, one before and one after the debate, the
Sunday Times featured pieces by its religious affairs correspondent,
John Whale. As the son of a former Bishop of London, he was perhaps
particularly well placed to comment on the organisation and politics of
the Church of England. His prediction of the outcome of the debate
was accurate: 'The Church of England will this week distance itself
from the government's policy on nuclear weapons.' He outlined the
three main positions in the debate represented by the Bishops of
London, Salisbury and Birmingham and forecast, again correctly, that
Salisbury would lose but that Birmingham's amendment, which
argued for no-first-use of nuclear weapons, would carry the day and
hence create a gap between the Church's position and the
government's. What Whale also did was to draw attention to a well-
attended conference of Christian Conservatives (mostly Anglican)
which had just taken place and to the rapturous reception accorded to
the journalist Paul Johnson, who had stated that the evil of nuclear
weapons was outstripped by the evil of possible Soviet domination.

On February 13, Whale had a centrepiece article entitled 'The
Church political'. He suggested that the vote went the way it did
because the Church remains deferential to its hierarchy:

> Unilateralism went down heavily – the vote was three to one – because
> the Archbishop of Canterbury strongly resisted it; no-first-use scraped
> through because a figure of almost equal seniority and weight, the
> Bishop of Durham, spoke up for it.

At the heart of Whale's article, however, was a statement about the
relationship between moral judgements and specific recommendations. He supported the view that Church leaders had to get down to
specifics. The effect of doing so is that two different kinds of discourse
intermingle. The Bishop of Birmingham had said in the debate that
there could never be a moral justification for a first nuclear strike: 'The

intention is not defence but naked aggression in the form of pre-emptive action. The nature of the act is evil. It is deliberately to loose hell on earth.' Yet, as Whale points out, this is current NATO strategy for stopping a Soviet tank attack on West Germany, so the moralist becomes a strategist whether he wants to or not. Whale's conclusion is that if Michael Heseltine can come into the Ministry of Defence and express his opinions, without any specialist experience, then the Bishops of Birmingham and Salisbury, with a good knowledge of defence issues to call on, certainly have the right to offer guidance and advice on such matters.

The *Guardian's* coverage of the debate merits comment for several reasons. On both the day of the debate and the day after the leading editorial was devoted to the issue. 'What binds the Synod and Mr Bush?' asked the *Guardian*, referring to the American Vice-President's current tour of Europe for discussions on defence policy. The article pointed to the widespread anxiety in Europe and the United States about the adequacy of received theories of nuclear deterrence and the increasing concern about the growing stockpile of nuclear weapons. This was linked to a lack of confidence in President Reagan, doubts about the intentions of the US to negotiate seriously with the Russians on arms reductions and a feeling that policy in the West lacks substance. The last paragraph of the editorial sought to connect the two concurrent events, the Bush visit and the Synod debate, as a way of symbolising the policy dilemmas of the West:

> It is that void [in Western policy] in their own humble way, which the Salisbury team sought to fill. They seek (in a rather more measured way than Mr Foot) to dispose of Britain's own small segment of nuclear armoury. It is – and this should be clearly understood – only a small beginning in their terms. It is giving away something that does not much matter: something that could not be used independently in any remotely foreseeable combat, something which if considered one-to-one (the doughty US alone against the USSR) automatically undercuts all NATO's case about the importance of the nuclear balance to deterrence. The question, of course, is what one would get in return for the gesture: and the sad answer, alas, is probably very little. But the context – displayed clearly enough in all the Synod's likely amendments today – is not any longer one where that single, sad answer suffices. We have reached a point where the obscenity and finality of the holocaust in waiting must be made to retreat by one means or another rather than allowed inexorably to advance. That is the message Mr Bush must take home with him: by one means or another.
>
> Guardian, 10.2.83

Next day, the first editorial declared: 'The Synod declines to stand pat'. It took the view that the Conservative Party, while no doubt very pleased that the recommendations of the 'Church and the bomb' report were rejected (it obtained 23% support from Synod), would be unhappy with the Bishop of Birmingham's amendment 'which plainly repudiated the first use of nuclear weapons in any circumstances'. The whole decision is interpreted within the wider context of the Geneva arms control talks. If they failed, the likelihood was, it was argued, that the Bishop of Salisbury's warning that the balance of terror can no longer be regarded as a stable force would gather support. The editorial concluded:

> The message from Church House is thus sharply different from that which Mr George Bush came to Britain hoping to hear; it is also, no doubt, sharply different from that which he will have heard in Downing Street. But it was the product of the same kind of doubts and uncertainties which now agitate the country as a whole. And they much more certainly reflect the mood of ordinary people in Britain that the proclaimed certainties emanating from high places.
>
> *Guardian*, 11.2.83

On the same day the paper carried a half-page report from Martyn Halsall of the Church debate with a photograph of the Synod in session under the heading: 'Compromise decision rejects any NATO first use of nuclear weapons. Synod throws out unilateralism by three to one'. Extracts from a number of speeches were given, the most extensive being that of the Archbishop of Canterbury. His opposition to the report was explicitly linked to his fear that its recommendations would undermine the Geneva negotiations, put the NATO alliance in disarray and strengthen United States isolationism.

In addition, there was a front-page story from Halsall headed 'Church rejects unilateral stance and favours "no-first-strike". There were photographs of the Bishops of Birmingham, Durham and Salisbury at the top of the page. Alongside the Halsall story and also under the photographs, David Fairhall, the defence correspondent, had written a piece headed 'Heseltine begins peace assault'. This referred to an address given to Tory women at the Conservative Central Office:

> he outlined the government's fundamental approach to nuclear deterrence and disarmament, reiterating its commitment to Trident, to NATO's 'dual track' decision on Cruise missile deployment and its continued refusal to yield to Opposition demands for a 'dual key' or British safety catch on these new weapons.

He also re-stated his refusal to debate the issues on a public platform with CND. In this respect the distance between the government and the Church of England was signalled. At the same time, the government's opposition to peace campaigners generally is indicated, a matter which is connected with a wider campaign initiated and co-ordinated by the government.

The Church and the Bomb debates on TV news – 10 February 1983

> It's been a long time since the Church of England found itself at the centre of so much attention. Queues for the public gallery were forming two hours before the debate began. Teams of police, unneeded as it happened, were on hand in case anti-nuclear demonstrators should disrupt proceedings. The debate was covered live by radio and television in Britain, and attended by thirty overseas broadcasting organisations. The issue – whether to back the recommendations of the report *The Church and the Bomb*.
>
> BBC1, 21.00, 10.2.83

What exactly was the Synod of the Church of England debating? The Chairman of the Church's Board for Social Responsibility, the Bishop of London, put a motion to the Synod concerning Britain's nuclear weapons policy. An amendment was tabled by the Bishop of Salisbury in support of the working party's report, *The Church and The Bomb*, which he had chaired. In the event of that amendment falling, as it did, the Bishop of Birmingham had tabled another amendment, proposing Britain adopt a no-first-strike policy. This amendment was carried. The motion and the two amendments are given in the box overleaf.

The debate had been signalled in advance as a potential clash with government policy. Perhaps the Church of England, sometimes caricatured as 'the Tory Party at prayer', was moving leftwards and was going to embrace the Labour Party's policy on disarmament. Was the established state Church going to speak with a different voice from that of the government?

The headlines of the main evening bulletins on the four channels put it this way:

> Hello, good evening. First the main news of the day. The Church of England has voted to reject the policy of unilateral disarmament.
>
> Channel 4

> The Church of England's governing body, the Synod, has firmly rejected the idea of unilateral disarmament by Britain.
>
> BBC1

The Church and the Bomb debate

Bishop of London's motion	Bishop of Salisbury's amendment	Bishop of Birmingham's amendment
15. That this Synod recognising:	34. **Leave out** all words after 'HM Government'' and **insert:**	55. '**Leave out** all words after 'international situation'' and add:
(a) the urgency of the task of making and preserving peace; and	(a) to announce the UK's intention of carrying out, in consultation with its allies, a phased disengagement of the UK from active association with any form of nuclear weaponry, involving:	and (c) that it is not the task of the Church to determine defence strategy but rather to give a moral lead to the nation;
(b) the extreme seriousness of the threat made to the world by contemporary nuclear weapons and the dangers in the present international situation,		(i) affirms that it is the duty of Her Majesty's Government and her allies to maintain adequate forces to guard against nuclear blackmail and to deter nuclear and non-nuclear aggressors;
calls upon HM Government, together with our allies in NATO,	(i) bringing to an end the Polaris strategic nuclear system, and cancelling the order for the proposed Trident replacement;	
(i) to reduce progressively its dependence upon nuclear weapons in its programme for defence; and	(ii) discontinuing all nuclear weapons wholly or mainly of British manufacture;	(ii) asserts that the tactics and strategies of this country and her NATO allies should be seen to be unmistakably defensive in respect of the countries of the Warsaw Pact;
(ii) to work to strengthen international treaties especially as they apply to the possession and use of such weapons.'	(iii) negotiating Britain's withdrawal from the manning of nuclear weapons systems manufactured by others;	
	(iv) negotiating an end to agreements for the present or future deployment of nuclear weapons systems on British soil;	(iii) judges that even a small-scale first use of nuclear weapons could never be morally justified in view of the high risk that this would lead to full-scale nuclear warfare;

(b) to invite other governments to make positive responses to the British initiative by comparable measures either of renunciation or restraint;

(c) to continue to prosecute vigorously disarmament negotiations of all kinds; and

(d) to devote resources to positive programmes for the building of peace and the fostering of international confidence along the lines indicated in the remaining recommendations of **The Church and the Bomb** (namely nos. 2–17 and 21–22)'.

(iv) believes that there is a moral obligation on all countries (including the members of **NATO**) publicly to forswear the first use of nuclear weapons in any form;

(v) bearing in mind that many in Europe live in fear of nuclear catastrophe and that nuclear parity is not essential to deterrence, calls on Her Majesty's Government to take immediate steps in conjunction with her allies to further the principles embodied in this motion so as to reduce progressively **NATO**'s dependence on nuclear weapons and to decrease nuclear arsenals throughout the world.

The Church of England has voted overwhelmingly against Britain banning the Bomb.

ITN

Here at home the Church of England has had its most important debate of the week, some say its most important since the war, on the issue of nuclear policy. As predicted on *Newsnight* two nights ago, they voted against unilateralism.

Newsnight, BBC2

So the inference was clear:

The Church of England, the State Church, pillar of the establishment, today firmly ended speculation that it was flirting with the defence policy of the Labour left.

Channel 4

And:

Mrs Thatcher will no doubt be relieved that the Church has voted down the Bishop of Salisbury and his unilateral report *The Church and the Bomb*.

Newsnight, BBC2

The word 'left' in the sentence is redundant in the sense that the amendment was consistent with the policy of the Labour Party. To refer to the left is a coded way of speaking about 'extremism' in this cultural context. It diminishes the strength of the unilateralist position in the Labour Party. Of course, as the Bishop of Salisbury's motion made clear the unilaterism in the proposal was not seen as an alternative to multilateral disarmament, but was seen in the context of multilateralism. Channel 4 reported the Bishop of Salisbury as having made 'an impressive speech, surely one of the most cogent marshallings of the arguments for unilateralism ever assembled' but it is the dichotomy between unilateral and multilateral that is typically reinforced.

In the Channel 4 news, moreover, the opening statement about the Church debate and the later developments of the story is separated by references to the British Secretary of Defence, the Prime Minister and the visiting American Vice-President all commenting on disarmament. Since the statements they make are left without comment or challenge, they serve to contextualise our understanding of the Church debate. This section of news is linked with the word 'meanwhile':

Meanwhile down the road from the Synod, Michael Heseltine has been talking about the Bomb to a group of Conservative women. He opened his speech by stressing that he was Secretary of State for Defence, not

Attack, and went on to explain the government's stance on disarmament: 'No sane person could hold my job for a moment without becoming preoccupied with how to achieve negotiated arms control and arms reducton. I believe that if we are to do this, we must maintain forces strong enough to deter aggression, while at the same time pursuing security at low levels of force on both sides. The so-called "peace campaigners" present these as opposites, but in negotiating with a hardheaded power like the Soviet Union they must go hand in hand.'

Newscaster: In the Commons the Prime Minister affirmed that President Reagan's zero option is not a 'take it or leave it' option, but she went on to stress that it is the ultimate goal, because it would provide the very best possible result for those who believe in safe-guarding our way of life. The United States Vice-President George Bush left London today at the end of his seven-nation European tour. Before he went he stressed that his attitude on disarmament had changed little:

Bush: I have heard only one argument, only one, against our proposal. You know what it was? The Soviet Union doesn't like it. It's not good to negotiate, but again it takes a united strong alliance to stay firmly together and that's what I think we've got as I leave after this eleven-day trip.

Meanwhile, as they say, back at the Synod the Church had actually passed the Bishop of Birmingham's amendment. This endorsed the view that all countries should publicly forswear the first use of nuclear weapons in any form. This was only very briefly referenced on BBC1 and ITN's main evening news bulletins. These programmes have the largest news audiences. Yet this position is quite at variance with British government and NATO policy, and was identified as such on BBC2's *Newsnight*. No bulletin pointed out, however, that the no-first-strike pledge had been publicly made by the Soviet Union at the UN Special Session on Disarmament 1982.

The example we have used of special-event news leads us to suggest that the arrangement and juxtaposition of news information is a form of impression management. After all, the positive decision of the Church on the no first-strike issue could have been the focus of attention and it would presumably have been somewhat more embarrassing to the government had that been the case. Even when it is mentioned in the account there are also techniques that may be deployed to diminish its significance. The conclusion of the Channel 4 bulletin illustrates both the sustaining power of the 'anti unilateralist' story and the discounting of the other issues raised:

Bishop Montefiore's amendment was passed by 275 votes to 222. So the debate ended with the Church of England firmly opposed to unilateral disarmament, but opposed, too, to a central plank in NATO doctrine, the commitment to be the first to use nuclear weapons if conventional forces can't contain a Russian advance. But does any of it matter? If the Church had joined the unilateral disarmers it would have been a huge embarrassment to the Tory Party, the government, especially in election year, and probably the Head of the Church, The Queen herself. It could have cost the Church dear in cancelled covenants from wealthy rightwing supporters, but that was avoided, even though Synod decisions like these aren't actually binding on anybody.

Channel 4

A day in the life of the Church became a day in the life of the media. Did it really matter? Did we really want to hear a group of serious-minded people calling the nation and the government to a position of no-first-strike? We would have to have been very attentive to tease out the potential significance of that message.

It would be a mistake to suppose that the concern of the Churches with the issue of nuclear war is to be equated with the presence or absence of media coverage. In this respect it is worth recalling the observations of two Church groupings which met later in 1983. The World Council of Churches at its Vancouver Assembly, July/August 1983, came out with a statement that is at variance with the kind of assumption typically enunciated on television news bulletins:

Nuclear deterrence can never provide the foundation for genuine peace. It is the antithesis of an ultimate faith in that love which casts out fear. It escalates the arms race in a vain pursuit of stability. It ignores the economic, social and psychological dimensions of security and frustrates justice by maintaining the status quo in world politics. It destroys the reality of self-determination for most nations in matters of their own safety and survival, and diverts resources from basic human needs. It is the contradiction of disarmament because it exalts the threat of force, rationalises the development of new weapons of mass destruction, and acts as a spur to nuclear proliferation by persistently breaking the 'good faith' pledge of disarmament in the Non-Proliferation Treaty, thus tempting other governments to become nuclear weapon states. It is increasingly discredited by first-strike and warfighting strategies which betray the doubts about its reliability.

Not surprisingly, in the light of that statement, the World Council of Churches went on to recommend a mutual and verifiable freeze on the development, testing and deployment of nuclear weapons and delivery vehicles. We may pause to wonder what would be the significance of information that was structured on those assumptions, with alternative views being treated as misguided, as opposed to the dominant notion of deterrence as a regrettable necessity for keeping the peace.

In November 1983, the British Council of Churches produced its statement 'On Making Peace in a Nuclear World'. There we read:

> This Council does not question the right of every nation to self-defence. It recognises that this and all nations have legitimate security interests. In view of the present threat to survival, however, it is becoming increasingly clear that traditional understandings of security are no longer adequate. It is now necessary for nations to move (if possible in a United Nations context) towards a framework of common security, an expression of rational love for our enemies, a love that is both in their interests and ours, a love that seeks to avoid steps that they will perceive as threatening.

The Council went on to support an agreed and verifiable freeze between the United States and the Soviet Union. It also urged that the United Kingdom, while remaining within NATO, should phase out British nuclear weapons and should not replace Polaris with Trident missiles. It also supported the view that Britain should support a no-first-use policy and posture within NATO, thus adding its collective weight to the view which prevailed in the Church of England Synod a few months earlier and on which this chapter has focussed.

TEN

Easter '83: Peace Signals?

Easter demonstrations: media coverage

The week of the Easter demonstrations, 1983, provided a good example of the exchanges involved in the propaganda war. Diplomatic moves, propaganda stunts, government pronouncements and arms control initiatives all culminated in the major demonstrations that weekend in Britain and on the Continent.

Immediately preceding the demonstrations President Reagan announced his interim zero option offer to the Soviet Union. On the eve of the main CND protest march– a linking of arms between Aldermaston, Greenham Common and Burghfield - it was announced that Soviet diplomats were being expelled from several European capitals, including Britain. It was stated in London that three Soviet diplomats were being sent home for actions inconsistent with diplomatic activities, a phrase usually taken as a euphemism for spying. The same day, Thursday, which coincided with the beginning of the CND protests, the Secretary of State for Defence, Micheal Heseltine, paid a visit to the Berlin Wall. The CND blockade of Burghfield on Thursday was followed by the main demonstration on Good Friday. The Secretary of State for Defence, on his return to Britain that same day, gave a press conference. The weekend saw further demonstrations in Scotland at Faslane and on the Continent. Events were completed by the Soviet Foreign Minister, Andrei Gromyko, who called a press conference in Moscow to announce his country's response to the interim zero offer. How did the press and television news cover these events?

Press coverage[1]

There was in general little critical press reporting of the US interim zero option offer and much space was given to the government viewpoint throughout the week. The protests, by and large, we singled out as publicity stunts, with little attempt made to solicit the opinions of any who participated. Whereas the Heseltine visit to the Berlin Wall was reported at face value, or in a supportive manner, much of the CND coverage was tied in with Soviet actions or intentions.

> Reagan Administration officials and European diplomats acknow-ledged . . . that President Reagan's compromise offer on medium-range missiles would almost certainly be rejected by Moscow, but they felt it was nonetheless essential in the battle for the political support of Western Europeans. 'That's what this negotiation' with the Soviet Union 'is all about', a ranking State Department official said. 'It all comes down to whether we or the Russians are more convincing to the Europeans, and whether the Europeans will back new American missile deployments or will block them,' the official said.[2]

In London, The *Times* (31.3.83) indicated that the offer was designed to defuse the peace movement protests. Indeed, when the US officials realised that Good Friday was not a normal publishing day for the press in Western Europe they brought the announcement forward in time for the Thursday press, so that it would precede the Easter demonstrations.

The interim zero option went unreported in the *Daily Star* but in other tabloid papers there was some coverage. The *Sun* tagged a couple of sentences on to a piece about Michael Heseltine's visit to the Berlin Wall.

> The government welcomed President Reagan's compromise plan for the European arms negotiations. The President offered to cut back American deployment plans if the Russians reduce their medium-range rockets.
>
> 31.3.83

The *Daily Mirror* heralded Reagan's new deal on disarmament, while the *Daily Express* and *Daily Mail* devoted more attention to the interim zero option than the other tabloids. The article in the *Daily Express* took up nearly a third of a page, yet there was no mention of any possible flaws in the proposals. The newspaper simply contented itself with outlining NATO's position. The *Daily Mail* was more jaunty about it all. Under the headline 'Match this, Reagan tells the Russians' it stated: 'President Reagan last night threw down the gauntlet to Russia over missiles in Europe', and went on to quote at length from his speech. It outlined the reasons for the Soviet rejection of the original zero option. These were listed as NATO's refusal to count in British and French missiles and US intermediate systems on planes and ships. The *Mail* further stated that, as a result of Moscow's rejection, the European members of NATO had pressured the US into making a new offer: 'Were the Russians to dismiss this compromise, they would look intransigent.' The *Mail's* use of the word 'compromise' is noteworthy, as the new Reagan offer did not include either British or French missiles. Yet they had already noted that this had been one of the factors responsible for the Soviet rejection of the original zero option.

The *Mail* accompanied the article with a leader entitled 'Out of the bunker'. It applauded the new offer and claimed that Reagan was willing to 'meet the Russians half-way'. The leader concluded by placing its confidence in hard-headed negotiation rather than 'one-sided disarmament' (a phrase much used by government supporters).

The coverage of the interim zero option in the tabloid press was sparse and uncritical. No objections to the proposals were raised or noted nor was any attention given to the underlying rationals of the proposals. The coverage in the quality press was, as one might expect, more comprehensive. However, the approach taken in *The Times* and the *Daily Telegraph* resembled that of the tabloid press in its underlying assumptions. The *Daily Telegraph* devoted 200 column centimetres to the interim zero offer.The only element of criticism appeared at the bottom of the back page. *The Times* presented a picture of a massive Soviet lead of 1,000 missile warheads in land-based nuclear weapons without mentioning the existence of contrary interpretations regarding the 'balance'. 'It was sensible of Mr Reagan,' *The Times* thought, 'to have sought an interim agreement.' He had given his negotiators greater scope to negotiate. The *Guardian* was critical of the new move from Washington. The *Financial Times* reported that, although reasonable on the surface, the proposals would be unacceptable to the Soviet Union. In addition to concern over sea-based cruise missiles it mentioned that the Soviet Union could hardly be expected to agree to limit its Asian systems without Chinese participation. It went on to say:

> These detailed issues are overshadowed by the much more general question raised by the apparent revision of US strategic policy....All

arms control negotiations between the superpowers have been based on a common understanding that large-scale deployment of anti-ballistic-missile systems would be highly destabilising and dangerous. . . . This has, at the very least, been shaken by the President's television speech . . . . [Soviet doubts] can only have been reinforced . . . by the violence of the President's rhetorical attack on the Soviet Union.

These comments stand in contrast with the reporting in other papers. The propaganda element in the offer is not dwelt upon. Yet it is instructive to compare this uncritical, even supportive coverage with the observations of Lawrence Freedman:

> Those responsible for the [NATO two-track] programme hoped from the start that the addition of an arms control offer to the force-modernisation plans would be sufficient to deflect the opposition. It was never envisaged that arms control would lead to the abandonment of the plans for 572 Cruise and Pershing missiles, but sufficient slack was built into the numbers to allow for substantial reductions in the name of arms control.[3]

The press reporting of the US offer contrasts with its treatment of the Soviet response. Like the Americans, the Russians sought to portray themselves as champions of peace. Their military statements were based on the problematic concept of balance. As did the West, they referred to their nuclear weapons as being a simple modernisation and not a qualitative change. All the newspapers concurred with NATO that the Soviet rejection was too hasty. Three of them, however, devoted attention to the Soviet position, The *Sunday Mirror's* 'Russia fears us' echoed the *Observer's* 'Kremlin despairs of dealing with Reagan'. These newspapers, together with the *Sunday Times*, while regretting the rejection, cautiously welcomed Reagan's offer, but noted the genuine nature of Soviet misgivings.

The rest of Fleet Street reported the Soviet response firmly within the context of the propaganda war. The *Telegraph* declared: 'Gromyko avoids the real issue', while the *Express* stated: 'Gromyko sounds off in the propaganda war'.

The British press gave a good deal of coverge to the CND actions at Burghfield, Greenham and Aldermaston. All the papers carried the main demonstrations on the front page and many presented large double-page photo-spreads. However, the demonstrations and the peace movement were packaged together with other events of the week, with the Secretary of State for Defence's comments receiving attention. Particularly instructive was the connection drawn with the expulsion of the Soviet diplomats from Britain. The *Daily Star* had a front-page headline: 'Spies alert over peace army.' It told its readers:

> spies were kicked out as a warning to the Kremlin not to meddle in the peace movement. Intelligence cheifs believe that Russia's spymasters have tried to use CND...the good intentions of thousands of ordinary people could be exploited to sabotage the arms talks.
>
> *Daily Star*, 31.3.83

Other papers made similar points albeit in less crude fashion.

The press reports also highlighted the financial costs incurred by the demonstrators and the inconvenience of their protests. *The Times* reported that the Greenham women's action in December had cost £57,000, while on its front page the *Daily Mail* stated: 'Villages under siege by CND'. The *Express* combined both stories noting 'the soaring cost of peace demos' and 'residents making defence plans'. Thousands of people descending on small areas is undoubtedly a cause for concern for the inhabitants. The inconvenience that is caused does not get the same amount of prominence with a sporting or royal occasion. Much coverage was given to CND's decision to hand out passes to local residents during the blockade of the road leading to the Burghfield weapons factory. Adverse comment from residents and the local MP received considerable attention. Finally, much of the coverage focussed on the *Sun's* front-page picture of a person in a bunny outfit climbing into the Greenham base. Such a focus can serve to trivialise the issue and tends to distract from the wide cross-section of people who were present.

Television peace news[4]

'Good evening. Propaganda battles over nuclear weapons dominated the world stage in Easter week,' (*News Review*, 3.4.83). The awareness of the propaganda element permeating the nuclear debate was indeed evident in television news coverage, more so than in the generality of press coverage. As with the press, the interim zero option announcement, the Heseltine visit to the Berlin Wall, The expulsion of Soviet diplomats from Britain, the Gromyko press conference, all figured as well as the peace demonstrations in Britain and on the Continent. How was the peace issue contextualised and what questions does it raise?

While the reporting of the interim zero option did convey a sense that the President was willing to be more flexible in his approach to

Good evening. Propaganda battles over nuclear weapons dominated the world stage in Easter week

BBC *News Review* 3.4.83

arms control, the reports also signalled clearly that he was aiming his remarks at European public opinion. Nor was the timing of the announcement seen as accidental since it immediately preceded the peace demonstrations in Europe. This awareness was also shown in the coverage of the President's announcements on the original zero option and START. At the same time opposition to the interim zero option was identified as coming from CND and the Soviet Union. Other opponents, including some who took the original decision to deploy the new missiles, were not mentioned. The *Daily Telegraph*, on the bottom of its back page, did at least quote Paul Warnke, the chief US negotiator of SALT II, when he said: 'If we agree not to deploy ground-launched Cruise missiles, that is of very little interest to the Soviets if we remain free to deploy sea-launched Cruise missiles' (31.3.83).

In this sense the extent of opposition to the proposal is not indicated. What, after all, were we to expect from the Soviet Union since an ITN newscaster had, in introducing the report, said: 'The President said the Soviet Union had launched a propaganda campaign to separate America from its allies and its allies from each other'? Still, in the ITN report the correspondent's view was that 'Russia is certain to find little that is acceptable in the new proposals.' In the course of his report he points out that the Russians would have to accept much deeper cuts than the Americans. This is based on the calculation that there were 1,000 SS-20's in the Soviet Union (an aggregate of the European and Asian fronts), that the US intention was to deploy 572 Cruise and Pershing II missiles in Western Europe and that the proposed reduction was thought to be down to 300 on each side. The correspondent notes that because of their mobility the Americans were still rejecting the Soviet view that the count of SS-20s should not include Asian-based systems. They also did not accept the Russian view that British and French missiles should be included in the negotiations.

The BBC report also stated categorically: 'Moscow looks certain to reject the American offer'. The correspondent does not outline all the points made in the ITN bulletin but the correspondent's comment towards the end of his report is: 'But the Americans are still giving nothing away on some important points like their refusal to include British and French missiles in the negotiating package.' Hence the question as to who is the more intransigent or the more flexible does not invite an unambiguous response from the viewer. The next day BBC reported that NATO had formally endorsed the interim zero option but that Moscow Radio had dismissed it as 'an old idea in a new wrapping'.

On Easter Sunday, the official Soviet response to the interim zero option was presented by Mr Gromyko, the Soviet Foreign Minister, at a Moscow press conference. Both BBC and ITN covered it. The ITN Sunday evening bulletin pointed out that such conferences were rare and that Mr Gromyko complained about people who talked about lofty morals at the same time as they were preparing for war. Using still photographs of Mr Gromyko the report itemised three main objections which the Soviets had to the US proposals. In each instance, however, the American reply was also cited:

- 162 British and French missiles not included.
  American reply: These are tactical weapons and not in the same category as SS-20s.
- Missiles on US planes and ships not included.
  American reply: It has never ruled out agreements to cover them.
- Russian 'right' to move SS-20s to Asia.
  American reply: They could easily be moved back again to the European area.

These replies are then reinforced by a statement from the British

Foreign Secretary. The newscaster said that Mr Pym was quick to reply calling the Soviet position untrue and deliberately misleading:

> *Pym:* I think it's immensely serious that the Russians are always saying no. When are they going to stop saying no, no, no? It's rather like the Stalin period when they kept on saying *niet*, which is Russian for no. They have the preponderance now as I've proved out of their own statements and I think it's immensely serious. The only reason they are sitting down now and appearing to negotiate is because we have said that we will modernise our own weapons. They've modernised theirs. They have the advantage and the preponderance and that is what is unbalanced.

The BBC1 evening news bulletin was similar in that it outlined the three main Soviet objections to the interim zero option proposal and also used a statement by Francis Pym as a reply. Again Pym said the Russians were being deliberately misleading as to what the figures are: 'they're always trying to negotiate on a false basis of figures. However, in introducing the item the reporter in Moscow said it was a 'clear announcement that the American proposals are unacceptable' and that Mr Gromyko had made a 'crisp statement'. He reported that Mr Gromyko had suggested that the Americans did not want to reach agreement since they knew the proposal would be rejected. It was, the correspondent thought, 'a smooth performance by Mr Gromyko'.

The BBC2 *News Review* on Easter Sunday, after its opening statement about propaganda battles (noted at the head of this section), telescoped the two press conferences, Reagan's and Gromyko's. The written statements underneath the pictures of the two policiticians are cryptically presented. They do, however, give the kernel of the organisation of the story and it is also instructive to see how the ensuing item is contextualised:

A White House speech

Nato Ambassadors present but

real audience is public opinion

mainly European public opinion

Voice-over: President Reagan wanted people in Europe to see that America could be flexible.

Nato governments supported the plan. But Russia, as predicted, dismissed it out of hand.

Gromyko: President Reagan, he said, was claiming to champion lofty moral values while preparing for war.

The plan ignored many allied weapons in Europe but would scrap some in Soviet Asia.

Meanwhile, the Soviet news media gave great prominence to the latest Greenham Common protestors.

For present purposes a brief comment on Mr Heseltine's visit to the Berlin Wall will suffice. This was openly acknowledged by Mr Heseltine to be a propaganda exercise and it was recognised as such by the media. This raises the question of what we are to make of news values which choose to cover what was palpably a public relations exercise. After all the government has a routine opportunity to assert and explain its policy on arms control and defence. When the government decided to take on the peace movement and send Mr Heseltine to Berlin at the taxpayers' expense the news media colluded with him and in doing so the presentation of the peace demonstrations was influenced. No doubt this was done in the name of balance, but the peace demonstrators do not have the regular access to television news bulletins that the powerful in our society can command. If one person's balance is another person's bias then those who hae the power to balance as they see fit should perhaps, from time to time, explain and justify what it is they are doing.

Demonstrations

On the day of CND's arm link between Greenham, Burghfield and Aldermaston, the demonstration was the main item on both channels. In both cases over five minutes were devoted to the protest. In quantitative terms the CND organisers had some reason to be pleased with the coverage they received. What kind of coverage was it?

Television news did not endorse the government's view of the peace movement. The notion, for example, of a Kremlin-manipulated demonstration is not carried (although as in other peace protests reference is made to counter-demonstrations which do imply such a view). The picture of human chain demonstration at Greenham and the Glasgow 'die-in' the next day (Saturday) as well as the protest at Faslane submarine base on the Clyde (Sunday) was far from unsympathetic. The news laid stress on how good-natured, well meaning and committed the protesters were: 'Critics might argue with their viewpoint but surely not with their commitment' (ITN, 22.00, 1.4.83).

CND spokespersons were given access to explain their view on the nature of the protest:

> This has been the most moving, imaginative and I think hugely successful demonstration of all time in Britain. We have demonstrated again we oppose the manufacture of nuclear weapons, and the deployment of new weapons and the research into any future nuclear weapons. We will have none of it.

> Extract from Joan Ruddock (Chairperson of CND) speech, ITN, 22.00, 1.4.83

Bruce Kent (General Secretary of CND):

> The object is not just to mass the numbers but really to show people these Cruise missiles here and we have the research center at Aldermaston and we have the bomb factory. This is what I call nuclear valley and we are warning people that, with the first strike weapons and the first use weapons coming, this country is drifting towards nuclear war.

> ITN, 22.00, 1.4.83

In the reporting, protesters themselves were given access to state their reasons for being on the demonstration:

> It will achieve national and I hope worldwide press, and I hope that we can put our points of view forward.

> BBC1

> We are going into a new lunatic age and somebody has to stand up and be counted. I thought I must be there to be counted with them.

> BBC1

> We're ordinary British people who feel strongly that we want a peaceful future, and we're not going to get it with nuclear weapons on our territories.

> ITN, 22.00

> To show exactly what we feel about these nuclear weapons, and why we're here - and that's why I'm here and my daughter, because I want a tomorrow's world for her.

> ITN, 22.00

> Mrs Thatcher should be doing something for peace instead of telling us what we should be doing. What's she done for peace?

> ITN, 22.00

The ITN reporter did not seek to play down the scale of the demonstration. He concluded by saying: 'The sheer size of the rally will give added weight to those who are opposing the siting of new

American missiles not only in Britain but also anywhere in Europe.' (ITN, 22.00, 1.4.83).

Yet, threaded into the report, the correspondent still feels obliged to refer to the government's position, despite the fact that this is routinely reported on news bulletins, apart from high days and holidays. So he tells us: 'Mrs Thatcher has made no secret of her distaste for this weekend's protest, nor her belief, shared by President Reagan, that these people are at best misguided, and at worst dangerous and subversive' (ITN, 22.00, 1.4.83). Thus, besides being contextualised by accounts of the Heseltine visit, the report is permeated with references to the official government position, as though the CND protests cannot be presented simply in their own terms.

This was also true of the BBC evening bulletin with opening and closing references to the omni-present Mr Heseltine:

> It was, said the organisers, the most moving and successful demonstration of all time in Britain. According to the Defence Minister, it was misguided and naive. Either way, tens of thousands of people stood shoulder to shoulder along what the protesters call 'nuclear valley' in Berkshire.
>
> BBC1 21.00, 1.4.83

The report from the demonstration itself did stress the widespread support for the protest:

> They came to Berkshire in their thousands...an army of CND supporters from all over Britain. And they quickly filled the narrow country roads leading to the nuclear bases. Most arrived in fleets of coaches, all convinced of the value of their protest....demonstrators of all ages...and a variety of lifestyles. They were united by their opposition to nuclear weapons. For some it was clearly a family outing....and even members of the women's peace camp seemed in a holiday mood as they enjoyed a joke at the expense of the police. But the mood became more serious with the formation of the human chain along what's become known as 'nuclear valley'. It stretched fourteen miles from Greenham Common to the weapons factory at Burghfield...and also included the Aldermaston research centre. The symbolic joining of hands was the reason they'd come here... and the line was unbroken.
>
> BBC1, 1.00, 1.4.83

However, after film of both the British and West German protests it shown, Mr Heseltine is given the last word. It is not exactly a benediction:

> So I have got the simplest of messages for those who march today. You

do so in freedom and that freedom is your right and I am charged with its defence, however much I may deplore the inconvenience and the cost you impose on the majority of us who don't share your views. But don't believe for one moment that we will risk that freedom, our freedom as well as yours, by following you along a naive and reckless road.

Thus topped and tailed, sympathetic though the report of the event was, the story was sandwiched between Heseltine negatives. This same Heseltine statement was used in the early and late evening bulletins on both BBC and ITN. In making the point that the majority did not share the demonstrators' views, Mr Heseltine's position was not beyond dispute. The previous evening BBC2 *Newsnight* had cited poll evidence which indicated that, while the majority of the population were opposed to unilateral nuclear disarmament, all the polls concurred that the majority of the population was against the installation of Cruise missiles. The Gallup poll figure cited was 54% *against* Cruise missiles in Britain, and 32% *for*.

Although television news was aware of the propaganda war surrounding the peace and defence issue, it remains the case that decisions have to be made as to what to show. It is, for example, common to reference any counter-demonstration, however tiny, and sometimes with visual illustration of their objections. In the case of the Easter demonstration, the BBC reporter comments: 'Up above, someone clearly had doubts about the exercise.' We are then shown in vision the streamer from a plane reading, 'CND Kremlin's April Fools A similar example occurred in October 1983, when the reporter noted with visual accompaniment: 'A minor counter-demonstration' which 'accused CND of being communist, neutralist and defeatist' (BBC1, 19.25, 22.10.83).

Another decision to be made is which speakers to cover. This is best illustrated from the June 1982 and October 1983 rallies, which were more speaker-oriented than the Easter 1983 link-up. We have appended lists of the speaker programme for each occasion. For 6 June, both ITN and BBC carried extracts from speeches by Tony Benn and Arthur Scargill out of a list of some twenty-four. For BBC this selection was regarded as inevitable:

Religious groups were much in evidence, making this more than just a political gesture against the Americans who want to site their nuclear missiles in Britain. Inevitably though it was the political speeches which received most attention, favourable or otherwise.

BBC1, 17.50, 6.6.82

Similarly in the October demonstration we heard a brief extract from a Neil Kinnock speech out of a list of twelve. There is of course nothing inevitable about this. Other speeches could have been cited over and above those that were chosen, to give perhaps a greater representative sense of the occasion.

This points to a more general problem about the coverage of peace demonstrations. Demonstrations are in themselves ritualised events, expressions of the deep feelings which thousands of people have about the nuclear issue – deep enough to make them want to identify with the movement. However, it is not an obvious vehicle for the expression of rational argument, especially if coverage of the speeches is restricted. It becomes easy for opponents to depict this as an emotional movement rather than as a reasoned opposition containing people who are at best well meaning but naive, and at worst subversives playing on the fears of the population. If coverage of CND tends to be restricted to such occasions on television news, along with incidents such as Bruce Kent's address to the British Communist Party or his supposed difficulties with his Church or with Cardinal Hume, then the central argument of the peace movement, that the system of deterrence is unstable and precarious, is unlikely to be articulated consistently and clearly in any regular way. Deterrence may be a simple idea but it has a range of connotations and implications that are rarely unpacked on the news. Perhaps its axiomatic status overstates its credibility. It certainly diminishes the consideration of alternative possibilities.

Timetable for speakers at the CND national demonstration, Sunday 5 June 1983

12.30   Entertainers.
 1.20   Pat Comerford (Irish CND).
        Myrtle Solomon (Ch. War Resisters International).
        Jennifer Armstrong (Coord. East Anglia Alliance against Nuclear Power).
        Judith Hart MP.
        Andreas Christodoulides (Mem. PASOK Exec., on behalf of Andreas Papandreou).
 1.50   Entertainers
 2.10   Dr Kenneth Greet (Sec. Methodist Conference).
        Isobel Lindsay (SNP).
        Shorty O'Neill (Nat. Fed. Aboriginal Land Councils).
        Susan Lamb (Bridgend Peace Camp).
        Dr Petur Riemarsson (Ch. Iceland Campaign Against Military Bases).

2.40   Entertainers.
3.00   Helen John (Greenham Common Peace Camp).
       Takako Tatematsu (V. Pres. Japanese Women's
       Organisation. Dir., Gensikyo).
       Major Van der Wetering (Pres. Dutch Military Council for
       Peace & Security).
       Charlotte Wager (Schools Against the Bomb).
       Prof. Michael Pentz (V. Ch. CND).
3.30   Entertainers.
3.50   Arthur Scargill (Pres. NUM).
       Maj-Britt Theorin (Swedish Social Democrat MP).
       Sue Younger (Ch. Young Liberals).
       Terry Provence (US Freeze Campaign).
       Live telephone link with Bruce Kent in New York at
       United Nations.
4.20   Entertainers.
4.40   Edward Thompson.
       Annajoy David (Youth CND).
       Tony Benn MP.
       Joan Ruddock (Ch. CND).
       Presentation of the joint European Declaration with
       representatives of the European peace movements.
5.30   Finish.

Running order for Hyde Park

12.30	Entertainments	Roland Muldoon.
		The Amazing Mendezies.
		Benjamin Zephaniah.
		Frankie Armstrong.
2.00	Speakers	Bishop Trevor Huddleston
		(Pres. National Peace Council).
		Youth.
		Su Lamb (Greenham Women
		Against Cruise).
2.35	Entertainments	The Flatlets.
		Robyn Archer/Cut and Thrust
		Co.
3.05	Speakers	Paddy Ashdown, MP.
		(Liberal Party).
		Edward Thompson (Co-founder,
		END).
		Alva Myrdal (International
		telephone link with Swedish
		Nobel Peace Prize winner).

3.25	Entertainments	Spartacus R.
3.45	Speakers	Ron Todd. (TGWU Nat. Organiser and Vice-Pres. CND). Dorothy Cotton (US Freeze Movement).
4.05	Entertainments	Jim Morris.
4.25	Fundraising speech	Professor Mike Pentz (Ch. SANA and Vice Ch. CND).
4.30	Speakers	Neil Kinnock (Labour Party). Bruce Kent (General Secretary CND). Joan Ruddock (Ch. CND).
5.00	We Shall Overcome ...	

ELEVEN

The Current Affairs Prism

What part have current affairs programmes played in the area of peace, defence and disarmament questions? We take as our point of departure two short articles by Peter Fiddick: 'Is TV properly reflecting the public concern with nuclear weapons?' and 'Doomsday debates that fit their pigeonhole'. The second of these is essentially an updating and amplification of the first. Fiddick reviewed the way in which the nuclear issue has come back on to the agenda of television since 1979 and raised a number of questions as to what it all signified. We take matters a step further by considering some more recent current affairs programmes and the formats and formulae within which they tend to operate.

Fiddick reminds us that in addition to treatment of the nuclear issue on regular current affairs programmes such as *Panorama*, *Weekend World* and *World in Action*, there is evidence of additional coverage. Among the examples he cites are *QED*; the BBC's popular science programme showed Mick Jackson's film *A Guide to Armageddon*. This sought to demonstrate what would happen if a one-megaton bomb was exploded above St Paul's Cathedral, and thereby give some appreciation of the power of today's nuclear weapons. Channel 4's all-women current affairs programme *Broadside* opened with a film on Greenham Common and the women's peace movement; it later looked at the effects of exposure to nuclear contamination on British servicemen and Australian Aborigines as a result of the weapons test programme in Australia during the 1950s. *Everyman*, the BBC's religious affairs programme, also looked at the Greenham peace protest. Although Fiddick does not mention it, *Everyman* also produced a film report by Peter France entitled *What's Wrong with the Bomb?*. This was an account of the World Council of Churches hearing

277

on nuclear weapons and Christain conscience, which took place in Amsterdam in November 1981. There have been presentations of the defence debate made by Jonathan Dimbleby–his documentaries on *The Bomb* and *The Eagle and the Bear*–by John Pilger in *The Truth Game* and by Max Hastings in *The War about Peace*.

Fiddick comments in his *Listener* article:

> On the face of it, all this adds up to not a bad record of television, the main national communication medium, dealing with one of the most pressing subjects of national concern. If some researcher were to ferret out all the reports, discussions and documentaries, the list would seem quite long, I do not doubt, and the approaches suitably various, exposing different facets of a complicated and changing bundle of issues.

Before touching on Fiddick's doubts and questions as to what this signifies, let us look at some examples of programmes that have been screened since May 1983. Most of this is within the current affairs framework, although we also make brief reference to other kinds of coverage, notably Channel 4's Nuclear Week in May 1983, which took on added significance since it was in the middle of the British General Election campaign.

As far as current affairs programmes are concerned, there are three main formats: (1) the structured debate; (2) the film report plus studio discussion; (3) the film report without studio discussion.[3]

1. *The structured debate*

The debate format is not uniform. Different programmes may operate different ground rules relating to turn-taking, the use of witnesses, the possibilities of cross-examination and ways of evaluating the outcome. For example, on 4 May 1983, BBC2 featured *The Great Nuclear Arms Debate*. This was in fact an American CBS programme, briefly introduced for a British audience by Charles Wheeler but chaired by CBS's Walter Cronkite. Four contributors in London, New York, Florence and Bonn respectively were linked up by satellite. These were Michael Heseltine, the British Secretary of Defence, Henry Kissinger, a former US Secretary of State, Paul Warnke, formerly a US SALT negotiator, and Egon Bahr, the chief opposition spokesperson on arms control for the Social Democratic Party in West Germany.

The debate lasted ninety minutes and was on the subject of the deployment of Cruise and Pershing II missiles in Europe. Cronkite soberly told his audience that there would be no concession to entertainment. The debate was preceded by a short film with voice-over commentary. This referenced the post-war growth in the arms race with long- and short-range weapons, the signing of SALT I and the refusal on the part of the USA to ratify SALT II in the aftermath, it was said, of the Soviet involvement in Afghanistan. The Soviet refusal to accept President Reagan's zero option was noted. The growth of the peace movement in Europe and the USA including the proposal for a nuclear freeze was also presented as part of the climate in which the current Geneva arms talks were taking place. A formal resolution was then put for debate: 'The United States should proceed with its scheduled deployment of nuclear weapons in Europe.' There was to be no formal voting on the resolution; at the end of the debate, which concluded in the early hours of 5 May in Britain, although it occupied prime time on American TV, Cronkite simply said that he would leave the outcome of the debate to the audience 'and perhaps to history'.

The procedure for the debate was elaborated at the outset: each speaker had $5^{1}/_{2}$ minutes to begin with; they then had 4 minutes each to reply to points that others had made; each then had 4 minutes' summary time; and finally there was time for a less rigidly organised exchange of views. Cronkite simply facilitated the turn-taking. Essentially this was a discussion about the strategy and tactics of arms control negotiations, especially the Geneva INF talks. As such the language of the debate was couched in political and military terms. Heseltine and Kissinger supported the dual track position of NATO and its timetable, whilst Warnke and Bahr expressed reservations. Bahr appeared the most sceptical and suggested that fruitful discussions and negotiations were not possible on the basis of present positions and that both sides needed to negotiate seriously. There was, however, no account of how NATO arrived at its dual track strategy and why its modernisation programme had been linked to the deployment of SS 20s by the Soviets. Was the rationale primarily military or political? Nor, as Cronkite mentioned at the end of the programme, was there a contribution from the nuclear freeze lobby, which would have produced an alternative perspective on what was on narrowly defined arms control debate.

The restricted terms within which this debate was conducted led to criticism from Professor Michael Pentz, a leading figure in CND. In a letter to the *Guardian* he challenged the accuracy of the figures relating to nuclear weaponry cited by Kissinger and Heseltine. He concluded:

This non-debate showed yet again that the exclusion of serious critics of

NATO policy from 'the nuclear debate' is depriving the public of its right to know about and to judge an issue of vital importance to its security and survival.[4]

Such critics are not always excluded on current affairs as we shall show; nevertheless this objection reminds us that, even when the chairman of the debate was non-interventionist, the selection of the participants was a crucial editing decision. It remains possible that relevant and considered views on the topic in question may be ommitted even when a large amount of time is allocated, as on this occasion.

In a debate screened on 29 May 1983, as part of Channel 4's Nuclear Week, CND did play a leading role. The resolution was: 'Nuclear weapons are immoral and serve no military purpose. Britain should give them up unilaterally.' This was chaired by Peter Jay, an experienced journalist and a former British Ambassador to the United States. The resolution was proposed by Monsignor Bruce Kent, General Secretary of CND, and opposed by Keith Ward, Professor of Moral and Social Theology at Kings College, London. Each side was given thirty minutes to put forward their case. They were allowed to call two witnesses to support their case, who were also subject to cross-examination by the opposing side. This gave something of a court room atmosphere to proceedings, which was added to by the fact that a panel of twelve people, selected by a market research company 'because they have an open mind on this issue', was present to vote on the issue. In the event seven supported the motion, four opposed and one abstained. At the end of the programme Jay asked a number of the panel why they voted the way they did.

Given the title of the debate it was not surprising that the arguments were couched in both moral and military terms. Bruce Kent referred to just war theory, arguing from the principle of proportion that the use of nuclear weapons is wholly disproportionate to any objectives imaginable and therefore was immoral. He argued that first use of nuclear weapons was part of NATO's doctrine and that first strike capacity was now more feasible with the advance of technology. In consequence, he maintained, the modernisation of nuclear weapons was destablishing in its effect and that, moreover, in military terms Britain's possession of nuclear weapons was senseless since their use against the Soviet Union would be suicidal. He used as his witnesses Dr Paul Rogers, Senior Lecturer in Peace Studies at Bradford University, and Ms Sheila Oates, General Secretary of the National Peace Council.

Keith Ward based his case on the right to self-defence in a violent world, arguing that the possession of nuclear weapons served to defend the values of the rule of law, democracy and civilisation. There are, he maintained, no self-evident absolutist truths in this situation and the realist has to think about the likely consequences of proposed actions. The possession of nuclear weapons was therefore not immoral in itself and could defend Britain against nuclear blackmail. He concluded that his view took better account of the complexities of the matter. As witnesses he used two colleagues from Kings College, the Professor of War Studies, Lawrence Freedman, and the Principal, General Sir John Hackett, formerly of NATO High Command. The arguments used by both sides covered very similar ground to that of the Church and the Bomb debate, which we have already discussed.

2. The film report plus studio discussion
We take three examples of this format. The first is *Weekend World's Inquiry on the Bomb*, shown on 22 May 1983, on Channel 4. Brian Walden provided the voice-over to the film and interviewed the studio participants in an unusually long programme lasting 1 hour 40 minutes. He introduced the programme by telling us that the Bomb was second only to unemployment as an election issue. The film that followed sought to pursue the question, how and why did we get to our present predicament?

In his voice-over commentary Walden started from the Second World War. He proceeded to reference Hiroshima, the post-war European settlement, the formation of NATO, Britain's decision to go nuclear, the development of Soviet nuclear weapons and the movement of the USA's position from one of mutually assured destruction (MAD) to flexible response. This was the story, said Walden, of how we developed nuclear weapons to defend against foreign tyranny but today doubts are expressed about its wisdom. The story he told with the aid of archive film was elaborated and assisted on the way by comments from military and strategic experts including Professor Margaret Gowing, Colonel Jonathan Alford, Professor Lawrence Freedman, Philip Windsor, Phillip Williams, Professor Michael Howard and David Bolton. Institutional affiliations of these people included Oxford University, the LSE, the Institute for Strategic Studies, the Institute of International Affairs, and the Royal United Services Institute.

Walden then interviewed three senior representatives of the main parties: Micheal Heseltine (Conservative) John Silkin (Labour) and

David Owen (SDP Alliance). The programme was in the run-up to the election and Walden as interviewer centred his questions on what he regarded as problematic in each party's position. Heseltine is asked about how a Tory government will handle a continuing protest movement. Silkin is questioned about the 'realism' of Labour's unilateralist position on nuclear weapons and Owen about the niceties of no-first-use and no-early-use policy in relation to NATO's nuclear strategy.

The position of the presenter in this kind of format is very powerful and in a sense the more so since he is not ostensibly offering us a 'personal view'. He tells us at the beginning of the programme that we are dealing with complex military and diplomatic matters but claims that the film will set out the facts. Yet the selection of facts and their interpretation is fraught with methodological problems. The presenter is also an interpreter. In that respect Mr Walden's own political background as a former Labour MP opposed to unilateral nuclear disarmament over an extended period should be recalled. The choice of 'experts' to reinforce the implicit line in the programme is also crucial and simply nuances aspects of the philosophy of deterrence. In a strong attack on the programme, E. P. Thompson of END wrote:

> What was offensive about this operation was the fact that anyone familiar with the literature will know that these 'experts' were hand-picked and rehearsed by Mr Walden to confirm the prejudices which Mr Walden has long held, and that for every 'expert' offered the presenter could have (if he had wished to be objective) found an expert with equal or greater authority to offer a contrary view. And most of the questions proposed by Walden to these experts were not matters of information at all, which require expert research, but were matters of political choice and value as to which these gentlemen have no more right to claim authority than any other citizen.[5]

In the studio interviews that followed the initiative is also very much with the interviewer. The participants were segregated from each other in the conventional arrangements and the presenter becomes the mediator of the message through the questions he chooses to ask.

The second example of this format is the BBC's programme *A Matter for Joint Decision*, screened in November 1983. This was presented and chaired by John Tusa, when Heseltine, Silkin and Owen as political adversaries and party spokesmen were again involved in the studio discussion. Was there, could there be, should there be, dual control over the use of American nuclear weapons based in Britain? This issue was explored in a film report by David Henshaw.

The reason for taking up the issue was anchored to an opinion poll which indicated that 55% of the population was against the installation of Cruise missiles and 45% for it. At the same time 82% as against 18% was reported as being in favour of the presence of nuclear weapons in Britain. In the case of Cruise, however, only 4% of the population thought that the USA should have sole control, whilst the overwhelming 96% supported dual control if the missiles were to be installed.

The film report was designed to show, mainly through interviews with US politicians and military people, that despite declared 'understanding' dual control was not a serious reality and over the past thirty years never has been. The US airforce has been in Britain continuously since 1948, when it first arrived for what were described as goodwill and training purposes. General Len Johns of the USAF, who was in Britain between 1948-52, pointed out that alert and could have been made ready if necessary. Professor Margaret Gowing took the view that the then Prime Minister, Clement Attlee, did not realise the implications of what he was doing and made no agreements about the use of the bases. Dean Acheson, then US Secretary of State, had taken the view that the British could not interfere with the United States' constitutional right to declare war. He would accept, therefore, no agreement on the use of the bases, which none the less increased in number under Attlee and other post-war Prime Ministers. The position essentially taken up in the film report was summed up in the response of the US arms control negotiator Paul Warnke, that the country which physically controls weapons makes the decision and that therefore joint controls are effective until it counts! This view was also expressed by former Secretary of State Robert MacNamara. A definite line is taken in the film report even though it is not billed as a 'personal view'.

The subsequent studio discussion with the politicians was not segregated as in the previous example but involved some interchange between them. Heseltine claimed that the film misrepresented the position, which was that joint control was a reality. Silkin said it was all very disturbing and that there were a number of occasions when American bombers had flown off on an alert without consultation. Owen said that dual control was possible and that the film was ridiculous because it had omitted to mention the period of the Thor missile, 1959-62, when joint control was a reality. It was, he said, safer for this country to be involved in the launch mechanism and that was why the then Prime Minister, Harold Macmillan, had been prepared to pay for it. The concluding part of the programme then allows a turn of the political wheel in which we hear: (1) that we actually have dual control, (2) that we do not and cannot, (3) that we do not but could and should.

A final example of this format is the *Panorama* programme of 21 November 1983. Fred Emery, a regular presenter, opened the programme by referring to the fact that the film *The Day After* had just been shown in the USA and that in Britain we were facing the advent of the Cruise missile. He poses two questions: Are we on the verge of a hair trigger strategy with no time for second thoughts? And are we making the world more dangerous? As with the previous example, use is made of public opinion polls, in this instance a specially commissioned *Panorama*/Marplan poll. Four questions and responses were reported:

1. Should Britain accept American Cruise missiles?

	Nov. 83	*Oct. 83*	*May 83*
Yes	42%	37%	34%
No	47%	48%	54%

2. Has American action over Grenada made you more or less likely to trust the Americans?

More likely	17%
Less likely	58%

3. There should be a physical device to prevent firing without British consent ... 76%
No such safeguard is necessary ... 17%

4. Britain should not keep any nuclear weapons ... 29%
Britain should keep nuclear weapons ... 64%

Whereas in the previous example the responses to the questions aggregated to 100%, here they do not. In the first case the 'don't know' category is ignored, whereas in this case the 'don't knows' are not listed but are implicitly taken into account. But in both instances we can see that from the interpretation of a perceived concern based on poll findings the programme identifies an issue and then proceeds with a film report.

In his film report Peter Taylor explores how it was that the West developed the 'dual attack' approach to arms control and the problems this has brought in its train. The case developed by Taylor was that the reasons for the decisions on Cruise and Pershing II deployment were political and not military. This was prompted by Herr Schmidt, then

West German Chancellor, who feared that the strategic parity of the USA and the USSR, as he saw it, might lead to a refusal on the part of the USA to support Western Europe, and especially West Germany, in the event of a Soviet attack. This anxiety that the USA might 'decouple' from the Western European alliance was all the greater since Schmidt feared that the other members of the alliance might not come to West German's aid in that event. Hence the deployment of United States land-based nuclear theatre weapons, in Schmidt's view, could be seen as a guarantor against decoupling. He successfully argued for this policy within NATO and this was approved in December 1979. According to Raymond Garthoff, a former SALT negotiator, the development of SS 20s was seen as part of the Soviet modernisation programme and in military estimations did not call for additional requirements of deployment or a special necessity to deter the Soviets from deploying SS 20s. Taylor also cited a secret discussion document – 'Theatre modernisation and arms control – prepared by the Americans before the Schmidt initiative which supports this view. This could of course provide a context in which President Reagan's subsequent zero option offer would not be regarded as a serious negotiation by the Soviets. Garthoff suggested that there was nothing surprising about the Soviet rejection of the zero option.

In his report Taylor counter-balances the views of Garthoff with those of Kenneth Adelman, the United States arms control negotiator, who argued that NATO must keep up its deterrent strength. He also contrasted in interviews the differing positions of Helmut Schmidt and Willy Brandt. Brandt, a former Chancellor, now represents the majority view in the SDP, which regards the deployment of Pershing II in West Germany as undesirable.

Two themes emerge in the film: first, that the hearts and minds of the people in the Western alliance have been disaffected by a clumsy policy which has raised many worries; and second, that the effects of deployment will be profoundly destabilising. In particular, Professor John Erickson, an Edinburgh University defence specialist, argued that Pershing II has 10–11 minutes' flight time from launch to target. The Soviets believe, he said, that their command and control centres are under threat by the new weapons and that this severely restricts their military options. Launch on warning becomes their most workable option.

Following the film report, Emery chaired a studio discussion with Michael Heseltine and Dennis Healey, representing the government and the opposition. This hinged on the issue of how far the dual track policy, if it led to the deployment of Cruise and Pershing II, enhanced or diminished collective security. On all aspects of the issue the two men were opposed: the necessity of the policy, its effect on decoupling and destabilisation, and the dangers inherent in it as an element of flexible response strategy. Heseltine supported the policy and the position of Helmut Schmidt. Healey did not and also cast doubt on the good faith of the US negotiators. He pointed out that Adelman, the man in charge of negotiations, had gone on record at one time as saying that arms control negotiations are a sham, whose only purpose was to soothe public opinion at home and abroad.

3. The film report format

Here we cite three examples taken from late 1983. We see that this format can take the character of investigative journalism.

On *Panorama* (5.9.83), Tom Mangold, following a brief introduction from Fred Emery referencing the Korean airliner which the Russians shot down, gave us a report entitled *Beyond Deterrence*. This was filmed in the United States and the interviewees comprised military men, strategic specialists and scientists. Mangold referenced President Reagan's endorsement of the militarisation of space (23 March 1983), the ultimate goal of which was to eliminate the threat posed by strategic nuclear missiles. He cites this as an example of the extension of the arms race and as a concomitant to the doctrine of flexible response, which has taken the place of the earlier deterrent doctrine of mutually assured destruction. Mangold proceeds to bring forward specialist witnesses such as Dr John Steinbruner, Director of Policy Studies at the Brookings Institute, to suggest that with or without extensions into space the whole defence system is vulnerable. Because of this central vulnerability of the command posts and communication networks there is tremendous pressure on both sides (although they deny it) to go for a pre-emptive strike. This can create great tension between political and military decision-makers. Even the President of the USA is viewed as a poor command and control risk. Whether he would reach his jumbo jet in the eight minutes required is doubtful and in any case he would then have no means of communicating with Moscow. Thus the pre-emptive strike would cause very great confusion as a result of the vulnerabilities of the system.

It is in this context that the planned deployment of Cruise and Pershing II is set. The Soviets see them as targeted on Moscow and their command posts. Given the short flight times of Pershing II the options open to the Russians are very limited. The argument followed is that they will be constrained to follow a launch on warning policy and that this is a very risky situation. The extension of defence into space to deal with pre-emptive strikes constitutes the strategic defence plan which goes 'beyond deterrence'. Mangold draws attention to critics who see this as further contributing to the arms race and causing greater instability. Dr Sidney Drell, Professor of Physics at Stanford University, described the whole approach as 'the fallacy of the last move'. Since the time scales for decision have become so short we are living in a hair trigger situation where human decisions are heavily constrained by computers. Hence computer errors can precipitate the fateful exchanges. In a similar vein Dr Desmond Ball of the Department of Strategic Studies at the Australian National University concluded that the question of control is central and that the political control of such technical systems is the most difficult one can possibly envisage. People are deluding themselves if they have confidence in such arrangements.

We can see in this example that Mangold is questioning the rationality of the arms race and the direction it is taking. To do so he employs a combination of scientific and strategic specialists to expose what he sees as the contradiction and dangers implicit in the developing tendencies. Even though he interviews those who support the arms race into space, such as Edward Teller and the head of the Pentagon's Defence Advanced Research Projects Agency, Dr Robert Cooper, it is clear where Mangold's sympathies lie. This comes out in the programme and also in articles in the *Listener* based on his investigation. There he writes of a new instability which could lead to a witting or unwitting pre-emptive strike:

> Even if both superpowers were to develop these new systems in roughly equal time-scales and achieve rough parity, the technological time-scale of warfare will have been changed by several orders of magnitude. Today we still have a precious few minutes – not many, but perhaps enough – to think, reason, cool down and judge against the destruction of the Northern Hemisphere.
>
> In President Reagan's brave new world of strategic defence, those minutes will have been replaced by milliseconds; and human judgement and compassion by the circuits on a silicon chip.
>
> How can that prospect enhance international security?[6]

The second example is a BBC *Newsnight Special* presented by John Tusa in November 1983. This is introduced by an anonymous announcer – 'John Tusa talks to leading defence experts about new ideas on NATO's strategy that could lead to a nuclear-free Europe.' Tusa, in his film report, records the views of senior politicians and military commanders who regard NATO's current policy as 'suicidal, misguided and unnecessary'. They include Robert MacNamara, General Jochen Loser, a former West German NATO chief and Admiral Noel Gaylor. The opinion of Lt General Mikhail Milstein, Senior Researcher at the US–Canada Institute, was also obtained. The overall argument was that the deterrent strategy of NATO was not credible and that a system of defence based on conventional weapons was an available alternative to deal with the Soviet 'threat' in Europe. This was both possible on the basis of new anti-tank weapons and financially credible. And there is no good reason to suppose it would lead to a decoupling of the United States from Western Europe. To move in this direction would take away the need for tactical nuclear weapons and possibly in time go beyond that. So Tusa interpreted his role as presenting the early stages of a debate within NATO of an alternative defence policy that would diminish the reliance of both East and West on nuclear weapons and with it the possibility of judgemental mistakes that could lead to nuclear war.

The third and final example of this kind of investigative journalism is *TV Eye's* programme in November 1983, *Here Comes Cruise*. After a brief introduction from Alastair Burnett, who described Cruise as the most controversial weapon in the present nuclear debate, Peter Prendergast gave his film report. This consisted of a simulation of what was involved in moving Cruise out of Greenham to an appropriate launching-base. A convoy of the exact size and dimensions with replica missiles on board was moved from Greenham some twenty-two miles away to a place just outside the village of Whitchurch in Hampshire.

Air Vice Marshall Stuart Menaul described the weapon in positive terms as very efficient, small, flying subsonic but at reasonably high speed, difficult to detect and not easy to shoot down. Colonel Jonathan Alford said the purpose of moving the weapon out of the base was to keep the other side guessing. Three *vox pop*. interviews were conducted at Whitchurch. Their responses ranged from 'It's got to come. You can't stop progress', to 'They won't work anyway' and 'We can't have peace and destruction at the same time.'

But what is Cruise for? Prendergast outlined the scenario for possible use in relation to a Soviet conventional attack on West Germany where they had obtained the upper hand. Colonel Alford saw the missile as primarily a deterrent but noted that it could be directed at Soviet military bases, which of course implies first use possibility. Frank Barnaby, a former Director of the Stockholm Peace Research Institute, claimed that the missile was accurate to within fifty metres and since it carried very large warheads could destroy military targets. But it was slow and he questioned the usefulness of its strategic and tactical role. Later in the programme the disarmament analyst Dan Smith claimed that if Cruise was used, or the Russians thought it was about to be used, the consequence would be a massive retaliation. Furthermore, although he thought the concept of parity was a ludicrous idea, the Russians work with it. They are behind at present and will want to catch up.

Some doubt was cast upon the usefulness of moving Cruise about the English countryside. Defence analyst Owen Greene pointed out that there are so many defence sites in central and southern England that there are considerable limits as to where the convoy could end up if these were to be avoided. He argued that the Russians would follow the same logic and have all these possibilites targeted. Therefore the weapon was very vulnerable to attack.

Prendergast brought two senior politicians, Dennis Healey (Labour) and Francis Pym (Conservative), down to the site at Whitchurch and interviewed them separately. Healey claimed the weapon was militarily useless because vulnerable to attack; that it raised the risk of a nuclear attack on Britain; that it made disarmament more difficult and that it weakened public support for NATO. Pym argued that it would convince the Kremlin that, even though they are stronger than us, the price for attacking us was too high to pay. Cruise filled a gap in the West's deterrence strategy, he maintained. It would not be a British finger on the button, however. Professor Lawrence Freedman took the view that despite talk of a British veto in the end it was an American decision. The programme concluded that arguments over whether Cruise is the price of peace or the height of folly will go on.

Satire and opinion

In the last week in May 1983, Channel 4 produced a cluster of programmes on the issues of defence disarmament. These had been scheduled before the announcement of the General Election and therefore were additional to the discussion of these matters which the forthcoming election was provoking. The programmes represent a variety of styles, formats and emphases which take us beyond the current affairs mode in some instances.

One new approach to the presentation of the topic of nuclear war was *It'll all be over in half an hour*. This consisted of three late-night programmes on successive evenings in which Jonathan Dimbleby explored a number of questions, which were illustrated by songs and sketches. With a mixture of satire and black humour, the programmes questioned the rationale for the arms race.

The first programme focussed on the in-built momentum of the arms race. It elaborated the significance of President Eisenhower's warnings about the need to control the military-industrial complex. It looked at the ways in which modernisation of weapons systems took place, often in secret as in the case of the Chevaline programme to update Polaris. The role of deterrence theory was then questioned in the light of modernisation programmes since, it was said, new weapons can create new rules and in particular there was now talk of winning a nuclear war. Consequently, nuclear deterrent theory was turned on its head.

The second programme looked at the issue of civil defence. It suggested that we tend to live with images of past wars which are totally inappropriate to a nuclear war. It criticised the government for its unwillingness to give adequate information about the impact and effects of nuclear attacks. It suggested that *Protect and Survive* was thoroughly unsatisfactory as a guide to citizens as to what to do in the event of nuclear war and that there is no coherent civil defence policy except that, in David Owen's words, 'The governors will go underground, the governed will stay on top.' Civil defence, nevertheless is portrayed as being inextricably linked with military strategy. To provide adequate civil defence for all the people would be enormously costly and could sharpen the fear of war, whereas for the deterrence threat to remain credible it is necessary for us to appear resolute and not fearful of war. Against this, Dimbleby suggested, perhaps the less you fear war in the present circumstances the more likely it becomes.

The third and last programme looked at the position of Europe in the context of current nuclear strategic thinking. This considered the doctrine of flexible response, argued that the concept of a limited nuclear war was a dangerous fallacy and encouraged strategists to think of Europe as a principal battleground. Scepticism was expressed about the conduct of arms negotiations insofar as disarmament talks are actually accompanied by increases in nuclear weaponry, in the name of the modernisation. It was argued that the real debate about disarmament must go beyond simplistic labels of unilateralist and multilateralist. Attention was drawn to the views of Lord Mountbatten, Lord Carver and Sen. Edward Kennedy as departures from orthodoxy. The conclusion was drawn that there is no longer a consensus on nuclear strategy in Europe, and that is partly a result of the growth of the peace movement in Europe and its impact on the political parties. Consequently, we have reached a critical moment in a critical debate.

These programmes could be described as anti-establishment in their general thrust. Nor did they ignore the position of the Soviet Union and its responsibility to promote peace through disarmament. They were a new departure in style. With the memorable exception of the comedian Jasper Carrot reading out portions of *Protect and Survive* in the course of one of his programmes, it is difficult to think of nuclear defence issues being handled in this format. The songs were reminiscent of those of Tom Lehrer first heard some two decades or more earlier.

For the three days in which *It'll all be over in half an hour* was shown there were also three *Opinion* programmes. In each case these were shown directly following the anti-nuclear satirical programme; in each case also the chosen spokesman defended the policy of nuclear deterrence. These were straight to the camera talks with only slight camera movements around a head and shoulders focus. The sequencing of these programmes could be interpreted as an attempt at balance.

Michael Howard, Professor of History at Oxford University, spoke on the case against unilateral nuclear disarmament. His argument was that we cannot disinvent nuclear weapons and return to the garden of nuclear innocence and that the concept of deterrence was the worst system for keeping the peace except for all the others. Policy should be based on the attempt to maximise the deterrent effect while minimising the chance of use. The realistic approach, he argued, to keeping peace was through arms control agreements. Alternatives such as nuclear-free zones in Europe, or absolute moral positions such as pacificism, would, he judged, have the unintended consequence of destabilising the world and creating terrible uncertainly. We have to take to account of the consequences of our actions rather than having utopian views about world government or bringing about a new international order. We can stabilise the peace if we are clear headed.

He concluded with the observation that it is unwise in a minefield simply to get up and run.

Lord Cameron, a former Chief of Defence Staff, argued the case for a nuclear defence policy for Britain. He started from a similar position to Professor Howard: nuclear weapons cannot be disinvented. Millions of people did not take the Nazi threat seriously; it would be just as mistaken to ignore the Soviet threat today. Lord Cameron described the Soviet arms position as representing a real but marginal advantage over the West, and justified the NATO doctrine of flexible response. He went on to justify from his standpoint the deployment of Cruise and Pershing, NATO's first strike position, Britain's independent nuclear deterrent and the decision to install Trident as a replacement for Polaris (preferring the larger D5 to the C4 system).

Roger Scruton, Reader in Philosophy at Birbeck College, London, entitled his talk, 'The Illusions of Disarmament'. This was a very explicit attack on CND. He likened this 'so-called peace movement' to Hitler's Nuremberg pre-war rallies, where crowds supported him with a mystical enthusiasm for a cause they did not understand. He likened the CND movement to a millennarian religion with an apocalyptic longing to be rid of the dilemmas of the real world. CND's concentration on the horrors of nuclear death, he suggested, were the equivalent of hell-fire sermons, yet their solutions were ludicrous and irrational. The emphasis of his talk was to categorise CND as irrational, a term which recurred. Against this he set his assessment of the Soviet threat, and its disposition to over-run its neighbours. Therefore, we are bound into a system of deterrence through circumstances beyond our control: without this power to repel and deter Soviet leaders we would be subjected to moral blackmail.

The *Opinion* programmes were very different in style to the caberet satirical programmes which preceded them. They give the speaker the opportunity to state a position and then develop or seek to justify the grounds for that view. They are in effect visual radio talks.

Conclusion: gesture without motion?

While the role of nuclear weapons in defence has clearly come on to the agenda of television, the extent of the initiative should not be overstated. In Fiddick's view public concern has run ahead of the media. It is relevant to observe how public opinion polls are themselves used and even commissioned by current affairs programmes. These can, as we have seen, serve the function of legitimising the case for examining the topic under discussion as being a matter of public concern. There is, Fiddick suggests, a general awareness of the sheer killing power of the new generation of nuclear weapons. Hence the internal contradictions of poll findings – with strong support for Britain remaining in NATO and retaining a nuclear capability, but strong opposition to Cruise and Trident — make some kind of sense. If this assessment is deep rooted then it will not easily go away. Moreover, since 1979–80, with the advent of the Thatcher and Reagan administrations, the nuclear question has more sharply divided political establishments. The working consensus that existed for over a decade, such that in Britain it was not even a subject for parliamentary debate, has dissolved. To this extent, as Fiddick observes, television was knocking on an open door. Once the issue had become controversial and a source of dissent, politicians and defence experts would be ready to express their point of view on current affairs programmes. As we have seen from the examples discussed, some of them appeared on several occasions. Current affairs programmes tend to operate in the responsive rather than the initiating mode so far as public discussion is concerned.

Yet some programmes do come to be defined as problematic and not only in the current affairs framework. In such cases controversy may precede the showing of the programme, if indeed it is shown. Peter Watkins' film *The War Game* has become a *cause célèbre*. Originally made for the BBC sixteen years ago, it has still not been shown on television. Lord Normanbrook, the then Chairman of the BBC, held the view that it risked swinging public opinion against the government's defence policy. It seems that oppositional arguments are more likely to be seen as problematical. The dropping of the proposal to give E. P. Thompson the floor for the Dimbleby Lecture in 1981 is a well-known recent example (although the Reith Lectures shortly afterwards were given over to the thoughts of a NATO strategist). Nicholas Humphrey, the psychologist, did manage to deliver his Bronowski Lecture in which he argued the case for nuclear disarmament, but the Bronowski Lectures have been discontinued. His was the last to be delivered. 'I could have told you five minutes after the lecture that there'd never be another one. I think it's basically a political thing,' said Mrs Bronowski.[7] More recently there were delays to the screening of John Pilger's *The Truth Game* until another programme could be made to 'balance' it. Pilger's 'personal view' had to be balanced by Max Hasting's 'personal view', *The War about Peace*, although how many people watched both programmes is a matter for speculation. If *The War about Peace* had been made first would there have been a mirror-image controversy? If so, would it have been resolved in the same way? We cannot think of an instance where a 'safe' programme has been balanced by a 'provocative' one.

This suggests that TV current affairs, documentaries and opinion programmes are the site of considerable cultural and political struggle. There are very able people working in this area of television and they have been able to probe some aspects of government and NATO policy. But there are programmes which get knocked back or delayed and are defined as problematical. Such disputes and their outcome help to define the limits of pluralism in a democratic society. From time to time, erratically but not randomly, intended programmes are identified by senior administrators within the BBC or the IBA as risky. The ensuing rows, if the dispute becomes public, may be embarrassing to those administrators since they may be accused of political censorship; but from another point of view, the government's, it may be regarded as a sign that they are taking a responsible view of their duties. Nevertheless the positions taken up by the senior authorities in broadcasting do not have to be predetermined – as the IBA's screening of *The Day After*, whilst refusing Secretary of State for Defence Michael Heseltine an official right of reply, demonstrates.

In a *Times* article, 'Balance: TV's eternal victim',[8] David Hewson asked: 'Is there not good reason to believe that television as a medium is chronically unsuited to the notion of impartiality altogether, except in the rigid form of editorial *diktat*?' The artificiality of the concept, supported as it is by *ad hoc* or mechanistic notions of balance, should be stressed. It is not only a question of supposedly setting one 'personnal view' against another – Pilger versus Hastings – but of recognising that in programmes with experienced journalists such as Tusa or Mangold, personal views are also being presented; or at the very least a line of thought with references and implications is developed. Hewson's concluding question is worth repeating: 'If there can be a free-for-all in the market place of television drama, which makes up the most popular part of the broadcasting constituency, can a loosening of the reins on news and current affairs be long delayed?'

Conclusion

Towards the end of 1984 the BBC television journalist Michael Buerk went to Ethiopia. His report on the famine proved to be a great stimulus to aid relief. Millions of people were moved to respond to this enormous need, and governments were provoked into action. No one could suppose that the reporter was indifferent to what he saw. His professional skills, with a proper care for accuracy and reliability, did not result in an impartial neutral account. Clearly he was on the side of the starving and the effect of his reports showed us just how powerful the mass media can be in certain circumstances. While there can be arguments about the causes of such a famine and the long-term solutions, with varying scientific, political and economic connotations, it is an overriding concern with human welfare which insists that' something be done.

Is it not the same with the issues of war and peace in a nuclear age? The growth of the nuclear stockpile is part of the reality of our times. The destructive consequences of their use are attested to by scientists and medical specialists the world over. To develop mass media oriented towards peace is simply to work from the assumption that at the level of basic human values one cannot be impartial about matters that potentially affect the survival of the species and even the planet. What is the significance of a perspective?

In 1980, UNESCO published the MacBride Report, *Many Voices, One World*. This included some discussion of the responsibilities of the media in relation to the goal of peace. In a key paragraph we read the following:

'The primary function of the media is always to inform the public of significant facts, however unpleasant or disturbing they may be. At times of tension, the news consists largely of military moves and statements by political leaders which give rise to anxiety. But it should not be impossible to reconcile full and truthful reporting with a presentation that reminds readers of the possibility – indeed, the necessity – of peaceful solutions to disputes. We live, alas, in an age stained by cruelty, torture, conflict and violence. These are not the natural human condition; they are scourges to be eradicated. We should never resign ourselves to endure passively what can be cured. Ordinary men and women in every country – and this includes a country depicted as 'the enemy' – share a yearning to live out their lives in peace. That desire, if it is mobilised and expressed, can have an effect on the actions of governments. These statements may appear obvious, but if they appeared more consistently in the media, peace would be safer.[1]

It would be inappropriate to blame the mass media for failures of political imagination on the part of those who are responsible for the peace of the world. Clearly, too, journalists can be on the receiving end of censorship, disinformation and propaganda campaigns from powerful pressure groups. What this does point to, however, is the need for critical journalism, an approach which does not accept unquestioningly the official line or the press hand-out. Alternative sources of information can provide some check on the reliability of data and can affect the texture of a news story. In the field of defence and disarmament there are research institutes with specialist academic knowledge. The United Nations Institute for Disarmament Research, the Stockholm Institute for Peace Research, the International Institute for Strategic Studies in London and the Armament and Disarmament Information Unit at the University of Sussex all provide the kind of detailed information which can serve the press.

What the informed or sceptical journalist knows is that he or she is likely to be on the receiving end of claims and statements, some of them seeking to gain advantage in the propaganda war of words. The ability to put the knowledgeable question, or to check relevant sources so that contradictions, inconsistencies or factual errors may be exposed, is important. Even to be aware of the technical problems in counting weapons or the linguistic problems in distinguishing between strategic, theatre, tactical and intermediate weapons – with their overlapping elements and hidden ambiguities – helps to avoid some of the pitfalls, which politicians and official spokespeople wittingly or unwittingly create. As we have seen, the whole discussion of intermediate-range nuclear forces has been beset with these problems. Definitions of which weapons are to be, or should be, included differ between the parties, and this can lead to different tabulations and inferences. Paradoxically this may generate an awareness of the spurious concreteness which underlies much apparently factual discussion.

Writing in 1982, the journalist Jonathan Dimbleby, who has an impressive record in this field, maintained:

> If the media were now to display a little more zeal in pursuit of nuclear truths they could transform our understanding not only of the Geneva talks, but of their relationship to other, no less urgent issues: the controversy over flexible response; the doctrine of limited nuclear war; the concept of 'balance' in a world of nuclear overkill; the prospect of another dangerous spiral in the arms race; the risk of an accidental holocaust that begins ludicrously from miscalculation or misunderstanding; and, finally, to that gravest of all the question of whether the prevailing strategies are protecting the peace or driving us towards the abyss. It is surely not too much to insist that common sense requires the debate to begin in earnest without delay.[2]

Far from limiting or attempting to control the media by the advocacy of one particular line, such an agenda would be more pluralistic in its implications. Concepts of deterrence, threat and security would be open to more, not less, scrutiny. Since enormous consequences flow from the application of these concepts in policy-making, this has to be a gain if the public's right to know is to be anything more than a slogan.

Those who trade in cold war rhetoric may object that to allow such critical scrutiny in this 'sensitive' area is dangerous and even subversive. But there is a growing belief in some parts of broadcasting that such criticism should be developed. A good example of this was in a recent Channel 4 report on the Afghan war. It contrasted the television images of the conflict in the West and in the Soviet Union.

> Back in the USSR, viewers get an entirely different perspective of the Afghan war. While the West sees pictures of gunships and Mojahadeen attacks, Soviets are shown a war against poverty, ignorance and disease . . . . We in the West don't hear much about the torture and mutilation of civilians by the Mojahadeen. By the same token Soviet television doesn't broadcast the fact that while many children will live because of Soviet doctors and nurses others will die from Soviet bombs. The media are locked into their respective cold war attitudes.
>
> *Kabul Autumn,* Channel 4, 17.12.84

In the British context a particular responsibility is placed upon broadcasters. Given a popular press which shows little sign of responding seriously to public issues, the broadcasters with their large audiences, especially for news programmes, are presented with both a challenge and an opportunity. A pessimistic view would argue that the constraints on broadcasters are so powerful and their own professional codes so deep-rooted that any change is impossible. We do not think so. Those who produce media output that may be constrained by powerful forces but they are not totally determined by them. They did have some opportunity to point to alternative possibilities and proposals and not simply to reflect official definitions of reality. Perhaps the most important recent example was the production of *Threads*. In screening this play about the effects of a nuclear war on Sheffield, the BBC in some measure redeemed its failure to show *The War Game* and also revealed that policies can shift on such matters. The subsequent scientific documentary on nuclear winter also underlined what serious broadcasting to the nation can accomplish.

The way these matters are presented, analysed and evaluated will help to shape public perceptions of our situation and what can be done about it. Nuclear weapons, we are often told, cannot be disinvented, and certainly not by broadcasters; but the causes and consequences of the arms race and the cold war can be critically exposed.

Notes

Introduction

1. C. F. Barnaby and G. P. Thomas, *The Nuclear Arms Race, Control or Catastrophe?*, Frances Pinter, 1982.
2. The report of a working party under the chairmanship of the Bishop of Salisbury, *The Church and the Bomb, Nuclear Weapons and Christian Conscience*, Hodder & Stoughton, 1982.
3. E. P. Thompson and Dan Smith, *Protest and Survive*, Penguin, 1980.
4. Philip Towle, Iain Elliot and Gerald Frost, *Protest and Perish. A Critique of Unilateralism*. Institute for European Defence and Strategic Studies, 1982, p. 9.
5. Crispin Aubrey, ed., *Nukespeak. The Media and the Bomb*, Comedia, 1982.
6. E. P. Thompson, *Beyond the Cold War*, Merlin Press, 1982.
7. In Michael Clarke and Marjorie Mowlam, eds., *Debate on Disarmament*, Routledge & Kegan Paul, 1982, p. 97.
8. Final Document of the Special Session of the United Nations General Assembly Devoted to Disarmament, 1978, para. 2; reprinted along with other useful documentation on this topic in Marek Thee, ed., *Armaments, Arms Control and Disarmament*, UNESCO, 1981.
9. See Sverre Lodgaard, 'Taking stock of the United Nations special session devoted to disarmament', in Thee, op. cit., pp. 244–9; Richard Pollak, 'Covering the unthinkable, the UN disarmament session and the press', *The Nation*, Vol. 234, 17, May 1981; Tapio Varis, 'Media coverage of disarmament-related issues', *Current Research on Peace and Violence*, 1/1983, pp. 52–64.
10. Robert Harris, *Gotcha! The Media, the Government and the Falklands Crisis*, Faber, 1983, p. 151.

1 Making Good News

1. Dr Bernard Donoughue (Prime Minister's Chief Policy Adviser 1974–9) in BBC *Panorama*, (8.3.82).
2. Joe Haines (Press Secretary to Harold Wilson) in *Panorama* above.
3. It is too trite to say simply that most newspapers and television tend either to the political centre or the right wing. They vary over particular issues and in relation to

their own audiences. Still, support for the political left is largely absent in the national media (e.g. for the left of the Labour Party). The recent sharp move to the right in politics and 'Thatcherism' produced misgivings among many television journalists and also among some normally 'conservative' newspaper – especially over the rise in unemployment. The 'success' of the Falklands conflict largely eclipsed the fears of the right-wing press, and the general dominance of right-wing politics has ushered in some more stringent controls in television – though not in all areas. See for example the pressure of *The Friday Altnerative* on Channel 4 and the evidence in this book on the coverage of the Falklands conflict.

4. Richard Francis, letter to *New Statesman*, 20.4.79.
5. Quoted in *Panorama*, op. cit.
6. D. Leigh, *The Frontiers of Secrecy*, Junction Books, 1980 p. 33.
7. See *More Bad News*, Routledge & Kegan Paul, 1980.
8. *Really Bad News*, Writers & Readers Co-operative, 1982, p. 14.
9. Sometimes these were sent directly to us as the people concerned could not attract much attention from the media.
10. For more detailed examples of this see Chapter 5.
11. Duncan Campbell, *New Statesman*, 12.3.82.
12. James Bellini, *Rule Britannia*, Jonathan Cape, 1981, p. 210..
13. See their evidence to the Parliamentary Defence Committee on the *Handling of Press and Public Information during the Falklands Conflict*, published HMSO, 8.12.82.
14. Brigadier Caldwell. Spoken at a seminar on Defence and The Mass Media. Quoted in P. Knightly, *The First Casualty*, Quartet, 1983, p.379.
15. Air Vice Marshall Menaul was later a resident military expert for ITN during the Falklands conflict.
16. House of Commons Defence Committee, *The Handling of Press and Public Information during the Falklands Conflict*, HMSO, 8.12.82, Vol. II, p. xxxviii.
17. In their evidence to the Defence Committee, ITN noted that at times stories had to pass through *six* separate layers of screening; from (with the Forces) the local military authority and the MoD press officer, to (London) the Director of Public Relations, Chief PR Officer, the Clearing Committee and the Secretary of State; op. cit., Vol. II, pp. 66–7.
18. Quoted in Robter Harris, *Gotcha*, op. cit., p. 61.
19. BBC NCA minutes, 28.6.82.
20. NCA minutes, 27.7.82.
21. For more detailed account of this see the evidence given to the House of Commons Defence Committee; op. cit., Vol. II, pp. 254–74.
22. Robert Harris, *Gotcha*, op. cit., p. 110.
23. Leonard Downie, *Washington Post*, reprinted in *UK Press Gazette*, 6.9.82.
24. Journalists who were with the Task Force had wished to indicate this, but the feeling was apparently not shared by the programme controllers in London.
25. David Nicholas, speaking on *The Friday Alternative*, 7.1.83.
26. *Gotcha*, op. cit., p. 150.
27. In practice, it does not do this – as we showed in *Really Bad News*, op. cit. It tends, for example, to report the views of the right wing of the Labour Party more than the left and to endorse the views of the right in interview questions.
28. See Chapter 3.
29. There is an extended discussion of 'relatives' on the news and 'public opinion' in Chapter 3.
30. BBC evidence to House of Commons Defence Committee, op. cit., Vol. II, p. 43.
31. Derek Jamieson, quoted in *Gotcha*, op. cit., p. 109.
32. *Listener*, 3.6.83.

33. Op. cit., Vol. II, p. 76–7.
34. See Chapter 3.
35. Evidence to Defence Committee, op. cit., Vol. II, p. 72.
36. For a detailed analysis of the polls and public opinion see Chapter 3.
37. Evidence to Defence Committee, op. cit., Vol. II, p. 77.
38. Dr John Gilbert.
39. Evidence to Defence Committee, op. cit., Vol. II, p. 100.
40. Evidence to Defence Committee, op. cit., Vol. II, p. 61. The BBC were so taken aback by this exchange that they made a second submission to the Defence Committee later in 1982, giving further evidence.
41. Kim Sabido, quoted in *UK Press Gazette*, 14.6.82.
42. His letters home were published as *Message from the Falklands*, ed. H. Tinker, Junction Books, 1982, p. 189.
43. Robert Fox, *Listener*, 15.7.82.
44. D. Tinker, op. cit., p. 182.
45. Max Hastings, 'How the Admiral upset the Army', *Evening Standard*, 23.6.82.
46. Evidence to Defence Committee, op. cit., Vol. II, p. 67.
47. Barry Cox, speaking at the Edinburgh International Television Festival, 1982.
48. The point at issue was broadcasts which reviewed what was being said in the newspapers – including those which were against the war.
49. Evidence to Defence Committee, op. cit., Vol. I, p. xiii.

2 Fighting the War

1. *Aviation Week and Space Technology*, 26.7.82, p. 25; Michael J. Gething, 'The black back raids', *Defence Magazine Special*, November 1982, p. 69.
2. Max Hastings, BBC2, 22.50, 15.6.82.
3. Minutes of evidence, House of Commons Select Defence Committee on Handling of Information during Falklands Conflict, 1982.
4. Ibid.
5. *New Civil Engineer*, 19/26, August 1982.
6. Evidence to Defence Committee, op. cit., Vol. II, p. 158.
7. Ironically, it probably was the intention of the raid to get one bomb on the runway – but it clearly did not have the effect of putting the runway out of operation.

3 The Home Front

1. Servicemen too know the human costs of the fighting from direct experience; but the conditions of their service prevent them from expressing their views in public.
2. There are two possible exceptions: one woman is shown getting married (BBC1, 22.10, 8.5.82), but this is obviously before her husband leaves for the South Atlantic; and a group of women are shown talking to their MP (BBC1, 21.00, 26.5.82), but they are talking about waiting for information about their husbands.
3. The BBC's Assistant Director General notices this too. The NCA minutes of discussion about interviewing relatives record: 'Certainly, ADG said, he would seek the sacking of any reporter who asked "How did you feel?"' (NCA, 8.5.82); 'The return of the *QE2* had been another example of superb coverage marred by constant repetition of "How did/do you feel?" ADG said enough was enough' (NCA, 15.6.82).

4. At that week's NCA meeting, the BBC's Director of Public Affairs 'suggested special caution in the weeks ahead, over the question "has it all been worth it?"' (NCA, 15.6.82).
5. A *Newsnight* feature dwelt on the differences: 'Argentine politics are not Western ones ... Argentina's sense of relentless economic decline ... The Falklands conquest is almost the only symbol of greatness that the country has .... Argentina is a deeply fragmented society with each interest group bent on self-advancement to the detriment of and the exclusion of the others. Decisions are impulsive, not subject to outside checks and balances; miscalculations are easier to make in such a system. And besides, in their personal and national culture, a man never climbs down, never admits he's wrong, and it all makes Argentina a very difficult country to deal with' (BBC2, 22.40, 23.5.82). Some of the same criticisms ('economic decline', 'only symbol of greatness', 'deeply fragmented society', 'miscalculations', 'never climbs down') could be applied to Britain, it is not done. Instead Argentina is held up as the country with problems.
6. Latin American Bureau, *Whose Crisis?*, 1982.

5 The Propaganda War

1. Cited in Alva Myrdal, *The Game of Disarmament. How the United States Run the Arms Race*, Spokesman, 1980, p. 29.
2. Gwyn Prins, ed., *The Choice: Nuclear Weapons Versus Security*, Chatto & Windus, 1984, p. xv.
3. David Martin and Peter Mullen, eds., *Unholy Warfare. The Church and the Bomb*, Blackwell, 1983, p. 40.
4. Cited by Eugene J. Carroll, 'Nuclear weapons and deterrence', in Prins, op. cit., p. 8.
5. Cited in George W. Ball, 'White House roulette', *New York Review of Books*, 8.11.84, p. 5.
6. Jeff McMahan, *Reagan and the World*, Pluto Press, 1984, pp. 53-4.
7. Strobe Talbott, *Deadly Gambits*, Knopf, 1984.
8. Grethe Vaerno, 'A public opinion strategy', *NATO Review*, No. 3/4, 1983, pp. 28-9.
9. Ibid, p. 31.
10. Cited in Malver Lumsden, 'Nuclear weapons and the new peace movement', *World Armaments and Disarmament*, SIPRI Yearbook, 1983, p. 120.
11. Central Office of Information, *The Policy of Deterrence*, February 1984. p. 1.
12. Ibid., p. 2.
13. *Statement on the Defence Estimates 1981*, HMSO, 1981, p. 13.
14. Ibid., p. 13.
15. Central Office of Information, *Trident: Britain's Strategic Deterrent*.
16. Douglas Hurd MP, quoted in *Guardian*, 31.1.83.
17. See for example: 'Thatcher in Hitler warning to CND', *Sunday Times*, 13.2.83; 'Tories zero in on "later day appeasers"', *Guardian*, 14.2.83; 'Heseltine's stealthy way with nuclear disarmers', *Guardian*, 14.2.83; 'Heseltine brands CND a red tool', *Mail*, 23.4.83; 'Tory smear tactics revealed by CND', *Guardian*, 30.4.83; 'Roots of Tory smear against CND', *Observer*, 8.5.83.
18. Mary Kaldor, 'Is there a Soviet military threat?' in Clarke and Mowlam, op. cit., p. 37.
19. The Report of the Alternative Defence Commission, *Defence Without the Bomb*, Taylor & Francis, 1983, p. 62.

20. Dusko Doder, 'New Moscow fear of encirclement', *Washington Post*, Sept. 1980; reprinted in *Guardian Weekly*, 21.9.1980.
21. Jonathan Steele, *World Power: Soviet Foreign Policy under Brezhnev and Andropov*, Michael Joseph, 1983.
22. Gwyn Prins, *Defended to Death: A study of the nuclear arms race*, Penguin, 1983, p. 203.
23. Ibid.

6 Breaching the Peace at Greenham Common

1. Sometimes there seems to be a reluctance to even mention women. The report on Greenham Common on BBC1, 17.45, 11.12.83, uses the word 'women' only once, substituting 'people' twice and 'demonstrators' three times. Other TV news coverage reveals a stereotyped approach to women and their role in the family–see the analysis of women's role during the Falklands War in Chapter 3.
2. This is not to say that their analysis of political parties is adequate. See the chapter on TV coverage of the Labour Party in *Really Bad News*, Writers & Readers, Cooperative 1982.
3. Beeban Kidron and Amanda Richardson, *Carry Greenham Home*, NFTS, 1983. This film has now been shown on Channel 4.

7 Say It with Figures

1. Daniel Frei, *Risks of Unintentional Nuclear War*, Croom Helm, 1983. See especially pp. 72 ff.
2. Report of the UN Secretary General, *Nuclear Weapons*, Frances Pinter, 1981, pp. 113–14.
3. Gwyn Prins, ed., *Defended to Death*, Penguin, 1983, p. 85.
4. See, for example, Yevgeniv N. Kochetkov, 'The position of th USSR on nuclear weapons and arms control', *Annals of the American Academy*, 469, September 1983, pp. 137–43.
5. Thomas J. Hirschfield, 'Reducing short-range nuclear systems in Europe: an opportunity for stability in the eighties', *Annals of the American Academy*, op. cit., p. 80.
6. Lawrence Freedman, 'Nuclear arms control', in Phil Williams, ed., *The Nuclear Debate*, Catham House Special Paper, Routledge & Kegan Paul, 1984, pp. 36–7.
7. Jeff McMahan, *Reagan and the World*, op. cit., p. 55.
8. Simon Lunn and Hefferson Seabright, 'Intercontinental nuclear weapons', in *World Armaments and Disarmament, SIPRI Yearbook 1983*, Taylor & Francis, 1983, p. 8.

8 Talking of Peace

1. *Final Document of the Special Session of the United Nations General Assembly Devoted to Disarmament*. 1978, para. 13; reprinted in *Armaments, Arms Control and Disarmament*, op. cit., pp. 217–43.
2. Ibid., para. 18.
3. Independent Commission on Disarmament and Security Issues (Palme Commission), *Common Security*, Pan Books, 1982.

9 The Church and the Bomb

1. John Austin Baker, Bishop of Salisbury, 'People and the bomb', in David Martin and Peter Mullen, eds., *Unholy Warfare. The Church and the Bomb*, Blackwell, 1983, p. 221.
2. Ibid., p. 81.
3. Ibid., p. 154.
4. Ibid., p. 155.
5. Ibid., p. 156.
6. Paul Abrecht and Ninian Koshy, eds., *Before It's Too Late. The Challenge of Nuclear Disarmament*, World Council of Churches, 1983.
7. Graham Leonard, Bishop of London, 'The morality of nuclear deterrence', in Martin and Mullen, op. cit. p. 193.

10 Easter '83: Peace Signals?

1. In this section we have been able to draw on material prepared by Dan Plesch and Pat Wilson and we thank them for making it available to us.
2. Cited in Jeff McMahan, *Reagan and the World*, op. cit., p. 66.
3. Ibid., p. 69.
4. We acknowledge with thanks the help of Brian McNair in the peparation of this section. In addition to matters not touched on in this book his forthcoming work will develop some of the points made here.

11 The Current Affairs Prism

1. *Listener*, 21.4.83.
2. *Guardian*, 9.8.83.
3. Attempts to look at a number of current affairs programmes rather than individual instances are still rare. One recent study which attempts to classify and analyse them as a form of actuality television (in which are included news bulletins, topical, current affairs and documentary programmes) is Philip Schlesinger, Graham Murdock and Philip Elliott, *Televising 'Terrorism': political violence in popular culture*, Comedia 1983.
4. *Guardian*, 27.4.83.
5. E. P. Thompson, 'Gatekeepers to the nation's politics', *END*, Aug.–Sept. 1983, pp. 20–21.
6. Tom Mangold, 'President Reagan's arms race into space goes beyond deterrence', *Listener*, 9.9.83.
7. Quoted in *Guardian*, 17.7.82.
8. *The Times*, 14.11.83.

Conclusion (Section Two)

1. S. MacBride, *et al.*, *Many Voices, One World*, UNESCO, 1980, p. 177.
2. Jonathan Dimbleby, 'The media and defence: past and future problems', in Michael Clarke and Marjorie Mowlam, eds., *Debate on Disarmament*, Routledge & Kegan Paul, 1982, p. 109.

Appendix 1 Theoretical Issues Raised By Opinion Polling

The relationship between public opinion, public opinion polls and the reporting of polls is not straightforward. The issues we point to here are, by and large, well known to most social scientists but we think they are worth noting because of the role which opinion polls have come to play in our society.

The information conveyed by opinion polls is usually the product either of face-to-face or telephone interviewing. The kind of knowledge this gives us can be problematical. The interviewer–interviewee encounter is itself a social relationship and interviewers are trained to try to establish a 'successful' relationship so that they can sustain communication and accomplish the basic objectives of the interview. From an examination of the literature on interviewing, Cicourel concluded:

> The nature of responses generally depends on the trust developed early in the relationship, status differences, differential perception and interpretation placed on questions and responses, the control exercised by the interviewer, and so forth. The validity of the schedule becomes a variable condition within and between interviews.
> Aaron V. Cicourel, *Method and Measurement in Sociology*, Free Press, 1964, p. 99

Cicourel's statement embraces more than problems about the wording of questions, but even that should give pause for reflection. Forty years ago, Hadley Cantril delineated eleven types of 'poor' questions. These referred to questions too vague to permit precise answers; obscure in meaning; misunderstood because they contain technical or unfamiliar words; not adequately circumscribed, not providing exhaustive alternatives; containing too many possibilities of choice; carrying unforeseen implications; giving only surface references; containing stereotypes; likely to elicit stereotyped answers; and referring to matters which mean nothing to some of the sample. (Hadley Cantril *et al.*, *Changing Public Opinion*, Princeton University Press, 1944). Cantril's list has its own in-built problems, but for the most part we have to take on trust that these criteria are met by opinion pollsters.

The interview itself is an unusual social situation. Catherine Marsh has pointed out that the notion of an opinion is a very individualistic one:

> ... any of the usual activities undertaken in arriving at a view on an issue, such as discussing it with others, are forbidden in the interview situation, as the interveiwer is supposed to elicit those views that the respondent holds as an individual. Fundamental to this approach is the idea that everybody holds an opinion about everything. Further, it is held that these opinions are fixed and latent, with the potential to cause actions and verbal behaviour; responses to questionnaire items can therefore be treated as indicators of underlying attitudes. But this is a perversion of the way in which people have ideas, interact with one another and change their views.

> Catherine Marsh, 'Opinion polls – social science or political manoeuvre?',
> in John Irvine, Ian Miles and Jeff Evans, eds., *Demystifying Social Statistics*,
> Pluto Press, 1981, p. 270

The opinion pollsters can reasonably remind us that they have a good record on predicting General Elections. We should remember, however, that we are relating a clearly understood intention – that of voting or not for a particular party – which refers to a specific event in the near future and which involves the respondent in a direct way. There is a close relationship between attitudes and behaviour. Yet this cannot be treated as a paradigm case for all attitude studies – where the relationship between feelings, beliefs, intentions and behaviour may be much more problematical and uncertain. In such cases it is not clear what the variously tabulated results signify. In practice we are offered interpretations as to the significance of poll findings: these are speculative inferences rather than logical deductions based on validated axioms.

An instructive example of what happens when pollsters comment on their own work is provided by Robert Worcester and Simon Jenkins's article in *Public Opinion*, June/July 1982, 'Britain rallies round the Prime Minister'. This was a commentary on a series of surveys carried out by MORI for various clients – the *Daily Star, Sunday Times, Economist* and BBC's *Panorama* – in relation to the Falklands conflict. These were a mixture of telephone and fact-to-face interviews. No distinction is made in the discussion of the findings. The samples were quota not random samples and included re-interviewing from a panel in some instances. Again there is no discussion of the methodological significance of this or any caveats made. As Marsh points out:

> Quota samples have the advantage of speed, but the error margins around the results are known to be a lot wider than with random sampling designs. It is good practice to report the error margins with all results, but this is done infrequently.
>
> p. 276

Worcester and Jenkins write:

> Initially, there was some doubt in the British public's mind about the importance of retaining British sovereignty over the Falklands if it resulted in the loss of British servicemen's lives (44% said it was important enough, 49% disagreed).
>
> p. 54

Notice here how 'the British public's mind' becomes a collective entity, derived from an individualistic methodology. The implication is further that the phrase 'retaining British sovereignty' is meaningful to the respondents and its implications understood. The question as to how many lives would the British be justified in losing in order to retain sovereignty was not asked. As Worcester and Jenkins acknowledge, the issue of 'proportionality' is very hard for pollsters to elucidate. Yet it is just there that moral and political issues are crucially interwoven. Without some specification around this problem it is difficult to know how to interpret the findings.

Worcester and Jenkins proceed to interpret their own findings in a way which raises more questions than it solves. Consider the following:

> By mid-May 'the patience of the British war cabinet with the drawn-out negotiations process had worn thin and that of the public with it. Continued British attacks on the Port Stanley airfield, the failure of the Haig initiative, of the Peruvian plan and of the United Nations negotiations all led to a widespread acceptance of the inevitability of escalation of the conflict. When asked, 'If negotiations break down, which of the following options do you favour?' 59 per cent of the sample were by then for a full-scale invasion of the Falklands, and 34 per cent even felt Britain should bomb military bases in Argentina.
>
> p. 55

But we cannot tell from the evidence of the opinion polls whether the statements in the first two sentences are true or not. We do not know the level of awareness of the public concerning negotiations at the United Nations. To describe these negotiations as a failure is to omit the fact that negotiations were still in progress and that a ceasefire resolution was subsequently tabled at the UN Security Council, but was vetoed by Britain. The question used to buttress the contention that the public's patience was wearing thin begins with the hypothetical, 'If negotiations break down', which allows for the possibility that many respondents would still prefer a negotiated settlement. Indeed, given the circumstances and the qualifying 'if' of the question it might be regarded as mildly surprising that only 59% were in favour of a full-scale invasion.

Another example of speculative inference based on poll findings is embodied in the following comment:

> By that time (i.e. 23 May) a majority [54%] felt that Britain should retain the Falklands for ever; but a majority was also in favour of handing the islands over to a United Nations trusteeship (51% favourable, 43% against by 25-26 May). This overlap probably reflected a deep-seated conviction that victory was essential to restore British status and pride — yet subsequent compromise was inevitable.
>
> (p. 55)

'Probably' is a strong word to apply as an explanation to findings which might as plausibly to put down to confusions and uncertainties. In order to give some meaning to the poll findings the authors provide an intuitive judgement about how they connect with phenomena outside the scope of the poll itself. The *ad hoc* nature of this kind of theorising should be recognised for what it is, otherwise we lend undue authority and credibility to the activity on which it rests.

The opinion poll is a social invention which has its roots in market research and election studies. It has typically operated in the context of doing work for client organisations such as political parties, businesses, the press and broadcasting. When the polls are made public the reporting-back process through the media can be subject to various filters. From the original findings (with all their methodological problems that are usually left unremarked) more selection, simplification, compression and re-emphasis can take place. In this way we learn what 'the public', in which we are included, are supposed to think about this or that. It thereby plays a part in the social process, which it purports to describe and define; it becomes part of the social milieu within which issues are discussed and evaluated.

APPENDIX 2

The Peruvian peace plan

Introduction

The President of Peru, Belaunde Terry, launched his initiative to bring about a peaceful settlement to the Falklands conflict immediately following the collapse of US Secretary of State Alexander Haig's shuttle diplomacy at the end of April. The details of the conception, negotiation and collapse of the initiative are confused and even contradictory. Even with hindsight it is far from easy to obtain a clear picture of the events surrounding the initiative. However, from a detailed study of the world press of the time, and the material published subsequently, it is possible to reconstruct some of the circumstances surrounding the initiative. There were two distinct phases to the Peruvian initiative.

Phase 1. May 1-3

On 1 May, Belaunde Terry put forward several suggestions to bring about a negotiated settlement. While he arranged to conduct negotiations with Argentina, US Secretary of State Haig agreed to continue to mediate with London. Mr Haig was in direct contact with the British Foreign Secretary, Francis Pym, who was in Washington that weekend, and the British Ambassador in Lima was reported to be in direct contact with the Peruvian Foreign Ministry. An Argentine delegation was also reported as arriving in the Peruvian capital that weekend. Belaunde Terry who was in direct contact with Haig felt sufficiently confident of the progress being made in the negotiations that on 2 May he appeared on television in Peru to announce that both Britain and Argentina had agreed in principle to cease hostilities. (*Daily Telegraph,* 3.5.82; *The Times,* 3.5.82).

The *Daily Telegraph* reported (3.5.82) that the military junta in Buenos Aires was 'still in session early today' considering a seven-point plan put forward by Peru. *The Times* reported (3.5.82) that according to US sources the 'Peruvian initiative had been discussed with Mr Pym in general terms as part of a general review of ways of resolving the crisis.' A State Department official acknowledged that Mr Haig had been in contact with both Mr Pym and President Belaunde but emphasised there was 'no agreement on anything' (ibid.). The spokesman did add that the initiative 'cannot be dismissed out of hand' (*Daily Record*, 13.5.82). The *Washington Post* (4.5.82) carried reports of the visit of two Argentine officials to Lima and stated that 'the officials carried a detailed response to the plan transmitted to Argentina by Peru on Saturday'. The paper went on to report that 'counter-proposals by Argentina were possible' (4.5.82). Thus at the end of the first weekend of May it appeared that the Peruvian plan was at least under consideration by both Britain and Argentina.

However, late on 3 May the mediation effort apparently collapsed. An official communiqué was issued in Buenos Aires rejecting the seven-point plan. The *Daily Telegraph* stated that the communiqué 'referred to the sinking of the cruiser, the *General Belgrano*, as an aggravating factor in the refusal' (4.5.82). The communiqué, however, did cite another reason; the proposals were 'essentially similar to the last proposals made by the American government on April 27th which had already been studied and rejected by the Argentine Government' (*Daily Telegraph*, 4.5.82).

Reports elsewhere in the British and foreign press confirmed the failure of President Belaunde Terry's mediation effort. The *Washington Post* reported (4.5.82):

> following a National Council meeting on the Falklands, Administration sources, citing Argentina's Sunday turndown of the initiative, said its chances of acceptance in Buenos Aires appeared literally to have been 'torpedoed' by the apparent sinking of an Argentine cruiser, the *General Belgrano*, by a British submarine.

The *Guardian* cited two adverse factors in the failure: 'premature publicity in Lima and the attack on the *Belgrano*', (5.5.82).

Dr Arias Stella, Peru's Foreign Minister, said on 5 May that the sinking of the *Belgrano* 'left Argentina with no alternative but to reject the peace proposals' (*The Times*, 6.5.82). Later in May, Belaunde Terry was to claim that a settlement had been close at hand but 'the very unfortunate sinking of the *Belgrano* at that point also sank all the peace proposals we had made' (*Daily Telegraph*, 31.5.82). The week following these events, the Peruvians issued their version of the circumstances surrounding the collapse of the initiative. They accused Britain of direct responsibility for the failure of the plan by the decision to sink the cruiser (*Guardian*, 13.5.82). Peruvian officials claimed that Britain deliberately escalated military action every time mediation showed signs of success (ibid). The Peruvians in their account of the negotiations stated that Argentina had put forward certain amendments to their initial proposals. These amendments were incorporated and, according to a report in the *Guardian*, 'after a flurry of telephone calls on the same Sunday between Lima, Washington and Argentina the three amended points were agreed' (ibid.). There appears to have been no report from official sources in London confirming that the British government had agreed to any amendment.

Thus from reports in the British and foreign press, as well as official sources in Lima, Washington and Buenos Aires, the Peruvian initiative collapsed on 3 May. The reasons given for its demise included the sinking of the *Belgrano*, premature publicity and similarity with previous US proposals.

The collapse of the mediation led Peru to pledge its support to Argentina in the South Atlantic conflict. Dr Arias Stella announced it would give Argentina all the aid it asked for (*Guardian*, 7.5.82). This included military assistance. 'On the same day Peru offered military aid to Argentina in its conflict with Britain' (*The Times*, 22.5.82). Peru's War Minister, General Cisueros, stated that 'Peru would provide military aid to Argentina if required to do so, to help fight the British naval Task Force' (*Guardian*, 4.5.82). Peru, therefore, as the USA did following the collapse of shuttle diplomacy, took sides in the conflict; however, on this occasion the unsuccessful mediator sided with Argentina.

Phase 2 3–7 May

The rejection of the initiative indicated by the Argentine communiqué on 3 May did not put an end to the efforts to use the proposals as a basis for a negotiated settlement. There was speculation in certain quarters that Argentina might still be interested in the plan. The *Washington Post* reported (4.5.82.) that the plan's 'status yesterday remained the subject of speculation after Argentina's confusing sequence of responses'. In its editorial that day the paper mentioned 'signs that some leaders in Buenos Aires remain interested in the Belaunde initiative'. Argentine officials responded to this by indicating (*Washington Post*, 4.5.82)

> that it was believed, at least by some sectors of the Argentine government, that what they described as the last US proposals to Argentina – transmitted through the Peruvian government been made only in an attempt to place more pressure on Argentina by forcing it to reject a plan it had already said was unacceptable.

Argentine sources accused the US of trying to 'draw in the international forum the image of a government deaf to whatever negotiated offer' (ibid). However, the Peruvian ambassador to the US confirmed that Argentina had renewed its interest in the initiative. He claimed that the initial rejection had been 'based on a misunderstanding' (*The Times*, 7.5.82).

The escalation of military action on 3 and 4 May apparently resulted in the US Secretary of State attempting to revive the plan. Haig launched what the *Financial Times* described as 'an urgent new diplomatic effort to solve the Falklands crisis by peaceful means' (6.5.82). The *Washington Post* reported (6.5.82) that 'diplomatic sources said a ceasefire was the immediate objective of an intense, highly secret round of diplomacy being conducted by Haig, working with the British and Belaunde with Argentina'. According to Peru's ambassador in Washington, Mr Pym, on his return to London, began to show more interest in the initiative (*The Times*, 7.5.82). The *Washington Post* said that the British government supported the new efforts as a result of 'mounting domestic and international pressure' (6.5.82). Argentina on the other hand accused Britain of 'trying to buy time until their reinforcements arrive' (ibid).

In an article entitled 'US–Peru seeking Falklands ceasefire' (6.5.82), the *Washington Post* outlined the state of the negotiations. The article talks of a new initiative, 'an offshoot of the proposals put forward by Belaunde last weekend only to be rejected by Argentina'. It proceeds to state that 'Argentina has expressed a willingness to discuss the idea further, and the sources said Haig, who has been in close touch with the Peruvians since the weekend, subsequently proposed modifications'. It was reported that Belaunde was 'working on Galtieri to show flexibility' on the view that sovereignty was not negotiable. Haig's attempts to get Britain to soften her demands were also commented on: 'Another big problem...stems from British Prime Minister Margaret Thatcher's insistence on wishes of islanders to be paramount.' The implication was that both sides were laying down preconditions. This was very much the view in the US media at the time. An ABC diplomatic correspondent expressed this opinion succinctly in an assessment of the chances for a peaceful settlement on the 5 May edition of *Nightline*:

> The fact of the matter is that both Britain and Argentina recognise that they are under very strong pressures in terms of world opinion to give the impression that they are willing to recognise the other side's point of view and willing to come to terms. But the fact of the matter is that the positions they are taking diplomatically haven't changed from before the time that all the trouble started.
>
> *Nightline*, ABC, 5.5.82

3 to 6 May was described by the British press as a period of 'frenetic activity'on the diplomatic front. Much of this activity was centred on Washington and London. US Secretary of State Haig met with the British Ambassador to the US. The Foreign Office reported events as 'moving very fast indeed' (*Daily Telegraph*, 6.5.82.). Both the Foreign Secretary and the Prime Minister informed the House that Britain had made a 'constructive contribution' to the new ideas put forward by US Secretary of State Haig (*The Falklands Campaign, Digest of Speeches 2 April to 15 June 1982*, HMSO, 1982, pp. 211, 218). The British government, compared to its tight-lipped attitude the previous weekend, was now very forthcoming on the state of the diplomatic negotiations. Mrs Thatcher however, went to pains before the House of Commons to emphasise caution. She questioned 'whether Argentina will respond in the same way' (ibid., p. 218), and warned that 'it would not be imposible – indeed it may well be likely - that the Argentines are concentrating on a ceasefire without withdrawal' (ibid., p. 219). This, she stated 'would be a very evident ploy to keep them in possession of their ill-gotten gains (ibid., p.

219). The Prime Minister seemed to be preparing the House for the failure of the new initiative. This was echoed by the Foreign Secretary: 'I should not like to raise undue hopes but I will do everything I can' (ibid., p. 190). Both went out of their way to stress Britain's good faith in the negotiations and cast doubt on Argentina's commitment to achieve a negotiated settlement. The Foreign Secretary assured the House that 'any obstructionism would not come from our side'(ibid.,p. 211). Mrs Thatcher did admit: It seems clear that they [the Argentines] are interested in a ceasefire' (ibid., p. 218). The *Washington Post* put this more strongly in its headline of 6 May: 'Argentina Urges Ceasefire; US, Peru Press Peace Plan'.

At this time the international environment was particularly difficult for the British government. International opinion had been firmly on Britain's side until the sinking of the *Belgrano*. Many countries, including some of Britain's staunchest allies, considered this an unwarranted escalation of the conflict. World opinion appeared to be moving against Britain. Ireland's Foreign Minister attested to this when he claimed that 'Britain was now the aggressor' (e.g. *Daily Record*, 7.5.82). Mrs Thatcher was also under pressure from backbench Tory MPs not to make concessions. They urged a swift conclusion of the conflict expressing fears that the longer negotiations continue, the greater the danger to the Task Force. (e.g. question of Nicholas Winterton MP to PM, *The Falklands Conflict, op. cit.*, p. 216).

On the evening of 6 May in a statement from the Foreign Office, the Foreign Secretary announced the collapse of the Peruvian initiative:

I am deeply disappointed that Argentine intransigence has once again frustrated a constructive initiative. Had they genuinely wanted peace they would have accepted the latest proposals put to them and would have a ceasefire in place by 5 p.m. tomorrow.

Mr Pym firmly laid the blame at Argentina's door: 'Argentine intransigence has once again led it to reject proposals for a diplomatic solution' (Foreign Office Statement, 6.5.82). He made reference to Argentina' 'diplomatic obstructionism' and stressed Britain had accepted an interim agreement. The *New York Times* carried Mr Pym's statement and noted: 'First word of the plan's contents, as well as the report that it was not acceptable to Argentina, came from Foreign Secretary, Francis Pym, in London' (7.5.82).

Mr Pym's comments were fully reported in the British newspapers. The headlines of the quality press were: 'Peru's Ceasefire Move Collapse' (*The Times*); 'Ceasefire Diplomacy Collapses' (*Daily Telegraph*); 'Pym Saddened By Plan's Failure' (*Guardian*). All newspapers carried the FCO version. They also reported that the proposals were never formally put to Argentina. The Peruvians had not sent the package to Buenos Aires although 'the Argentines had been aware of the content' (*Guardian*, 7.5.82). It is reported the Peruvians decided not to put the plan formally to either side in spite of pressure from Britain's ambassador to do so. The Peruvians appeared to believe not enough progress had been made by Mr Haig to make the plan acceptable to Argentina.

There was, it was reported in some papers, no official rejection statement from Buenos Aires. The *New York Times* did not agree with this account. According to its report (7.5.82) the Peruvian plan 'was turned down by the Argentines when Peru presented it to them Wednesday night'. The *New York Times* London correspondent also reported that 'according to authoritative sources, the Argentine junta rejected the plan on Wednesday in a message to the United States' (7.5.82). There is a clear contradiction between these statements. One assumes that the 'authoritative sources' in London were government. However, dealing with diplomatic events of 6 May the *Guardian* (7.5.82). reported from the UN:

> one of the diplomats involved in yesterday's round of discussions described it as 'confusing'. At the end of the day the pattern appeared that Buenos Aires favours the UN plan proposals, while London and Washington prefer the Peruvian plan.

It seems during this period that while London focused on Haig's attempt to revive the Peruvian initiative, Buenos Aires concentrated on obtaining a ceasefire through the UN. Argentina accepted UN Secretary General's proposals on 6 May (*Guardian*, 7.5.82). The *New York Times* confirmed that 'the Argentines told the Peruvians that they would work for the time being only through Mr Perez de Cuellar' (7.5.82).

In reporting the collapse of the latest round of negotiations, the *Guardian* carrried a report, from its correspondents in Washington and at the UN, entitled 'Inflexible attitudes thwart diplomacy'. The article (7.5.82) began:

> Another effort to find a peaceful solution to the Falklands seemed to have come full cirlce last night. Despite protestations from Britain and Argentina of their readiness to seek ways to end the fighting, neither seemed ready to shift position sufficiently to allow progress'.

The *New York Times* (7.5.82) stated that

> the apparent consensus of informed diplomats and American officials here [the UN] today was that there has been no significant movement toward resolving the Falkland Islands crisis. Rather, there is an assumption that both Argentina and Britain, by their public statements and actions are trying to position themselves to lessen international and domestic criticism if major fighting resumes by the end of this weekend, as many officials believe it will.

This echoed the news expressed in the US media. Joe Kraft in the *Washington Post* (6.5.82) reiterated this theme in an article examining the problems confronting each side in negotiating a peaceful solution. He referred to the 'spur of necessity' under which the British government had put itself: 'Conditions in the South Atlantic dictate that military action be taken swiftly, not long postponed.' He also spoke of the inability of the Argentine decision-making apparatus to handle negotiations. Kraft saw both sides as having locked themselves into a military confrontation which they were unable to avoid. Doubt concerning Britain's negotiating stance were to be found in the British press. Geoffrey Parkhouse in the *Glasgow Herald* referred to HMG's insistence that Argentina respond first to any diplomatic proposals – 'we are the wronged party' – and stated: 'the result was that the junta was diplomatically wrong-footed as part of a sustained campaign by the new British diplomacy to cast Argentina in world opinion as the intransigent party in the dispute'.

Britain's role in the negotiations was subject to a great deal more scrutiny following the end of the conflict. Hugo Young reported a conversation he had with a member of the cabinet (*Sunday Times*, 4.7.82). According to the Minister,

> the purpose of the war cabinet's apparently intense search for peace had been, as he saw it, to make the British understand why they had to go to war; in other words to maximise the chances that they would face and tolerate the casualties that were sure to come. From this it was hard to avoid the conclusion that the peace efforts were in part a charade.

Alexander Haig was however to maintain his view that the Argentines were 'intransigent' and 'unwilling to negotiate'. It has been argued that Haig had an interest in portraying Argentina in the most unfavourable light. Gavashon and Rice in their book, *The Sinking of the Belgrano*, (Secker & Warburg, 1984), described Haig's briefing on his diplomatic efforts to the US Senate: 'Instead of their contributing positive proposals, they [the Argentines] were shown as rejecting Haig's. Instead of negotiating they were shown as intransigent' (p. 70). In the authors' view Haig had to be careful about too close an identification with Britain. They describe US policy in this respect thus (ibid., p. 75):

> Their reputation for throwing their own weight around had been inhibiting their foreign policy ever since the wars in Indo-China. Before they could back the British preparations for a massive counterstrike, they needed some moral ground for action. Argentina's 'intransigence' provided it.

Haig also had to convince the 'Latino lobby' in the Reagan administration of the correctness of siding with Britain. Thus it can be argued that Haig concurred with a British policy of portraying Argentina as unwilling to negotiate.

APPENDIX 3

News language on the *General Belgrano* and *HMS Sheffield*

This appendix is a record of language used in news bulletins between 3 and 15 May on the following themes:

A.   Survival statements on the *Belgrano*.
B.   Casualty statements on the *Belgrano*.
C.   Survival statements on the *Sheffield*.
D.   Casualty statements on the *Sheffield*.
E.   Statements suggesting the *Belgrano* was a threat and justifying the attack.
F.   Statements suggesting that the *Belgrano* was not a threat and criticising the attack.

It is as complete as we can make it allowing for a small loss through equipment failure. For reasons of space we could not include similar lists for all our case studies. But we thought it useful to include this as an indication of the basis on which our conclusions on news language in Chapter 2 are made.

Statements on survivors and 'survivability' of the *Belgrano* crew

outside the exclusion zone but who are nearby and would be allowed to come in and tow her away or take survivors aboard. We are still waiting for information. – Journalist with Task Force.

Are any of the ships of the Task Force standing by to take on any possible survivors, for example? – Journalist

Yes, *Hermes* broadcast an emergency message over the emergency frequency to ships in the area, and that is, all ships in the area, to look for survivors – Journalist with Task Force.

No, there will be the normal helicopter surveillance and sweep for survivors. All that can be done is being done to pick up survivors in the sea. – Journalist with Task Force.

ITN, 17.00, 3.5.82

316

According to military sources here, at least five Argentine warships are taking part in this search but if the cruiser has indeed gone down the chances of the crew's survival would seem remote. – Journalist.

The *Belgrano* was safe from immediate destruction by her thick armour-plating under the waterline but for that there might have been heavy loss of life amongst her crew of 1,000 men. As yet we don't know exactly when she went down, presumably her two escorting destroyers were able to go alongside to take off the survivors. – Defence correspondent.

BBC1, 21.35, 3.5.82

There is no news of whether there are any survivors – Newscaster.

Finally, Argentina has reported that its cruiser the *General Belgrano* has been sunk. Apparently Argentine ships are searching for survivors of her crew of 12,000 ... Will it be possible to get the Argentinians out of the Falklands without killing people? – Newscaster.

I believe – I believe so personally, and I also believe we are moving in a step-by-step manner with that aim – Admiral Weymiss

ITN, 22.20, 3.5.82

After the sinking of the Argentine ship *General Belgrano*, up to 600 sailors are still missing but 40 have survived – Journalist.

And he went on to express concern about any loss of life that resulted from the attack. So far, reports from Argentina say that 400 survivors from the *General Belgrano* have been rescued. – Journalist.

Fifteen more life rafts have been spotted and the Argentine sailors are hopeful of finding more survivors. – Journalist

BBC2, 1836, 4.5.82

but there is a good chance that a lot of them will have been saved. – Presenter

She had two escorts with her who may have picked up most of the men on board who could have survived the attack and were able to make their escape, but we just don't know yet. – Presenter

Are there any details or indications once again about the possibility of survivors, John? – Journalist

No. There's considerable confusion about that, Donald. Officially, the government here are saying absolutely nothing about survivors. – Journalist.

Now it could be that the other 5 or 600 were rescued in time but officially we really don't know – Journalist

Newsnight, BBC2, 22.15, 3.5.82

A vast search is going on in the South Atlantic for survivors from the Argentine cruiser *General Belgrano*. The latest reports say about 123 men out of a total crew now said to number over 1,000, have been picked up. Its 36 hours since the cruiser was torpedoed by a British submarine and the best chance of survival seems to be the modern life-rafts she was carrying. – Newscaster.

We asked an expert about the chances of the sailors surviving in the South Atlantic ... Argentine ships and aircraft are continuing their search in the South Atlantic for survivors of the cruiser *General Belgrano*. The ship sank after being torpedoed by a British submarine on Sunday. So far, the Argentines say 123 men have been rescued – Newscaster

The men who were picked up were in storm-proof life-rafts and according to the Argentine navy, there were at least 30 of these rafts on the cruiser. They are enclosed and . . . could take 20/30 seamen . . . latest survival gear. – Newscaster

On the question of survival in the South Atlantic, we will be talking later to a man who sells life-rafts in South America, and he knows the area well. – Newscaster

The *General Belgrano*, sunk by a British submarine, is believed to have been carrying a crew of over 1,000 – 130 of whom have been rescued. The rest were thought to be adrift somewhere in the South Atlantic; most probably in life-rafts. So, how long could they survive in craft like these? That's the question. With me now is Captain Bob Greenland who is a member of the Viking life-saving equipment company and is a master mariner. Captain Greenland, first of all, what is the chance of survival in those seas down in the South Atlantic in craft like these? – Journalist

Well, it depends to a great extent on the training the seamen have had. Properly trained, I feel reasonably confident myself that they could exist for a considerable period of time – three or four days quite easily. – Capt. Bob Greenland

It appears from reports we have had over the past few days that the ship was first damaged and didn't sink immediately, so presumably there's a good chance they could have got off – Journalist

Well, in my opinion they could have spent the time very wisely in preparing themselves to evacuate the ship and consequently, they probably, dependent on weather conditions, have got away. – Capt. Bob Greenland

How would they get into them? – Journalist

Well, the life-raft would have been thrown over the side, and they could probably have climbed in either down ropes or jumped into the water to be pulled in. – Capt.Bob Greenland

Well, assuming they have got into these inflatable lifecraft, how would they survive once in them? – Journalist

And providing they are dry when they get into it, they can keep warm and comfy in it for a long time? – Journalist

Assuming these life-raft are well equipped, as the Argentine navy has said, they would presumably have things like homing beacons as well, would they? – Journalist

Yes. They will be equipped with radio beacons to enable them to be located by any rescue operations that are taking place. – Capt. Bob Greenland

Meanwhile, the search is continuing in the South Atlantic for other survivors from the ship's 1,042 crew. – Newscaster

As the search continues for survivors of the Argentine cruiser . . . Newscaster

Argentine boats and planes which resumed their search at dawn today for more survivors from the sunken cruiser, have now rescued 400 of the ship's complement of 1,042 – Journalist, ITN, 13.00, 4.5.82

And in another development, an Argentine naval tug is reported to have picked up 400 survivors from the Argentine cruiser *General Belgrano*. – Journalist

400 Argentine sailors are reported safe from their sunken cruiser. – Journalist

It was feared there wouldn't be many survivors because of the extremely cold seas, but now it seems many of the sailors managed to get into-life rafts that were aboard the ship. – Journalist

BBC1, 17.00, 4.5.82

The 400 survivors already found are aboard the support vessel ... Navy spokesmen say they are optimistic about finding 300 more men alive. – Newscaster

where survivors are now being taken ... – Newscaster

The Argentine military authorities say 400 survivors have been picked up from the cruiser *General Belgrano*, which sank after a British submarine attack. – Newscaster

With the probability that more men from the *General Belgrano* are alive on life-rafts, its thought they're equipped with the latest survival gear. Francis Coverdale has been to a company in this country who makes similar equipment. – Newscaster

The *General Belgrano's* thought to have had 30 life-rafts similar in construction to this one and with similar survival kits, there'd be everything necessary to keep the men alive for up to six days. – Journalist

They would be most uncomfortable, but the main point about the whole thing is, once they are in it, they're pretty safe. – Captain Greenland

After the sinking of the Argentine cruiser, 400 men have been picked up. – Newscaster

BBC1, 17.40, 4.5.82

The Argentines say that 400 survivors have been picked up so far and are being taken to Ushaia but one agency report from Buenos Aires quotes naval sources as saying that the majority of the 1,000 crew are safe. – Newscaster

The Argentine military high command say that 400 survivors from the *General Belgrano* have been picked up, and the naval auxiliary vessel *Galshaga* is heading for the southern port of Ushaia packed with men. Official Argentine navy sources say there were hopes of finding a further 300 survivors. One agency report from the capital quotes other navy sources as saying the majority of the 1,000-strong crew are safe. – Journalist in Argentina

ITN, 17.45, 4.5.82

Almost 700 Argentines have now been rescued from the cruiser *Belgrano*. – Journalist

The latest word on that from official sources in Argentina is that 680 survivors of the one thousand man crew have been picked up and the search is going on for the other 300 or so. – Journalist

Argentina are continuing the search ... for survivors from the cruiser *General Belgrano*. The Argentinian military authorities say 680 sailors have now been rescued. – Newscaster

BBC1, 21.10, 4.5.82

Argentina says 680 rescued from the *General Belgrano*. – Newscaster

Meanwhile though the search continues for survivors from the sunken cruiser *General Belgrano*. – Journalist

the small Argentine patrol vessel ... with possibly 300 survivors aboard. – Journalist

ITN, 22.10, 4.5.82

He allowed the ship to go on floating and he allowed the Argentines to come and rescue the crew. – Admiral Roxburgh

Newsnight, BBC2, 4.5.82

refer to the score being evened after the sinking of Argentines' cruiser the *General Belgrano*, in which 800 crew members have now been rescued. – Journalist

BBC1, 12.30, 5.5.82

There's a feeling that the sinking of the *Sheffield*, coupled with the news of 800 sailors rescued from the cruiser *Belgrano*, has restored Argentine pride. – Journalist

ITN, 13.00, 5.5.82

At the same time the first group of survivors from the Argentine cruiser *General Belgrano* have been brought ashore. The *General Belgrano* was torpedoed by a British submarine on Sunday. 800 men have now been rescued and the searches still continuing for others. – Newscaster

Early Evening News, BBC1, 5.5.82

The Argentine's say there were around 700 survivors from the 1,082 men on board the *General Belgrano*, which was torpedoed on Sunday. The Argentine government . . . – Journalist

ITN, 17.45, 5.5.82

In Argentina, some 800 survivors have now been picked up after Sunday's sinking of the cruiser General Belgrano. 150 received an emotional welcome when they were flown back to the mainland. – Newscaster

Later today, survivors from the torpedoed Argentine cruiser seen here setting out on its fateful last patrol, are due to arrive back at mainland ports aboard the rescue ships. The search still goes on for more lifeboats of the *General Belgrano* which had 15 days provisions aboard for 20 people. – Journalist

BBC1, 21.05, 5.5.82

The Argentines say they've picked up about 800 of the 1,042 ... on their cruiser. Rescue operations are still going on. – Newscaster

BBC1, 22.05, 5.5.82

And as for the crew of the *General Belgrano*, the Argentines say they have rescued 800 and there could still be another 300 to account for. – Journalist

Newsnight, BBC2, 22.45, 5.5.82

The survivors from the Argentine cruiser the *General Belgrano* have been arriving ashore and the commander and his deputy were both amongst those rescued. They got a warm welcome back at the base at Bahia Blanca in southern Argentina. Argentina says that 800 men have now been picked up. – Newscaster

BBC1, 09.15, 6.5.82

The first survivors from the sunken Argentine cruiser *General Belgrano* . . . – Newscaster

The survivors of the *General Belgrano* were shuttled north ... The authorities here say 800 out of the crew of just over 1,000 were saved, some after spending more than 48 hours in fragile rafts. The survivors were given full military honours ... were allowed to greet their families and well-wishers. Many had thought their sons and husbands had been killed. News of what the Argentine government is calling 'the most successful naval rescue in history' has been slow in coming out. – Journalist

BBC1, 12.30, 6.5.82, repeated in part or full BBC1, 17.05, 17.40, 21.00, *Newsnight*, BBC2, 6.5.82

We have reports from Buenos Aires and from above the icy waters of the South Atlantic and the men and the warships of Argentina which survived the British attacks. – Newscaster

News of Argentina's reaction to the peace plans came as scores of sailors from the torpedoed cruiser the *General Belgrano* were reunited with their relatives amidst emotional scenes. – Newscaster

Meanwhile as the planes bringing the first of the survivors from the *General Belgrano* touched down, a huge crowd waited at the air base. 70 men came in on this first plane and all day more continued to arrive.

Each survivor was personally greeted by a top naval officer ... successful rescue operation. Considering they had spent 48 hours in fragile rafts, in the freezing sea, they all looked suprisingly well. During the day the reunions continued as over 300 as an estimated 800 men came home, including the captain of the sunken cruiser. The survivors have already asked if they can be sent back to sea, as soon as possible. – Journalist

ITN, 13.00, 6.5.82

The search continues for any other survivors from the cruiser *Belgrano* which was sunk for four days ago. The Chileans are helping in the rescue. – Newscaster,

ITN, 13.00, 6.5.82

We flew out into the South Atlantic in search of the huge rescue operation which Argentina had launched to find 100s of seamen from the sunken cruiser *Belgrano* .... Four days after the *Belgrano* disaster, the South Atlantic and most of the Beagle Channel were calm, ensuring the best conditions for the survivors .... Though Ushwaia has no ship repair facilities, it is a supply point and it was here that the first 500 survivors of the *Belgrano* were brought .... which we filmed a month ago trespassing in Chilean waters, now acting as a main life-saver with over 100 aboard. – Journalist

ITN, 13.00, 6.5.82

Some of the survivors from the *General Belgrano* ... reunited. – Journalist

BBC1, 17.05, 6.5.82

400 survivors ... reunited ... The Argentines say 800 men are safe ... search continues for the rest. – Newscaster

As I said, the Argentine navy said it's still searching for survivors from the sunken warship . More than 750 have been picked up. scaster

ITN, 17.45, 6.5.82

Argentine television has been relaying pictures of the reunion of survivors from the cruiser *General Belgrano*, with their families. – Journalist

BBC1, 21.00, 6.5.82

The first survivors from the Argentine cruiser *General Belgrano* ... reunited with their families.

Newsnight, BBC2, 6.5.82

The Argentines say up to 800 of the 1,000-strong crew have been rescued. – Newscaster

May 7 BBC1, 21.00, 7.5.82, repeated

Chile is helping ... small groups of survivors ... adrift. – Newscaster

Buchard returns from the South Atlantic with scores of survivors from the torpedoed *General Belgrano*. The voyage ends in the Beagle. ... the rescue effort. Small groups of survivors are still believed adrift. So there are extra lifeboats. – Journalist

BBC1, 12.30, 21.00, 7.5.82, repeated

The photo was taken by a member of the *Belgrano's* crew after he'd taken to a lifeboat. – Journalist

BBC1, 21.30, 9.5.82

Statements referring to potential and actual Argentine casualties in the attack on the Belgrano

is thought the *Belgrano*, which has around 1,000 men on board, is still afloat, but it is not known if there are any casualties. – Journalist with Task Force

We do not know yet whether any casualties have gone overboard or whether there are any casualties at all. We must assume that there are. – Journalist with Task Force

ITN, 17.00, 3.5.82

Then, no other details were given, whether there had been any Argentine casualties nor how serious the damage was. – Journalist

BBC1, 21.35, 3.5.82

Of the 1,000 men on board, 600 are still missing, but the air and sea search of the South Atlantic still continues. – Newscaster

BBC2, 18.35, 4.5.82

There must be fears of a grave human disaster as well. – Journalist

normally has a crew of about 1,000 maybe 1,200 men. Local radio is saying that the boat is missing with only 500 men aboard. – Journalist

Well, Donald, it depends entirely on the … on whether a lot of lives have been lost. – Journalist

Well if a lot of lives have been lost — Argentine lives - this can be a major diplomatic setback for Britain. – Journalist

there was no question of major casualties at that point. – Journalist

If there is a great flap now about Argentine lives being lost, then a lot of countries are going to say this has created a totally new situation. – Journalist

if it turns out that the cruiser *General Belgrano* has been lost with some loss of life. – Journalist

if the reports about the sinking of the *General Belgrano* are confirmed and if a great number of Argentine lives have been lost. – Journalist

Newsnight, BBC2, 22.16, 3.5.82

The big question is, how many have perished? There could be as many as 900 men still not accounted for. – Newscaster

An official statement a short while ago said more than 1,000 men had been on board the *General Belgrano* and at least 900 including the captain and the sons of three admirals were still missing. – Journalist

the losses for us … it is only the men … training men … about this sad news of course. – Ad. Fernando Milla

some time out of radio contact, and has now sunk. We have no reason to disbelieve this account. We have no knowledge of Argentinian casualties. – Mo D.

There is no formal comment yet from the States Department about the sinking of the *Belgrano* and the presumed heavy loss of life. – Journalist

needless loss of life on a large scale. – D. Healey M. P.

BBC1, 12.30, 6.5.82

So far, they have given no official casualty figures. One United Nations report says 500 crew have been lost. – Newscaster

As for the fate of the *Belgrano* itself, the Ministry of Defence said it had no reason to disbelieve Argentine's suggestions that the ship had been sunk with anything up to a thousand or more men on board. – Newscaster

Meanwhile, Labour's Shadow Cabinet met at noon and its clear that if 500 or more men have been lost in the *Belgrano*, Labour will be very critical. – Journalist

Fifteen life-rafts are reported to have been sighted this morning, but there are dwindling hopes here that anyone else will be found alive. – Journalist

The sons of three Argentine admirals and the captain of the cruiser are believed to be among those who perished. – Journalist

I believe the *Belgrano* is really a very sad question. More for the crew than for the cruiser itself. We are sad because the lives of course. – Ad. Fernando Milla

ITN, 13.00, 4.5.82

Was there no way of warning the Argentines without loss of life? – Newscaster

ITN, 13.00, 4.5.82

but up to 600 are still missing. – Newscaster

He went on to express concern about the loss of life. – Newscaster

Mr Speaker, it must be a matter of deep concern to the House at the loss of life from these engagements, including the sinking of the *General Belgrano*. – John Nott

That leaves up to 600 men not accounted for, yet according to Argentine figures about the crew, 15 ships are still searching for the missing men. – Newscaster

these men are missing and its their loss and the emotion it aroused. – Newscaster

any losses is a loss especially the men ... training men ... its important for the lives ... It makes people angry. It, eh, angry is not the word, but sad.. – Ad. Fernando Milla

but while there were regrets at the loss of life... – Journalist

When Tony Benn suggested . and that the Prime Minister was rejoicing in the loss of life. – Jouranlist

BBC1, 17.40, 4.5.82

Mr Pym said,'Our relief that British lives have not been lost is inevitably tempered by our deep regret at Argentine casualties.' – Journalist

Mr Foot called the cruiser's sinking 'a tragic loss of life'. – Journalist

Commons today rose several degrees when Mr Tony Benn said the majority of the people would not be rejoicing with the Prime Minister at the loss of life when the ship was torpedoed without a declaration of war, as Mr Benn put it. – Journalist

The heavy loss of life on the *Belgrano* has severely shocked the Argentines. – Journalist

The Argentines all say they will hold on to the Falklands whatever the price they have to pay, and even with the cost now being counted in the blood of hundreds of their young. – Journalist

casualties don't seem to be as high as feared. – Journalist

...could draw the conclusion that the recent tragic loss of lives associated with their cruiser would contribute to continuing intransigence. – Mr Haig

BBC1, 21.10, 4.5.82

However, the sinking of the *Belgrano* with its loss of life has convinced Mr Haig that further heavy losses of Argentine lives are likely. – Journalist

ITN, 17.45, 4.5.82

All Labour leaders were critical of the possibly high loss of life. – Newscaster the Falklands dispute had been transformed over the weekend from the war of words and a blockade into one with serious casualties. – Journalist

From a diplomatic point of view, the sinking of a capital warship with the inherent loss, risk of loss of life. – Journalist

An administration spokesman said the United States regretted the loss of life on the *Belgrano*. – Journalist

. . . others, perhaps as many as several hundreds are still missing. – Newscaster

BBC1, 21.10, 4.5.82

it is thought likely that more than 300 Argentine sailors have perished. – Journalist

has set sail and is now beyond the Beagle Channel trying to assist in the rescue of the victims of the British attack on the Argentine cruiser *Belgrano*. – Journalist

a majority in Britain will not be rejoicing with the Prime Minister at the loss of life when the ship . . . when the ship. – Tony Benn from House of Commons

We can't have young Argentinians sent to the bottom of the ocean – Eric Heffer M. P.

ITN, 22.10, 4.5.82

the routine statement about the loss of life. – Journalist

Now the concern expressed in the Commons about the sinking of the *Belgrano* was essentially concern at the scale of the human disaster there, earlier. The probable loss of 100s of lives of Argentines sailors who were pictured only days ago proudly sailing off on the second largest of their navy's ships. – Journalist

Newsnight, BBC2, 4.5.82

and I might add, have grieved over the loss of people even in Argentinian ships. – Tony Benn, M. P.

Others take the view that now that both sides have suffered loss of life, the way may be open for peace, and express the hope that, appalling as the losses are, it may provide the pressure – Journalist

ITN, 13.00, 5.5.82

But the loss of their own cruiser and hundreds of their young men. – Jouranlist

ITN, 13.00, 5.5.82

continued that the fight must go on. But commentators here who have heard of the British losses were saying that they hope that both sides would now see the need for . – Journalist

ITN, 17.45, 5.5.82

But naval sources there have not revealed how many were lost or injured when their ship was torpedoed. – Newscaster

BBC1, 21.05, 5.5.82

. . . no rejoicing here at the loss of the British destroyer . . . But they know now that the war is costing them more than just lives . . . economy ailing . . . Journalist

ITN, 22.05, 5.5.82

military propaganda, adopting a tone not shared by service families in the south of the country, where losses from the *Belgrano* have been sustained. – Journalist

that as sailors were saddened by the sinking of the Argentine cruiser and the loss of life it involved. – Journalist with Task Force

Newsnight, BBC2, 22.45, 5.5.82, repeated BBC1, 09.15, 6.5.82

The Argentines have never said exactly how many men were on board but its thought that another 200 may have perished. – Newscaster

BBC1, 09.15, 6.5.82

The *General Belgrano* had a complement of 1,242 men. So far there is no news of the estimated 200 sailors who are still missing, presumed dead. – Newscaster

ITN, 13.00, 17.45, 22.00, 6.5.82, repeated

...supplies to go to the rescue of drowning Argentinians in the South Atlantic. – Journalist

ITN, 17.45, 22.00, 6.5.82

This doesn't take account of those lost in the sinking of the cruiser *General Belgrano*. – Newscaster

BBC1, 12.30, 21.00, 7.5.82, repeated

but that doesn't include about 370 men missing from the cruiser *General Belgrano* which was torpedoed last Sunday. – Newscaster

ITN, 22.00, 7.5.82

the Argentines say more funerals will take place soon when it's established how many want down with the *General Belgrano*. There were reported to have been over a thousand men aboard. The Argentines, claims only 800 have been rescued so far. – Journalist

BBC2, 18.55, 8.5.82

Argentina had also issued the casualty figures for the *General Belgrano*, sunk by a Royal Navy submarine twelve days ago. They say that out of a crew of 1,100, 301 are still missing and 20 bodies have been recovered. – Journalist

BBC2, 19.00, 15.5.82

Statements referring to potential or actual Sheffield survivors or/and references to survivability

Crew abandon burning ship: all those picked up. – Newscaster

All the crew who abandoned ship were picked up, but the Ministry of Defence says its feared that there were some casualties. – Newscaster

Now if there has been a direct hit on the operations room, how many men, do you think, would have stood a good chance of getting off ship? – Journalist

ITN, 22.10, 4.5.82

...was picked up...-Naval wife

Mrs McClaferty heard her son Peter was safe.-Reporter

He had been picked up.-Mrs McClaferty

ITN, 13.00, 5.5.82

Sheffield was set on fire and finally the crew were forced to abandon ship. Everyone who left the ship was rescued.-Journalist

BBC1, 17.00, 5.5.82

Other Royal Navy ships picked up survivors.-Newscaster

The resulting fire burned for four hours before the ship was abandoned.-Newscaster

Survivors from the *Sheffield*...-Newscaster

So when did you finally hear that your husbands had been picked up?-Newscaster

Early evening news, BBC1, 5.5.82

...that he was picked up and they didn't know whether...any injuries yet.-Naval wife

One woman...heard that her son had been picked up safely.-Newscaster

His wife can't believe he's coming home.-Journalist

ITN, 17.45, 22.05, 5.5.82

The order was given to abandon ship...and the rest of the Task Force picked up survivors.-Newscaster

BBC2, 19.35, 5.5.82

Several hours before the news came that their husbands were safe.-Newscaster

I just wanted to know if he was one of the casualties or if was safe.-Naval wife

Before the order was given to abandon ship...-Newscaster

BBC1, 21.05, 5.5.82

...of the woman who got good news about her son.-Journalist

ITN, 22.05, 5.5.82

He survived, but the first his wife heard was the bare fact...Journalist

I heard the good news that my husband was one of the survivors.-Naval wife

The survivors of HMS *Sheffield* are still scattered about the fleet. Their names are being gathered and sent to London.-Journalist

All who had survived this long were picked up.-Journalist with Task Force

Newsnight, BBC2, 22.45, 5.5.82, journalist with Task Force repeated BBC1, 9.15, 6.5.82

The Commander of HMS *Sheffield* was...taken aboard *Hermes* after he was rescued. Back home his wife...heard with relief that he was safe. – Newscaster

BBC1, 09.15, 6.5.82

Survivors from HMS *Sheffield* are still scattered about the fleet. – Newscaster

BBC1, 12.30, 6.5.82

The captain of HMS *Sheffield*...paying tribute to...the crew. Most of the sailors survived the tragedy. The captain said...they had saved themselves. – Journalist

Some of the sailors rescued...were taken to...*Hermes*. – Journalist with Task Force

Captain...order abandon ship...praised crew for their conduct. – Journalist with Task Force

men were incredible . . . company really saved themselves. – Capt. J. Salt

BBC1, 17.05, 6.5.82

Many know that their husbands are safe but everyone helps. – Journalist

ITN, 17.45, 6.5.82

Many know their men are safe. – Journalist

ITN, 22.00, 6.5.82

The survivors from HMS *Sheffield* are to be brought home . . . The MoD announcement about the survivors came on the day...diplomatic efforts...The news about *Sheffield* survivors was given at an MoD news conference. – Newscaster

BBC1, 18.00, repeated BBC2, 18.55, 8.5.82

Survivors of HMS *Sheffield* are presently...brought home. All survivors will be given leave.

BBC1, 18.00, repeated 22.10, BBC2, 18.55, 8.5.82

Arrangements are being made to bring more than 250 survivors from HMS *Sheffield* home as soon as possible. – Newscaster

ITN, 21.45, 8.5.82

The *Sheffield* survivors are coming home... The survivors from destroyer *Sheffield* are to be brought home. – Newscaster

BBC1, 22.10, repeated BBC2, 23.10, 8.5.82

Statements referring to potential and actual casualties on **HMS Sheffield** and statements on casualties/grief

the ship's company abandoned ship. All who abandoned her were picked up. It is feared that there have been a number of casualties. – MoD

BBC1, 21.10, 4.5.82, repeated same bulletin, repeated ITN, 22.10, *Newsnight*, BBC2, 4.5.82

As a result of that the ship had to be abandoned and undoubtedly there have been quite considerable casualties. – Defence correspondent

Of course if we get any more developments on that particularly grave incident ... –Newscaster

Well even before tonight's *tragic news* from the Ministry ... Falklands dispute ... transformed ... into one with serious casualties ... some Conservatives are beginning to lose hope ... that efforts can succeed before there is more bloodshed. Tonight they've had *tragic confirmation* of that. –Journalist

In naval terms it more than offsets the loss of the cruiser *Gerneral Belgrano*, and in human terms its possible the casualties may be high. – Defence correspondent

There is no indication, yet, here at the Ministry of Defence about the number of casualties, but to recap on what the Ministry spokesman said a few moments ago: all those who abandoned her were picked up but it is feared there have been a number of casualties. From a very, very, sombre Ministry of Defence in Whitehall, back now to the studio. – Journalist

BBC1, 21.10, 4.5.82

HMS *Sheffield* hit by Argentine missile. Some casualties feared. – Newscaster

Very briefly Admiral Wemyss your thoughts this evening on the loss of the *Sheffield*. – Journalist

These are friends of mine. I am very sad. – Admiral Wemyss

The Opposition leader, Mr Foot described tonight's news as 'grave and tragic'. – Newscaster

support falls away very sharply indeed once we talk about the loss of British life, and that loss, probably on a serious scale, has now happened. – Journalist

Are you among those who tonight are saying, 'I'm afraid I told you so. That I always said there would be losses like this'? – Journalist

Well, I must say, from the beginning I did warn that, once the thing got under way, it wasn't going to be an easy walkover and we could well have lots of casualties ourselves. – Eric Heffer MP

Now we are in a shooting war and contrary to what a lot of people thought, we are of course now getting casualties of our own. – Eric Heffer MP

We can't have more of our young people's lives lost. – Eric Heffer MP

ITN, 22.10, 4.5.82

Grim news ... HMS *Sheffield* ... sunk ... it is feared there have been a number of casualties. –Journalist

And in view of tonights terrible news – Journalist

In other words, this tragic incident doesn't ... in your view ... detract from the ... exercise which the Task Force is attempting to carry out? – Journalist

Well, it's grim news and of course, one's heart goes out to the families and the next of kin and I hope there are not as many as we fear, eh, casualties. – David Owen MP

... vessels in the immediate area which picked up those who had abandoned ship. Nearly all the ship's company and the captain are accounted for. However I regret to say that initial indications are that twelve men are missing and there are likely to be other casualties. – John Nott

> deep sorrow for the families of the casualties on the *Sheffield*. – D. Healey MP

> *Newsnight* BBC2, 4.5.82

Wednesday's headlines are of course dominated by the attack on HMS *Sheffield* with the loss of about thirty British lives. – Newscaster

the first British casualties since the Falklands crisis began. – Newscaster

we will be asking a Falkland Islander whether he thinks the first British casualties are going to change any minds on the islands. – Newscaster

This covers the dead, the missing and the wounded. – Newscaster

The number of sailors who perished still stands at around thirty . and he will give details of the casualties. Next of kin are being informed at the moment and we expect a list of those who perished later this afternoon. – Journalist

The Ministry here are naturally taken aback by what has happened, but that they know full well that casualties are inevitable; their purpose as he said, is to keep casualties and risks to a minimum. – Journalist

You can't have a war without some casualties and some are worse than others. – Capt. J. Lamb (stepfather of Capt. Salt)

Sheffield was hit it was . . . *Hermes* to which casualties were ferried. – Journalist

The instinct of the majority of Conservatives is to carry on, accepting sadly that there are bound to be casualties. – Journalist

Now that the first British blood has been spilled could this change attitudes on the islands? – Newscaster

How worried are you that because of the latest casualties from HMS *Sheffield* that sympathy is no longer with the Falkland Islanders? – Newscaster

If they send the fleet to the South Atlantic they cannot withdraw after some casualties. None of us likes to see casualties either British or Argentinian. – J. Cheek, Falkland Island Council

The loss of *Sheffield* has hit hard the town of Portsmouth. – Journalist

There was a feeling of shared grief between the widows of the *Sheffield* men who died, wives of those who survived. – Newscaster

And from Buckingham Palace has come a statement from the Queen. It says she is concerned and saddened by the tragic news of the loss of HMS *Sheffield*. – Newscaster

> BBC1, 12.30, 5.5.82

The number of men who died on HMS *Sheffield* is still thought to be about thirty. – Newscaster

> BBC1, 12.30, 5.5.82

Whitehall sources also said a short while ago that the next of kin of 87 crew members from HMS *Sheffield*, and that includes dead, missing and wounded, have now been contacted by the Ministry of Defence. Last night the Defence Secretary Mr Nott said it was feared that up to thirty men may have died. – Journalist

This morning the mood inside the Ministry was far more relaxed. It was as if casualties had been feared all along and now the fears had been realised. – Journalist

Throughout the night the Ministry of Defence has been contacting the next of kin of everyone on HMS *Sheffield*, in many cases to report sailors dead, wounded or missing. In other cases to report the safety of loved ones. The full casualty list will not be released until every next of kin has been informed. – Journalist

The grim news of the British losses in the South Atlantic...Mrs Thatcher herself was said to be deeply concerned about the casualties in the fighting. – Journalist

could't there be a feeling amongst British people that we don't want those who have died already to have died in vain? – Newscaster

The Queen...saddened by the tragic news of the loss of HMS *Sheffield*. – Newscaster

The House of Commons will be united this afternoon, as it was last night, in pride at the courage of our troops and with grief and sorrow for those who have been killed and their families. – Norman St John Stevas MP

The loss of life on both sides is horrifying. – Norman St John Stevas MP

London awoke to the latest news of *Sheffield* and her casualties. – Journalist

The Navy's welfare department is taking on the grim task of making contact with families who have suffered losses. – Journalist

News of the casualties, covering dead, missing and wounded...relayed to families. – Journalist

Queen saddened by the tragic loss of the ship. – Newscaster

Men have died, men on the same side have died...they want to get on with it. – Journalist

The list of casualties won't be released . . . survivors have been picked up . . . there could be an element of double counting of dead and wounded. – Newscaster

. . . precise details of who was killed and injured in the destruction. – Newscaster

The shock of losing their destroyer and as many as 30 men...left and emptiness. – Journalist

ITN, 13.00, 5.5.82

30 British sailors are still missing after the attack on HMS *Sheffield* by Argentina. – Journalist

The latest news of the casualties from the destroyed British ship HMS *Sheffield*, is that 30 men are still missing. It is feared that they died after the ship was hit by a missile. News of the attack has shocked the country. Today, the Queen, whose son Prince Andrew is serving on the aircraft carrier HMS *Invincible,* said she was deeply concerned and saddened by the deaths. – Journalist

...discuss the first British losses in the Falklands conflict and this afternoon, Mr John Nott the Defence Secretary told concerned MPs of the grief everyone felt at the *Sheffield's* loss. – Journalist

Two cities especially have been mourning the loss of HMS *Sheffield*. – Journalist

BBC1, 17.00, 5.5.82

The shocked city of Portsmouth mourns the loss of HMS *Sheffield*. The number missing from the destroyer is still put at 30 after the Argentine...–Newscaster

The Defence Secretary Mr Nott told MPs this afternoon that 30 men are still missing from the destroyer *Sheffield*.–Newscaster

The latest information I have is that about thirty men are still missing. A further number sustained injury and they are being well cared for under medical supervision. We have no further details of casualties at the present time...The thoughts of the whole House are with them at this sad time.–John Nott

...among the British casualties...–Newscaster

the Queen deeply concerned and saddened by the loss of HMS *Sheffield*.–Newscaster

The first many of them knew about the tragedy...several hours before the news came that their husbands were safe.–Newscaster

just wanted to know if he was one of the casualties.–Naval wife

The families of the dead and injured are receiving personal visits.–Newscaster

Early evening news, BBC1, repeated 21.05, 5.5.82

30 British seamen were killed in the attack on the *Sheffield* by an Argentine missile. The Ministry of Defence say that 87 are either dead, missing or wounded.–Newscaster

Its still not known exactly how many British sailors were killed in the attack on the destroyer *Sheffield*; Mr Nott told the Commons the latest figure is still about 30. The MoD say they contacting 87 families of men who are either dead, missing or wounded.–Newscaster

Today the city was in mourning. Flags flew at...Local councillors, meeting this afternoon, offered condolences to the families of crewmen killed or injured. Men have died, men on the same side have died...–Journalist

Men have died, men on the same side have died . . . –Journalist

He said about 30 men from *Sheffield* are still missing.–Newscaster

held in Sheffield Cathedral . . . for the sailors who died.–Newscaster

ITN, 17.45, 5.5.82

But the day's been completely overshadowed by the loss of HMS *Sheffield*. MP of all parties . . . expressed sympathy for the relatives of those who've lost their lives.–Journalist

After last night's British losses and the political pressures they've brought ...–Journalist

crew abandoned ship. The more seriously injured . . . brought to *Hermes*.–Journalist

statement said the Queen was deeply concerned and saddened by the tragic news of the loss of HMS *Sheffield* . –Newscaster

The Pope has spoken of profound shock and grief over the sad news from the South Atlantic. He called for prayers for victims of both sides.–Newscaster

Have you any message at all for the wives of those unfortunate sailors who have perished?–Journalist

I only hope that the loss of their lives will achieve something. – Naval wife

The full list of casualties still isn't known. – Journalist

The shock of losing their destroyer and as many as 30 men ... – Journalist

grim task of making contact with ... families who've suffered losses. – Journalist

ITN, 17.45, repeated 22.05, 5.5.82

After Argentine's missile attack on HMS *Sheffield*, 30 men are still missing. And Foreign Secretary Mr Pym says the losses on both sides now makes a diplomatic solution even more urgent. – Newscaster

John Nott has told the House of Commons ... 30 men from HMS *Sheffied* are still missing. – Newscaster

Mr Pym said recent losses on both sides showed the need for diplomacy. – Newscaster

BBC2, 19.35, 5.5.82

Portsmouth mourns HMS *Sheffield*. Thirty of the destroyer's crew are still missing. – Newscaster

It's been a day of mourning here at home. – Newscaster

MPs were told that here are still thirty men missing from the destroyer HMS *Sheffield*. – Newscaster

MPs were anxious for news of the casualties on the *Sheffield* and of new diplomatic initiatives to settle the dispute before any more lives are lost. – Newscaster

Buckingham Palace say the Queen has been following events in the South Atlantic closely and is deeply concerned and saddened at the loss of life. – Newscaster

30 men are still missing after the Argentine missile attack – Newscaster

BBC1, 21.05, 5.5.82

Portsmouth mourns its dead. – Newscaster

How many more lives will have to be lost before the government fully realises that there can be no purely military solution to this crisis? – D. Canavan MP from House of Commons

The Ministry ... 87 families ... thought to be dead, missing or wounded ... 30 are now presumed dead. – Newscaster

Mr Haig expressed his concern at the loss of life to the British Ambassador. – Newscaster

The Queen sent her own message ... it said, I have been much distressed by yesterday's tragic events ... grateful ... convey message of deep sympathy to relatives of all who lost their lives. – Newscaster

And the Prince of Wales ... joined the Princess to send our deepest sympathy to the wives and families of those who lost their lives so couragously. – Newscaster

Today Sheffield City Council called for UN mediation to stop more loss of life. – Journalist

Though there have been very nasty casualties ... down below would be more. – Admiral Wemyss

The lesson of the tragic loss of *Sheffield* . . . –D. Healey MP

ITN, 22.05, 5.5.82

Both sides are counting the death toll of the naval battle, from HMS *Sheffield* 30 men dead and missing but 87 families have been contacted by the Defence Ministry in connection with relatives killed, missing or wounded. – Journalist

Full impact from the losses of HMS *Sheffield* are only now beginning to be felt. The Defence Ministry still hasn't released the exact casualty list, but 87 families are being contacted about relatives either killed, wounded or missing. Now for all the relatives, the suspense since the announcement of the loss of the ship, must have been agony. For at least thirty, the true agony is only just now beginning. – Newscaster

They should continue the strategy and hope these men's lives and families haven't been lost and altered so much for nothing. To withdraw now, it would mean these men's lives have been wasted. – Naval wife

Casualties will be assessed. About twenty men are still missing, there are two seriously injured and about a score who have minor injuries and shock . . . helicopters set off towards it carrying doctors and fire-fighting equipment and bringing back casualties. – Journalist with Task Force

BBC1, 09.15, repeated 12.30, 17.05, 6.5.82

Brian Hanrahan was apparently talking about there being 20 men missing instead of 30 as we thought earlier, and let's hope that is right, and two seriously injured. – Journalist

Casualties have taken place on both sides. – C. Price, Labour MP

Put the Argentines off the Falklands . . . otherwise all the casualties will have been in vain. – M. Mates, Tory MP

I'm not saying we should take fright because there have been casualties on both sides. – D. Crouch, Tory MP

We knew there would be casualties, war is war and produces casualties. – D. Crouch, Tory MP

Some Conservatives want to go on . . . whatever the casualties. – C. Price, Labour MP

We can't alter our principles because we've suffered casualties. – M. Mates, Tory MP

Can all that be done without very, very serious casualties, far worse than the *Sheffield*? – Journalist

What casualties are we prepared to take? – K. Hunt, military expert

BBC2, Newsnight, 22.45, 5.5.82

Officially the number of dead from the *Sheffield* is still put at thirty. Other men were seriously injured. – Newscaster

BBC1, 09.15, 6.5.82

The Pope described as deeply anguished by the death toll in the battle . . . – Newscaster

A full list of the casualties suffered in the Argentine missile attack . . . is due. – Newscaster

ITN, 11.55, 6.5.82

Having acknowledged the tragic loss of the *Sheffield* we really mustn't now go on to assumed that all our ships are going to be sunk. – S. Menaul
> ITN, 13.00, 6.5.82

I have however an announcement to make about the casualties sustained in HMS *Sheffield*. 20 officers and men must now be presumed dead, 24 of the crew sustained injuries . . . only one of these is on the seriously ill list. The further 242 survivors are all well . . . . Details of those presumed dead and of the one man on the seriously ill list are now being issued. – MoD
> ITN Newsflash, repeated BBC1, 21.00, ITN, 22.00, 6.5.82

. . . the number of sailors who died have still not been given. – Journalist
> BBC1, 17.05, 6.5.82

The official list of casualties from . . . *Sheffield* is expected. – Newscaster
In the confusion over casualties from HMS *Sheffield*, one mother suffered the ordeal of being told first that her son was missing, then that he wasn't, then again he'd been lost. Andrew Swallow is . . , listed as missing after . . . his mother believed that he had died and then that he was alive. – Newscaster
> BBC1, 21.00, Repeated with variations, *Newsnight*, BBC2, 6.5.82

. . . found safe . . . then unaccounted for . . . probably died for his country. – Mrs Swallow
The MoD is expected . . . about the casualties from HMS *Sheffield*. – Newscaster
> BBC1, 17.40, 6.5.82

many of the men who were casualties on HMS *Sheffield* have families in Gosport. – Newscaster
You've had the job . . . letting the women know their husbands are missing. – Journalist
> ITN, 17.45, repeated 22.00, 6.5.82

The MoD now say that 20 men are presumed dead and 24 were injured in the attack . . . one man is in a serious condition and the 242 other men on board have been transferred . . . to ships. – Journalist
> BBC2, 19.30, 6.5.82

Official casualty figures from HMS *Sheffield*, 20 sailors presumed dead and 24 others injured, one of them seriously.
Mr McDonald spoke to reporters about the casualties caused when HMS *Sheffield* was hit . . .
Now for more about the loss of two Harrier jets and the casualty figures from HMS *Sheffield* . . .
As details of casualties were passed to Britain. The Navy stepped up its help and advice for bereaved families and those worried about their relatives. – Newscaster
> BBC1, 21.00, 6.5.82

the homes of lost 20 men in HMS *Sheffield* . . . – Newscaster
Portsmouth lives tonight with the news that 20 of HMS *Sheffield's* men are dead. Nearly all the 20 men lost from HMS *Sheffield* came from the South Coast. – Newscaster

Here is the full list of the dead, officers and men, as given today by the Ministry of Defence. [*Individually listed on screen.*] The names of the 20 dead, or presumed dead, aboard HMS *Sheffield* which was destroyed in the South Atlantic this week. Those sailors on *Sheffield* are the first to be killed in battle action aboard a British warship since the second world war. 24 of their shipmates were injured; only one seriously. Remarkably the remaining 242 crew men escaped unhurt. The fatalities suggest the administrative deck bore the brunt of the damage. Amongst those killed were three officers and eight of the *Sheffield's* catering staff. Andrew Swallow from Bembridge on the Isle of Wight was just eighteen; the youngest man to die. 20 year old Neil Goodall . . . . His girl friend heard of his death while on holiday in Greece. His mother who lives in Middlesex said, 'My son never joined the Navy to die for something as wasteful as this.' [*All dialogue spoken by the newscasters.*]

There is no mistaking the feeling of desolation here. Ten of the dead came from the Portsmouth area . . . but everyone shares in the sense of loss . . . who are missing . . . . And the anxious waiting goes on, with the fear that tomorrow might bring news of more deaths or war injuries. – Journalist

They are proud that their loved ones gave their lives in this way. – Editor, *Daily Star*

None of the families we interviewed tonight were related to anyone who had been killed on the *Sheffield*. – Newscaster

ITN, 22.00, 6.5.82

And the Ministry also confirmed today that 20 officers and men from HMS *Sheffield* must now be presumed dead. Another 44 sustained injuries. Among those listed dead are eight cooks. – Journalist

BBC2, *Newsnight*, 6.5.82

Prayers were said for the 3 pilots and the casualties from HMS *Sheffield*. – Journalist

BBC1, 17.40, repeated 21.00, 7.5.82

Apart from their anti-submarine role the helicopters will provide a support and delivery service for the Task Force. It was Sea-Kings which buried the casualties from HMS *Sheffield*. – Journalist

BBC1, 17.40, 7.5.82

We expected losses and we warned ministers of losses . . . sad because of the loss . . . of life. – Admiral Lewin

BBC1, 21.00, repeated ITN, 22.00, 7.5.82

Two nights ago the body of one of those who died in the missile attack on the HMS *Sheffield* was buried at sea . . . . The simple service and the commital to the sea, served too as a memorial to all those who died in the fire.

More than 1,000 people attended a memorial service at Sheffield Cathedral tonight for the men who died on the missile attack on HMS *Sheffield*. – Newscaster

Both men died when an Exocet missile fired by an Argentine aircraft hit . . . – Journalist

. . . those who were saved; those who were injured; and those who had given their lives for queen and country. – Rev. Frank Curtis

ITN, 18.30, 9.5.82

And a memorial service tonight for the Britons who died in HMS *Sheffield* . . . –Newscaster

Uppermost in most minds is the loss of HMS *Sheffield* and the men who died in her. –Newscaster

Early arrivals were the widows of two of the men who perished, petty officer Antony Norman and Chief Chef Michael Toole. –Newscaster

It was a highly emotional occasion, most for those who had suffered direct loss and for the citizens of Sheffield. –Newscaster

BBC1, 21.30, 9.5.82

She will now be a grave for the men whose bodies remain abroad. –Journalist

BBC1, 17.40, repeated 21.00, 10.5.82

HMS *Sheffield* . . . wrecked 6 days ago by an Argentine missile attack which claimed 20 lives has sunk. –Journalist

BBC2, 19.20, 10.5.82

She sank soon afterwards to her grave in the South Atlantic. –Journalist in Task Force

ITN, 22.00, 10.5.82

Statements on the *Belgrano* as a 'threat' or giving justification to the attack

Shooting started in the early hours around the Falkland Islands 200 miles total exclusion zone. The submarine *Conqueror* made two direct hits on the *General Belgrano*. It is not known how badly she has been hit. –Newscaster.

The MoD say the attack on the *Belgrano* was because it posed a significant threat to the Task Force. It is not clear whether the ship was just inside or just outside the 200 mile limit. –Newscaster

What I can say is that the cruiser was operating South of the Falklands Islands with two escort vessels. This group of warships presented a significant threat to our ships in the area of the Falkland Islands. –MoD

The attack on the *General Belgrano* took place in the late afternoon and was said to be fully in accordance with the rules of engagement of the British Forces in the South Atlantic. –Newscaster

It seems the *Belgrano* and its two support ships were at the edge of the 200 miles total exclusion zone in the Falklands when the British submarine attack came. It was, said the Ministry of Defence, 'a significant threat' to the Task Force. –Newscaster

Our reporter on board the Task Force flag ship has told us that the *Belgrano* had been shadowed for some time as it nosed in and out of the exclusion zone. –Newscaster

What we are trying to find out, from Admiralty staff aboard *Hermes*, is whether she has power to take herself back outside the exclusion zone. –Task Force Reporter

All I can say is that in the case of the cruiser yesterday, that was a serious threat to our forces, and so they took action. –Mr Pym

So I hope that as a start at any rate, the Argentines will respect that total exclusion zone, respect it. – Mr Pym

ITN, 17.00, repeated 22.20, 3.5.82

The submarine attack on the cruiser was eight hours earlier, just outside the zone south of the Falklands, according to the MoD. – Newscaster

So far it has shown that it can enforce the sea and air blockade. – Task Force Reporter

BBC1, 18.00, repeated 21.35, 3.5.82

The warships presented a significant threat to our ships in the area of the Falklands Islands. – MoD

Were these incidents separate or were they related? That's a key question, because if there is a connection, it could mean the Argentines were attempting some kind of pincer movement to break the British naval blockade. – Defence correspondent

BBC1, 18.00, 3.5.82

Just outside the exclusion zone . . . – Newscaster

BBC1, 18.35, 3.5.82

It's now more than 70 hours since Britain sank an Argentine patrol boat within the exclusion zone and more than 24 hours since the Royal Navy torpedoed the *Belgrano*, just outside. – Newscaster

So, victory once again for the Task Force. What Rear-Admiral Woodward needs to know is what that cruiser was doing so far south. Was it intended as a surprise attack on the Task Force off the Falklands or on South Georgia? If those patrol boats were in the north, does that mean the Argentines are planning a combined attack using land-based aircraft, submarines and the Argentine carrier? – Defence correspondent

Yesterday, there was a very real threat to that zone, posed by a cruiser. – Mr Pym

That military activity has been directed to securing the total exclusion zone of which we gave notice. – Mr Pym

If the need arises as the Task Force commanders decided it did last night, when the Argentine cruiser was attacked, military action will be taken. – Journalist

As you will appreciate, if there is a threat to our own ships and to our own men, we have no—no possible option but to respond to that threat. Our first duty is to protect our own men, and the *General Belgrano* was a threat to our men and therefore it was quite correct that she was attacked by our submarines. – Mr Nott

The Argentine government knows there is one quick and simple way to avoid casualties to their personnel and loss of their ships and aircraft. It is to keep out of the zones declared by us and to cease threatening and attacking air forces. – Mr Nott

BBC1, 21.35, 3.5.82

She was attacked by a nuclear powered submarine just outside the maritime exclusion zone off the South Falklands. The Ministry of Defence in London say the cruiser and her escorts were a threat to British forces and had been dodging in and out of the zone. It is possible she may have been trying to see if British assault force was on its way. – Newscaster

The attack on the *General Belgrano* was said to be fully in accordance with the Rules of Engagement issued to British Forces in the South Atlantic. We now know those rules of engagement are wide-ranging and allow the Task Force to attack any ship or aircraft that comes close to the Fleet. – Journalist

What happened yesterday was that the *Belgrano*, along with its two escort vessels, came close to the edge of the 200 mile total exclusion zone. – Journalist

And all I can say is, that in the case of the cruiser yesterday, that posed a serious threat to our forces, and so they took action. – Mr Pym

It is our solemn purpose to achieve the military objectives to which reluctantly we have been compelled, using the minimum of force . . . commensurate of course with our overriding duty, to defend our own ships, aircraft and men. – Mr Nott

The Ministry of Defence in London says the *General Belgrano* had been manoeuvring in and out of the maritime exclusion zone. That's it for tonight. Goodnight. – Newscaster

> ITN, 22.20, 3.5.82

Mr Nott also explained why the cruiser, the *General Belgrano*, was attacked outside the exclusion zone. He said the arms the cruiser and its escorts carried, presented a threat to the Task Force. – Newscaster

> BBC2, 18.35, 3.5.82

Within the past hour the Defence Secretary, John Nott, has been speaking to newsmen for the first time since the invasion of South Georgia. And he insisted that last night's attack on the Argentine cruiser, *General Belgrano*, was completely justified. He said that the government had been compelled to use force. – Presenter

At that state Mr Nott had not heard the report from Buenos Aires recently, that the cruiser had sunk, but he did defend the torpedoing of the cruiser, as we have heard, saying that Britain had no possible option but to attack the cruiser even although it was outside the 200 mile exclusion zone. – Presenter

What seems to have happened in the past 24 hours is that there have been two separate attempts by the Argentine navy to close on the British Fleet. – Journalist

When a British submarine moved in on three Argentine warships just outside the 200 mile blockade zone, the British say, even though the Argentines were outside the zone, they were still a threat to the Task Force, which declared an additional defensive zone around itself ten days ago, no matter where it moved inside or outside that 200 mile zone. Now these ships, unlike the cruiser, were clearly infringing the British blockade zone, so whether or not they were a threat to the British fleet, they were in breach of the declared British blockade. – Journalist

[*Sinking wrong decision?*] No. The imposition of pressures necessitated the exclusion zone and for that reason, and hopefully in order to safeguard not only British lives but Argentine lives on the Falkland Islands, and most important of all, the Falkland Islanders lives, then, pre-emptive action of that kind or responsive action of other kinds that has taken place, is necessary. That is part of the function of the Task Force. – Neil Kinnock MP

> *Newsnight*, BBC2, 22.15, 3.5.82

Well just a few minutes ago at the Ministry of Defence here in London they made a statement about the *General Belgrano* and her escorting ships. They gave further details of the attack by a British submarine on Sunday and they say the cruiser and two destroyers were a threat to British planes and ships. – Newscaster

This force, because of its position relative to our Task Force and because of its weapon capability overall, posed a major threat to our ships. In accordance with the warning given to the Argentinian government on 23 April, the cruiser was then attacked by an RN vessel. – MoD

Although the government insists that the Argentine cruiser was in a position to pose a major threat to the Task Force, there has been no indication of how far away the cruiser was from the fleet. While it was outside the 200 mile exclusion zone the Argentines had been warned that the danger zone was extended to cover the fleet. – Journalist

The spokesman said he had no specific information as to whether there were any potential British targets within the *Belgrano's* sights at the time of the attack, but he pointed out that the task force commander has to take, in his words 'many factors' into account and choose the best moment to attack. – Journalist

The *General Belgrano*, as we know, was skirting the edge of the total exclusion zone, and certainly within the sights of its 15 guns there could have been British forces, so the Task Force commander took the decision that it was justified to attack the cruiser. – Journalist

BBC1, 12.30, 4.5.82

The MoD say . . . the Argentine cruiser posed a major threat. – Newscaster

As for the cruiser *Belgrano*, she for some time had been in the general area in which she was attacked. She may have been going in and out of the total exclusion zone or perhaps skirting it. She was accompanied by two Argentinian destroyers. The cruiser was armed with 15 6″ guns with a range of 13 miles and the short-range Sea-cat missiles which posed a threat to our aircraft engaged in operations in the total exclusion zone. Both of the destroyers were fitted with exocet missiles which have a range of over 20 miles. This force, because of its position relative to our Task Force and because of its weapon capability overall, posed a major threat to our ships. In accordance with the warning, given to the Argentinian government on 23 April, the cruiser was therefore attacked by an RN vessel. – MoD

Government sources this morning were saying, 'We are not apologising'. The Argentines have been warned. Keep clear of the British fleet. – Journalist

The government's attitude to criticism, both at home and abroad, is that if it was right to send the Task Force, no one should be surprised when Britain uses that force. – Journalist

Britain's UN representatives have been maintaining that attacks on the Argentine navy by the Task Force have been in self-defence. – Newscaster

With me in the studio now is Rear-Admiral Martin Wemyss. How was the *Belgrano* such a threat to the lives of British servicemen? – Newscaster

It is not the *Belgrano* alone, with her 15″ guns but also the two escorts with her, both of whom were fitted with Exocet. An exocet is a very potent little missile. I know it because I did the trials of it in our Navy. – Ad. Wemyss

So they could, if they had been allowed to move into the zone and perhaps fire those missiles, it could have resulted in serious loss of life of British servicemen? – Newscaster

This is the only reason we would have taken out that cruiser. – Ad. Wemyss

And would the British forces be satisfied that the cruiser was about to embark on hostile action? – Newscaster

I'm perfectly certain in my own mind that this action was not taken until that surface action group of ships became a positive menace. – Ad. Wemyss

ITN, 13.00, 4.5.82

Earlier the Prime Minister, Mrs Margaret Thatcher, strongly defended the decision to fire on the Argentine cruiser, the *General Belgrano*. She said she regretted the loss of life, but the government's first duty was to protect Britain's forces. – Newscaster

Sunday brought the attack, on the *General Belgrano*, the Argentine cruiser. She was attacked outside the 200 mile zone around the islands which Argentine ships have been warned to keep away from. – Newscaster

BBC1, 17.00, 4.5.82

Mr Nott told MPs that the Task Force Commander would have ignored the threat from the cruiser at his peril. – Newscaster

The Defence Secretary also referred to the Argentine cruiser, *General Belgrano*, and explained why it was attacked outside the exclusion zone. He said the armaments the cruiser, and its destroyer escorts carried, guns and missiles with ranges up to 20 miles, presented a threat that the Task Force commander could ignore at his peril. – Newscaster

But our first duty must be the protection of our own ships and men [hear, hear]. There may be further attacks on our forces, and they must be allowed to act in self-defence. We cannot deny them that right. – John Nott

She, and the Defence Secretary, Mr Nott, were defending the action of the force in torpedoing the Argentine cruiser as necessary for the safety of our ships and men. – Newscaster

There were no regrets at the action. The torpedo attack had been necessary to protect the fleet. – Journalist

The Defence Secretary, John Nott . . . the cruiser, though old had substantial fire power from her guns. It was within hours, he said, of the Task Force. The commander could only have ignored it at his peril. – Journalist

Mr Nott, however, was adamant. The attack had been necessary. The threat was real. He wasn't saying any more. – Journalist

As I told the House, the cruiser and its escorting destroyers were in fact only hours steaming time away . . . – Mr Nott

In the Commons, Mrs Thatcher spoke of the worry she had hourly, that the Argentine navy might break through and attack the British Task Force. – Newscaster

BBC1, 17.40, 4.5.82

[Headline:] The government defends the torpedoing of the *Belgrano*, says British lives were at risk. – Newscaster

Good evening. The Prime Minister has defended the sinking of the Argentine cruiser the *General Belgrano*. She said it was one of three ships which posed a serious threat to our fleet and if we hadn't fired, lives would have been at risk. – Newscaster

Two former Labour Defence Ministers asked why the two escorting destroyer, which had much more modern equipment, and fewer sailors, were not attacked. Mr Nott insisted the cruiser's big guns were very dangerous. – Journalist

The main points again—Mrs Thatcher told the Commons the Argentine cruiser the *General Belgrano* was torpedoed because it was a serious threat to the fleet. – Newscaster

ITN, 17.45, 4.5.82

Our first duty is to our own forces . . . there on our orders and we must look after their safety, our second duty is . . . to use minimum force, but that cruiser, and associated destroyers . . . not far from the exclusion zone. They do pose a very obvious threat to the men in our task force and had we left it any later it would have been too late and then I might have had to come to the house with the news that some of our ships had been sunk. – Mrs Thatcher

ITN, 17.45, repeated versions also on BBC1, 17.40, BBC1, 21.10
ITN, 22.10, Newsnight, BBC2, 4.5.82

Mrs Thatcher also revealed, 'The worry that I live with hourly, that Argentine naval and air forces will get through to our forces.' – Journalist

ITN, 17.45, 4.5.82

Mrs Thatcher says she is sorry for any loss of life but she defends the sinking. – Newscaster

. . . insisted that the attack had been fully justified. – Newscaster

There is no condemnation of Britain . . . and among the public . . . a feeling that the British have got away with it. In fighting back they've done what they have said they would do. And perhaps a little bit more. – Journalist in USA

Mr Nott insisted that the House must not put the Task Force at risk. – Journalist

The action did take place, we believe, just outside—35 miles outside the total exclusion zone, but as I told the House, the cruiser and its escorting destroyers were, in fact, only hours steaming time away. – John Nott

BBC1, 21.10, 4.5.82

Early today in the Commons, Mrs Thatcher strongly defended the attack on the Argentine cruise the *Belgrano*. She said everyone regretted the loss of life, but Britain's first duty was to protect its own forces. – Newscaster

Mrs Thatcher justified that action by saying the government's first duty was to protect the lives of British servicemen. There was clear evidence she said, of aggressive intent by the Argentines. The *Belgrano* and the two escorting destroyers were an obvious threat to our forces. Had we left it any later it would have been too late. – Journalist

May I make it perfectly clear that the worry that I'm left with, hourly, that the Argentine forces may attack, both naval and air, may get through to ours and sink some of our ships and I'm sure that will also be very much in the Right Honourable Gentleman's mind and our first duty is to our own forces who are there, at our orders and with our support, and we must look after their safety. – Mrs Thatcher

Mr Nott also found himself defending the government against the opposition accusations about the sinking of the *Belgrano*. The Task Force commander could have ignored the threat from the cruiser only at his peril, he said. Tackled by Mr

Healey, Labour, Mr Nott, confirmed that three Argentine ships had been 30/35 miles outside the total exclusion zone, only hours steaming time away from the Task Force. – Journalist

. . . but the group was hours away from our Task Force. – John Nott

Mr Speaker, we are—insofar as we are engaged in military operation, we are doing so under the United Nations Charter in self-defence. – Mr Pym

ITN, 22.10, 4.5.82

I think what's happened today shows that the attack was a justified attack against a vessel which was posing a real threat to the Task Force and which was closing on it, and I think it was an attack which a military commander was right to take in the circumstances and I'm sorry that Dennis criticises that. – Charles Onslow MP

There was also a statement from the Defence Secretary, Mr Nott. He said that the sinking of the *Belgrano* was justified on the grounds, as he put it, our first duty must be the protection of our own ships and men. – Presenter

There was clear aggressive intent on the part of the Argentine ship, fleet and government. You can see that first in the claims. They had previously claimed that they had sunk HMS *Exeter*, damaged *Hermes*. That they had brought down eleven Harriers. This was clear evidence of Argentine aggressive intent . . . remember the persistent attacks throughout the whole of Saturday . . . repelled by . . . our people. – Mrs Thatcher

Newsnight, BBC2, 4.5.82

But the loss of the *Sheffield*, it is felt, puts the *General Belgrano* in a different light. The Task Force clearly had to do what it did for its own protection. – Journalist

ITN, 13.00, 5.5.82

Mr Nott revealed today that it was the submarine commander who decided to fire the torpedo which sunk the *General Belgrano*; that he did so, said Mr Nott, within rules of engagement approved by the cabinet. – Journalist

ITN, 22.05, 5.5.82

Well, I rather see this as an attempt to avoid a repetition of that controversy, by giving advance warning that we regard all naval vessels and military aircraft as, of themselves, presenting a threat to us, rather than having to explain with regard to any particular vessel that in the circumstances at that moment, it did represent such a threat. – Professor Rosalyn Higgins

ITN, 22.00, 7.5.82

The first picture of the sinking of the Argentine cruiser the *General Belgrano*, appears on the front page of tomorrow's *Daily Mail*. The ship was torpedoed a week ago on the edge of the 200 mile exclusion zone. – Newscaster

ITN, 18.30, 9.5.82

Statements that the *Belgrano* was not a threat and the British attack was unjustified

The cruiser had been operating outside Britain's 200 mile exclusion zone, for several days. – Task Force reporter

General Belgrano was an old World War II cruiser; had 15 big guns and a crew of

1,000 to man them. Despite its fire power, it was perhaps the least worrying of the serious threats to the Task Force. – Task Force reporter
BBC1, 18.00, repeated 21.35, 3.5.82

The first incident was more than 200 miles south of the Falklands, outside Britain's total exclusion zone. – Defence correspondent

In Argentina we have just received a government statement that said Britain had brought a new level of aggression to the conflict by her attack on the cruiser the *General Belgrano*. – Newscaster

The military junta's version of the submarine attack contradicts British reports that the Argentine cruiser posed a significant threat to the fleet. A communique tells that the *General Belgrano* was torpedoed outside the zone, declared by both countries around the Falklands Islands. – Journalist
BBC1, 18.00, 3.5.82

The attack took place at 8 o'clock our time yesterday evening outside the 200 mile exclusion zone South of the Falklands. – Newscaster
BBC2, 18.45, 3.5.82

The question Argentines are asking tonight is why the British fleet attacked the cruiser when it was outside the total exclusion zone and was not defying the British blockade. – Journalist

My government believe that that is a case of gunboat diplomacy that was widely practised during the nineteenth century. – Sr J. Herra Vegas

Argentina called the torpedo attack on the cruiser a 'new aggression' by the British government. – Newscaster
ITN, 22.20, 3.5.82

Mr Nott was then asked a question about the attack last night on the Argentine cruiser *General Belgrano*. Was this the minimum use of force to which the government is committed.? – Journalist
BBC1, 21.35, 3.5.82

Do you think the government so far has taken a wrong decision? For example, in shelling the airport, in sinking or trying to sink the cruiser? – Presenter

The *General Belgrano*, an old ship, due to be scrapped, came under torpedo attack from Royal Navy submarines when, according to the Argentines anyway, it was cruising just outside the 200 miles exclusion zone. – Journalist in Argentina
Newsnight, BBC2, 22.15, 3.5.82

Our correspondent in Beunos Aires said one newspaper carried the headline 'English murderers'. – Newscaster
BBC2, 18.35, 4.5.82

Costa Mendez, . . . that he is outraged at the sinking of the *Belgrano*. – Newscaster
BBC2, 18.35, 4.5.82

The Argentines say the *Belgrano* was hit by a torpedo 36 miles outside the British blockade zone. – Newscaster

This morning the newspapers have been calling the British 'murderers'. – Newscaster

A communiqué said that the sinking of the ship, 36 miles outside the so-called exclusion zone, had been a treacherous act of aggression. Here in the capital there is a deep sense of shock. One newspaper carries a huge headline saying 'English murderers'. Another calls Mrs Thatcher a crazy killer who could only be compared with Hitler for her violation of the rules of war. – Journalist in Argentina

Also this afternoon, the Shadow Foreign Secretary says he is concerned about Britain losing international support after the sinking of the *Belgrano*. – Newscaster

Are you concerned that there's a danger Britain will lose international support now, because of this . . . ? – Journalist

. . . the international support we have had is our most priceless asset, and it would be jeopardised if world opinion felt that we had been responsible for needless loss of life on a large scale . . . – D. Healey MP

> BBC1, 12.30, 4.5.82

The Argentines have now given a precise location of the attack. It was, they say, 36 miles outside the 200 mile blockade imposed by the British around the Falklands. – Newscaster

The Argentine government has called the attack on the *General Belgrano* 'a treacherous act of aggression in violation of the United Nations Charter'. They claim the cruiser was at least 36 miles outside Britain's 200 mile exclusion zone. – Journalist in Argentina

A government communiqué said that so far, Argentina has limited herself to defensive action against British attack. – Journalist

. . . Defence Minister, Mr Paddy Power, who this morning called Britain aggressors. [He said] 'Obviously the British themselves are very much the aggressors now.' – Journalist

. . . do you think that the sinking of the *Belgrano* was really necessary? – Journalist

When they backed Britain with sanctions two weeks ago, they did not mean to back the use of so much military force by Britain. – Journalist

Some Labour leaders, like Mr Healey, are concerned that its bound to weaken world support for Britain. – Journalist

They accuse Britain of sharply escalating the fighting. – Journalist

> ITN, 13.00, 4.5.82

The Argentines say that the *General Belgrano* was 36 miles outside the exclusion zone when it was torpedoed on Sunday. – Newscaster

> BBC1, 17.40, 4.5.82

newspaper headline says just two words: 'English murders'—another calls Mrs Thatcher a 'crazy killer' to be compared with Hitler. – Journalist in Argentina

The government called the sinking of the *General Belgrano* 'an uncalled act of aggression' and the people are outraged. – Journalist in Argentina

The Irish Defence Minister said his government regarded Britain as the aggressor. – Journalist

> BBC1, 17.40, repeated 21.10, 4.5.82

Argentina has written to the United Nations Secretary General calling the attack a totally unlawful and cruel operation and Costa Mendez described the sinking of the *General Belgrano* as 'a treacherous act of aggression in violation of the UN Charter'. – Journalist in Argentina

Argentine newspapers were comparing Mrs Thatcher with Hitler. – Journalist in Argentina

What do you think about what the British did to the cruiser *Belgrano*? – Journalist in Argentina

Well, I think that it is a crazy decision. – Argentinian citizen

Irish government have been the most outspoken with their Defence Minister, Mr Power, calling Britain the aggressor . . . The British are very much the aggressors now, he said. – Journalist

Argentina denounced the escalation of the conflict. – Journalist

Mr Healey said the attack on the *Belgrano* was already damaging Britain's world support . . . . Mr Tony Benn said . . . people would not be rejoicing with the Prime Minister . . . when the ship was torpedoed without a declaration of war. – Journalist

ITN, 17.45, 4.5.82

Government were pressed hard to give more exact details of the circumstances surrounding the attack which happened outside the so-called total exclusion zone surrounding the Falklands. – Newscaster

Reaction in Argentina to the sinking . . . has been one of outrage. – Newscaster

. . . may weaken or even destroy the possibility of negotiations . . . . That the operations of the last few days have already cost us a great deal of support among our European allies . . . – D. Healey MP

BBC1, 21.10, 4.5.82

Why? The question was constantly asked in the House today. Why was such a level of force have to be used against this ancient cruiser? After all, the government admitted that she and her two destroyer escorts were actually outside the 200 mile blockade zone around the Falklands when the British submarine made its attack 48 hours ago. And what many in the Commons wanted to know was, how can we be sure that the *Belgrano* really was a threat, an immediate threat to the British Fleet? And just how close really was she to any of the British ships? Well, Mr Nott steadfastly refused to be precise; he just said the *Belgrano* was closing on the Task Force, only hours steaming away. Now admiral, can I come back to you and ask why do you think the British didn't wait to let the cruiser get clearly within the exclusion zone? – Newsnight presenter questions Admiral Roxburgh (some replies are included in the 'threat' categories)

Well I don't think the exclusion zone comes into this particular argument. The exclusion zone was a moral exclusion zone; that is, an exclusion zone round the forces themselves, wherever they are. I'm sure that the *Canberra* is being protected from fierce attacks, 1,000 miles north of the exclusion zone. She will be protected by her escorts . . . he obviously made up his mind in his judgement according to the instructions he had, that this ship was going to pose a threat to our other forces. – Ad. Roxburgh

And yet it was only hours steaming away . . . – Presenter

Well, whether it was 35 miles or whether it was fifty miles, he might not . . . that might not have occurred again. – Ad. Roxburgh

Hours could mean 300 miles, Mr Healey said in the Commons? – Presenter

Yes, but will you have to wait to hear what the actual facts were, but I am saying that the captain of the submarine was the man who would make the judgement. He made the judgement. The fact that it was 35 miles outside is neither here nor there to my mind. – Ad. Roxburgh

The government has failed to justify the attack on the cruiser yesterday. It's not clear that the British Task Force was at risk when the cruiser was attacked . . . and it was inevitable . . . that it was bound . . . to strengthen the Argentine desire for revenge and to make negotiation less possible, and I think that was an error. It think its essential if we sent the Task Force . . . it should operate with minimum of force and I fear its been used in a way . . . which makes negotiations less likely and its not clear there was political control when the Argentine cruiser was attacked. – Dennis Healey MP

Newsnight, BBC2, 4.5.82

The Argentine government has accused Britain of escalating the fighting . . . – Journalist

Mr Healey warned that the sinking would lose Britain's support around the world. – Journalist

There is deep concern . . . in case certain types of military action—and I think that the attack on the cruiser *General Belgrano* may be an instance of this—intended . . . to back up negotiation, may weaken or even possibly destroy negotiation as a long term solution. – Dennis Healey MP

We can't have young Argentinians sent to the bottom of the ocean. – Eric Heffer

ITN, 22.10, 4.5.82

The captain claimed the cruiser was well outside Britain's 200 mile exclusion zone when the submarine attacked. Captain Bonzo gave a graphic account of how two torpedoes struck the warship, one exploding in the engine room. The decks, he said, became red hot. Two decks collapsed, killing and trapping crew members resting below . . . . But others did not survive the battles at sea. – Journalist in Argentina

BBC1, 18.00, repeated BBC2, 18.55, BBC1, 22.10, 8.5.82

Captain Bonzo denied that the *Belgrano* had posed a threat to the British fleet when it was attacked. He claimed his cruiser was steaming at a slow 10 knots towards the Argentine mainland when it was hit. – Journalist in Argentina

ITN, 21.45, 8.5.82

INDEX

and Falklands ceasefire plan, 162–71; and Peruvian Peace Plan, 146–51; Resolution 502, 162–4, 165–7, 168, 169; Report of Secretary General on Nuclear Weapons, 216–7; First Special Session on Disarmament, ix, 230; Second Special Session, viii, 230, 259; press coverage of, 238–45; TV news coverage of, 231–8
United States, 5, 11, 147, 148, 160, 170, 176, 180–1, 183–4, 212
United States Arms Control and Disarmament Agency, 180
Ustinov, Marshal, 190

Vaerno, Grethe, 183–4
Vietnam, 8, 19
Vincent, John, 250

Wain, Christopher, 7
Walden, Brian, 281–2
Walsh, Robin, 16
Ward, Keith, 280–1
Warnke, Paul, 224, 278–90, 283
Washington Post, 11, 33, 59, 61, 128, 147, 163, 167, 191
Watkins, Peter, 293

Weekend World, 138, 204–5, 277, 283
Week In, Week Out, 97
Weinberger, Caspar, 179, 180, 188
Weymss, Martin, 31, 55
Whale, John, 252–3
Wheeler, Charles, 182, 237, 278
Wightman, John, 243
Williams, Philip, 281
Windsor, Philip, 281
Woodward, Sandy, 47, 60
Women
coverage of during Falklands conflict; as wives/mothers, 98–105; waiting at home, 105–7; views of, 107–11; image of, 118–21
Women and Families for Defence, 213
Worcester, Robert, 306–7
World Council of Churches, 234, 260, 277

Young, Hugo, 147, 315

Zero Option, 217–23; interim proposal, 261; press coverage of, 262–5; TV news coverage of, 266–9
Zuckerman, Lord, 249